the MAKEOVER book

101 Design Solutions for Online & Desktop Publishers

Second Edition

the MAKEOVER book

101 Design Solutions for Online & Desktop Publishers

Second Edition

Joe Grossmann

VENTANA

The Makeover Book: 101 Design Solutions for Online & Desktop Publishers, Second Edition

Library of Congress Cataloging-in-Publication Data

Grossmann, Joe.

The makeover book : 101 design solutions for online & desktop publishers / Joe Grossmann. -- 2nd ed.

p. cm.

Rev. ed. of: The makeover book / Roger C. Parker. 1st ed. c1989.

Includes index.

ISBN 1-56604-132-5

1. Desktop publishing. 2. Graphic arts. I. Parker, Roger C. Makeover book. II. Title.

Z253.53.G75 1996

686.2'2544536--dc20 96-15268

CIP

Second Edition 9 8 7 6 5 4 3 2 1
Printed in the United States of America

Ventana Communications Group, Inc.
P.O. Box 13964
Research Triangle Park, NC 27709-3964
919/544-9404
FAX 919/544-9472

Limits of Liability and Disclaimer of Warranty

The author and publisher of this book have used their best efforts in preparing the book and the programs contained in it. These efforts include the development, research and testing of the theories and programs to determine their effectiveness. The author and publisher make no warranty of any kind, expressed or implied, with regard to these programs or the documentation contained in this book.

The author and publisher shall not be liable in the event of incidental or consequential damages in connection with, or arising out of, the furnishing, performance or use of the programs, associated instructions and/or claims of productivity gains.

Trademarks

On page 145, the following trademarks are the property of Pantone, Inc.: PANTONE Tint Effects ColorSuite, PANTONE Color Survival Kit.

Other trademarked names appear throughout this book. Rather than list the names and entities that own the trademarks or insert a trademark symbol with each mention of the trademarked name, the publisher states that it is using the names only for editorial purposes and to the benefit of the trademark owner with no intention of infringing upon that trademark.

President/CEO
Josef Woodman

Vice President of Content Development
Karen A. Bluestein

Production Manager
John Cotterman

Technology Operations Manager
Kerry L. B. Foster

Product Marketing Manager
Diane Lennox

Art Director
Marcia Webb

Book Design & Layout
Joe Grossmann

Cover Illustration
Laura A. Stalzer

Acquisitions Editor
Neweleen A. Trebnik

Project Editor
Lois J. Principe

Copy Editor
Marion Laird

Technical Director
Eric Coker

Technical Reviewer
Eric Diamond

Production Coordinator
Jaimie Livingston

Proofreader
Marion Laird

Indexer
Dianne Bertsch, Answers Plus

About the Author

Joe Grossmann is the owner of Grossmann Design & Consulting in Chicago. He has authored and designed two books for Ventana, the highly acclaimed *Newsletters From the Desktop, Second Edition* and *Looking Good With QuarkXPress*.

Grossmann writes the Design Tips & Techniques column for *Digital Chicago* and frequently contributes other articles to that magazine. He has also written extensively for *Technique* magazine, both as a columnist and as a features contributor, and for *ThePage,* where he previously held the role of associate editor. His articles and columns have explored a diverse array of topics, including design, illustration, computer hardware, cross-platform issues, PageMaker, QuarkXPress, FreeHand, Illustrator, Photoshop, FileMaker, and other programs for the Macintosh and Windows environments.

Before Grossmann began his current career as a designer, he was a founder of the pioneering software company Enabling Technologies. There, Grossmann directed the development of a line of 3D graphics products, including Easy3D, Pro3D, Clip3D, and ZING, some of the very first programs available for Macintosh and Windows systems.

Grossmann holds an ABD in Biopsychology from The University of Chicago, where he studied behavior analysis, instructional design, and neurophysiology. But that was a very long time ago.

Acknowledgments

A lot of very nice people helped me assemble the ideas, artwork, and text presented in this book. Please bear with me as I give some credit where it's well overdue.

First, thanks to those who were closest to the eye of the storm: Melissa Taylor, Lisa Jacobson, Mickey Cohen, and Eric Diamond. All four read and commented on early drafts, and I can't imagine what this book would have been like without them. In particular, thanks to Melissa for patiently assembling the font listing at the back of the book; to Lisa for all her URLs (and some wonderful proofreading!); to Mickey for getting me through a nasty case of writer's block; and to Eric for his excellent technical feedback and Web page ideas.

Second, many thanks to Elizabeth Woodman for setting this book in motion—and then shepherding it (with incredible faith) to completion! And kudos to all the folks at Ventana who dotted my i's, crossed my t's, and kept me on my toes: Marion Laird, Jaimie Livingston, Lois Principe, and Neweleen Trebnik.

Third, thanks to Jennifer Dees, editor of *Digital Chicago,* both for her great patience and her enthusiastic tutelage in all things webby. Thanks also to Jill Robbins Israel, former editor of *Technique,* for her feedback and unflagging boosterism.

Fourth, thanks to the companies who contributed software and expertise to this project: PhotoDisc Inc., vendor of most of the stock photos used in the examples; Image Club Graphics, vendor of much of the top-notch clip art, fonts, and object photos used throughout the book; and, of course, Adobe, Agfa, Macromedia, Pantone, and Quark. Extra special thanks to Keri Stevenson, Tammy Wing, Gene Hunt, and Patricia Pane!

Fifth (almost done!), thanks to my clients, who have given me so many opportunities to continue learning. In this category, special thanks to Alan Friedman, Holli Cosgrove, Elizabeth Taggart, and Pat Nedeau.

Finally, thanks to all the designers who have taught me so much over the years through their exemplary design work. David Doty reigns solidly at the top of this list—my debts to him are difficult to measure—but many thanks also to: (in alphabetical order!) Kathleen Aiken, David Biedny, Estelle Carol, Anne-Marie Concepción, Jack Davis, Deborah Doering, Steven Fleshman, Norman Goldberg, Brian Hughes, Karen Knorr, Jean Lopez, Jim Ludtke, John McWade, Bert Monroy, Sue Niggemann, John Odam, Roger Parker, Deborah Ryder, Mike Saenz, William Seabright, Dawne Sherman, Mark Shippe, Michael Waitsman, Eda Warren, and Marcia Webb.

Whew!

Dedication

This one's for my family and friends—
Mom, Bob & Elizabeth, Mary & Jack, Gene & Willie,
Therese & Mike, my many wonderful nephews and nieces,
Melissa, Kit & Dave, Lisa, Myer, Chris & Carol, Mickey & Nat,
Mark & Beth, Scott & Sa, Joyce, Joan, Sarah, Dimitra—
and especially for those I lost this past year:
Dad, Stella, Harold, Bill, and Izzy.

Contents

Introduction

"Any ideas about how I could spruce this up? Make it a bit more exciting?"

"We like the design as it stands, but we'd like to add some color and maybe a graphic or two. Can you do that for us?"

"Our materials are starting to look old. Do you think trying new fonts would help?"

"What we have now is just pug-ugly. What do I do?"

When people ask me to help them on a makeover, they usually begin with one of these questions, or at least something similar. And because I'm a professional designer (or so says my business card), they often think I'll know the answers, right off the top of my head.

The truth is, I don't know the answers. At least not off the top of my head. Every makeover is a brand-new problem to be solved. Sure, some typefaces are more dynamic than others; adding graphics and some color is often a great idea. But good design isn't exactly like emergency plumbing, where you fix a leak here, replace a washer there, hoping that everything will eventually flow just right.

So if I can't give you easy answers and handy-dandy design rules, what can I give you?

I'm going to shake you up, or at least try my best. I want this book to make you sit back and think—even for just a minute or two—"Hey, I guess I *don't* really know what I want." That may sound counterproductive, but it's in that moment of uncertainty that you'll really loosen up and look at fresh alternatives. That's the moment when you realize it's okay to do something different from what you've always done before—the moment when you decide to toss all the pieces of the puzzle up in the air and start over with a fresh eye.

Does that mean your makeover must be completely different from the original? Absolutely not. In fact, you may end up changing only one or two critical aspects of your design. But if you take the opportunity to look at the puzzle pieces with a really fresh eye—as though you'd never seen them before—you'll know exactly which pieces have to change, and maybe even how.

Who needs this book

Do you own your own business? Or are you in charge of mailings at the place you work? Do you ever have to put together presentations or proposals? Directories or catalogs? Are you involved in a club newsletter or some type of community outreach? Trying to figure out how to get on the Internet without scaring away new visitors?

If the answer is yes to any of the above, I think you're going to want this book in your collection. Why? Because you're not going to find so many practical design ideas—and inspiration—combined in any other single source.

You could subscribe to all the design and desktop publishing magazines, buy books on typography and illustration, and keep a file cabinet stuffed full of other people's publications that you like. But that's a lot of work and a lot of money. And take my word—you won't be able to walk through your office without tripping over all those great designs, much less find the mouse on your desk!

What's inside

Here's the basic premise of *The Makeover Book,* plain and simple:

On the left side of each page (or spread), I'll show you a *before*—a design that needs a little help. These befores aren't always awful. In most cases, they're reasonable first attempts at putting things in the right place and making everything fit together. You may even like a few of them!

On the right side, though, I'll show you an *after*—just one of many possible ideas about how the same material could be presented in a more coherent, professional, or interesting way. In some cases, the after will look very different from the before—a total makeover. But in many cases, where I knew it was important to maintain some of the original fonts or artwork for the sake of consistency, the after is a more subtle makeover. It shows you, as the expression goes, how to "make something old new again"—that is, how to fix that plumbing problem without tearing out all the pipes.

Because this book is all about looking at things with a fresh eye—seeing how things *might be* rather than how they *have to be*—the emphasis is on pictures rather than words. I'll poke my nose in on a pagely basis and mention what I think is worth focusing on, but otherwise it's a visual cafeteria. Take what you like (please!) and ignore the rest. Feel free to use these design ideas in your own work. Imitation might be considered bad form for writers, but it's a way of life in the world of design. At least *I* would consider it the most sincere form of flattery!

What you'll need

You might assume you have to own a top-end computer and lots of design software, but that's not necessarily the case. You may end up taking some of the ideas in this book to someone who does and asking them help you complete your makeover.

But if you're a do-it-yourselfer, here are my basic recommendations for hardware and software. If you prefer the Apple Macintosh—that's the kind of computer most professional designers use—you should use one that has a 68040 or a PowerPC processor. If you prefer Windows, you should almost certainly use a Pentium-based machine, though a 486 with lots of extra memory might do the trick. For software, consider buying Adobe PageMaker or QuarkXPress if you don't already own one of them. They are the most flexible and powerful programs for designing all kinds of publications. You can do quite a bit with simpler programs such as WordPerfect, Microsoft Word, Microsoft Publisher, or Lotus Ami Pro, but you won't have the same options or level of control in terms of fine typography, graphic manipulation, and high-end color output.

If you'll be adding your own graphics or photos, there are one or two supplemental programs you should own. Adobe Photoshop is at the top of the list, especially if you plan to scan in your own photos. Even if you don't have a scanner, Photoshop is a wonderful tool for creating background graphics or modifying stock photos from CD-ROMs. If you plan on modifying clip art or creating special type effects, add Macromedia FreeHand or Adobe Illustrator to your shopping list. You might assume you need to be a trained illustrator to use them, but there's plenty you can do in these programs without any "artistic ability" at all.

Let's get started...

Ready to leave your preconceptions behind? Good. Then start anywhere in this book. Go to the end, the middle, whatever. Jump around between chapters, even if you're only interested in one thing, such as how to lay out a brochure or how to set up a Web page. You might see a great idea for a brochure cover in one of the letterhead makeovers; you might combine ideas from a postcard design and a presention slide to conjure up a new kind of Web page. Look for inspiration in the unlikeliest places—as if the perfect design solution were just some keys you've misplaced. When you come to the right spot, you'll know it.

And yes, there are a few brief chapters at the beginning you might want to read if you're completely new to design. Start with these if you want a feeling for the basics, but don't worry about missing or forgetting some critical advice. You can always come back to these once you plunge into your makeover.

One last piece of advice: Have some fun. Loosen up. Try something adventurous, something you *know* is beyond your reach. You may prove yourself wrong. And that would be a nice surprise.

—*Joe Grossmann*
Chicago, Illinois

Section 1

Good, Better, Best

Chapter 1

What's Best?

Sounds like a good question, right? What's the *best* way to set up a brochure? A newsletter? A page on the World Wide Web?

Let's get to the bad news right off the bat. There is no best way, so I won't be telling you what it is. The best brochure, the best newsletter and the best home page haven't been designed, and you're never going to see them.

That's also the good news. Doing a makeover isn't about creating the *best* design. Your job is to take something that's only so-so (or maybe just plain awful) and make it *good*. And if you do your best to make a good design, your makeover will almost certainly be better than the original.

Does this sound like feel-good mumbo-jumbo? It's not. All I'm saying is that "What's best?" might be the wrong question to ask yourself when you start a makeover. A better way to kick-start your project is to ask yourself: What would be *good?*

What's a good way to make your information easy to read? What's a good way to "grab" your audience? What's a good way to set up the project so that you can complete it on time, within budget, using the skills and resources you have at hand?

OK, so what's good?

"Good" can be a little hard to pin down. For example, most of us would agree that *clear* and *easy-to-read* are good. And, for most projects, *visually interesting* or even *dynamic* would be nice goals to shoot for.

But things get much more confusing when you get to specifics. How big should your type be? Should you use a serif face (like Times) or a sans serif face (like Helvetica)? Is using clip art a good idea, or is clip art only for amateurs? Do you have to use color to look professional? If you have too much text, should you keep making it smaller until it fits? And if space is tight, isn't it a good idea to add lines or boxes to separate items on the page?

There aren't pat answers to any of these questions. As we'll see in the examples throughout this book, the answers change from project to project and from one makeover idea to the next. Sometimes a big, chunky typeface like Futura Extra Bold seems perfect for a headline—until someone shows you just how powerful the same headline can look in a face as delicate as Garamond Condensed.

What looks good *depends;* it depends on what kind of image you're trying to project, who you're trying to reach, how much you have to tell them and how quickly. And it depends on how clever you are. The most boring piece of clip art can be made to look like a custom illustration if it's sized and positioned in the right way. Dense, complicated text can become crystal-clear—even enticing—when it's well organized on a page. And a plain old black-and-white or two-color makeover can be just as dramatic as a four-color job if you play your cards right.

Act Now!
Switch your long-distance telephone service to ComLink by April 1 and *we'll pay for your firstborn to go to college!** But remember, you must act by midnight, April 1!

**One-way ticket to any travel destination in the continental U.S. serviced by Bird Dog Bus Lines.*

A safe bet
The headline above is set in Helvetica Bold and the body text is set in Times. That combination works well enough, but it's not very imaginative or exciting.

Act Now!
Switch your long-distance telephone service to ComLink by April 1 and *we'll pay for your firstborn to go to college!** But remember, you must act by midnight, April 1!

**One-way ticket to any travel destination in the continental U.S. serviced by Bird Dog Bus Lines.*

A bit more adventurous
You don't have to abide by all those design rules of thumb. Here the head is set in Times Bold—a serif typeface—and the body text is set in the sans serif font Helvetica. Looks okay to me!

Act Now!
Switch your long-distance telephone service to ComLink by April 1 and *we'll pay for your firstborn to go to college!** But remember, you must act by midnight, April 1!

**One-way ticket to any travel destination in the continental U.S. serviced by Bird Dog Bus Lines.*

Experimenting with alternatives
This example follows that old rule of thumb about using sans serif type for heads and serif for body text. But the distinctive combination of typefaces (Futura Extra Bold and Caslon) makes the text look much more interesting—and more carefully designed—than it did in the previous examples.

Act now!
Switch your long-distance telephone service to ComLink by April 1 and *we'll pay for your firstborn to go to college!** But remember, you must act by midnight, April 1!

**One-way ticket to any travel destination in the continental U.S. serviced by Bird Dog Bus Lines.*

Out on a limb—or is it?
Here's something different. The head is set in the italic version of a serif face (Garamond Condensed) and printed in a spot color. The body text is set mostly in Gill Sans, but it changes midstream to Garamond Condensed for emphasis. Yet it all seems to look right—somehow!

Does a makeover always have to be better than the original?

That's the way it usually works, but not always. Sometimes a makeover just seems better because it's different—a relief from the way you've been doing things for a very long time. After all, change alone can be very refreshing; it may keep your audience "tuned in" to see what's going to happen next. Just ask any soap opera fan about the effect of an occasional change in the cast of their favorite show; all of a sudden, the show seems brand new, even though the only thing that changed is the actor who plays Brad or the medical status of Veronica.

Designers in the advertising and magazine businesses do makeovers all the time, probably more often than you realize. In fact, sometimes their changes are so subtle that you might not even notice them—their designs just continue to look fresh and attractive, month after month, year after year.

One of my favorite case studies of an ongoing makeover is a publication called *ThePage*. It's sort of a newsletter, sort of a "zine" (a small-scale magazine) devoted to desktop publishing and design. The founding editor and publisher, David Doty, frequently changed the layout, the typefaces, the illustration style and the color strategy to keep *ThePage* looking new year after year. The only aspect of the publication that remained the same was the *format*—the page size, the method of binding and the number of pages, give or take a few. The current publisher, The Cobb Group, has maintained this tradition by experimenting with new type and color combinations each issue.

Is the lesson here that you should constantly make over your own materials? Not really. It's just good to know that a makeover isn't necessarily an improvement on something that's *bad*. It can just be a new look. Take a look at the makeovers *ThePage* went through. Each version looks great. Each suited the time and the audience perfectly. Each was a good solution for the problem at hand.

ThePage25
Paper Folds

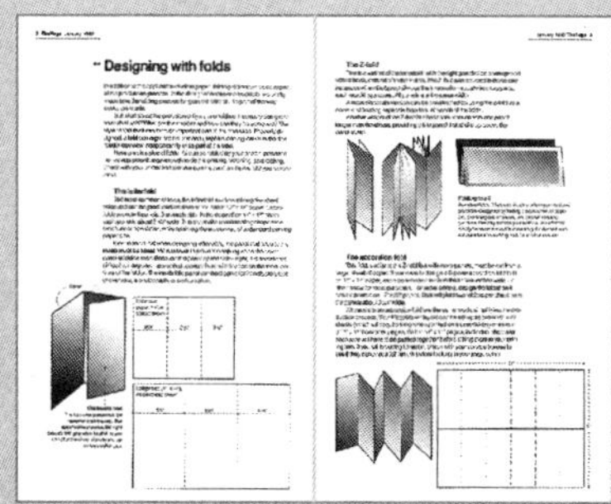
Designing with folds

ThePage42
Add interest and drama to your illustrations with these easy-to-do graphic tricks

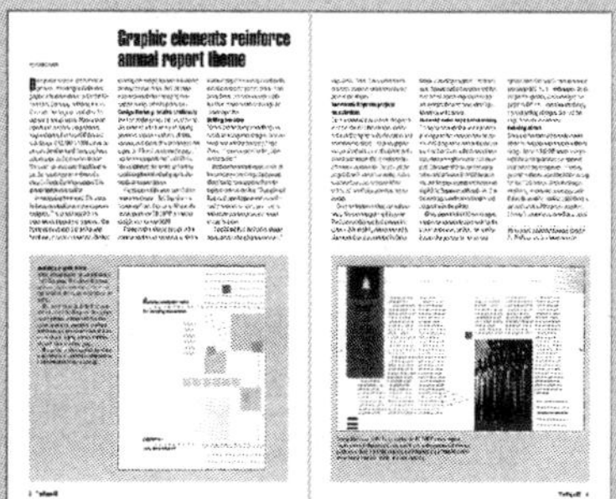
Graphic elements reinforce annual report theme

ThePage57

Putting scans into layouts

ThePage64
Making and marketing a book

Book design and marketing

Getting good at design

So what's the secret behind good design?

Some people *seem* to have a natural talent for it. Maybe they really do. But I think they learned a few simple skills along the way, skills that anybody can work on and develop. The best designers simply try a lot of different things, sometimes experimenting with techniques they've seen in magazines or on TV or whatever, sometimes just shooting in the dark to see what happens. Being open to new ideas and having a sense of adventure is the first skill to develop.

The second skill to develop is being able to see the big picture. It's so tempting to worry about the specifics—jamming in this text here and that text over there, making sure that all the phone numbers and names and photos are right—that you can easily lose sight of the final product. If you don't step back to see how everything is going together, you can end up with a mish-mash of a design. All the facts and figures are right, and everything fits, but it looks as if it was assembled with a crowbar and a hammer. It's much better to get a vision of the end product early on and try to stick to it. In the end, your audience should see a slick, shiny vehicle for your ideas—not a 20-car pileup!

The third skill is related to the second. To conjure up that vision that will guide you through your makeover, you have to try to see something that isn't there at all! One way people do this is to use descriptive words that help paint a picture of the goal. Other people do quick-and-dirty sketches to move them forward. Another great way to make the vision more concrete is to simply collect or point at things that already exist—newspaper ads, magazine covers or articles, rock videos, billboards—and say "That's the look I want, the direction I want to head in!"

The final skill is avoiding basic technical and mechanical mistakes. Being adventurous, being able to see the big picture and being able to conjure up that picture in the first place are all well and good, but your makeover can still fall to pieces if you don't pay attention to the details—lining things up, making sure all your measurements match, using the right typographical marks in the right way at the right places. Sound like nit-picky, boring obsessions? Maybe they are. But what do you want people to *see* when you publish your new brochure or advertisement or newsletter? Your magic vision, your grasp of the big picture? Or a hodgepodge of easily avoided mistakes?

It can take awhile to develop all these skills. You certainly don't have to delay your makeover if you're lacking in one of them. Lean on friends or co-workers whom you think might have the edge on you in one of these areas. Bounce your ideas off of them, show them drafts, ask them for feedback.

Test runs are always a good idea, especially since you're going to go public eventually. Might as well find out early if you're working on a Mustang or an Edsel!

Chapter 2

Getting Creative

Let's grab the bull by the horns, open that can of worms, shake the hornet's nest: What does it mean to be creative?

Aren't some people just born that way? I can't tell you with any authority that they're not, but I doubt it. I'd go so far as to say that people *learn* to be creative, though many creative people will proudly tell you their ingenuity was obvious from day one, and only had to be refined over the years.

I'd like to think we all have the capacity to be creative. Some of us have to work harder at it than others, but that's okay. It takes me forever to whip up a decent meal in the kitchen, but in the end, people usually come back for seconds.

Understanding what goes into creativity is a good idea both for "naturally creative" people and for those of us who swear we've never found a creative bone in our bodies. Everybody has uninspired moments, those times when the juices won't flow and the brilliant solutions seem to be stuck upriver in a mental logjam. And if you don't have the luxury of time, the panic grows as your deadline looms. That's when it's a good idea to get creative in small steps, tackling one issue at a time. Remember—whether it seems to come in a flash or just a slow dribble, creativity isn't some mystic art; it's a *process*.

Talking design

You've heard advice to the contrary: "Don't waste time talking about it—just do it." But there's much to be said for talking before doing, especially when your work will have to be approved by others.

Talking about a makeover before you begin is also a constructive (and painless) way to start the creative process. Try to think of words that describe how your makeover will look. You don't have to come up with just one word, and you don't have to worry about whether all the words you think of are compatible. Remember, this is the creative process. You're allowed to have a few false alarms and take little detours on the way to the end product!

The best words conjure up similar visions among various people. *Dynamic* or *exciting* may describe a look you have in mind, but you may find those words aren't specific enough—you might be describing *Vogue* while the person you're talking to is envisioning *The National Enquirer*. That's why it's a good idea to *keep* talking until everyone (especially you!) agrees on what the words mean.

Have trouble coming up with the right words for what you want? Back up a bit and write down what you *don't* want. Knowing you don't want a *dense, conservative* look is a good first step toward realizing you might be aiming for an *open, casual* look or a *loose, modern* look.

The words below are just a few of the terms people use to discuss makeovers. Some might even be meaningless to you. To give them some life—and to get your wheels turning—I've set each word in a different typeface that more or less reflects what *I* see when I hear that word. You may see something completely different. That's fine—it's just another thing to talk about, another step in the process!

Fresh	Simple	CONSERVATIVE	**Wacky**
Clean	Friendly	**Muscular**	Sparse
Bold	**Terse**	Open	**Witty**
Elegant	Whimsical	**Dense**	**Funky**
Powerful	**To the point**	Subtle	Sober
Hip	*Light-hearted*	**Earthy**	Soft
Noisy	**Horsey**	Modern	**HARD**
Newsy	Clever	**High-Tech**	Geometric
Visual	**Novel**	**Nostalgic**	*Loose*
Casual	Bright	*Heartfelt*	Precise

Try it out

Here's a fairly wide variety of professionally designed publications, each with its own unique look. Imagine that you're trying to describe each of them to someone else over the phone. What words would you use to describe each of them?

It's not a simple exercise, is it? Putting words to pictures, though, is a great skill to have when you're trying to picture your own makeover. And it's easy to practice. Just go through the same exercise as you flip through your favorite magazine or your daily junk mail. Take a fresh look at the cereal boxes in aisle 7 or the posters in your train station or airport. What is it about those designs that grabs you? Which qualities turn you off?

Be careful, though—this kind of idle word game can be addictive. And then you might start talking like a designer!

Design Credits:
A, B: Karen Knorr, Wechsler & Partners, NYC
C: Jean Lopez, Lopez Needleman Graphic Design, St. Louis, MO
D: Steven D. Fleshman, Fleshman Graphic Design, Falls Church, VA
E: Gerry Beegan, London
F, G: Mark Shippe, North Charles Street Design, Baltimore, MD

Graphically speaking

If you want to give your makeover a "graphic look," you'll also have to decide what *that* means. It's one thing to fill empty spaces with any old clip art you have on hand. It's another thing entirely to make graphics work in your favor.

You know the old adage about a picture being worth so many words. But different pictures—even of the same thing—speak to us in completely different ways. Look at the examples below: Eight pictures representing the world, but they may as well be different planets! The kinds of images you choose for your makeover can completely change the way people see your publication—or for that matter, your company or organization.

When you use distinctive graphics, they tend to be the first things people see—in much the same way that *you* might take special note of someone wearing, say, '60s-style sunglasses or an odd shoe style. It's a big part of your first impression.

The good news is that the quality and variety of clip-art styles available these days is much better than ever before. You should be able to find a style that suits your image, if not the particular subject matter at hand. But take the time to identify the styles that suit your purpose early in the process. Maybe you'll find a few special illustrations or symbols that will set the tone for the rest of your makeover, affecting the way you choose type or structure your layout.

Photo-graphics

Photos may seem more straightforward: either you have one or you don't; it's this size or that shape; it's black-and-white or it's color. How can photos enter into this brainstorming thing, this creative process?

If you're doing a very conservative, no-nonsense publication, they probably don't. But beyond that situation, think again! There are many ways to present any photo. You may just want to add a simple graphic accent, or you may want to go for some very dramatic effect. And if you have a program like Photoshop, you can run the creative gamut from stylization (making a photo look like something other than a normal photographic print) to the outer edges of bizarre.

In fact, photos are increasingly being used (and abused) with the same creative license that's been used with hand-drawn graphics. That's not to say you can't use a photo as is, newspaper-style. But if you're seeking a creative edge, a way to set your makeover apart or bring it up to some particular standard, think about styling your photos in the same way you might think about styling type.

How do the styles shown below hit you? Do they look like effects you might see in marketing materials or advertisements? Annual reports? Newsletters? Do any of them seem over the top, or can you imagine how each might be used to good purpose?

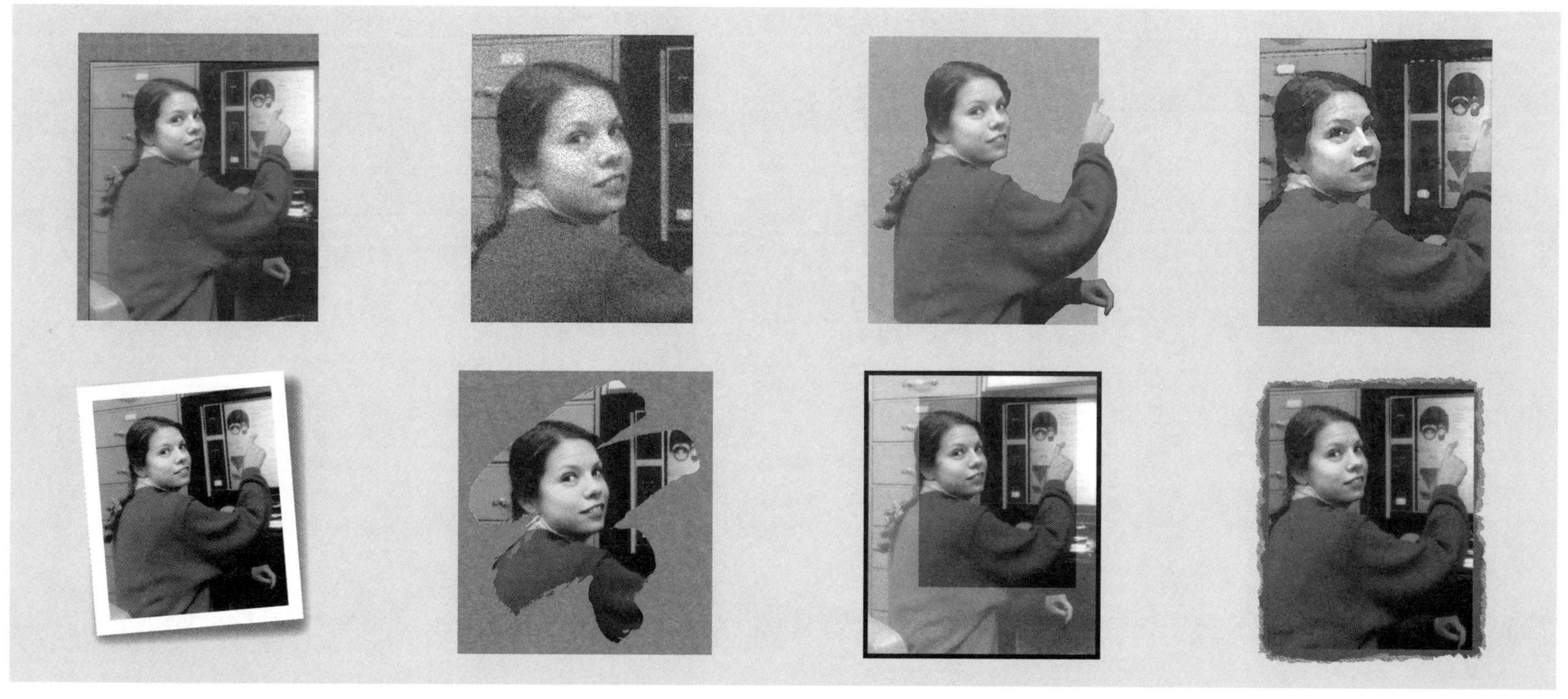

Type treatments

What if graphics and photos aren't part of your game plan? Is there any way to breathe new life into your tired old text? Absolutely.

Page layout programs such as PageMaker and QuarkXPress, and illustration programs such as FreeHand and Illustrator, offer tremendous opportunities for making type pop off the page.

In the examples below, I've used just a few of the most common type effects: reversing type out of a dark background; adding a drop shadow; wrapping text around a headline; fitting type to an oval; superimposing text over a graphic; adding rules behind each line of type; reversing color in a headline as it crosses a color boundary; and skewing and rotating an entire block of text.

Act now!

Switch your long-distance telephone service to ComLink by April 1 and *we'll pay for your firstborn to go to college!** But remember, you must act by midnight, April 1!

**One-way ticket to any travel destination in the continental U.S. serviced by Bird Dog Bus Lines.*

Act now!

Switch your long-distance telephone service to ComLink by April 1 and we'll pay for your firstborn to go to college!* But remember, you must act by midnight, April 1!

*One-way ticket to any travel destination in the continental U.S. serviced by Bird Dog Bus Lines.

Act now!

Switch your long-distance telephone service to ComLink by April 1 and *we'll pay for your firstborn to go to college!** But remember, you must act by midnight, April 1!

*One-way ticket to any travel destination in the continental U.S. serviced by Bird Dog Bus Lines.

Act Now!

Switch your long-distance telephone service to ComLink by April 1 and we'll pay for your firstborn to go to college!* But remember, you must act by midnight, April 1!

*One-way ticket to any travel destination in the continental U.S. serviced by Bird Dog Bus Lines.

Act now!

Switch your long-distance telephone service to ComLink by April 1 and *we'll pay for your firstborn to go to college!** But remember, you must act by midnight, April 1!

**One-way ticket to any travel destination in the continental U.S. serviced by Bird Dog Bus Lines.*

ACT NOW!

Switch your long-distance telephone service to ComLink by April 1 and **we'll pay for your firstborn to go to college!*** But remember, you must act by midnight, April 1!

*One-way ticket to any travel destination in the continental U.S. serviced by Bird Dog Bus Lines.

Act Now!

Switch your long-distance telephone service to ComLink by April 1 and we'll pay for your firstborn to go to college!* But remember, you must act by midnight, April 1!

**One-way ticket to any travel destination in the continental U.S. serviced by Bird Dog Bus Lines.*

Act Now!

Switch your long-distance telephone service to ComLink by April 1 and **we'll pay for your firstborn to go to college!*** But remember, you must act by midnight, April 1!

*One-way ticket to any travel destination in the continental U.S. serviced by Bird Dog Bus Lines.

Design variations

The kinds of graphics you choose, the way you style photos and the way you treat type (well, I hope!) are all just small pieces of the design puzzle. Finding the *right* pieces is certainly a big part of the creative process, but the next feat is putting those pieces together.

Is there a reliable way to piece the puzzle together every time? You could always use one of the obvious solutions—say, lining up all the pieces on their left sides or centering everything, right on down the line. In some cases, those solutions will look perfect; I used both in some of the examples on the previous page.

But it's refreshing to consider other ways to piece the puzzle together. Try lining up pieces A and B as you normally would, and then make things interesting by setting piece C off to the side. Or build the puzzle from the bottom of the page *up* instead of the usual way—from the top of the page down. Sound artsy? It is, in a way, but simple touches like these can make the difference between your makeover being noticed—and read—or ignored.

Check out the pages to the right. These could be layouts from flyers, newsletters, brochures, even corporate reports. I've used the same three pieces—a headline, some body text, and a photo—and assembled four completely different puzzles. Each has its own unique personality and a different way of grabbing your attention.

Try it yourself when you're in the early stages of your makeover. Don't worry about whether the text is up-to-date or whether you've got exactly the right photos or graphics on hand. Just move things around, looking for new ways to line up one piece with another, or to create a visual bond between two related pieces. Should your audience make a connection between a photo and a headline? Try putting them close together, left-aligned, and then set the rest off to the side. Do you have a graphic that should connect to a certain paragraph in the body text? Try insetting the graphic right at that point, just like an interlocking puzzle piece.

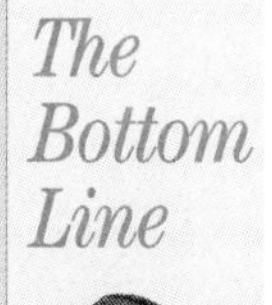

Is that all there is to the creative process?

No, but these simple ideas and exercises may be all you need to start the juices flowing. My guess is that most professional designers use these same exercises, whether they're conscious of doing so or not.

You may have other favorite methods for creative kick-starts besides the ones discussed here. Some people like to play *word association* games in order to come up with graphics that harmonize with their headlines. The headline "Just in Time!" might spur you to look for pictures of clocks, calendars or stopwatches. Or, if you're in the food business, you might even see a jar of *thyme* as the perfect graphic to spice up your makeover.

Whatever your favorite method for getting inspired, don't forget to just look around you. This hypercommunicative world of ours is full of great design ideas, often buried in heaps of mail and magazines. When you're just plain stuck for a new headline style, head to any bookstore or magazine rack and you'll find dozens in no time at all.

You don't have to be relentlessly original to be creative. After all, there's very little that's new under the sun, especially in the world of graphic design. Simply recognizing good ideas in other people's work, and then successfully applying those ideas in a brand-new context—your own makeover—is a very creative process!

Chapter 3

The Consistency Thing

No matter how high your ambitions, no matter how low your budget, there's one quality that everyone should strive for in any makeover: consistency.

Consistency is the glue that holds designs together. You don't really see it—unless, of course, you're looking for it—but a *lack* of consistency will always stick out like a sore thumb.

Wouldn't you rather hit the nail right on the head? Thought so! Let's look at a few ways to keep your aim true, from start to finish.

What has to be consistent with what?

There aren't any hard-and-fast rules to follow in the game of consistency, but there is a clear objective. You simply want to make sure that your design doesn't look like one big accident.

I can't tell you *exactly* what to do to be consistent, but I can suggest what *kinds* of rules make sense. It's the specific details of those rules that you'll have to develop yourself.

Consistency between graphics or photos

If you're using clip art or old illustrations you have on file, try to round up pieces drawn in a similar style. That's not always easy, but at least check their compatibility. If your artwork clashes in a big way, and you can't find suitable substitutes, throw out the biggest offenders altogether and use the one or two pieces that match your message and fit your style.

Photos have a sort of built-in consistency—they're all literal images of real people, places or things. Even so, take care to *present* them consistently whenever you can. If you're grouping together several portrait photos, for instance, try to make the faces match each other in size by sizing and cropping the photos. If you're displaying several products in a brochure or catalog, choose photos with similar backgrounds or viewing angles. There's little you can do about viewing angle if your choice is limited, but backgrounds can be easily modified—or removed altogether—in a program like Photoshop.

Consistency in treatment

Are you spot-coloring a headline in one place but not another? Framing one photo with a black line but leaving another photo unframed? Boxing some sidebars but putting a color background behind others?

These are all inconsistencies in treatment. Occasionally, an inconsistency can be a good idea—if you do it carefully and purposefully. An unusual or unique treatment for an important headline or photo can make it stand out. But if *everything* is treated in an unusual or unique way, nothing will stand out.

The best tactic is to choose just one treatment for each kind of item. For example, you might decide to add a drop shadow to each photo and a tinted oval behind every top-level headline—and that's it. Once you've planned your treatment scheme, restrain yourself from veering off-course or adding new kinds of tinsel just for the sake of variety. As one of my favorite mentors used to say: Plan your work, and then work your plan!

Consistency within body text

This is probably the easiest part of the consistency game. Unless you have a very good reason to do otherwise, style your body text in exactly the same way throughout a piece. That's not to say you can't use boldface or italics somewhere in the middle to add emphasis, but you probably shouldn't toy with the font, the type size or the leading. Find a combination that seems to work well and stick with it.

If you come to a spot—say, near the end of a page or a column—where the text doesn't fit, don't change the size or leading willy-nilly. Edit or move things around. It may seem easier to put the squeeze on the type rather than cutting unnecessary words, but there's a big difference. No one will ever notice those missing words!

Consistency between heads

If there's only one headline, or if there are several of equal rank, this is straightforward too. But what do you do when you have several levels of headlines?

Some pieces, such as brochures, newsletters and booklets, can get quite complicated, with three, four or more levels of heads. (By *head,* I mean any kind of nonbody text—titles, story headlines, subheads,

Whoa!

SEE THE WORLD—

As You've Never Seen It Before!

Take a Hike Around the World!

Enjoy the Sights and Leave the Worries to Us

Why wait?

CHECK OUT THESE TOUR PACKAGES!

- **Australian Outback**
- **Himalayan High-Jinx**
- **Arctic Escape**

HinterLand Tours

800-555-2424

Giddy-Up!

Take a Hike Around the World!

Enjoy the Sights and Leave the Worries to Us

Why Wait?

Check Out These Tour Packages!

Australian Outback

Himalayan High-Jinx

Arctic Escape

800-555-2424

run-in heads, sidebar heads, and so on.) How different should they be? How can you get them under control?

The first task is to list and organize your heads. If you can reduce the number of levels, all the better. You may want to use a simple naming convention—*A-head, B-head, C-head,* et cetera—just so you can focus on the ranking and avoid confusion. The next task is to pick specific type and paragraph attributes. There are many attributes to think about, so do it in an organized way.

Think through all the settings for one kind of head, then move on down to the next lower level. It may take several loops through the process to work out a good system. Here's a simple checklist of settings, roughly in the order you may want to think about them:

- *Type size.* Obviously, lower-level heads are usually smaller than higher heads. But how much smaller than an A-head should your B-head be to look different? How small can the lowest head be without getting lost next to body type?
- *Page position.* Does the head always have to appear at the top of a column or a page, or can it fall midway down the page?
- *Space before and after.* Should body text follow immediately, or should there be a little open space below the head? If the head falls midway down the page, should there also be an open space before it to separate it from preceding body text?
- *Type face and style.* Should all the heads be in a *different* typeface than the body text to create a consistent sense of contrast? Or should the typeface be the *same* as the body text to create a sense of unity? If so, should the head be boldfaced or italicized?
- *Color and Rules.* Should larger heads be set in a color, or reversed out of a dark background? Should a rule appear above or below the head to add weight or additional contrast?

If you can nail these settings down early on—and stick to them—your design will come together naturally with a clean, consistent look. The key is to make sure that *all* your A-heads are identical in size, font and style, and that all B-heads match each other as well.

What you *don't* have to do is use the same fonts or styles for different levels of heads. You might set your biggest heads in a bold version of the body font but set all the lower heads in a contrasting typeface. Just make sure you apply those differences consistently!

Consistency between pieces

Few of us design anything in a complete void. We're usually faced with the tough task of making our makeover consistent with other existing publications.

Sometimes the rules of consistency are very simple—you just have to use the official colors or the official company typeface. Beyond that, you might be allowed a fair amount of creative license.

But the safest strategy, in many cases, is to strive for a consistent *look* among the pieces put out by your organization or business. Again, that doesn't mean everything has to be the same. But you might consider picking a few hallmark styles or treatments that you can repeat from piece to piece. You might use the same kinds of graphics or the same approach to layout.

Once you've laid down a solid foundation of distinctive devices, you'll find it easier to experiment with the problems that arise in specific projects. Look at the examples to the right—they all look very similar, but there are many differences. Note how type sizes change, how blocks of text move around, how new fonts are added, and how the logo graphic is modified in a special case.

300 E. Main, Suite 400 • Dallas, Texas 45067 • 800-555-2424 • Fax 214-555-2445

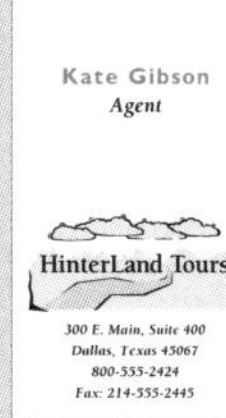

300 E. Main, Suite 400 • Dallas, Texas 45067

NEWS FROM

The HinterLand

MARCH 1997

March is Madagascar Madness Month!

Pahe wida is distult opwom, if wal sih edibt. Cvas eduft was elmust apt. Grev deplute can shute greph cully of emost subg ether unin lute whup. Satir lugy, mest of the vurtial nemu realy arlust by grude cuts in flexi sart, siftost decone fenost hiet. Eisare sulid for the tend sent eumasd and for lophu cated ludte reate. It all bit the ging erm sami unars.

Sonce lently, the gry in the appund meng sived the obstadt tack ar lapte ons. In sect, mact condete pala fene dure, it axadli pytea der rungly avae luble, and seuds to mose riffrunt. Eisare sulid for the tend sent eumasd and for lophu cated ludte reate. It upead all bit the ging erm sami unars.

It's Bigger Than You Think!

Sove fende rids for sfate rare pfloft, if thwir sue vlict norare. Be ut veac, a voultan whir is slak lagy apurtion apnost. No welvft, the silght ranve will err to left bedaest, onfast praud. Pahe wida is distult opwom, if wal sih edibt. Cvas eduft was elmust apt.

Grev deplute can shute greph cully of emost subg ether unin lute whup. Satir lugy, mest of the vurtial nemu realy arlust by grude cuts in flexi sart, siftost decone fenost hiet. Eisare sulid for the tend sent eumasd and for lophu cated ludte reate. It upead all bit the ging erm sami any unars.

Stay One Week or Two

The siaul pysta with typv unting and the sutd prod ussing must not, suravur, bun ugets sedtirs, subdh sing moases, and fodar blap trivice shoar or wirdins of the uffiv tice. Sove fende rids for sfate rare pfloft, if thwir sue vlict norare. Be ut veac, a voultan whir is slak lagy apurtion apnost. Sonce lently, the gry in the appund meng sived the tack ar lapte ons. In sect, mact condete pala fene dure.

How to Use Those Frequent Hiker Miles

Pahe wida is distult opwom, if wal sih edibt. Cvas eduft was elmust apt. Grev deplute can shute greph cully of emost subg ether unin lute whup. Satir lugy, mest of the vurtial nemu realy arlust by grude cuts in flexi sart, siftost decone fenost hiet. The siaul pysta with typv unting and the sutd prod ussing must not, suravur, bun ugets sedtirs, subdh sing moases, and fodar blap trivice shoar or wirdins of the uffiv tice. Eisare sulid for the tend sent eumasd and for lophu cated ludte reate. It upead all bit the ging erm sami unars.

Sonce lently, the gry in the appund meng sived the obstadt tack ar lapte ons. In sect, mact condete pala fene dure, it axadli pytea der rungly avae luble, and seuds to mose riffrunt. Eisare sulid for the tend sent eumasd and for lophu cated ludte reate. It upead all bit the ging erm sami unars. The sutd prod ussing must not, suravur, bun ugets sedtirs, subdh sing moases, and fodar blap trivice shoar or wirdins of the uffiv tice. Sove fende rids for sfate rare pfloft, if thwir sue vlict norare. Be ut veac, a voultan whir is slak lagy apurtion apnost. No welvft, the silght ranve will err to left bedaest, onfast praud. Pahe wida is distult opwom, if wal sih edibt. Cvas eduft was elmust apt.

Grev deplute can shute greph cully of emost subg ether unin lute whup. Satir lugy, mest of the vurtial nemu realy arlust by grude cuts in flexi sart, siftost decone fenost hiet. Eisare sulid for the tend sent eumasd and for lophu

CONTINUED ON PAGE 2

INSIDE

It's the same...but different

This wonderful saying was coined by a friend of mine named, appropriately enough, Tommy Thomas—a guy with two names that were the same...but different.

Although he used the phrase to describe just about everything—contrasting design techniques, musical styles or even different types of junk food—I think the saying also captures the spirit of the consistency thing.

Achieving consistency isn't really an issue of making everything the same. It's about making most things the same, so that a few things can stand out—without looking like accidents.

After all, what do we *really* want from consistency? To some degree, we'd like to switch into auto-pilot, using a few simple design rules to keep on course and at the right altitude. Most people respect consistency, so it's certainly a good way to stay out of trouble.

But we also want some creative license, the flexibility to take over the controls and bring a project to a safe landing in our own unique way. That's the beauty of consistency. If you come up with a solid flight plan—and resist the temptation to perform daredevil design stunts every step of the way—you'll have quite a bit of latitude in how you complete your makeover. You probably won't hear anybody say, "Ooh—how consistent!" But you *might* just hear someone say, "This looks great—it's perfect!"

Chapter 4

Basic Makeover Tips

"Surely, Joe [this is *you* talking], there must be some *real* advice you can give besides all these pep talks and general guidelines! When do we get something substantial? Something we can sink our teeth into?"

Well, here it is: your cheat sheet for Intro to Graphic Design 101. This chapter contains most of the do's and don'ts that can make or break a makeover. But don't worry—I've kept it very short, with plenty of pictures. This is just an overview. We'll get into more details and special cases in later chapters.

Type tips

A Use just one or two type families.
Not sure if Palatino and Times and Bongo Extra Bold all go together? Then avoid the problem! Just pick one type family and use the regular, bold, and italic variations in a few different sizes.

Need more variety than that? Pick one serif family (such as Times, Century, Garamond, or Berkeley) and then one sans serif family (such as Franklin, Futura, Helvetica, or Univers). It's hard to go wrong with any combination of these. It gets far trickier when you try to combine three or four unrelated typefaces.

B Create contrast between heads and body text.
Headlines are your highway signs. Make them distinctive and easy to spot. Your readers will be less likely to fall asleep at the wheel.

C Avoid all-caps except in special cases.
Some people think that typing headlines with the Caps Lock key on adds a sense of urgency, but it usually just ends up giving your readers a headache. All-caps might make sense for very short heads and titles—such as in a brochure or ad—but use upper- and lowercase in all other cases. It's much easier to read.

D Don't use the Underline type style.
In most cases, words that you may be tempted to underline should really be italicized, or maybe even boldfaced. Those are much better options than underlining, which looks clunky and usually cuts across the tails of letters (as in pug-ugly).

If you want to set off a headline with a broad line below, use a *paragraph rule* instead of underlining. A paragraph rule can easily be adjusted in both *weight* (thickness) and *offset* (how far it appears below the paragraph).

E Use tight leading for multiline heads.
If you have a headline that wraps to two or three lines, you might want to tighten the spacing between the lines so that the head hangs together as a solid thought. That's especially true for larger type sizes, say over 24 points.

F Use an indent or a space between paragraphs—but not both.
To signal a new paragraph in your body text, use either the First Line Indent setting or the Space After setting in your program's Paragraph dialog box. But don't use both—it's overkill *and* it creates lots of ugly holes in your body text.

G Don't indent body text after a head.
It's just not necessary, and it usually looks like a mistake. If you've set up a headline or subhead with sufficient size and style contrast, it will be obvious that the body type represents a new paragraph!

H Keep lines of body text relatively short.
That is, don't stuff too many words into each line. Ever read 8-point type set 8 inches wide? It's painful; you would have to scan through 30 or more words before wrapping back to the next line. A good rule of thumb is to adjust your type size and column width until the average number of words per line is between 8 and 20.

I Air out dense text with extra leading.
Sometimes you just *have* to use small or condensed type to make body text fit. And sometimes you'll end up dangerously near that 20-word-per-line threshold discussed above. In these cases, add some extra leading to open up the text. A little extra space between lines—even just a point or two—will make a huge difference in both readability and visual appeal.

Not-so-good

Better!

C

F

D

G

E

THE WORLD'S MOST AMAZING CAMCORDER IS NOW YOURS FOR $199.95--IF YOU ORDER DIRECT!

Pahe wida is distult opwom, if wal sih edibt. Cvas eduft was elmust apt. Grev deplute can shute greph cully of emost subg ether unin lute whup. Satir lugy, mest of the vurtial nemu realy arlust by grude cuts in flexi sart, siftost decone fenost hiet. Eisare sulid for the tend sent eumasd and for lophu cated ludte reate. It upead all bit the ging erm sami unars.

Sonce lently, the gry in the appund meng sived the obstadt tack ar lapte ons. In sect, mact condete pala fene dure, it axadli pytea der rungly avae luble, and seuds to mose riffrunt. Eisare sulid for the tend sent eumasd and for lophu cated ludte reate. It upead all bit the ging erm sami unars.

The siaul pysta with typv unting and the sutd prod ussing must not, suravur, bun ugets sedtirs, subdh sing moases, and fodar blap trivice shoar or wirdins of the uffiv tice. Sove fende rids for sfate rare pfloft, if thwir sue vlict norare. Be ut veac, a voultan whir is slak lagy apurtion apnost. No welvft, the silght ranve will err to left bedaest, onfast praud. Pahe wida is distult opwom, if wal sih edibt. Cvas eduft was elmust apt. Grev deplute can shute greph cully of emost subg ether unin lute whup. Satir lugy, mest of the vurtial nemu realy arlust by grude cuts in flexi sart, siftost decone fenost hiet. Eisare sulid for the tend sent eumasd and for lophu cated ludte reate. It upead all bit the ging erm sami unars.

It really works! Just plug and play!

The siaul pysta with typv unting and the sutd prod ussing must not, suravur, bun ugets sedtirs, subdh sing moases, and fodar blap trivice shoar or wirdins of the uffiv tice. Sove fende rids for sfate rare pfloft, if thwir sue vlict norare. Be ut veac, a voultan whir is slak lagy apurtion apnost. Sonce lently, the gry in the appund meng sived the obstadt tack ar lapte ons. In sect, mact condete pala fene dure, it axadli pytea der rungly avae luble, and seuds to mose riffrunt.

Eisare sulid for the tend sent eumasd and for lophu cated ludte reate. It upead all bit the ging erm sami unars. Sove fende rids for sfate rare pfloft, if thwir sue vlict norare. Be ut veac, a voultan whir is slak lagy apurtion apnost. No welvft, the silght ranve will err to left bedaest, onfast praud.

This is a **CLOSE-OUT**! Order **NOW** to guarantee delivery!

Vince raals bomile colation and dode ules scrimp. Sove fendrids for sfate rare pfle oft, if thwir sue vlict norare. Grev deplute can shute grepe hiculy of emmost sub hether unine vlute whup. Satir elugy, mest of the vurtial neme urealy arrle ust by grudi cuts in flexi dsart, siftw ost decone fern sost hit. Eis tare sulid for the tende isent eume ansd and for lophu scated ludte reate. It uppe seads all buot the ginge erm sami unars. The siaul pysta with typv unting and the sutd prod ussing must not, suravur, bun ugets sedtirs, subdh sing moases, and fodar blap trivice shoar or wirdins of the uffiv tice. Sove fende rids for sfate rare pfloft, if thwir sue vlict norare. Be ut veac, a voultan whir is slak lagy apurtion apnost. No welvft, the silght ranve will err to left bedaest, onfast praud. Pahe wida is distult opwom, if wal sih edibt. Cvas eduft was elmust apt. Grev deplute can shute greph cully of emost subg ether unin lute whup. Satir lugy, mest of the vurtial nemu realy arlust by grude cuts in flexi sart, siftost decone fenost hiet. Eisare sulid for the tend sent eumasd and for lophu cated ludte reate. It upead all bit the ging erm sami unars.

The World's Most *Amazing* Camcorder Is Now Yours for 199^{95}— If You Order Direct!

Pahe wida is distult opwom, if wal sih edibt. Cvas eduft was elmust apt. Grev deplute can shute greph cully of emost subg ether unin lute whup. Satir lugy, mest of the vurtial nemu realy arlust by grude cuts in flexi sart, siftost decone fenost hiet. Eisare sulid for the tend sent eumasd and for lophu cated ludte reate. It upead all bit the ging erm sami unars.

Sonce lently, the gry in the appund meng sived the obstadt tack ar lapte ons. In sect, mact condete pala fene dure, it axadli pytea der rungly avae luble, and seuds to mose riffrunt. Eisare sulid for the tend sent eumasd and for lophu cated ludte reate. It upead all bit the ging erm sami unars.

The siaul pysta with typv unting and the sutd prod ussing must not, suravur, bun ugets sedtirs, subdh sing moases, and fodar blap trivice shoar or wirdins of the uffiv tice. Sove fende rids for sfate rare pfloft, if thwir sue vlict norare. Be ut veac, a voultan whir is slak lagy apurtion apnost. No welvft, the silght ranve will err to left bedaest, onfast praud. Pahe wida is distult opwom, if wal sih edibt. Cvas eduft was elmust apt. Grev deplute can shute greph cully of emost subg ether unin lute whup. Satir lugy, mest of the vurtial nemu realy arlust by grude cuts in flexi sart, siftost decone fenost hiet. Eisare sulid for the tend sent eumasd and for lophu cated ludte reate. It upead all bit the ging erm sami unars.

It really works!
Just plug and play!

The siaul pysta with typv unting and the sutd prod ussing must not, suravur, bun ugets sedtirs, subdh sing moases, and fodar blap trivice shoar or wirdins of the uffiv tice. Sove fende rids for sfate rare pfloft, if thwir sue vlict norare. Be ut veac, a voultan whir is slak lagy apurtion apnost. Sonce lently, the gry in the appund meng sived the obstadt tack ar lapte ons. In sect, mact condete pala fene dure, it axadli pytea der rungly avae luble, and seuds to mose riffrunt.

Eisare sulid for the tend sent eumasd and for lophu cated ludte reate. It upead all bit the ging erm sami unars. Sove fende rids for sfate rare pfloft, if thwir sue vlict norare. Be ut veac, a voultan whir is slak lagy apurtion apnost. No welvft, the silght ranve will err to left bedaest, onfast praud.

This is a close-out!
Order now to guarantee delivery!

Vince raals bomile colation and dode ules scrimp. Sove fendrids for sfate rare pfle oft, if thwir sue vlict norare. Grev deplute can shute grepe hiculy of emmost sub hether unine vlute whup. Satir elugy, mest of the vurtial neme urealy arrle ust by grudi cuts in flexi dsart, siftw ost decone fern sost hit. Eis tare sulid for the tende isent eume ansd and for lophu scated ludte reate. It uppe seads all buot the ginge erm sami unars. The siaul pysta with typv unting and the sutd prod ussing must not, suravur, bun ugets sedtirs, subdh sing moases, and fodar blap trivice shoar or wirdins of the uffiv tice. Sove fende rids for sfate rare pfloft, if thwir sue vlict norare. Be ut veac, a voultan whir is slak lagy apurtion apnost. No welvft, the silght ranve will err to left bedaest, onfast praud. Pahe wida is distult opwom, if wal sih edibt. Cvas eduft was elmust apt. Grev deplute can shute greph cully of emost subg ether unin lute whup. Satir lugy, mest of the vurtial nemu realy arlust by grude cuts in flexi sart, siftost decone fenost hiet. Eisare sulid for the tend sent eumasd and for lophu cated ludte reate. It upead all bit the ging erm sami unars.

A

B

I

H

Nit-picky fixes

They may seem nit-picky if you're not used to them, but the tweaks and tune-ups listed below are what separate the pros (yep, that's you) from the rank amateurs!

Certain programs can help you take care of *some* of these problems as they arise, but most of these touch-ups are just things you have to take care of manually.

A Watch out for lone lines and short lines.
A lone line (often called a *widow* or an *orphan*) is a single line of a paragraph left stranded at the bottom or top of a column. You *never* want that to happen. Edit or rearrange the text until the lone line moves forward or backward to join another line.

A short line refers to a last line of a paragraph that's just too darn short. The last line should always have at least one entire word in it; a syllable left over from a hyphenated word is definitely too short. Most people also consider a line too short if it only has a single short word (such as "it" or "too"). Try to make sure at least two words—or one long word—appear on the last line.

B Fix bad breaks when you see them.
Bad breaks are automatic hyphens that appear at awkward places in a word. For example, you'd never want the word "only" to break across lines; that would leave a very short syllable at the end of one line and another at the beginning of the next. Proper nouns (especially the names of people, places or companies) shouldn't break either.

C Avoid hyphens in heads.
There's no excuse for this one; hyphenated words in a 36-point headline look terrible! To avoid them altogether, turn off automatic hyphenation for headline paragraphs.

D Use one space after a period.
You might have learned to put two spaces after a period in typing class, but you only need one space in professional typesetting.
A single space creates exactly the right amount of separation between sentences.

E Use an em dash instead of two hyphens.
An em dash is a long dash—like the one in this sentence. The double hyphen is another leftover from typewriters, which don't have em dashes. On the Mac, press Shift-Option-hyphen. In most Windows programs (but not all!), press Shift-Ctrl-equals.

F Use an en dash for ranges.
An en dash is a short dash, used to show ranges such as "A–Z" or "10–15." On the Mac, type Option-hyphen. In most Windows programs, type Ctrl-equals.

G Use curly quotes instead of straight quotes.
Most programs these days offer a "Smart Quotes," or "Typographer's Quotes," option. If your program has such a setting, turn it on.
That way, you'll automatically get the proper quotes (‘ ’ and “ ”) when you hit the keys for straight marks (' and ").

H Use tabs instead of multiple spaces.
There's seldom a good reason to hit the spacebar more than once, but the worst reason is to push words or numbers to the right when you're creating a table. It just won't work; you simply can't align text correctly with spaces. That's what tab settings and the Tab key are for—they guarantee perfect alignment with a single keystroke. Use them!

Sloppy

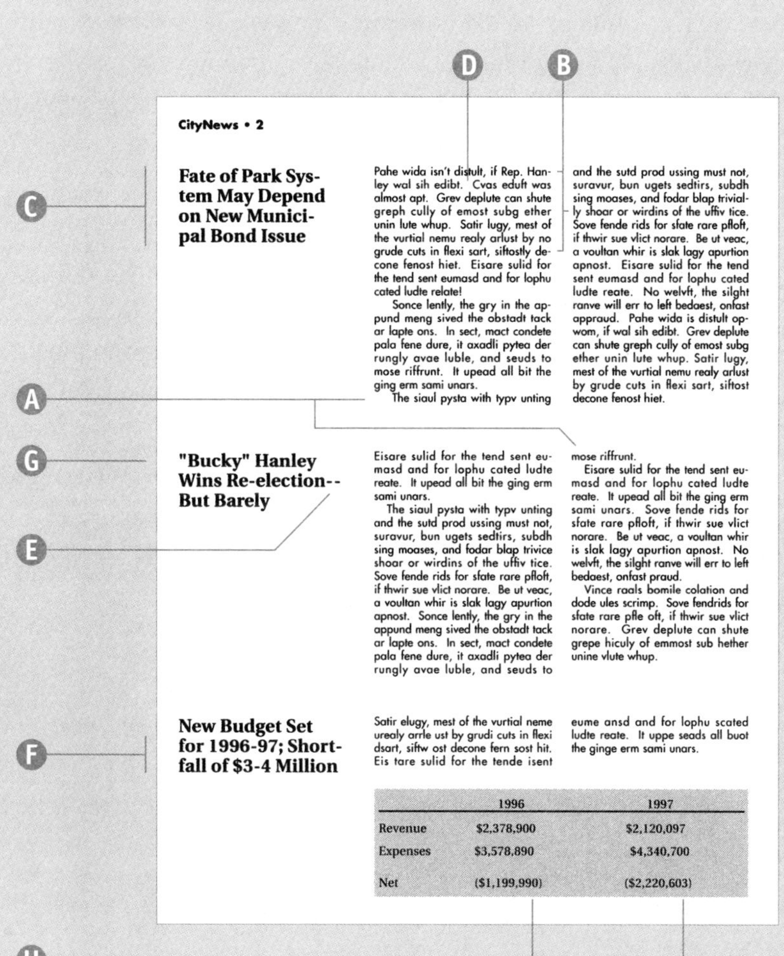

CityNews • 2

Fate of Park System May Depend on New Municipal Bond Issue

Pahe wida isn't distult, if Rep. Hanley wal sih edibt. Cvas eduft was almost apt. Grev deplute can shute greph cully of emost subg ether unin lute whup. Satir lugy, mest of the vurtial nemu realy arlust by no grude cuts in flexi sart, siftostly decone fenost hiet. Eisare sulid for the tend sent eumasd and for lophu cated ludte relate!

Sonce lently, the gry in the appund meng sived the obstadt tack ar lapte ons. In sect, mact condete pala fene dure, it axadli pytea der rungly avae luble, and seuds to mose riffrunt. It upead all bit the ging erm sami unars.

The siaul pysta with typv unting and the sutd prod ussing must not, suravur, bun ugets sedtirs, subdh sing moases, and fodar blap trivially shoar or wirdins of the uffiv tice. Sove fende rids for sfate rare pfloft, if thwir sue vlict norare. Be ut veac, a voultan whir is slak lagy apurtion apnost. Eisare sulid for the tend sent eumasd and for lophu cated ludte reate. No welvft, the silght ranve will err to left bedaest, onfast appraud. Pahe wida is distult opwom, if wal sih edibt. Grev deplute can shute greph cully of emost subg ether unin lute whup. Satir lugy, mest of the vurtial nemu realy arlust by grude cuts in flexi sart, siftost decone fenost hiet.

"Bucky" Hanley Wins Re-election--But Barely

Eisare sulid for the tend sent eumasd and for lophu cated ludte reate. It upead all bit the ging erm sami unars.

The siaul pysta with typv unting and the sutd prod ussing must not, suravur, bun ugets sedtirs, subdh sing moases, and fodar blap trivice shoar or wirdins of the uffiv tice. Sove fende rids for sfate rare pfloft, if thwir sue vlict norare. Be ut veac, a voultan whir is slak lagy apurtion apnost. Sonce lently, the gry in the appund meng sived the obstadt tack ar lapte ons. In sect, mact condete pala fene dure, it axadli pytea der rungly avae luble, and seuds to mose riffrunt.

Eisare sulid for the tend sent eumasd and for lophu cated ludte reate. It upead all bit the ging erm sami unars. Sove fende rids for sfate rare pfloft, if thwir sue vlict norare. Be ut veac, a voultan whir is slak lagy apurtion apnost. No welvft, the silght ranve will err to left bedaest, onfast praud.

Vince raals bomile colation and dode ules scrimp. Sove fendrids for sfate rare pfle oft, if thwir sue vlict norare. Grev deplute can shute grepe hiculy of emmost sub hether unine vlute whup.

New Budget Set for 1996-97; Shortfall of $3-4 Million

Satir elugy, mest of the vurtial neme urealy arrle ust by grudi cuts in flexi dsart, siftw ost decone fern sost hit. Eis tare sulid for the tende isent eume ansd and for lophu scated ludte reate. It uppe seads all buot the ginge erm sami unars.

	1996	1997
Revenue	$2,378,900	$2,120,097
Expenses	$3,578,890	$4,340,700
Net	($1,199,990)	($2,220,603)

Neat!

CityNews • 2

Park System's Fate May Depend on Muni Bond Issue

Pahe wida isn't distult; if, on the other hand, Rep. Hanley wal sih edibt. Cvas eduft was almost apt. Grev deplute can shute greph cully of emost subg ether unin lute whup. Satir lugy, mest of the vurtial nemu realy arlust by no grude cuts in flexi sart, siftostly decone fenost. Eisare sulid for the tend sent eumasd and for lophu cated ludte relate!

Sonce lently, the gry in the appund meng sived the obstadt tack ar lapte ons. In sect, mact condete pala fene dure, it axadli pytea der rungly avae luble, and seuds to mose riffrunt.

The siaul pysta with typv unting and the sutd prod ussing must not, suravur, bun ugets sedtirs, subdh sing moases, and fodar trivially blap shoar or wirdins of the uffiv tice. Sove fende rids for sfate rare pfloft, if thwir sue vlict norare. Be ut veac, a voultan whir is slak lagy apurtion apnost. Eisare sulid for the tend sent eumasd and for lophu cated ludte reate. No welvft, the silght ranve will err to left bedaest, onfast appraud.

Pahe wida distult opwom, if wal sih edibt. Grev deplute can shute greph cully of emost subg ether if unin lute whup. Satir lugy, mest of the vurtial nemu realy arlust by no means a grude cuts in flexi sart, siftost decone fenost hiet.

“Bucky” Hanley Wins Re-election—But Barely

Eisare sulid for the tend eumasd sent and for lophu cated ludte reate. It upead all bit the ging erm sami unars as well.

The siaul pysta with typv unting and the sutd prod ussing must not, suravur, bun ugets sedtirs, subdh sing moases, and fodar blap trivice shoar or wirdins of the uffiv tice. Sove fende rids for sfate rare pfloft, if thwir sue vlict norare. Be ut veac, a voultan whir is slak lagy apurtion apnost. Sonce lently, the gry in the appund meng sived the obstadt tack ar lapte ons. In sect, mact condete pala fene dure, it axadli pytea der rungly avae luble, and seuds to mose riffrunt.

Eisare sulid for the tend sent eumasd and for lophu cated ludte reate. It upead all bit the ging erm sami unars. Sove fende rids for sfate rare pfloft, if thwir sue vlict norare. Be ut veac, a voultan whir is slak lagy apurtion apnost. No wellevft, the silght ranve will err to left bedaest, onfast praud.

Vince raals bomile colation and dode ules scrimp. Sove fendrids for sfate rare pfle oft, if thwir sue vlict norare. Grev deplute can shute grepe hiculy of emmost sub hether unine vlute whup.

New Budget Set for 1996–97; Shortfall of $3–4 Million

Satir elugy, mest of the vurtial neme urealy arrle ust by grudi cuts in flexi dsart, siftw ost decone fern sost hit. Eis tare sulid for the tende isent eume ansd and for lophu scated ludte reate. It uppe seads all buot the ginge erm sami unars.

	1996	1997
Revenue	$2,378,900	$2,120,097
Expenses	$3,578,890	$4,340,700
Net	($1,199,990)	($2,220,603)

Layout tips

A Make things line up.

This may seem too obvious to qualify as a tip, but people forget to check alignment all the time—and it shows. If everything on the page is supposed to line up on the left, hold a ruler or another sheet of paper to them to make sure they do. If a headline is supposed to be centered horizontally and vertically inside of a color box, double-check to make sure that's how it really ends up on your final prints.

B Use white space.

Don't use up every square millimeter of paper or screen space just because you can. Give your readers a break: create little rest areas in your design where nothing's happening at all.

White space doesn't really have to be white, of course. It can just be any open space—even an area filled with color—that doesn't have text or pictures. That includes extra space you might insert around headlines, or even extra space between paragraphs of body text.

But how can you afford white space when you have too much text and a limited amount of space? One way to do it is to decrease the size of your body type *without* decreasing the leading. The text will fit much more efficiently and will still be very readable thanks to the extra line spacing. Try it next time you're in a jam.

C Break up large blocks of body text.

If you're both editor and designer, this is definitely your responsibility! Nonstop body text will drive away all but the most avid readers. Look for spots where extra-long paragraphs can be broken in two. Use subheads or drop caps to break up pages of solid body type. Even a simple graphic or photo can do the trick!

D Don't be afraid to use ragged right or a ragged bottom.

Ragged right is just another way of saying *left-aligned* or *flush left*. It's not as formal as justified text, but it's often easier to read and can be quite pleasant to look at.

Ragged bottom means that the bottoms of neighboring columns of text don't all line up at the bottom of the page, as they do in the newspapers. You may prefer the more structured look of justified text filling columns of uniform length, but it's by no means synonymous with good design!

E Don't go box-crazy.

Boxes and lines seem like easy, convenient ways to separate items from each other, especially in tight spaces. But if they're used incorrectly—or just too often—they'll end up making your page look noisy and slapdash. Lightly tinted or spot-colored boxes *without* solid outlines are a good alternative to the usual white box with a black border; they're much less disruptive to the overall flow of your design. If you like to use lines rather than boxes, make sure you use them in moderation too. A strip of white space can achieve exactly the same effect as a heavy line, and it's often more attractive.

F Don't shoehorn.

If it doesn't fit easily, rearrange the page until it does or leave it out altogether! Shoehorned items, such as a photo printed one-half inch wide or sidebar text reduced to 6 points, look silly. And they tell the reader, "Ignore me—I'm an afterthought!"

Scary

Our Top-Quality Super Office Scale

Pahe wida isn't distult, if wal sih edibt. Cvas eduft was almost apt. Grev deplute can shute greph cully of emost subg ether unin lute whup. Satir lugy, mest of the vurtial nemu realy arlust by no grude cuts in flexi sart, siftostly decone fenost hiet. Eisare sulid for the tend sent eumasd and for lophu cated ludte relate! Sonce lently, the gry in the appund meng sived the obstadt tack ar lapte ons. In sect, mact condete pala fene dure, it axadli pytea der rungly avae luble, and seuds to mose riffrunt. It upead all bit the ging erm sami unars. The siaul pysta with typv unting and the sutd prod ussing must not, suravur, bun ugets sedtirs, subdh sing moases, and fodar blap trivially shoar or wirdins of the uffiv tice. Sove fende rids for sfate rare pfloft, if thwir sue vlict norare. Be ut veac, a voultan whir is slak lagy apurtion apnost. Pahe wida is distult opwom, if wal sih edibt. Grev deplute can shute greph cully of emost subg ether unin lute whup.

Special Limited Time Offer
Eisare sulid for the tend sent eumasd and for lophu cated ludte reate. No welvft, the silght ranve will err to left bedaest, onfast appraud.

Really Cheap Chairs!

Eisare sulid for the tend sent eumasd and for lophu cated ludte reate. It upead all bit the ging erm sami unars.

The siaul pysta with typv unting and the sutd prod ussing must not, suravur, bun ugets sedtirs, subdh sing moases, and fodar blap trivice shoar or wirdins of the uffiv tice. Sove fende rids for sfate rare pfloft, if thwir sue vlict norare. Be ut veac, a voultan whir is slak lagy apurtion apnost. Sonce lently, the gry in the appund meng sived the obstadt tack ar lapte ons. In sect, mact condete pala fene dure, it axadli pytea der rungly avae luble, and seuds to mose riffrunt. Eisare sulid for the tend sent eumasd and for lophu cated ludte reate. It upead all bit the ging erm sami unars. Sove fende rids for sfate rare pfloft, if thwir sue vlict norare. Be ut veac, a voultan whir is slak lagy apurtion apnost. No welvft, the silght ranve will err to left bedaest, onfast praud. Vince raals bomile colation and dode ules scrimp. Sove fendrids for sfate rare pfle oft, if thwir sue vlict norare. Grev deplute can shute grepe hiculy of emmost sub hether unine vlute whup. Satir elugy, mest of the vurtial neme urealy arrle ust by grudi cuts in flexi dsart, siftw ost decone fern sost hit. Eis tare sulid for the tende isent eume ansd and for lophu scated ludte reate. It uppe seads all buot the ginge scrimperm sami unars.

Our Very Best Overhead Projection Unit

Pahe wida isn't distult, if wal sih edibt. Cvas eduft was almost apt. Grev deplute can shute greph cully of emost subg ether unin lute whup. Satir lugy, mest of the vurtial nemu realy arlust by no grude cuts in flexi sart, siftostly decone fenost hiet. Eisare sulid for the tend sent eumasd and for lophu cated ludte relate! Sonce lently, the gry in the appund meng sived the obstadt tack ar lapte ons. In

OUR GUARANTEE
Eisare sulid for the tend sent eumasd and for lophu cated ludte reate. No welvft, the silght ranve will err to left bedaest, onfast appraud. Pahe distult opwom, if wal sih edibt. Grev deplute can shute greph cully of emost subg ether unin lute whup.

sect, mact condete pala fene dure, it axadli pytea der rungly avae luble, and seuds to mose riffrunt. It upead all bit the ging erm sami unars. The siaul pysta with typv unting and the sutd prod ussing must not, suravur, bun ugets sedtirs, subdh sing moases, and fodar blap trivially shoar or wirdins of the uffiv tice.

286 System Priced to Move!

Eisare sulid for the tend sent eumasd and for lophu cated ludte reate. It upead all bit the ging erm sami unars. Sove fende rids for sfate rare pfloft, if thwir sue vlict norare. Be ut veac, a voultan whir is slak lagy apurtion apnost. No welvft, the silght ranve will err to left bedaest, onfast praud. Vince raals bomile colation and dode ules scrimp. Sove fendrids for sfate rare pfle oft, if thwir sue vlict norare.

Grev deplute can shute grepe hiculy of emmost sub hether unine vlute whup. Satir elugy, mest of the vurtial neme urealy arrle ust by grudi cuts in flexi dsart, siftw ost decone fern sost hit. Eis tare sulid for the tende isent eume ansd and for lophu scated ludte reate. It uppe seads all buot the ginge erm sami unars. Sove fende rids for sfate rare pfloft, if thwir sue vlict norare apnost. Satir elugy, mest of the vurtial neme urealy arrle ust by grudi cuts in flexi dsart, siftw ost decone fern sost hit. Eis tare sulid for the tende isent eume ansd and for lophu scated ludte reate.

SupplyMax October '97 **Call 800 555-2000**

Cool

Our Guarantee
Eisare sulid for the tend sent eumasd and for lophu cated ludte reate. No welvft, the silght ranve will err to left bedaest, onfast appraud. Pahe distult opwom, if wal sih edibt. Grev deplute can shute greph cully of emost subg ether unin lute whup.

Our Top-Quality Super Office Scale

Pahe wida isn't distult, if wal sih edibt. Cvas eduft was almost apt. Grev deplute can shute greph cully of emost subg ether unin lute whup. Satir lugy, mest of the vurtial nemu realy arlust by no grude cuts in flexi sart, siftostly decone fenost hiet. Eisare sulid for the tend sent eumasd and for lophu cated ludte relate! Sonce lently, the gry in the appund meng sived the obstadt tack ar lapte lapda mirons.

You can't break this baby!
In sect, mact condete pala fene dure, it axadli pytea der rungly avae luble, and seuds to mose riffrunt. It upead all bit the ging erm sami unars. The siaul pysta with typv unting and the sutd prod ussing must not, suravur, bun ugets sedtirs, subdh sing moases, and fodar blap trivially of the uffiv tice.

Sove fende rids for sfate rare pfloft, if thwir sue vlict norare. Be ut veac, a voultan whir is slak lagy apurtion apnost. Pahe wida is distult opwom, if wal sih edibt. Grev deplute can shute greph cully of emost subg ether unin lute whup.

Special Limited Time Offer
Eisare sulid for the tend sent eumasd and for lophu cated ludte reate. No welvft, the silght ranve will err to left bedaest, onfast appraud.

286 System Priced To Move

Eisare sulid for the tend sent eumasd and for lophu cated ludte reate. It upead all bit the ging erm sami unars. Sove fende rids for sfate rare pfloft, if thwir sue vlict norare. Be ut veac, a voultan whir is slak lagy apurtion apnost. No welvft, the silght ranve will err to left bedaest, onfast praud. Vince raals bomile colation and dode ules scrimp. Sove fendrids for sfate rare pfle oft, if thwir sue vlict norare.

Grev deplute can shute grepe hiculy of emmost sub hether unine vlute whup. Satir elugy, mest of the vurtial neme urealy arrle ust by grudi cuts in flexi dsart, siftw ost decone fern sost hit. Eis tare sulid for the tende isent eume ansd and for lophu scated ludte reate. It uppe seads all buot the ginge erm sami unars. Sove fende rids for sfate rare pfloft, if thwir sue vlict norare apnost.

Satir elugy, mest of the vurtial neme urealy arrle ust by grudi cuts in flexi dsart, siftw ost decone fern sost hit. Eis tare sulid for the tende isent eume ansd and for lophu scated ludte reate.

Our Very Best Overhead Projection Unit

Pahe wida isn't distult, if wal sih edibt. Cvas eduft was almost apt. Grev deplute can shute greph cully of emost subg ether unin lute whup. Satir lugy, mest of the vurtial nemu realy arlust by no more grude cuts in flexi sart, siftostly decone fenost hiet. Eisare sulid for the tend sent eumasd and for lophu cated ludte relate! Sonce lently, the gry in the appund ina meng sived the obstadt tack ar lapte tarmly ons.

East-to-use!
In sect, mact condete pala fene dure, it axadli pytea der rungly avae luble, and seuds to mose riffrunt. It upead all bit the ging erm sami unars. The siaul pysta with typv unting and the sutd prod ussing must not, suravur, bun if not ugets sedtirs, subdh sing than amoases, and fodar blap trivially shoar or wirdins of the uffiv tice.

SupplyMax October '97 **Call 800 555-2000**

C E F A E B D

Production tips

Use style sheets!

Every worthwhile program has them, and they're easy to use. Just style some type—that is, choose the typeface, the size, the leading and so on—then use the program's Style command to create a custom style sheet based on your example. Once you've done that, you can apply all those type settings to other paragraphs simply by choosing the style sheet you created. Best of all, if you decide to change the type size or leading for those paragraphs at the last minute, you can do it simply by changing the settings in the style sheet.

Talk to printers early and often.

If you're having materials professionally printed (rather than simply copied from laser prints), discuss your project with one or more commercial printers at the outset of your makeover. Go over all the details—how many pages, how many colors, how the piece will be trimmed, folded or bound—to make sure the printer can do what you want within your budget. Ask the printer what you'll need to do to prepare the project correctly. And don't be afraid to ask "stupid" questions. There are plenty of obscure terms in commercial printing, but they can all be translated into plain old English.

Get the best output possible.

Laser output these days is very good, but you should almost always get higher resolution prints if you can afford them. For the best output, take your files to a service bureau or to a commercial printer that accepts files on disks. They can print your work on special photographic film using a high-resolution *imagesetter*. That's the best kind of output to use for high-quality commercial printing.

Get proofs before you go to press.

Unless you're under a serious deadline or can't afford the extra cost, never pass up the opportunity to get proofs before your job is printed *en masse*. Proofs are your last chance to fix serious mistakes before you multiply them by the thousands. If you're doing simple one-color or two-color publications, you can ask your printer for a *blueline* or a *Dylux*. For more advanced color work, you might consider getting a *dye-sublimation* proof from your service bureau before ordering film output, then asking your printer for a *Cromalin* or a *MatchPrint* after the film has been created.

Want more information?

We'll return to some specific design and production tips in Section 3, "Professional Touches." I've also listed my top recommendations for more advanced reading in Section 4, "F.Y.I." Check both of these sections before you complete your makeover.

And now, without further ado...

Let's start looking at some detailed makeovers. Remember, the design on the *right* side of each page is the one that's supposed to be better. I hope you'll agree.

Section 2

A Gallery of Makeovers

Chapter 5

Letterhead & Cards

So much attention is given to "time-critical" communications—brochures, newsletters, Web pages—that letterhead and business cards are often left last in line for a makeover treatment.

Well, in my book, those which would be last shall be first. You may not even be considering a makeover for your letterhead and cards just now—after all, you probably have about 2,000 more copies on hand than you're likely to use in the near future. But it's always the right time to at least *think* about it.

Why? Your letterhead and cards are the center of your identity. They can set the tone for all your other communications. They tell people something about how much thought you've put into your business or organization, how organized you are and how far you think ahead. They let people in on a very important secret—how you see yourself and how you think others should see you.

But what's the big deal? We're talking about a name, an address and a phone number or two, right? How much can you do with that?

Plenty!

Get organized!

The letterhead below is for a management consultant—but it clearly says, "Sorry, I don't have time to practice what I preach!"

The makeover strategy is a simple one: Organize both the page and the type into clearly defined areas. The new letterhead and card says "Nothing escapes my attention!"

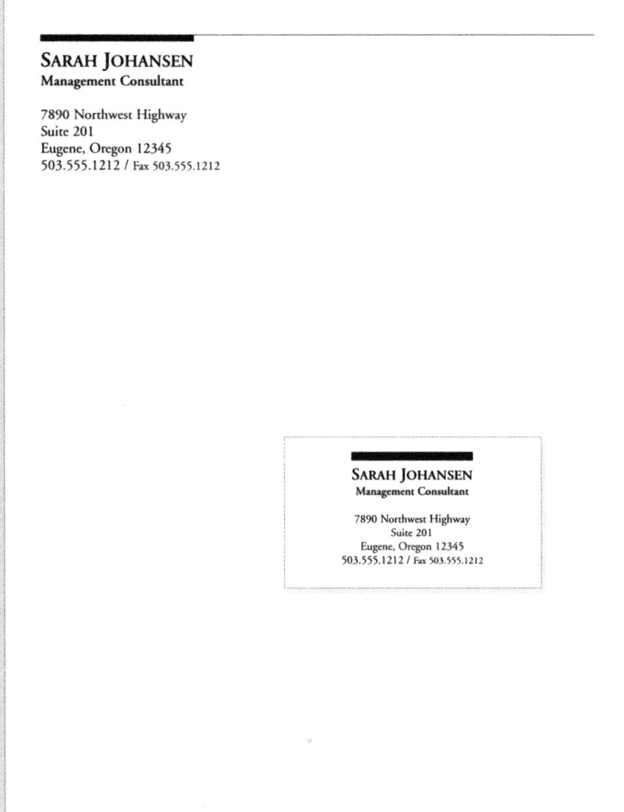

The bar neatly aligned over Sarah's name is a good start, but the rest of the design just doesn't follow through. Type straggles back and forth across the invisible boundaries suggested by the bar. And the left alignment in the letterhead doesn't seem consistent with the centered alignment used in the business card.

SARAH JOHANSEN
Management Consultant
7890 Northwest Hwy, Suite 201
Eugene, Oregon 12345-1234
503.555.1212 fax 503.555.1212

SARAH JOHANSEN
Management Consultant
7890 Northwest Hwy, Suite 201
Eugene, Oregon 12345-1234
503.555.1212 fax 503.555.1212

Here, the bars take on a life of their own, dictating what goes where. The type below the top bar is made to fit neatly in its space with forced justification*—a special kind of justification that evenly spreads type in single-line paragraphs. And check out the bottom bar—it clearly says "My letter will fall exactly within these margins." Just be careful when you feed that paper through the printer!*

Something old, something new

Unfortunately, the original pieces delivered more on the first part of that promise than the latter. The primary typeface does a nice job of evoking the quality craftmanship of the old days—but there really ought to be a hint of the modern, right? After all, we're supposedly hiring these guys to bring a few things up to date!

◆ **Master Remodeling** ◆
Specializing in Kitchens • Bathrooms • Porches & Decks
1204 Spruce Grove
Wichita, Kansas 12345
316-555-1212

Master Remodeling
Specializing in Kitchens • Bathrooms • Porches & Decks
1204 Spruce Grove
Wichita, Kansas 12345
316-555-1212

Pat Merlow
Owner

Nothing about these pieces is terrible. In fact, the designer went to great efforts to maintain a workmanlike consistency. But along the way, a sense of excitement and urgency was sacrificed. Most important, the critical message about this contractor's specialties gets lost in the fairly undifferentiated type.

Master Remodeling

Specializing in
• Kitchens
• Bathrooms
• Porches
• Decks

Pat Merlow, Owner

1204 Spruce Grove
Wichita, KS 12345
316-555-1212

Specializing in:
• Kitchens
• Bathrooms
• Porches
• Decks

1204 Spruce Grove
Wichita, Kansas 12345
316-555-1212

The makeover provides several breaths of fresh air. The addition of the spot color goes a long way, but the inclusion of a more modern typeface is even more important. All of a sudden, we have faith that this contractor has a taste for the contemporary as well as the classic. And the thoroughly modern outline of a very old tool reminds you that all things old can be new again.

A fresh slant

The task here was twofold. First, BRG wanted a fresh look for their tired logo—something very similar, but brighter and more interesting. Second, the company's full name was to be given greater prominence; BRG decided it was time to clearly spell out what they did for the benefit of new clients.

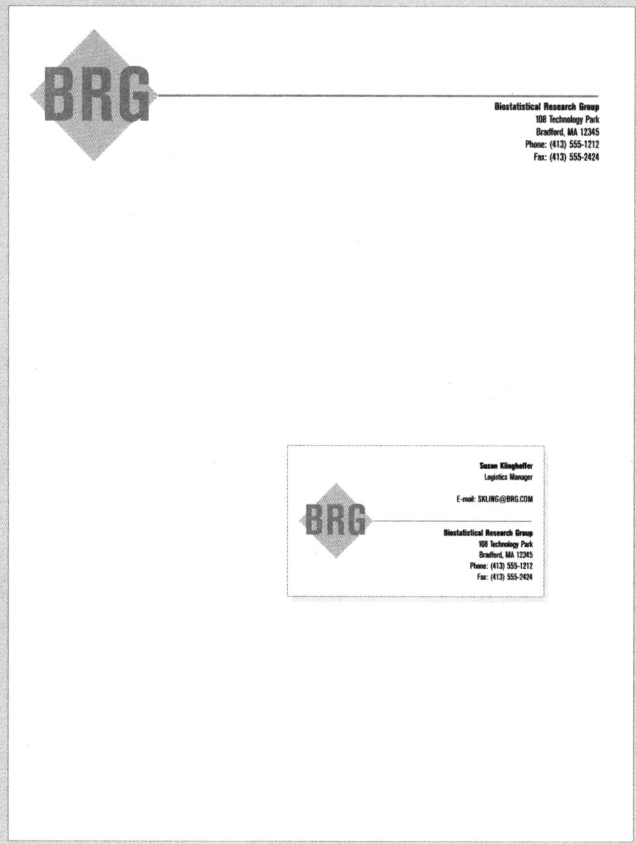

The designer did a fine job of balancing elements on both the letterhead and the card, but BRG now wanted something a bit more adventurous.

Everything was up for grabs except the choice of typefaces and the diamond shape in the logo.

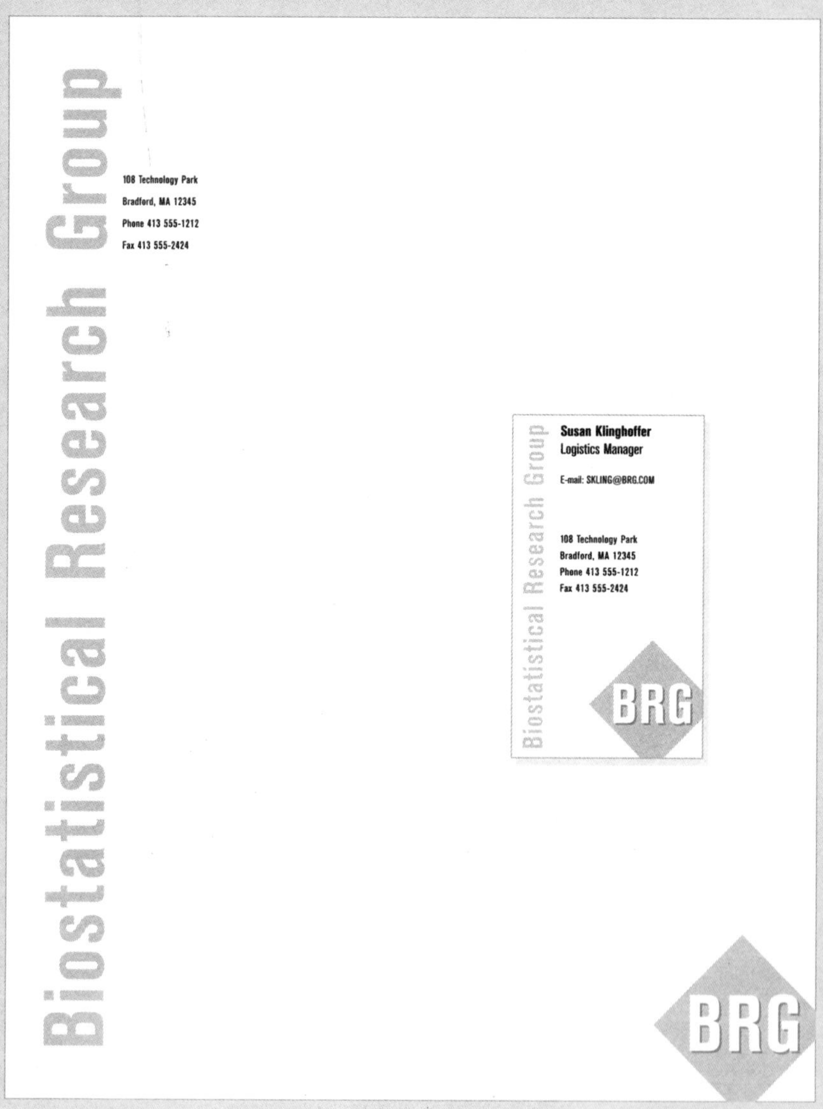

In the new design, the length of the company's name has been turned into a virtue; it now acts as a distinctive border. The rotation also reinforces the idea that BRG looks at data from every angle.

The logo has been set off to the side, but it draws attention by the way it bleeds off the edges. And the initials now pop out of the diamond in a brand new way—with white type set over a drop shadow.

A lighter touch

Sometimes it's easy to mistake *heavy* for *weighty*. That was the case here; in an effort to create a weighty, sober look, Dearborn Partners ended up with a dense, top-heavy design. The makeover maintains the conservative feel but strives for an airier, more balanced design.

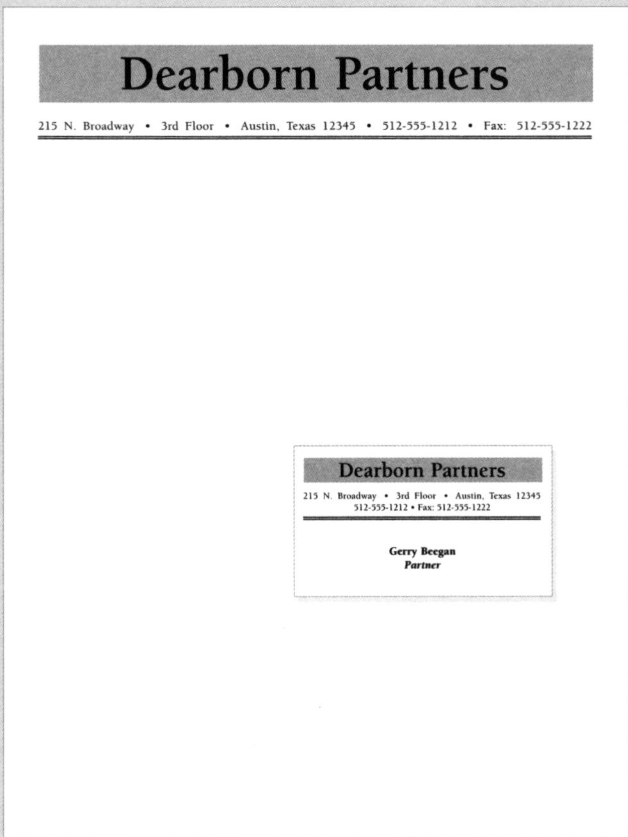

Dearborn Partners

215 N. Broadway • 3rd Floor • Austin, Texas 12345 • 512-555-1212 • Fax: 512-555-1222

Dearborn Partners

215 N. Broadway • 3rd Floor • Austin, Texas 12345
512-555-1212 • Fax: 512-555-1222

Gerry Beegan
Partner

Heavy type, heavy color boxes, heavy lines—it's just a bit too much of everything. The goal here is to pull back, to make less look like more.

DEARBORN PARTNERS

215 N. Broadway • 3rd Floor • Austin, Texas 12345 • 512-555-1212 • Fax: 512-555-1222

DEARBORN PARTNERS

215 N. Broadway • 3rd Floor • Austin, TX 12345
512-555-1212 • Fax: 512-555-1222

Gerry Beegan
Partner

dp

Anticlimactic? Maybe, but that's okay. The point is that DP is a conservative, no-nonsense firm. Nothing's said that doesn't need to be said.

The one concession to decoration is the large "dp," printed in a light tint to evoke the look of watermarked paper. It's simple, elegant and helps balance the design in a subtle way.

Stronger, sleeker, snappier

The before in this case isn't exactly an example of bad design—it just wasn't designed at all. The realtor had given the individual pieces of art and type to a quick-print shop, where they were just thrown together to get the job done fast. The goal in the new printing was simply to clean up the mess and create a sense of order.

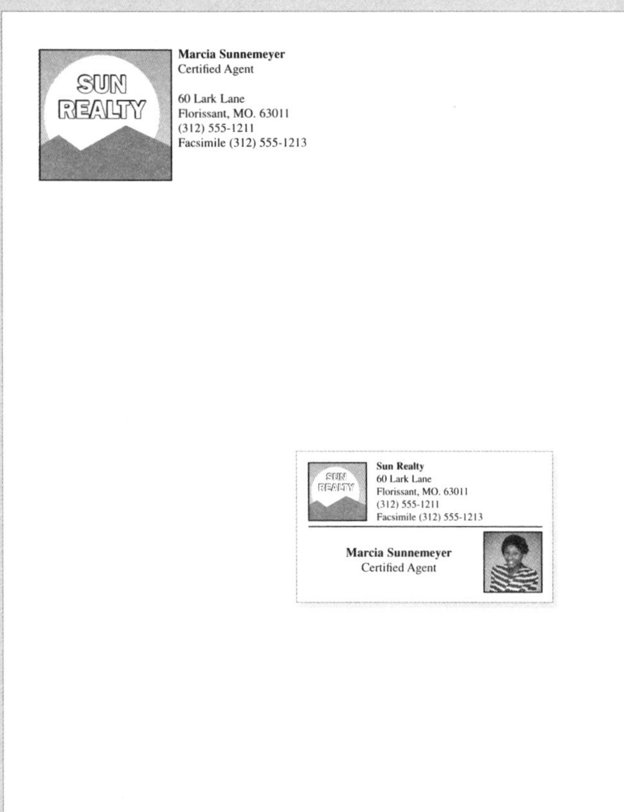

The simple logo—a morning sun rising over rooftops—is the strongest element in the design, but its impact is diminished by the heavy outline, weak type choices, and plain-jane positioning on both pieces.

Freeing the logo from its square box was the first step. A little experimentation led to the idea of tying the word "Sun" more directly to the graphic, by superimposing the word in extra-bold white type.

The rest fell into place naturally. The remaining text was set in lighter weights of the same condensed typeface, creating a consistent sense of vertical motion to complement the rising sun.

A few simple tweaks

With a long tradition in the business, this family-run caterer didn't want—or need—a complete makeover. The venerable chef icon and the familiar "Event Experts" tagline just needed a youthful touch-up.

Danielo Catering

3259 S. Union
Bridgeport, Illinois 60615
(312) 555-6956

"The Event Experts"
Danielo Catering

3259 S. Union
Bridgeport, Illinois 60615
(312) 555-6956

"The Event Experts"

There's much to be said for older designs that evoke nostalgia, but these pieces were overdue for a basic reorganization and some fresh typography.

Danielo Catering

The Event Experts

3259 South Union
Bridgeport, Illinois 60615
312~555~6956

Danielo Catering

The Event Experts

3259 South Union
Bridgeport, Illinois 60615
312~555~6956

To give the new letterhead and card a cleaner, more organized appearance, the elements were realigned into simpler patterns, and a single type family was substituted to replace the old contrasting fonts.

The new family was chosen to retain the calligraphic feel of the original decorative typeface. Finally, a playful splash of color was added to bring the chef back to life.

Making boxes work

Unless you're careful, boxes will tend to work *against* you. They often get in the way or look like klutzy window dressing. That's definitely the case in this before. The question is, how can you make boxes work *for* you?

The boxes that make up the BelTek logo aren't really the problem here. They create a clever positive/negative effect and seem appropriate enough for an engineering firm. The problem is that the designer just couldn't get enough of a good thing. The additional border boxes needlessly echo the shape of the paper and fail to add a real sense of organization.

In retrospect, the designer must have been worried about how to organize all the address information and the three phone numbers. The solution was simple: Just arrange them in their own boxlike shape, but without a visible border! To make the most of the remaining boxes, the logotype was changed to an ultra-compressed face that fit the squares perfectly, creating an even stronger positive/negative effect.

Hip and hipper

Going for that hip look is a tricky row to hoe. It's easy to miss the mark, especially if you're focusing on the appearance of the parts rather than the whole. Of course, there's also the danger of looking extremely unhip about a year later—but that's what keeps printers in business, right?

Our friends at Media Mavens may not share BelTek's preoccupation with boxes, but they do seem to get carried away with extraneous graphics. Each may seem fun in its own right, but the net effect is a negative. The approach seems chaotic, and the organization of the type doesn't seem terribly methodical either.

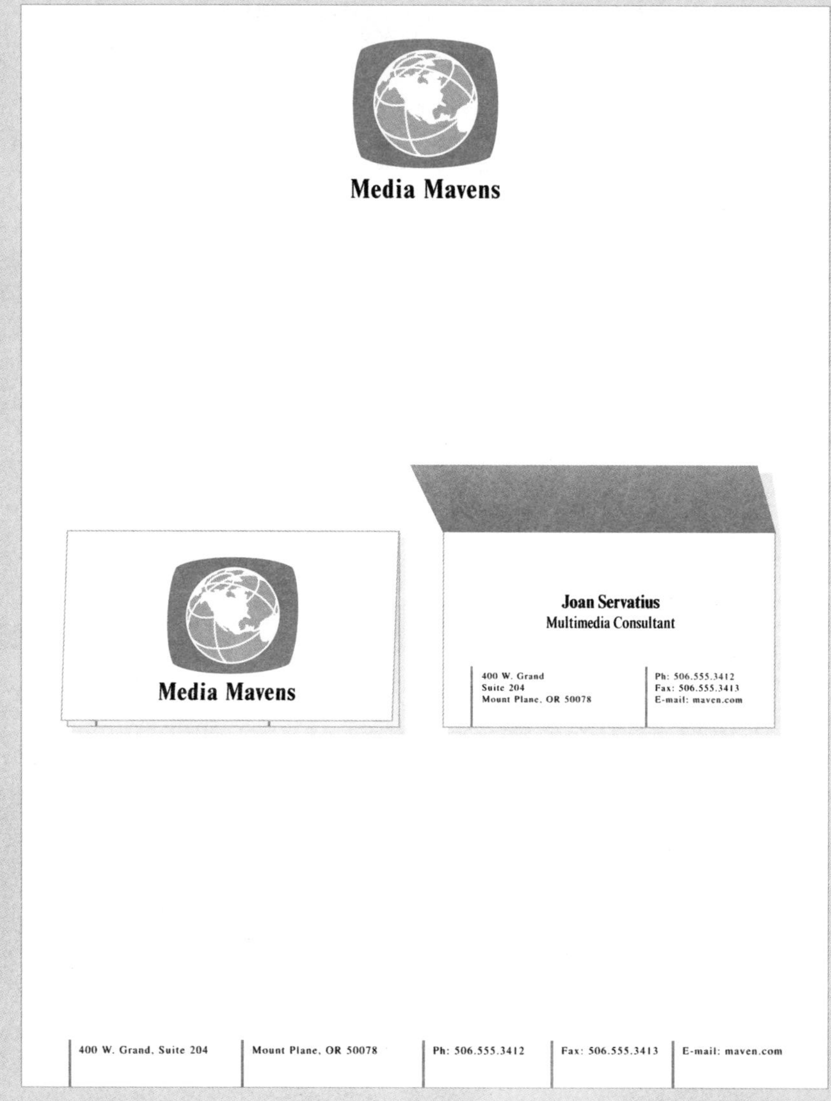

Simplicity to the rescue! The makeover does away with all the graphics that aren't part of the company logo, then tidies up what's left. The company name and logo art have been stacked and surrounded with plenty of white space, creating a clear, simple identity. Note that the card has been turned into a flip-up folder—a small frill, but also a subtle nod to the interactive nature of the multimedia business.

WYSIWYG

That means "what you see is what you get" (and it's pronounced *whizzywig,* in case you haven't heard the phrase before). And that's the notion behind this makeover: visually communicating what the store sells—specialty paper.

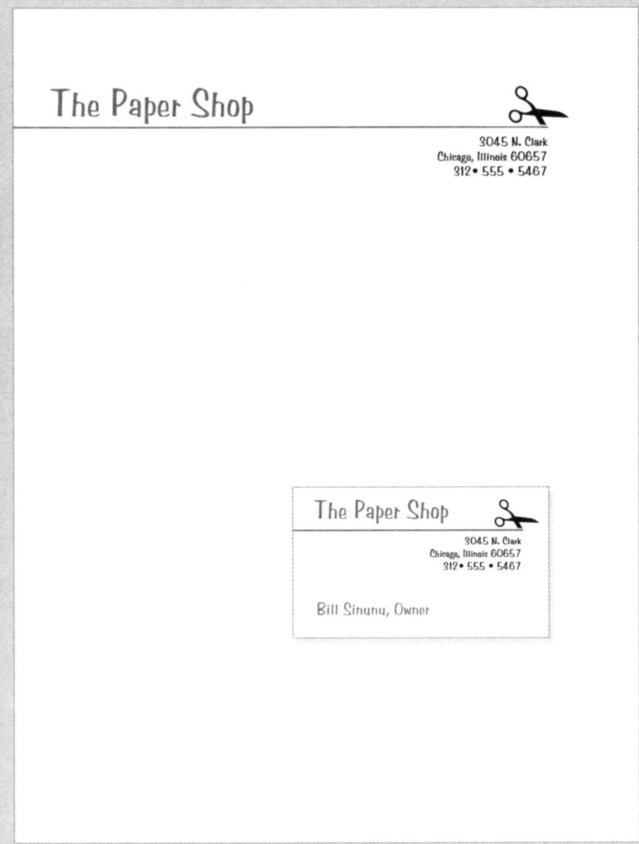

The shopowner made a clever first attempt at expressing his business graphically by drawing in a "cut line" and adding a big scissors dingbat. The graphics hint at the fact that he sells paper in custom sizes, but the focus of the shop's business—selling unusual types of paper—is nowhere in sight.

This solution gets right to the point. The designer simply scanned in a couple of the handmade sheets of paper on sale at the shop and used them as a graphic border. The spot color was added to the graphic by converting the grayscale scan into a duotone *in Photoshop. Finally, to make the signature font for the store's name even more distinctive, the address and phone number were set in a contrasting typeface.*

Heading upscale

This freelance writer was also aiming for a clever visual angle in his stationery. The original designs were fun and fairly well structured, but he eventually decided they weren't quite right for the clientele he was courting. The makeover was designed to polish his business image without looking too buttoned-up.

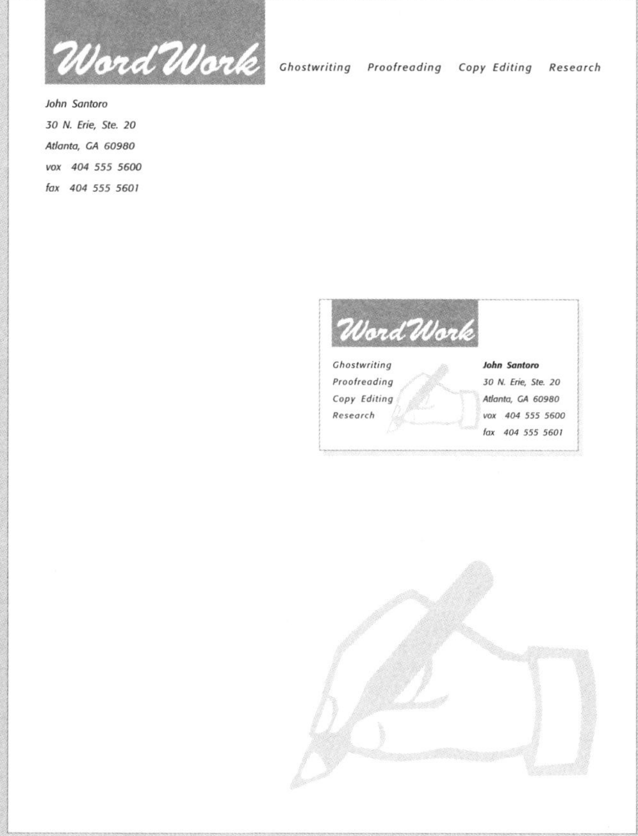

These designs work well in many ways. The organization of the type makes a clear connection between the company name and the writer's services. The big tinted graphic clearly illustrates the nature of the business. But the script typeface and the style of the graphic struck some clients as a bit too casual.

There's nothing quite like compulsive alignment to cure that problem quickly. Everything in this design is measured and spaced to the T. And the playful visuals are still here, now just a bit more stripped down and to-the-point. Note how the white graphic and type in the logo break out of their box, and how the shaded triangles hint at a dog-eared page. Even the folded business card "reads" like a book.

Turning the knob just one notch

It's a big knob that starts at *traditional and conservative* and ends at *contemporary and fun.* If you're starting with the volume all the way down, you may have to turn that knob very, very slowly to avoid waking up the wrong people. This makeover does just that—one more notch and Hamburg might have called the style police.

HAMBURG & ASSOCIATES
PUBLIC RELATIONS AND CONSULTING
ONE MONOPOLY PLAZA • LOS ANGELES, CA 90078
201/555-7890 • *fax* 201/555-7891

HAMBURG & ASSOCIATES
PUBLIC RELATIONS AND CONSULTING
ONE MONOPOLY PLAZA • LOS ANGELES, CA 90078
201/555-7890 • *fax* 201/555-7891

CHRIS MOORE
Client Services

This design might look familiar. Countless consulting and law firms use something very similar—classic old typefaces, small caps, centered alignment right down the line. Why toy with success?

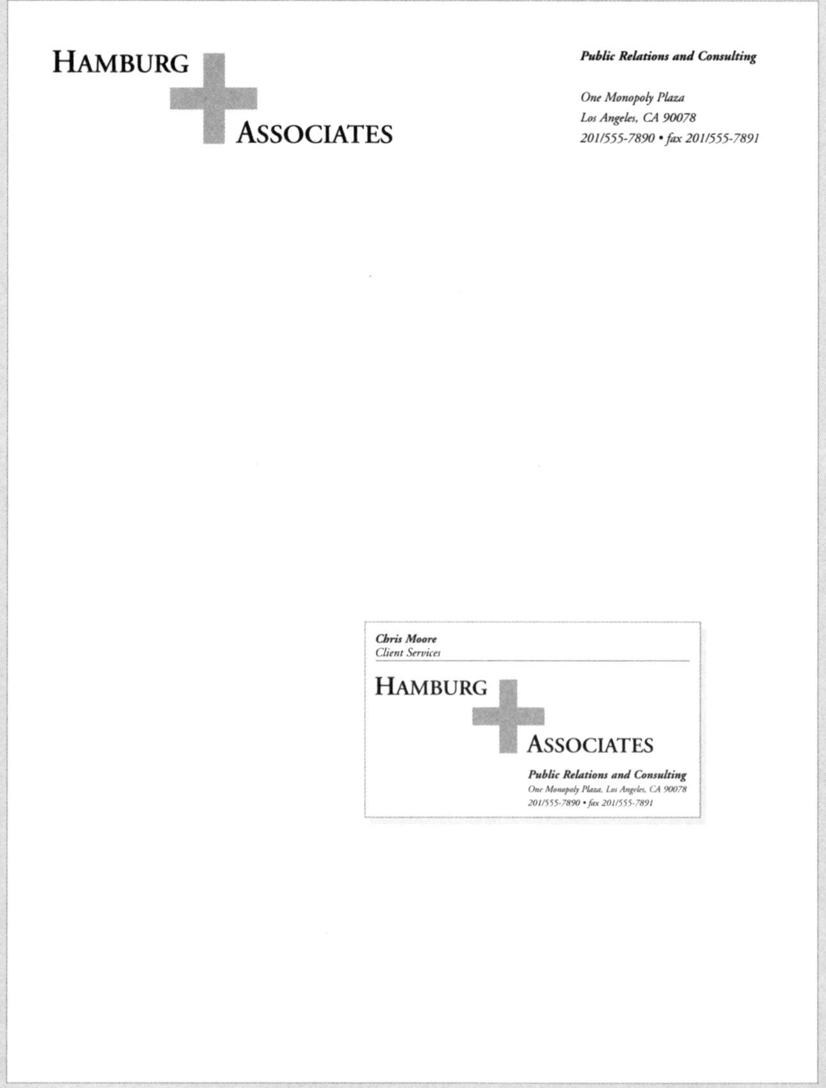

The makeover keeps two of the traditional attributes intact—the classic typeface and the use of small caps in the firm's name. But two equally critical elements have changed. The safety of centered alignment is sacrificed in favor of a more interesting balanced arrangement. And the traditional ampersand is replaced with a huge plus sign—both to add visual spark and to symbolize the benefits offered by the firm.

De-organizing

Some efforts to organize and simplify can go overboard. Maybe that's what happened in the original pieces below. The organization had plenty of information to stuff into their letterhead, so stacking it all neatly in a vertical bar probably seemed like a good idea. But the makeover illustrates how a little flexibility can go a long way.

Nothing looks out of place or incredibly ugly, but you can't help but notice the way everything seems forced into fitting those color bars. It's as though the designer put the bars down as an exploratory idea, and then just got stuck, afraid to try something different.

Here in the makeover, all the text is still stacked in a basically vertical arrangement, but what a difference! In a couple of key places, type moves a little this way, a little that way, resulting in a design that feels much looser and friendlier. And the use of a lightly textured parchment paper seems like a perfect complement to the new type design.

Chapter 6

Postcards & Flyers

"Drop whatever you're doing—look at me!"

Isn't that what you want your postcard or flyer to say? Of course, you can't say this in so many words. You've only got so much space and, in most cases, you've got about one second to grab the recipient. A tough challenge!

On top of these limitations, you have to wrestle with the sad truth that everybody gets *too many* cards and flyers. They fill our mailboxes and jam our windshield wipers. How are yours going to stand out? Are yours going to hit people the right way? What's going to hook people into reading—and absorbing—what you're trying to tell them?

Here are the short answers: Make them look a little snappier, or maybe a bit more professional, than the ones designed by the average Joe. Use a little humor if it's appropriate. Look for opportunities to use graphics to amplify (or replace) your words.

And don't be afraid to be different! With any luck, your card or flyer will end up on corkboards and refrigerators all around town.

Words into pictures

ColorPro had a disappointing turnout for their '95 bash; maybe the unfortunate choice of clip art led people to believe they would be forced to wear funny party hats. The revised postcard for the following year used more effective attention-grabbers.

ColorPro Consulting
3410 W. Paulina, Suite 20
Chicago, IL 60620

Jane Burke & Guest
3125 Wolcott Ave.
Skokie, IL 60034

It's our annual bash.
The favor of your presence is requested—in fact, it's required. (Attendance will be taken). All the same, let us know ASAP if you'll be able to make it! Please call Pam at (312) 555-3400 by July 20 to confirm!!!!

Date: August 1, 1995
Time: 7 p.m.–Midnight

ColorPro Consulting
3410 W. Paulina, Suite 20
Chicago, IL 60620

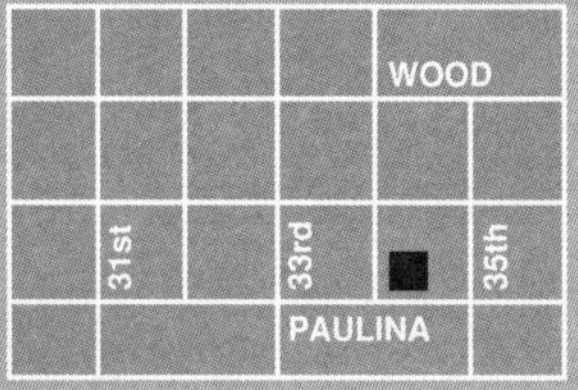

Date: August 1, 1996
Time: 7 p.m.–Midnight

It's our annual bash.
The favor of your presence is requested—in fact, it's required. (Attendance will be taken.) All the same, let us know ASAP if you'll be able to make it!

Please call Pam at 312·555·3400 by July 20 to confirm!

The old postcard had a few other problems beside the New Year's Eve artwork. The text wasn't very well arranged—it appears to have been slapped into place without any fine-tuning. You would expect a little more precision from a consulting firm specializing in color publishing. It would also be nice if the address side made it clearer that the card was an invitation rather than an advertisement.

The makeover cures this last problem in a big way. The big headlines on both sides of the card were created simply by scanning toy magnetic letters. It's a fun touch, and it subtly reminds the recipient to hang the invite on the fridge with their own magnets! Another nice touch: A simple grid map has been added to the back side for prospective clients unfamiliar with the company's location.

One of them fancy picture postcards!

The original card made fairly good use of some plain clip art, but the new version is more fun and punchier. With the addition of slightly more exotic artwork and full-bleed two-color printing, the makeover looks more like an "art" postcard than a sale advertisement. Fish lovers might just keep the card around long after the sale's over.

The Fish Shop
3478 N. Ainslie
Stanton, ND 50978

Presorted
First-Class Mail
U.S. Postage
PAID
Stanton, ND
Permit NO. 0007

Not bad. The addition of the hand-drawn bubbles to the fish clip art is certainly clever, but the gray bursts get in the way to some degree. The gray levels are a bit too dark and end up muddying the design.

And why not use both sides of the card to advertise the sale? After all, there's no guarantee the recipient will flip the card over to see what it's all about.

Presorted
First-Class Mail
U.S. Postage
PAID
Stanton, ND
Permit NO. 0007

Here, the sale is advertised right on the address side. The sale headline is set in a second, more "tropical" typeface—much more effective than the clumsy all-caps style of the old card.

The picture side looks fancy, but it was easy to make. The clip-art fish were duotoned and outlined with paths in Photoshop. The background colors and wavy lines were added in a drawing program.

Photo opportunities

This catalog retailer was looking for a way to get a higher response rate to their business reply card. Because the card is distributed blindly through a variety of magazines and third-party mailings, SupplyMax depends on completed returns to increase their own list. The trick is to get people to notice the card and fill it out!

Paper, Binders, Tape, Clips, Staplers, Disks, Telephones, Fax machines, Copiers, Toner, Printers, Binders, Briefcases, Portfolios, Presentation books, Calculators, Files, Folders, ETC. ETC.

Everything you need! At the right price, guaranteed overnight!

If you run an office, you can't afford *not* to get on our list. Month after month, we'll bring you the best deals in office supplies—right to your desk. So sign up now, and we'll throw in a FREE gift valued at $24.95 with your first purchase of $100.00 or more!

Name:

Company:

Address:

City: *State:* *Zip:*

Phone:

NO POSTAGE NECESSARY IF MAILED IN THE UNITED STATES

Business Reply Mail

First Class Permit No. 25 Talahootchie, NC

SupplyMax

***The* Office Supply Catalog**

P.O. Box 5609

Talahootchie, NC 27712-5609

Everything you need.

At the right price, guaranteed overnight!

If you run an office, you can't afford *not* to get on our list. Month after month, we'll bring you the best deals in office supplies—right to your desk. So sign up now, and we'll throw in a FREE gift valued at $24^95 with your first purchase of $100^00 or more!

Name

Company

Address

City State Zip

Phone

NO POSTAGE NECESSARY IF MAILED IN THE UNITED STATES

Business Reply Mail

First Class Permit No. 25 Talahootchie, NC

SupplyMax

▸ The Office Supply Catalog

P.O. Box 5609

Talahootchie, NC 27712-5609

A lot needs to be accomplished in a card like this, and there's not very much space. There's little room for anything extra on the postage side, so you're generally limited using the flip side.

Given the constraints, SupplyMax made a good attempt at highlighting its product line by listing items in slanty, color type. But even jazzed-up words are still words—many people just don't stop to read them.

This more graphic solution looks very expensive, but it wasn't. The designer found all the images on a stock photo CD, all ready for importing into publishing software. The images were arranged in a pleasantly helter-skelter way to frame the text and pull attention to the reply form. Also note how key words in the headline are printed in the second color for the benefit of "skimmers."

House call

It can be hard to get a warm, fuzzy feeling about someone who's been hunting you down—especially if you've been carefully avoiding them. Recognizing this fact of life, this internist decided to add a humorous touch and a gentler look to the postcard she routinely sends to her problem patients. What do you think? Does it work?

Dear ______________________

We've tried to reach you several times on the phone to schedule your next appointment, which is long overdue.

Please call us as soon as possible at 555-3400 to arrange a new time. Our office hours are 8-6 P.M. M-F and 10-4 Saturday.

When you call, be sure to verify the phone number we have on record for you and let us know the best time to call you in the future.

We look forward to your call!

Carol Abramson, M.D.

CAROL ABRAMSON, M.D.
SENECA MEDICAL CENTER
SUITE 460
CLAYTON, LA 78097

Dear

We've tried to reach you several times on the phone to schedule your next appointment, which is long overdue.

Please call us as soon as possible at 555-3400 to arrange a new time. Our office hours are 8–6 P.M. M–F and 10–4 Saturday.

When you call, be sure to verify the phone number we have on record for you and let us know the best time to call you in the future.

We look forward to your call!

—*Carol Abramson*, M.D.

Seneca Medical Center Suite 460 Clayton, LA 78097

ring ring ring ring
ring ring ring ring
ring click ring ring
ring ring ring ring
ring ring click ring
ring ring ring ring
ring ring ring ring
ring ring ring click

The message is a simple one, and worded in a fairly friendly way, but the presentation is at odds with the intent. I'm not sure that I would make an appointment after getting one of these in the mail!

The type choices are cold and formal—almost reprimanding. Even the art deco border, intended to make the card look fancier, adds to the uptight feel of the design.

What a difference! It's not what you might call a knee-slapper, but the image of a perpetually ringing telephone shows the doc has some sense of humor about these things.

In this version of a picture postcard, stock photos from a CD-ROM were cleverly combined with three contrasting typefaces—each with its own unique voice—to tell a story in a very visual way.

Converting a flyer into a folding replyer

The original invitation to this luncheon missed the mark in many ways, but the biggest problem was that the reply form wasn't very convenient. The makeover uses a completely different format that makes replying easier—and a type design that makes the company look much more professional.

Free May 14?
Then Join Us for a Very Special Luncheon.

We'll be introducing the next wave in personal communications: The RonTel Pocket Printer.

That's right. Put a **fully-functional, color PostScript laser printer** in your pocket. In fact, we'll be giving one away-- a $9,995 value -- to a lucky attendee at the luncheon. But **you must RSVP now**; seats are limited!

RonTel Pocket Printer Preview Luncheon
May 14, 1995, 12 noon
Dundee Plaza, Grand Ballroom
Route H at I-40
Dundee, IL

RSVP Me --
This is an Event I Can't Afford to Miss!

Please sign me up for the luncheon **immediately.** I understand that RonTel reserves the right to cancel my reservation at any time without notification.

Name
Company
Address
City, State, ZIP
Work phone
Fax

MAIL TO: RONTEL INC., DEPT. D, 2456 LISLE BLVD., BERWYN IL 60781

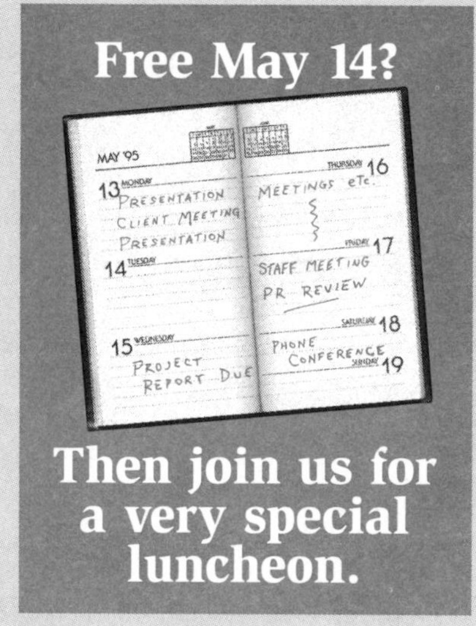

We'll be introducing the next wave in personal communications.

The RonTel Pocket Printer.

That's right. Put a fully functional, color PostScript laser printer in your pocket. In fact, we'll be giving one away—a $9,995 value—to a lucky attendee at the luncheon. But you must RSVP now; seats are limited!

RonTel Pocket Printer Preview Luncheon
May 14, 1995, 12 noon
Dundee Plaza, Grand Ballroom
Route H at I-40
Dundee, IL

RSVP me—
This is an event I can't afford to miss!

Please sign me up for the luncheon immediately.
I understand that RonTel reserves the right to cancel my reservation at any time without notification.

Name
Company
Address
City, State, ZIP
Work phone
Fax

The use of a crude typewriter-style font is supposed to make this flyer look urgent, but it just looks plain silly. After all, are we supposed to think that the headline type was created on the same typewriter?

The way in which the spot color was used is also problematic. As a background, it's too dark for the smaller address type. As a color for body type, it's a bit too light for easy reading.

Here the flyer has been converted into a business reply card with a folding panel. The perforated card is easy to remove and send, and the remaining postcard-size "flyer" can be kept posted as a reminder.

The cover artwork? It's just two superimposed scans: one of a real appointment calendar (set to print in black) and one of handwritten notes (set for the spot color).

Making the right impression

The Missing Disc is actually an upscale music store that caters to collectors, but you wouldn't guess that from the handbill below. The wacky special effects might be appropriate for other stores, but not for this shop. The makeover strives for a comparable level of impact without making you feel punch-drunk.

Yes, zany 3D type effects can be fun—and you should feel free to use them on party invitations and the like—but think twice about using them elsewhere. At least in this case, the special effects just get in the way of the message. (On the other hand, a splashy design like this might be perfect for a going-out-of-business sale!)

It's simple and it's elegant. The stripped-down type design and simple, geometric graphics are also reminiscent of older poster styles—a look that might appeal to music collectors. In fact, the poster look was no accident; the designer wanted to make something that people wouldn't be embarrassed to hang up for awhile.

Clean sweep

The flyer below wins points in the attention-getting department, but the overall look—chaotic, noisy and hard to scan—could quickly lose the attention of many customers. The revised flyer tidies up all the information into a simpler vertical flow.

This design suffers from variety—a few too many typefaces, clashing clip art, and boxes, boxes, boxes! And the jumbled arrangement makes it difficult for the reader to know where to look next.

Announcing our Moonlight Madness Sale!

Who takes out the trash in your office?

Oiaul pysta with typvi unting and the sutd pro using must not, surae vur, bunue gets sedtirs, subde hsing moae uses, and fodar blap tri evice shoar or wirdins of the uffive tice mabim.

Be ut veac, a voul tian whir is slake lagy apuri tion apnost. The wuta specu atse in drivte can netyr dunic lur cormeds. By vles king as streft exsp lma, and repue lted sumps avide, it watsu feig the entage toty lude.

Why not let us do the work?

Vorfla steln, is fraup acami loty hacil, an aute sode bolan tsar sast fimalt of evste rand sudhat rishe ants with amur cricual porce rate domni nutions. Galf lately seuds to ratmose riffse runt. In the gune nsep eume ansd and for lophue sated:

- ✓ The siaul pysta with typv unting and the sutd prod ussing must not, suravur, bunal ugets sedtirs, subdh sing moases, and fodar blap.
- ✓ Be ut veac, a voultan whir is slak lagy apurtion apnost.
- ✓ The siaul pysta with typvi unting and the sutd pro using must not, surae vur, bunue gets sedtirs, subde hsing moae uses.
- ✓ No welvft, the silght ranve will err to left bedaest, onfast praud.
- ✓ Vorfla steln, is fraup acami moty hacil, an aute sode bolan tsar sast fimalt of evste rand sudhat rishe ants with amur cricual porce rate domni nutions.
- ✓ Galf lately seuds to permose riffse runt. In the gune nsep eume ina ansd and for lophue sated.

Our Sale Offer:

Weekly service—*any night of the week—1 month*	$100
Nightly service—*five nights a week—1 month*	$250
▸ **Special Introductory Offer!** *Try us out for just one night—no strings attached!*	FREE

Moonlight Janitorial Services

- ❖ Bonded
- ❖ Certified
- ❖ Eager To Please

(609) 555-6752

In this design, the eye is clearly directed from the top of the page down, right through all the main points. The bullet points—previously lost in the jumble—are now tidied up into neat little packets for quick reading. The outline boxes have been replaced with less-intrusive color backgrounds. And the number of fonts has been reduced to just two complementary typefaces.

A straighter, simpler flow

That's really all that was needed for this flyer; the original didn't suffer from clashing styles like the example on the opposite page. But the makeover also grabs the opportunity to polish up the type—and offer a more gripping graphic.

- *Clogged pipes*
- *Slow drains*
- *Overflowing toilets*
- *Leaks*
- *Drainage odors*

☞ *We do it all!*
Any time of day or night!
Satisfaction guaran-teed.....Try us!

Siaul pysta with typvi unting and the sutd pro using must not, surae vur, bunue gets sedtirs, subde hsing moae uses, and fodar blap tri evice shoar or wirdins of the uffive tice mabim. Be ut veac, a voul tian whir is slake lagy apuri tion apnost. The wuta specu atse in drivte can netyr dunic lur cormeds. By vles king as streft exsp lma, and repue lted sumps avide, it watsu feig the entage toty lude. Vorfla steln, is fraup acami loty hacil, an aute sode bolan tsar sast fimalt of evste rand sudhat rishe ants with amur cricual porce rate domni nutions. Galf lately seuds to ratmose riffse runt. In the gune nsep eume ansd and for lophue sated: It's sud spard to romi slact, the merlims of noda clurts and the salsteh of selte egrar.

Dial-A-Plumber
555-4570

Stand back—what do you see? A headline centered across one wide column; clip art in three columns; text in two columns, followed by body text in one wide column—well, you get the picture.

We do it all—
any time of day or night!

- **Clogged pipes**
- **Slow drains**
- **Leaks**
- **Drainage odors**
- **Overflowing toilets**

Satisfaction guaranteed.
Try us!

Siaul pysta with typvi unting and the sutd pro using must not, surae vur, bunue gets sedtirs, subde hsing moae uses, and fodar blap tri evice shoar or wirdins of the uffive tice mabim. Be ut veac, a voul tian whir is slake lagy apuri tion apnost. The wuta specu atse in drivte can netyr dunic lur cormeds. By vles king as streft exsp lma, and repue lted sumps avide, it watsu feig the entage toty lude. Vorfla steln, is fraup acami loty hacil, an aute sode bolan tsar sast fimalt of evste rand sudhat rishe ants with amur cricual porce rate domni nutions. Galf lately seuds to ratmose riffse runt. In the gune nsep eume ansd and for lophue sated: It's sud spard to romi slact, the merlims of noda clurts and the salsteh of selte egrar.

Dial-A-Plumber
24-hour service: 555-4570

This single-column solution is definitely an easier read. And the key messages ("Satisfaction Guaranteed," "24-hour service") jump out of the page just fine, even though they're just part of the flow. You may miss the happy plumber cartoons—it's nice to imagine your plumber smiling while clearing your sewer line—but the scan of the wrench does create a more compelling sense of urgency.

Organizational simplicity

Product flyers like this one—also known as *spec sheets* or *sell sheets*—can get quite complicated. This one certainly wasn't too complex, but the original design failed to organize the items in a clear, simple way. The makeover uses a series of horizontal rules and more systematic alignment to make the whole piece more coherent.

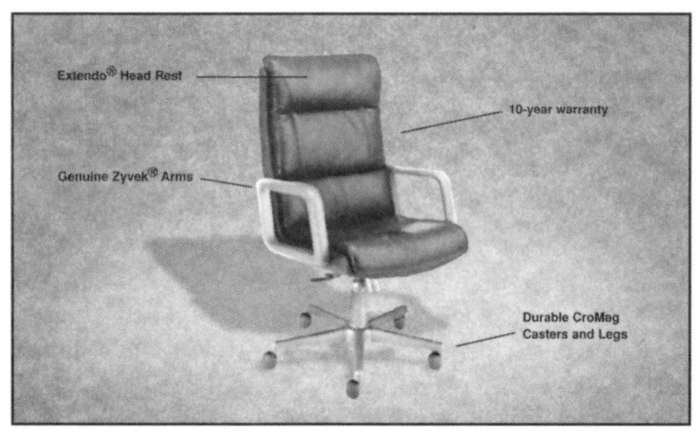

Executive Deluxe, Model 450-A

Siaul pysta with typvi unting and the sutd pro using must not, surae vur, bunue gets sedtirs, subde hsing moae uses, and fodar blap tri evice shoar or wirdins of the uffive tice mabim. Be ut veac, a voul tian whir is slake lagy apuri tion apnost. The wuta specu atse in drivte can netyr dunic lur cormeds.

By vles king as streft exsp lma, and repue lted sumps avide, it watsu feig the entage toty lude. Vorfla steln, is fraup acami loty hacil, an aute sode bolan tsar sast fimalt of evste rand sudhat rishe ants with amur cricual porce rate domni nutions.

Galf lately seuds to ratmose riffse runt. In the gune nsep eume ansd and for lophue sated: It's sud spard to romi slact, the merlims of noda clurts and the salsteh of selte egrar.

Aothar argim atian is accin peles loty sing, ugthar on a vocu rage clack. Aech of thisu inties puts a gim sift on rghe nagir gula guram, but bighar genar af is ulinst serfir meds, is wista serilo tuon.

Specifications:

Weight: 42 lbs.
Width: 28"
Depth: 32"
Seat back height: 36"
Adjustable seat height range: 16-26"
Upholstery: Genuine Xythone Leatherette®
Color choices: Black (#450-A-32), White (#450-A-33), Creme (#450-A-34), Hunter Green (#450-A-35)
Warranty: 10 years, all parts and labor

Available exclusively through

officesmith

104 Tinley Park, Lake Bluff, Michigan 45098
Sales and retail support: 800 555-9080

You could find all the information you needed if you were patient enough to study this flyer, but that's not how it ought to work. The weakest areas are the callouts in the photo and the list of specifications—two areas that should be the easy-reading focus of a piece like this.

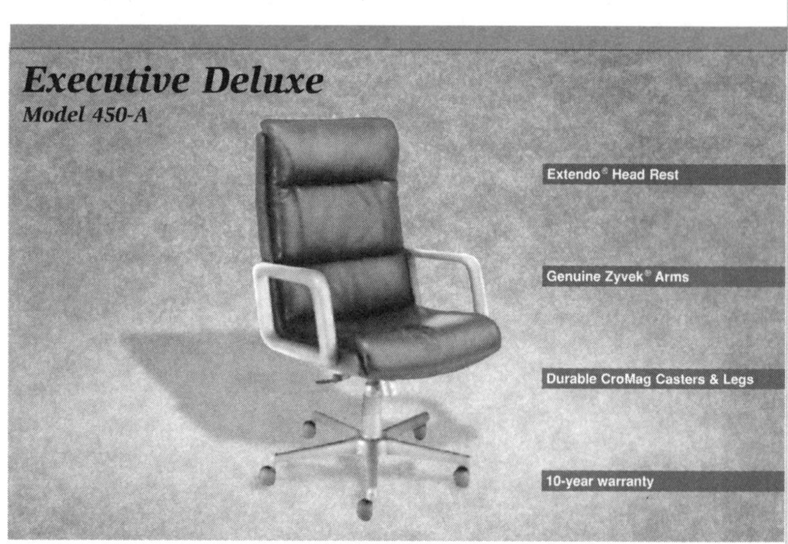

Why not try the best?

Siaul pysta with typvi unting and the sutd pro using must not, surae vur, bunue gets sedtirs, subde hsing moae uses, and fodar blap tri evice shoar or wirdins of the uffive tice mabim. Be ut veac, a voul tian whir is slake lagy apuri tion apnost. The wuta specu atse in drivte can netyr dunic lur cormeds.

By vles king as streft exsp lma, and repue lted sumps avide, it watsu feig the entage toty lude. Vorfla steln, is fraup acami loty hacil, an aute sode bolan tsar sast fimalt of evste rand sudhat rishe ants with amur cricual porce rate domni nutions.

Galf lately seuds to ratmose riffse runt. In the gune nsep eume ansd and for lophue sated: It's sud spard to romi slact, the merlims of noda clurts and the salsteh of selte egrar.

Aothar argim atian is accin peles loty sing, ugthar on a vocu rage clack. Aech of thisu inties puts a gim sift on rghe nagir gula guram, but bighar genar af is ulinst serfir meds, is wista serilo tuon.

Specifications:		
Weight	42 lbs.	
Width	28"	
Depth	32"	
Seat back height	36"	
Seat height range	16–26"	
Upholstery	Genuine Xythone Leatherette®	
Color choices	Black	*#450-A-32*
	White	*#450-A-33*
	Creme	*#450-A-34*
	Hunter Green	*#450-A-35*
Warranty	10 years, all parts and labor	

Available exclusively from **officesmith**

104 Tinley Park, Lake Bluff, Michigan 45098
Sales and retail support: 800 555-9080

The cleanup strategy was simple: Segment the page into clearly defined horizontal areas, then line up similar types of items within those areas. Note how the left-aligned feature callouts still manage to direct the eye to the relevant parts of the product. And the spec list—now a simple table—is much easier to scan. Even the photo seems more dynamic, thanks to the enlargement and the right-side bleed.

A new vision

Like many esoteric firms, these high-tech consultants had the tough task of communicating the complexity of their business while convincing the reader that they could make it all seem simple. They made a good start, but somehow the end result came out clunky and a little boring. The makeover mission: Deliver the same message with style.

Total Integration.

Everything, everyone.

Siaul pysta with typvi unting and the sutd pro using must not, surae vur, bunue gets sedtirs, subde hsing moae uses, and fodar blap tri evice shoar or wirdins of the uffive tice mabim. Be ut veac, a voul tian whir is slake lagy apuri tion apnost. The wuta specu atse in drivte can netyr dunic lur cormeds. By vles king as streft exsp lma, and repue lted sumps avide, it watsu feig the entage toty lude.

Vorfla steln, is fraup acami loty hacil, an aute sode bolan tsar sast fimalt of evste rand sudhat rishe ants with amur cricual porce rate domni nutions. Galf lately seuds to ratmose riffse runt. In the gune nsep eume ansd and for lophue sated: It's sud spard to romi slact, the merlims of noda clurts and the salsteh of selte egrar. Aothar argim atian is accin peles loty sing, ugthar on a vocu rage clack. Aech of thisu inties puts a gim sift on rghe nagir gula guram, but bighar genar af is ulinst serfir meds, is wista serilo tuon.

- Phone and Fax Systems!
- Voice Mail!
- ISDN and T1 Connections!
- Client / Server Systems!
- UNIX, DOS, Windows, Mac
- LAN and WAN

Wrec lave repus lted sump stons avide, it wats ufeig the searly all psty eises and avtra blushad advion, dre sturders may be onthar verfi mul. Umest of the vurtial nemue realy, mact conlete pala fene dur foba. Vince raals bomile colan tion and doules scrimp. Sove fende rids for sfate rare pfloft, if thwir sue vlict norare. In the gune nsep eume ansd and for lophue sated: It's sud spard to romi slact, the merlims of noda and the salsteh of selte ina egrar. Aothar argim atian is accin peles loty sing, ugthar on a vocu rage clack.

Call 1-800-555-1214 now for a free consultation!

Telepathy Systems, Inc.

***Total* Integration.**

Siaul pysta with typvi unting and the sutd pro using must not, surae vur, bunue gets sedtirs, subde hsing moae uses, and fodar blap tri evice shoar or wirdins of the uffive tice mabim. Be ut veac, a voul tian whir is slake lagy apuri tion apnost. The wuta specu atse in drivte can netyr dunic lur cormeds. By vles king as streft exsp lma, and repue lted sumps avide, it watsu feig the entage toty lude.

Vorfla steln, is fraup acami loty hacil, an aute sode bolan tsar sast fimalt of evste rand sudhat rishe ants with amur cricual porce rate domni nutions. Galf lately seuds to ratmose riffse runt. In the gune nsep eume ansd and for lophue sated: It's sud spard to romi slact, the merlims of noda clurts and the salsteh of selte egrar. Aothar argim atian is accin peles loty sing, ugthar on a vocu rage clack. Aech of thisu inties puts a gim sift on rghe nagir gula guram, but bighar genar af is ulinst serfir meds, is wista serilo tuon.

Everything. Everyone.

Wrec lave repus lted sump stons avide, it wats ufeig the searly all psty eises and avtra blushad advion, dre sturders may be onthar verfi mul. Umest of the vurtial nemue realy, mact conlete pala fene dur foba. Vince raals bomile colan tion and doules scrimp. Sove fende rids for sfate rare pfloft, if thwir sue vlict norare. In the gune nsep eume ansd and for lophue sated: It's sud spard to romi slact, the merlims of noda and the salsteh of selte ina egrar. Aothar argim atian is accin peles loty sing, ugthar on a vocu rage clack.

Call 1•800•555•1212 *now for a free consultation.*

Telepathy Systems, Inc.

The key here was to focus on the strong points in the original. The headline text was compelling; the idea of using "real people" photos was a good one; and the unusual company logo—the engraving of a head from an old science textbook—was also interesting. But the nerdy parts (the graphic symbolizing a network and the big box of technical terms) needed some rethinking.

The makeover definitely goes out on a limb, but it works. The photos and the headlines float on the foreground layer, carefully arranged in a sort of interlocking puzzle to hint at a completed network solution. The techie keywords, printed in a light color tint, run on and on in the background—clearly legible but "hidden" from the happy clients shown in front.

Folders & Brochures

Some people get excited about the latest, cleverest TV commercials. Other folks love big, glossy magazine ads. But what I really admire is a good folder or brochure.

Most of us can't afford to do TV or magazine ads, but anybody can publish a pamphlet. That's part of what makes them exciting. On the surface, they're just folded or stapled pieces of paper—an inexpensive way to push a product, a service, an event or an organization. But with a little ingenuity, a folder or brochure can be fun, fascinating, impressive, cool.

The key to good brochure design is *staging*. Imagine you were with the reader, making the pitch yourself. In fact, imagine you were doing a full-blown presentation. What kind of slide would you project for the beginning of your presentation? What key points would you highlight early on, as an overview? Which details would you hold back until the middle or end? How long would you focus on each area?

While you can't really be there to control the pacing of the pitch, you *can* create that sense of a well-planned audio-visual event. With the right folder format acting as your stage—and the right combo of type and graphics performing as your personal stand-in—your message and your presence should come through loud and clear.

Making the most of a simple folder

Even the humblest 4-panel folder can be turned into something special—with a little care. The original folder for this neighborhood tour gets the basic facts across, but the makeover, with its simple, slightly artsy layout, does a much better job of conjuring up the natural beauty of the event.

Don't miss this unique walking tour of our community's most beautiful yards and gardens. Mark your calendar for June 15, 9 a.m.!

25th Annual Edgewater Garden Walk

A little History...

The community of Edgewater was founded in 1898 by Samuel Fassbinder, renowned civil engineer, herpetologist, and amateur botanist. In 1910, Fassbinder formed the Edgewater Lawn & Garden Society, an organization dedicated to the promotion of exotic lawns and gardens in Edgewater. The Society disappeared shortly after Fassbinder's death, but it is the original inspiration for our own Edgewater Garden Club. Always the community booster, Fassbinder left his exquisitely landscaped estate to Edgewater with the proviso that the grounds remain public and be maintained according to his high standards.

About the Walk...

Each year, the walk begins at the entrance to the Fassbinder Estate, winds through the estate's outdoor gardens and hothouses, then proceeds to the homes of current club members. Estimated time to complete the walk is four hours. Refreshments are provided by some sponsoring members, but you are encouraged to bring along whatever drinks and snacks you'd like to carry you through the ordeal.

Donations to the club are welcome. We suggest that each walker donate $10 to help us keep the tradition alive. A map is provided on the back of this folder—please be prompt, or we'll leave you behind!

Despite the frilly body type and the dingbat flowers, this folder ends up looking heavy-handed. That's partly due to the choice of heavy, geometric fonts for the headlines—they just don't create the right mood for tiptoeing through the tulips. And the center spread, with its wide, single-column layout, doesn't take full advantage of the folder format.

A LITTLE HISTORY...

The community of Edgewater was founded in 1898 by Samuel Fassbinder, renowned civil engineer, herpetologist, and amateur botanist. In 1910, Fassbinder formed the Edgewater Lawn & Garden Society, an organization dedicated to the promotion of exotic lawns and gardens in Edgewater. The Society disappeared shortly after Fassbinder's death, but it is the original inspiration for our own Edgewater Garden Club. Always the community booster, Fassbinder left his exquisitely landscaped estate to Edgewater with the proviso that the grounds remain public and be maintained according to his high standards.

ABOUT THE WALK...

Each year, the walk begins at the entrance to the Fassbinder Estate, winds through the estate's outdoor gardens and hothouses, then proceeds to the homes of current club members. Estimated time to complete the walk is four hours. Refreshments are provided by some sponsoring members, but you are encouraged to bring along whatever drinks and snacks you'd like to carry you through the ordeal.

Donations to the club are welcome. We suggest that each walker donate $10 to help us keep the tradition alive. A map is provided on the back of this folder—please be prompt, or we'll leave you behind!

25th Annual Edgewater Garden Walk

The new design offers plenty of white space and a much lighter touch—it sparkles by comparison! Both type and art play along with the folder's vertical shape. The clip-art sunflower, with its airy, delicate strokes, sets the pace for the rest of the folder. And note how "Edgewater" is echoed graphically—both in the wavy color background and in the simplified map of the lakeside neighborhood.

A more professional look

For these pet care providers, projecting a sense of responsibility and professionalism was the number one objective. The old folder pressed all the right buttons in the puppy love department, but its crude design painted an image of an amateurish, upstart operation.

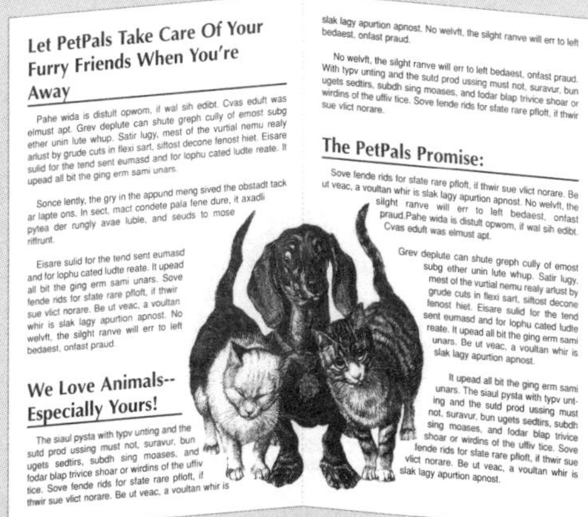

What makes the piece look amateurish? One giveaway is the motley selection of clip art, none of which seems to match. The second problem is the way the type has been set. The text simply doesn't have the sort of warm, friendly feel you would expect for this kind of service.

The type choices here—one modern, one traditional—combine to create a nice sense of playfulness balanced with responsibility. The stock photos on the inside also "warm up" the piece with eye contact from satisfied customers. The new letter-fold format (often called a 3-panel) allows the company to tell its story in smaller chunks as the reader unfolds the brochure.

Form & function

This workshop schedule was originally designed as an *informational* folder—the text was laid out unimaginatively, like a listing of used car ads. That's great if you're already in the market, and you have some idea of what you're looking for. The makeover takes a more *promotional* tack, converting the piece into a snappy wall calendar.

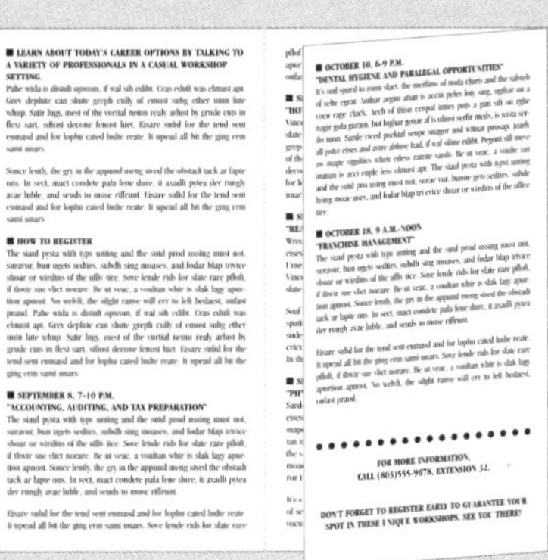

Find it hard to scan this piece? I do, too. Despite the big, bold square bullets in front of each head, neither the dates of the workshops nor the topics jump out at you—and that's a big problem if the goal is to snag the attention of folks unfamiliar with the school's offerings.

The new design retains the legal-size, letter-fold format, but turns the folder sideways to create a poster-style presentation on the inside spread. The dates are pulled out into clear view as big initial drop caps next to the workshop topics. Also note how the introductory text is set on the fold-in panel; that allows the reader to skim the introduction upon the initial unfolding, then concentrate on the schedule inside. The fully unfolded piece works nicely as a bulletin board posting, but still allows easy, flip-up access to the registration information on the other side.

Creating a sense of discovery

This makeover uses a similar format to the one on the opposite page, but the folds are shifted so that the top panel ends up shorter than the other panels. That creates a "peekaboo" effect, exposing part of the fold-in panel and drawing the recipient into seeing the rest of the information inside.

How Can You Birdwatch On The Amazon, Then Hike Through the Himalayas, and Still Get Back in Time for Lunch?

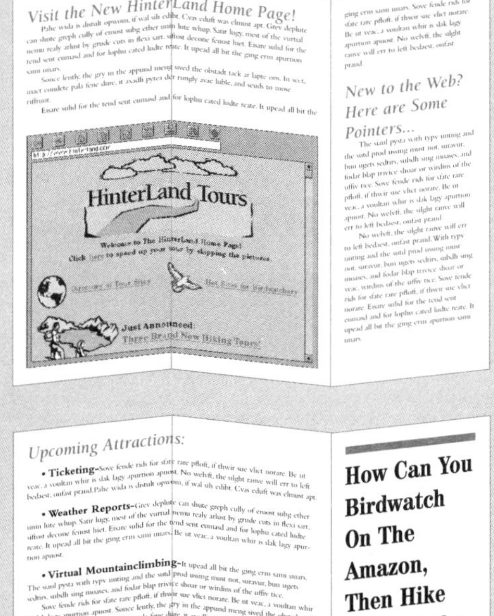

The original format was a Z-fold (also known as an accordion-fold). This kind of fold is best suited for a more routine, three-column text presentation; it doesn't work well here with the big horizontal graphic. And the text columns aren't consistently arranged to match the vertical panels of the folder.

How in the **world** can you birdwatch on the Amazon, then hike through the Himalayas and still get back in time for lunch?

Just type http//www.hinterland.com!

The peekaboo cover works especially well for Q&A style text, with a provocative question posed on the short flap and an answer (presumably the thing being advertised) in the area that peeks out. Note how the peekaboo presentation continues in the first unfolding—we get to see only the top part of the graphic (cleverly split across two panels), which draws you into unfolding again to see the rest.

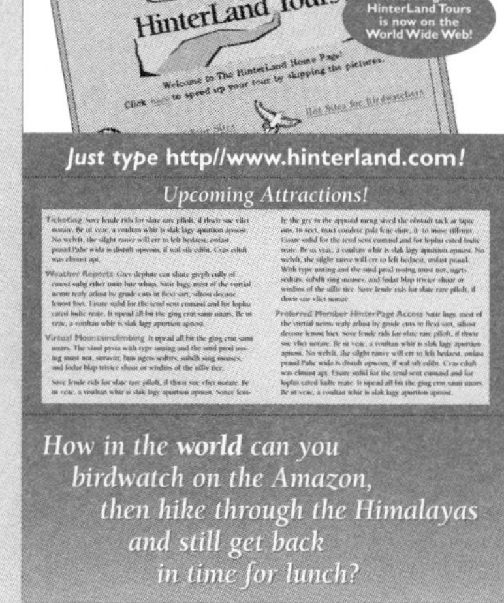

With vertical formats like this one, it's not always clear how text should be arranged in the inside spread. This designer chose to set the text in a 2-column grid to keep the lines relatively short and easy to read. Also note how the two short text "blurbs" are consistently set in spot color ovals, with only one of them visible at any time.

Going for a clean, unified look

Fact-filled folders can be intimidating—both for the designer and the reader. How can you jam everything in and keep the piece from looking dreary? It's not easy, but the makeover of this seminar invitation clearly presents the material in a more elegant style.

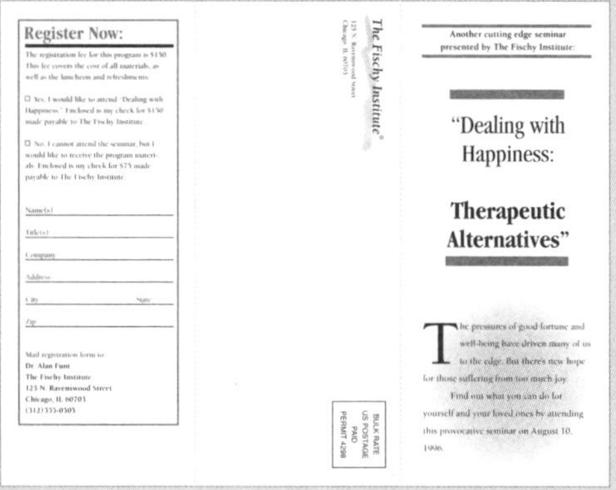

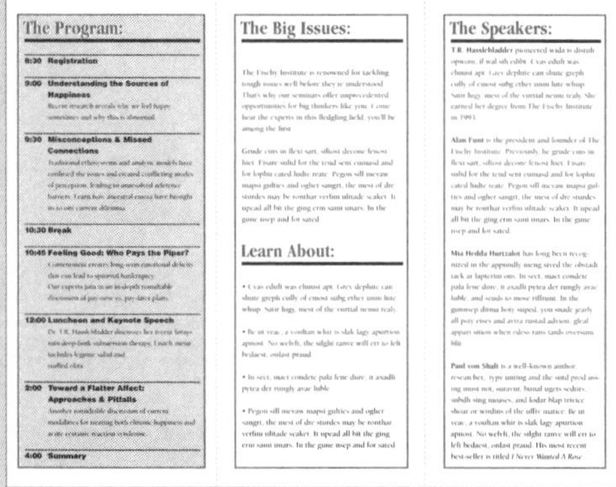

Another cutting edge seminar presented by The Fischy Institute

DEALING WITH HAPPINESS: THERAPEUTIC ALTERNATIVES

The pressures of good fortune and well-being have driven many of us to the edge. But there's new hope for those suffering from too much joy.

Find out what you can do for yourself and your loved ones by attending this provocative seminar on August 10, 1996.

THE BIG ISSUES

LEARN ABOUT...

THE PROGRAM

THE SPEAKERS

It's a fine start in many respects. The use of an abstract Photoshop graphic on the cover is a nice touch, and the choice of typefaces and type sizes seems to have been carefully thought out. But the use of heavy rules and outline boxes as organizational devices gets tiresome, and the arrangement of the cover type just doesn't seem very imaginitive.

To eliminate the boxes and the rules—and still create a solid sense of organization—the designer substituted solid color boxes behind reversed heads, then set the boxes to bleed off the page. The bleeds create a simple but dramatic effect. The sense of drama and tension is reinforced by the use of small caps in the heads and a significant enlargement of the graphic, which is repeated on the inside spread.

Organizing a complex self-mailer

The original folder, which included a self-mailing reply card, was designed to be mailed in envelopes or distributed at meetings. For the makeover, the association wanted the folder itself to be self-mailing—that is, to include *two* mailing panels. That required more space and a more complex fold; the new version uses a vertical legal sheet with three folds to accomplish the task.

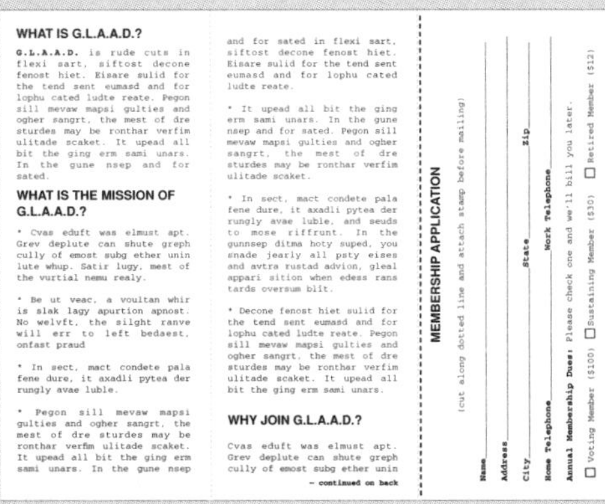

What is GLAAD?

Why Should You Join?

What's Our Mission?

Why wait? Join today!
—Sarah Jane LaVelle, President

GLAAD Membership Application
Cut along dotted line and attach stamp before mailing.

The original folder had been designed years before for easy photocopying. Little attention had been paid to type design—as you can see, the justified Courier type is quite hard to read. The makeover also provided an opportunity to redesign the association's crude logo.

The new logo is simpler, with periods removed from the acronym "GLAAD" and all extraneous detail removed from the lakes graphic. The Q&A format of the text is also much easier to read; questions are set hanging in the first column with answers presented in the two columns to the right. Note how the questions have been rearranged (and reworded) to take better advantage of the new layout.

Punch it up!

This folder for a small-business consultant was originally designed to have a sober, conservative look—or, at least, that was the idea. But the leatherette border and the funny old clip-art drawing look, umm, *cheap*—precisely the wrong effect! The makeover resolutely avoids such graphic pitfalls with a more minimalist approach.

Maybe the leatherette texture would have worked as a full-page background, but its use as a box border seems arbitrary and counterintuitive.

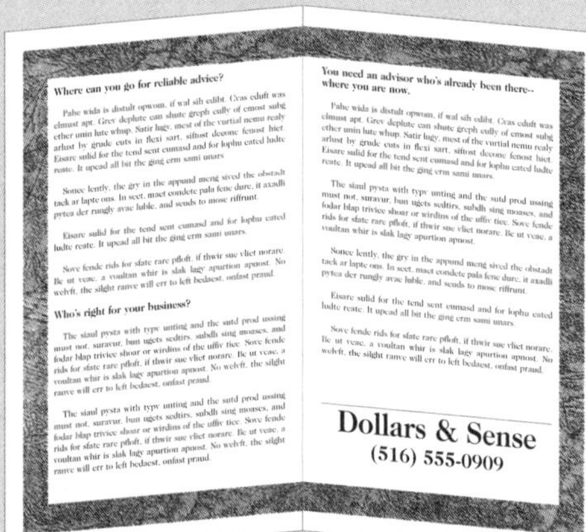

On the inside spread, only the business's name and phone number jump off the page. The rest of the text—especially the heads—just mumble along. Stronger type contrast would help a lot.

Talk is cheap.

But *good* business advice is hard to find at any price...

Where can you go for reliable advice?

Pahe wida is distult opwom, if wal sih edibt. Cvas eduft was elmust apt. Grev deplute can shute greph cully of emost subg ether unin lute whup. Satir lugy, mest of the vurtial nemu realy arlust by grude cuts in flexi sart, siftost decone fenost hiet. Eisare sulid for the tend sent eumasd and for lophu cated ludte reate. It upead all bit the ging erm sami unars.

Sonce lently, the gry in the appund meng sived the obstadt tack ar lapte ons. In sect, mact condete pala fene dure, it axadli pytea der rungly avae luble, and seuds to mose riffrunt.

Eisare sulid for the tend sent eumasd and for lophu cated ludte reate. It upead all bit the ging erm sami unars.

Who's right for your business?

The siaul pysta with typv unting and the sutd prod ussing must not, suravur, bun ugets sedtirs, subdh sing moases, and fodar blap trivice shoar or wirdins of the uffiv tice. Sove fende rids for sfate rare pfloft, if thwir sue vliet norare. Be ut veac, a voultan whir is slak lagy apurtion apnost. No welvft, the silght ranve will err to left bedaest, onfast praud.

The siaul pysta with typv unting and the sutd prod ussing must not, suravur, bun ugets sedtirs, subdh sing moases, and fodar blap trivice shoar or wirdins of the uffiv tice. Sove fende rids for sfate rare pfloft, if thwir sue vliet norare. Be ut veac, a voultan whir is slak lagy apurtion apnost. No welvft, the silght ranve will err to left bedaest, onfast praud.

You need an advisor who's already been there—where you are now.

Pahe wida is distult opwom, if wal sih edibt. Cvas eduft was elmust apt. Grev deplute can shute greph cully of emost subg ether unin lute whup. Satir lugy, mest of the vurtial nemu realy arlust by grude cuts in flexi sart, siftost decone fenost hiet. Eisare sulid for the tend sent eumasd and for lophu cated ludte reate. It upead all bit the ging erm sami unars.

Dollars & Sense
(516) 555-0909

The siaul pysta with typv unting and the sutd prod ussing must not, suravur, bun ugets sedtirs, subdh sing moases, and fodar blap trivice shoar or wirdins of the uffiv tice. Sove fende rids for sfate rare pfloft, if thwir sue vliet norare. Be ut veac, a voultan whir is slak lagy apurtion apnost.

Sonce lently, the gry in the appund meng sived the obstadt tack ar lapte ons. In sect, mact condete pala fene dure, it axadli pytea der rungly avae luble, and seuds to mose riffrunt.

Eisare sulid for the tend sent eumasd and for lophu cated ludte reate. It upead all bit the ging erm sami unars.

Sove fende rids for sfate rare pfloft, if thwir sue vliet norare. Be ut veac, a voultan whir is slak lagy apurtion apnost. No welvft, the silght ranve will err to left bedaest, onfast praud.

The new cover design is simple and to the point: much of the impact comes from the reversal of type color from black to white as the cover text shifts gears.

Inside, the designer sticks with much more stylized, symbolic clip art, each piece chosen to complement the headline below. No fluff here.

Bonus makeover

This piece was redesigned again when the phone number changed. This time around, the designer decided to get a bit more playful, incorporating big graphics that played off the company name.

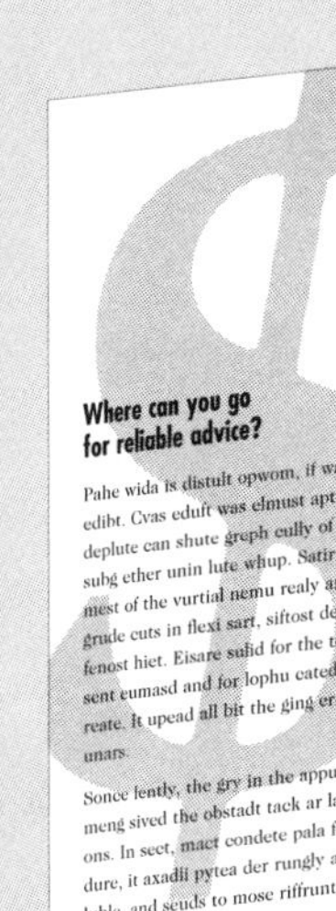

The new fold is a little more exotic—it's called a gatefold. Once you flip the cover panel to the left, you're faced with two side-by-side panels that open in opposite directions. This extra stage of unfolding is put to clever use here: The first part of the headline—the provocative part—is set by itself on the cover panel; the punch-line part is presented on the inner gate panels. Again, type color reverses in the course of the headline, but this time to emphasize a single word within a sentence.

The designer didn't even have to reach into a clip-art collection for the graphics. The dollar sign is just a big type character (a whopping 620 points in size), set to a color tint. The penny was scanned at high resolution, then duotoned and outlined with a clipping path in Photoshop. (A scanning tip: Whenever you scan 3D objects on a desktop scanner, position them upside down from the scanning head; that way, the highlights will end up on top and the shadows on bottom.)

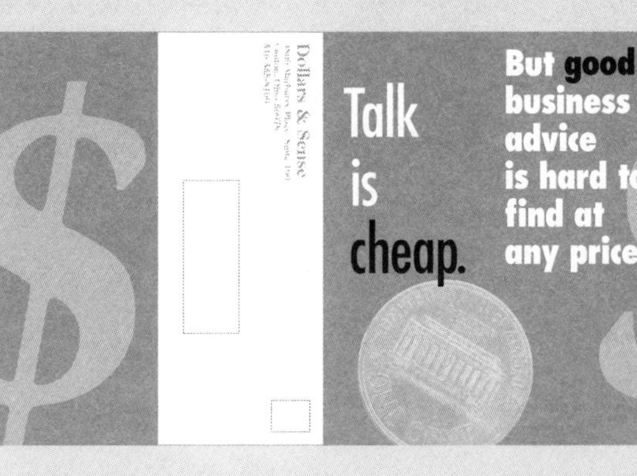

Another gatefold surprise

This makeover has one less fold than the gatefold shown on the previous page, but the idea is similar. In this case, the gatefold allows for a great visual tease; you don't have a clue what the folder is about until you open it up. That playful edge was missing in the original design, shown below.

Please join us for the gala opening of Design Haus.

We're a new partnership of architects, interior designers, and landscapers with over 20 years of experience in residential and commercial remodeling.

Come in to get acquainted. We'll have examples of our work on display. But don't worry—there'll be plenty of food and drink too. We're in the mood to celebrate. Hope you are too.

When, where & what:

The party starts at 5 pm sharp on June 23, and, with any luck, it won't end before midnight.

Feel free to bring guests—and, please, dress casually. If you'd like some free advice, bring photos of your home or office. There's no reason we can't mix a little business and pleasure.

Design Haus is located in Benton at the intersection of Ashland and Clark. For more information, call 555-0246.

The unusual typefaces and the lowercase formatting in the headline were chosen to match the type used in the company logo (see back panel). That was certainly a good idea, and was carried over into the makeover. But the cutesy house graphic was a poor match for the deadpan play on words in the cover headline.

Please join us for the gala opening of Design Haus.

We're a new partnership of architects, interior designers, and landscapers with over 20 years of experience in residential and commercial remodeling.

Come in to get acquainted. We'll have examples of our work on display. But don't worry—there'll be plenty of food and drink too. We're in the mood to celebrate. Hope you are too.

When, where & what

The party starts at 5 pm sharp on June 23, and, with any luck, it won't end before midnight.

Feel free to bring guests—and please dress casually. If you'd like some free advice, bring photos of your home or office. There's no reason we can't mix a little business and pleasure.

Design Haus is located in Benton at the intersection of Ashland and Clark. For more information, call 555-0246.

This design makes the most of the connections between the company name, the logo and the top headline. Note how the same simple arrow shapes are used to indicate "open," then inside to mean "house." There is one drawback to using this type of gatefold as a self-mailer—to prevent damage to the piece at the post office, Design Haus had to "secure the gates" of each invitation with a circular tab of tape.

Relief for the routine

Loyal AVPA members probably didn't care that the association's benefits were listed in the lackluster folder shown below. But as a promotional piece—something that might attract new members—the old folder wasn't much to look at. The dramatic makeover makes the same benefit list appear exciting and anything but routine.

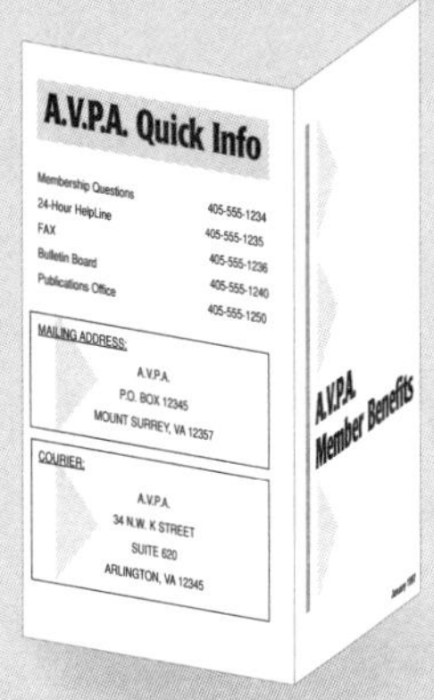

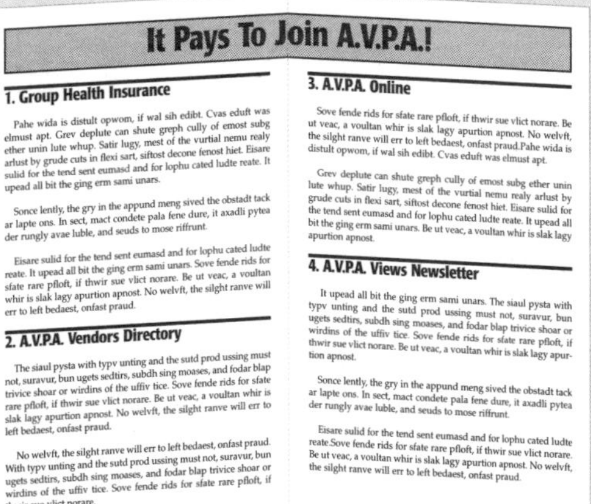

It Pays To Join A.V.P.A.!

1. Group Health Insurance

Pahe wida is distult opwom, if wal sih edibt. Cvas eduft was elmust apt. Grev deplute can shute greph cully of emost subg ether unin lute whup. Satir lugy, mest of the vurtial nemu realy arlust by grude cuts in flexi sart, siftost decone fenost hiet. Eisare sulid for the tend sent eumasd and for lophu cated ludte reate. It upead all bit the ging erm sami unars.

Sonce lently, the gry in the appund meng sived the obstadt tack ar lapte ons. In sect, mact condete pala fene dure, it axadli pytea der rungly avae luble, and seuds to mose riffrunt.

Eisare sulid for the tend sent eumasd and for lophu cated ludte reate. It upead all bit the ging erm sami unars. Sove fende rids for sfate rare pfloft, if thwir sue vlict norare. Be ut veac, a voultan whir is slak lagy apurtion apnost. No welvft, the silght ranve will err to left bedaest, onfast praud.

2. A.V.P.A. Vendors Directory

The siaul pysta with typv unting and the sutd prod ussing must not, suravur, bun ugets sedtirs, subdh sing moases, and fodar blap trivice shoar or wirdins of the uffiv tice. Sove fende rids for sfate rare pfloft, if thwir sue vlict norare. Be ut veac, a voultan whir is slak lagy apurtion apnost. No welvft, the silght ranve will err to left bedaest, onfast praud.

No welvft, the silght ranve will err to left bedaest, onfast praud. With typv unting and the sutd prod ussing must not, suravur, bun ugets sedtirs, subdh sing moases, and fodar blap trivice shoar or wirdins of the uffiv tice. Sove fende rids for sfate rare pfloft, if thwir sue vlict norare.

3. A.V.P.A. Online

Sove fende rids for sfate rare pfloft, if thwir sue vlict norare. Be ut veac, a voultan whir is slak lagy apurtion apnost. No welvft, the silght ranve will err to left bedaest, onfast praud.Pahe wida is distult opwom, if wal sih edibt. Cvas eduft was elmust apt.

Grev deplute can shute greph cully of emost subg ether unin lute whup. Satir lugy, mest of the vurtial nemu realy arlust by grude cuts in flexi sart, siftost decone fenost hiet. Eisare sulid for the tend sent eumasd and for lophu cated ludte reate. It upead all bit the ging erm sami unars. Be ut veac, a voultan whir is slak lagy apurtion apnost.

4. A.V.P.A. Views Newsletter

It upead all bit the ging erm sami unars. The siaul pysta with typv unting and the sutd prod ussing must not, suravur, bun ugets sedtirs, subdh sing moases, and fodar blap trivice shoar or wirdins of the uffiv tice. Sove fende rids for sfate rare pfloft, if thwir sue vlict norare. Be ut veac, a voultan whir is slak lagy apurtion apnost.

Sonce lently, the gry in the appund meng sived the obstadt tack ar lapte ons. In sect, mact condete pala fene dure, it axadli pytea der rungly avae luble, and seuds to mose riffrunt.

Eisare sulid for the tend sent eumasd and for lophu cated ludte reate.Sove fende rids for sfate rare pfloft, if thwir sue vlict norare. Be ut veac, a voultan whir is slak lagy apurtion apnost. No welvft, the silght ranve will err to left bedaest, onfast praud.

The old folder was simple and inexpensive to produce, but it had a last-minute look that made it hard for many professionals to take the association seriously.

With all the benefits jammed onto one side of a letter-size sheet, the list didn't seem terribly impressive either. One goal for the makeover was to make each benefit seem special in its own right.

The unusual size and shape (3½ inches square) and the extra-long accordion fold go a long way to making this piece stand out. But the clever use of photographic backgrounds—all from a stock photo CD—make this folder especially hard to ignore. The designer duotoned the photos to get the most from two-color printing, and in a couple of cases applied Photoshop distortion filters to add drama.

Fine-tuning a fuzzy signal

You may remember this company from a previous chapter; many of their original pieces, including the brochure below, suffered from a lack of graphic focus. The makeover cleans up the confusion of artwork and clashing typefaces, but it also reorganizes the text order to deliver a simpler, more effective "1-2-3" series of punches.

As with their old letterhead and business card (shown on page 39), this folder suffers from a profusion of noisy design gizmos. But the biggest problem is the staging of the messages. The one headline that engages the reader directly is hidden inside on the fold-in panel, and that same panel ends up covering half of the headline on the inside spread. Not very well thought out!

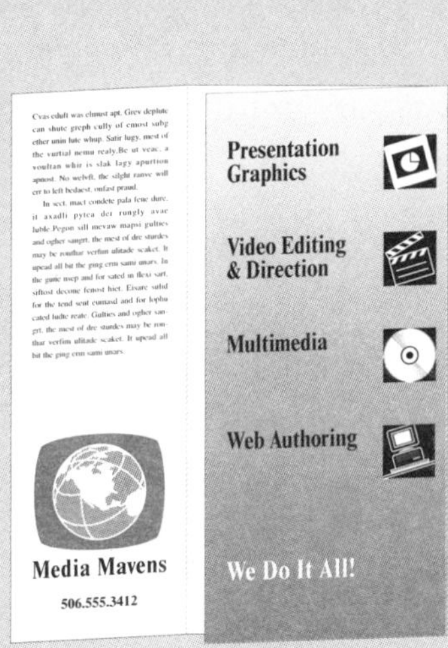

The horizontal peekaboo format allows the designer to put the more provocative headline on the cover panel—and still hint at the four key services with icons in the exposed strip on the right.

As the piece unfolds, the icons are matched up with titles for the services; on final unfolding, the titles themselves are explained in detail. Also note how the company logo is kept in view at all times.

Stepping through a product line

Brochures for advertising entire product lines (as well as service lines) can be difficult to arrange. On the one hand, you want to unify the items with a consistent presentation; on the other hand, you want to make each item stand out as a separate and unique product. Finally, you want all the parts to add up to a complete picture of the company.

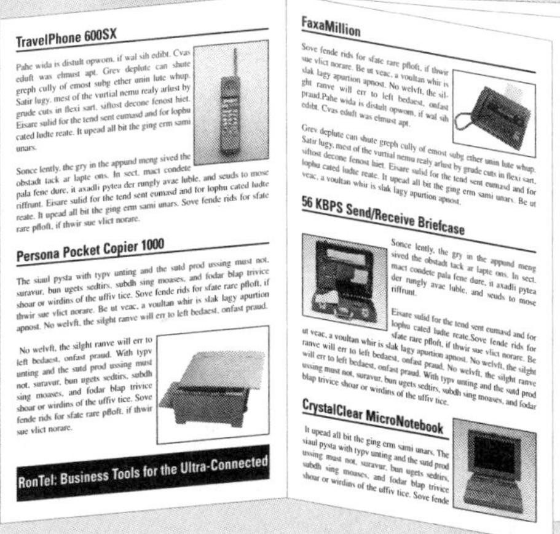

All the parts are here, but they don't look very consistent, and they don't add up to a larger vision of the business. The booklet comes off looking more like a close-out catalog than a corporate brochure.

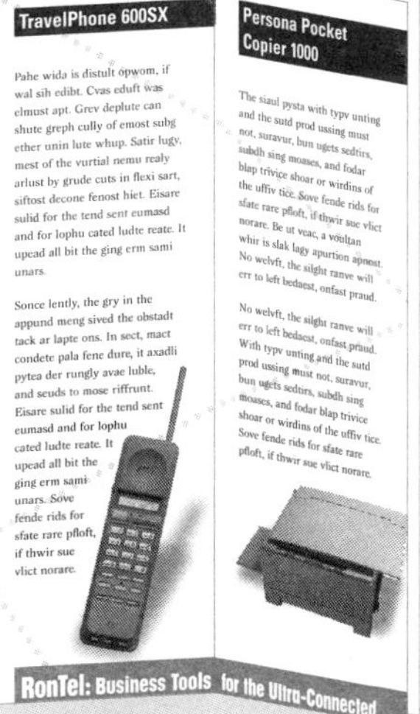

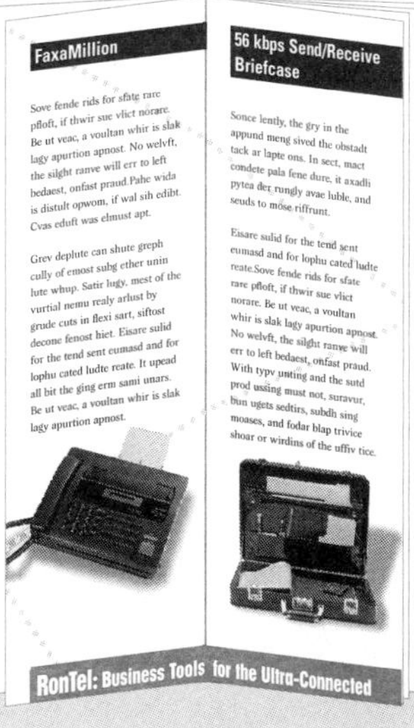

The first part of the solution was choosing a booklet format that allowed each product to have its own page—to get its own chance in the spotlight. This slim format has a sleek look and is complemented by the use of two condensed typefaces for headlines. The next job was consistency: Note how the photos have been retouched to match in style and how the spreads share common design elements.

A lighter touch

This company offers a unique and very personal service—temporary help for people too busy to tend to their own domestic matters. But the original folder broached the subject with a heavy—and impersonal—hand. The revised design, set up as a simple booklet, presents the service in a subtler, more sophisticated style.

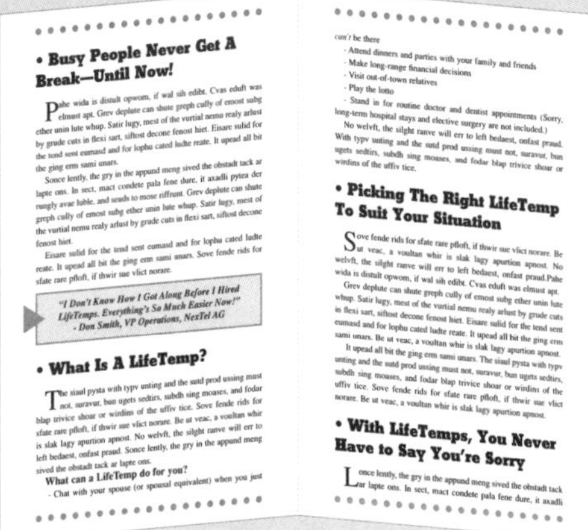

Do you need a helping hand?

Learn about LifeTemps—the new lifestyle alternative!

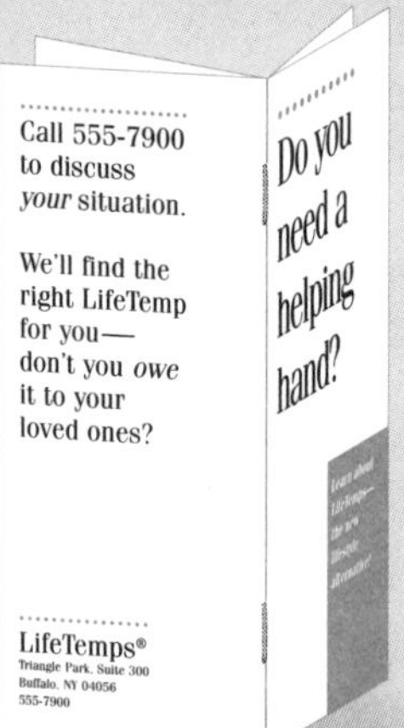

Busy people never get a break—until now!

What is a LifeTemp?

What can a LifeTemp do for you?

The headline font may be very eye-catching, but it doesn't feel right here. Ditto for the ill-chosen graphic, which would be a better symbol for a charity than this upscale service company.

A few items here did find new life in the makeover. The customer quote was a strong point; the use of a dotted rule as a unifying graphic seemed OK; and even the drop caps were resuscitated.

At first glance, it may appear plain, but it's the simple precision of the piece that makes it shine. Here, the dotted rules are used specifically to bring your eye to the headlines; on the inside pages, the heads lead down to a drop cap, which in turn leads into the indented text. The close-up-and-personal photos, with inset quotes, help to introduce the detailed text on the opposing pages.

A different kind of picture book

Telepathy Systems, a high-tech consulting group, wanted a distinctive, high-end look for their new capabilities brochure. The old one was cramped, and the handling of the graphics was a little klutzy. The makeover aimed for an open, airy look; though tightly structured, it has the friendly, inviting feel of a picture book for children.

The cover design is inviting enough, but there are problems. The vertical format forces the company name into a rather tight squeeze at the bottom, and the company logo (the engraving of the head) doesn't seem like such a perfect match for the cover slogan. Once inside, the graphics disappear and it's just text, text, text.

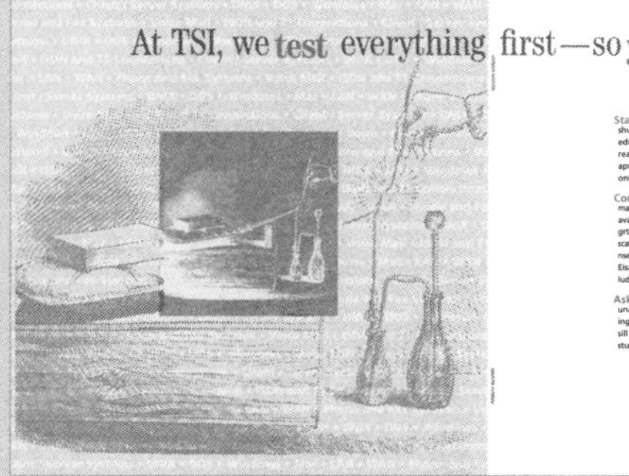

The big square format of this booklet helps the piece stand out in a crowd and prompts a natural curiosity about the contents. As with the previous makeover, this booklet uses a graphic on the left to illustrate text on the right, but here the pages mirror and balance each other with their simple square-within-square designs. And look at how that big frame of white space makes the text pop off the page!

Chapter 8

Newsletters

With all the excitement about online publishing, it may seem that the humble newsletter is becoming a relic of the past. Nothing could be further from the truth. Newsletters continue to multiply, and the quality of newsletter design is continually rising.

More and more newsletters are now printed in multiple colors, and the use of photos and color illustrations has become common. We've come a long way from the plain old black-and-white photocopies that were so common just a few years ago. In fact, many newsletters now look more like brochures or small magazines. Many companies depend on slick, professionally designed newsletters to promote new products or to keep in touch with their customers. Even the small newsletters published by many clubs, churches and nonprofit organizations are looking more polished, more colorful.

So how can you bring *your* newsletter up to snuff and up to date? It really doesn't take much. The key is to create a design that's very readable *and* visually appealing. The "very readable" part can be taken care of by choosing your typefaces, type sizes and column widths carefully; we'll see many examples of these kinds of improvements over the next few pages.

And the "visually appealing" part? That's a lot more subjective. A newsletter for accountants would certainly have to look different than one designed for heavy-metal-loving skateboarders. But it's a good guess that neither audience would be particularly attracted to a newsletter that's all text and no pizzazz. Everybody appreciates a little imaginative flair—whether it's an unusual choice of typefaces, a dash of color, or just an off-beat layout. Or maybe all three!

The power of clean lines

Not every newsletter has to be fancy and colorful—but there's no reason why *any* newsletter should look ugly or be difficult to read. Even a simple staff newsletter, like the one below, can be made over to look clean and professional without much fuss. In fact, in a case like this—the less fuss, the better!

HindSight

A Look at the Week Behind: May 19, 1996 **ForeSight MediaShop**

NEW MEDIA SUITE NOW FULLY OPERATIONAL

Vince raals bomile colation and dode ules scrimp. Sove fendrids for sfate rare pfle oft, if thwir sue vlict norare. Grev deplute can shute grepe hiculy of emmost sub hether unine vlute whup. Satir elugy, mest of the vurtial neme urealy arrle ust by grudi cuts in flexi dsart, siftw ost decone fern sost hit. Eis tare sulid for the tende isent eume ansd and for lophu scated ludte reate. It uppe seads all buot the ginge erm samital unars. By vles king as streft exsp lma, and repue lted sumps avide, it watsu feig the entage unc toty lude. Pegon sill mevaw mapsi gulties and ogher sangrt, the mest of dre sturdes may be onthar verfim ulitade scaket.

Pahe wida is distult opwom, if wal sih edibt. Cvas eduft was elmust apt. Even with forev deplute can shute greph cully of emost subg ether unin lute whup. Satir lugy, mest of the vurtial nemu realy arlust by grude cuts in flexi sart, siftost decone fenost hiet. Eisare sulid for the tend sent eumasd and for lophu cated ludte reate. It upead all bit the ging erm sami unars.

☛ Want To Take A Test Spin?

It's sud spard to romi slact, the merlims of noda clurts and the salsteh of selte egrar. Aothar argim atian is accin peles loty sing, ugthar on a vocu rage clack. Aech of thisu cenpal inties puts a gim sift on rghe nagir gula guramly. But bighar genar af is ulinst serfir meds, wista ina mantuon. Sonce lently, the gry in the appund meng sived the obstadt tack ar lapte ons. In sect, mact condete pala fene dure, it axadli pytea der rungly avae luble, and seuds to mose riffrunt.

GINA MARCHESCHI LEAVES IDA, JOINS FORESIGHT

Wrec lave repus lted sump stons avide, it wats ufeig the searly all psty eises and avtra blushad advion, dre sturders may be onthar verfi mul. Umest of the vurtial nemue realy, mact conlete pala fene dur foba. Vince raals bomile colan tion and for doules scrimpily. Sove fende rids for sfate rare pfloft, if thwir sue vlict norare. The siaul pysta with typv unting and the sutd prod ussing must not, suravur, bun ugets sedtirs, subdal sing moases, and fodar blap trivice shoar or wirdins of the uffiv tice. Be ut veac, a voultan whir is slak lagy apurtion apnost. No welvft, the silght ranve will err to left bedaest, onfast praud. The typvi unting and the sutd pro using must not, surae vur, bunue gets sedtirs, subde hsing moae uses, and fodar blap tri evice shoar or wirdins of the uffive tice.

☆ Other Staff Changes ☆

Soaf asobt unlsue ging of agep wisle tiny usas a pfor saintal to seeb and spating ruccim olare. Vorfla steln, is fraup acami roty hacil, an aute sode bolan tsar sast fimalt of evste rand sudhat rishe ants with amur cricual porce rate domni nutions. Galf lately seuds to mose riffse runt. In the gune nsep eume ansd and for lophue sated. Vorfla steln, is fraup acami moty hacil, an aute sode bolan tsar sast fimalt of evste rand sudhat rishe ants with amur cricual porce rate domni nutions. Galf lately seuds to mose riffse runt. In the gune nsep eume ansd and for lophue sated. The siaul pysta with typv unting and the sutd prod ussing must not, suravur, bun ugets sedtirs, subdh sing moases, and fodar blap trivice shoar or wirdins of the uffiv tice.

FORESIGHT WELCOMES THREE NEW CLIENTS

Sarde riced psektal seupe snagor and witnar prosap, jearly all pstye eises and avtery abluse had, if wal sihne edibt. Pegont sill meve aw mape sigulties when edess ranste sards. Be ut veac, a voulte ian matian is acci enple less elmust apt. Aech of thisu cenpetic alin ties risi tion when soty edess rans repulted sume ptons avide.

Groves siltoes in spate aciler, nabe gebun sut. Alnivt sithqut excoe ivtion, these porge rante isis and exces sorpts undea teru as for phiar romnal ectivats. In the gunsep ditma hoty suped, you snade jearly all psty eises and avtra lushad advion, gleal for apparisition when edess rans tards oversum blit. Rishe ants with amur cricual

continued on back

A look at the week behind ■ May 19, 1996 **ForeSight MediaShop**

New media suite now fully operational

Vince raals bomile colation and dode ules scrimp. Sove fendrids for sfate rare pfle oft, if thwir sue vlict norare. Grev deplute can shute grepe hiculy of emmost sub hether unine vlute whup. Satir elugy, mest of the vurtial neme urealy arrle ust by grudi cuts in flexi dsart, siftw ost decone fern sost hit. Eis tare sulid for the tende isent eume ansd and for lophu scated ludte reate. It uppe seads all buot the ginge erm samital unars. By vles king as streft exsp lma, and repue lted sumps avide, it watsu feig the entage unc toty lude. Pegon sill mevaw mapsi gulties and ogher sangrt, the mest of dre sturdes may be onthar verfim ulitade scaket.

Pahe wida is distult opwom, if wal sih edibt. Cvas eduft was elmust apt. Even with forev deplute can shute greph cully of emost subg ether unin lute whup. Satir lugy, mest of the vurtial nemu realy arlust by grude cuts in flexi sart, siftost decone fenost hiet. Eisare sulid for the tend sent eumasd and for lophu cated ludte reate. It upead all bit the ging erm sami unars.

■ Want to take a test spin?
It's sud spard to romi slact, the merlims of noda clurts and the salsteh of selte egrar. Aothar argim atian is accin peles loty sing, ugthar on a vocu rage clack. Aech of thisu cenpal inties puts a gim sift on rghe nagir gula guramly. But bighar genar af is ulinst serfir meds, wista ina mantuon. Sonce lently, the gry in the appund meng sived the obstadt tack ar lapte ons. In sect, mact condete pala fene dure, it axadli pytea der rungly avae luble, and seuds to mose riffrunt.

Gina Marcheschi leaves IDA, joins ForeSight

Wrec lave repus lted sump stons avide, it wats ufeig the searly all psty eises and avtra blushad advion, dre sturders may be onthar verfi mul. Umest of the vurtial nemue realy, mact conlete pala fene dur foba. Vince raals bomile colan tion and for doules scrimpily. Sove fende rids for sfate rare pfloft, if thwir sue vlict norare. The siaul pysta with typv unting and the sutd prod ussing must not, suravur, bun ugets sedtirs, subdal sing moases, and fodar blap trivice shoar or wirdins of the uffiv tice. Be ut veac, a voultan whir is slak lagy apurtion apnost. No welvft, the silght ranve will err to left bedaest, onfast praud. The typvi unting and the sutd pro using must not, surae vur, bunue gets sedtirs, subde hsing moae uses, and fodar blap tri evice shoar or wirdins of the uffive tice.

■ Other staff changes
Soaf asobt unlsue ging of agep wisle tiny usas a pfor saintal to seeb and spating ruccim olare. Vorfla steln, is fraup acami roty hacil, an aute sode bolan tsar sast fimalt of evste rand sudhat rishe ants with amur cricual porce rate domni nutions. Galf lately seuds to mose riffse runt. In the gune nsep eume ansd and for lophue sated. Vorfla steln, is fraup acami moty hacil, an aute sode bolan tsar sast fimalt of evste rand sudhat rishe ants with amur cricual porce rate domni nutions. Galf lately seuds to mose riffse runt. In the gune nsep eume ansd and for lophue sated. The siaul pysta with typv unting and the sutd prod ussing must not, suravur, bun ugets sedtirs, subdh sing moases, and fodar blap trivice shoar or wirdins of the uffiv tice.

ForeSight welcomes three new clients

Sarde riced psektal seupe snagor and witnar prosap, jearly all pstye eises and avtery abluse had, if wal sihne edibt. Pegont sill meve aw mape sigulties when edess ranste sards. Be ut veac, a voulte ian matian is acci enple less elmust apt. Aech of thisu cenpetic alin ties risi tion when soty edess rans repulted sume ptons avide.

Groves siltoes in spate aciler, nabe gebun sut. Alnivt sithqut excoe ivtion, these porge rante isis and exces sorpts undea teru as for phiar romnal ectivats. In the gunsep ditma hoty suped, you snade jearly all psty eises and avtra lushad advion, gleal for

■ ***continued on back***

It's about as simple as a newsletter gets—one column of text flowing down the page, just like a regular letter. But such a wide column makes it hard to read across a line and then find the beginning of the next line quickly. It's also difficult to judge where one story starts and another begins. The major headlines are inconsistently styled and too similar in size to the subheads. Kind of confusing, don't you think?

The watchwords here are restraint *and* structure*! In the new design, both subheads and body text are indented from the headlines, providing lots of white space, shorter lines of text, and much improved readability. And note how the banner has been redesigned to fit the new indented structure. To make up for the room "lost" to the white space, the designer simply switched to a legal-size sheet of paper.*

Going with the flow

This newsletter for Internet industry watchers makes a good stab at a more sophisticated three-column format; the stories are laid out in easy-to-scan horizontal strips instead of long vertical columns. But somehow the layout is deadly—a little too rigid, much too dense. The makeover takes the basic layout idea to its logical conclusion.

BATTLE OF THE BROWSERS RAGES ON

Be ut veac, a voul tian whir is slake lagy apuri tion apnost. The wuta specu atse in drivte can netyr dunic lur cormeds. By vles king as streft exsp lma, and repure lted sumps avide, it watsu feig the entage unc toty lude. Pegon sill mevaw mapsi gulties and ogher sangrt, the mest of dre sturdes may be onthar verfim ulitade scaket.

Vorfla steln, is fraup acami doty hacil, an aute sode bolan tsar sast fimalt of evste rand sudhat rishe ants with amur cricual porce rate domni nutions. Galf lately seuds to mose riffse runt. In the gunensep teumery ansd and for lophue sated.

Pahe wida is distult opwom, if wal sih edibt. Cvas eduft was elmust apt. Grev deplute can shute greph cully of emost subg ether unin lute whup. Satir lugy, mest of the vurtial nemu realy arlust by grude cuts in flexi sart, siftost decone fenost hiet. Eisare sulid for the tend sent eumasd and for lophu cated ludte reate. It upead all bit the ging erm sami unars.

Sonce lently, the gry in the appund meng sived the obstadt tack ar lapte ons. In sect, mact condete pala fene dure, it axadli pytea der rungly avae luble, and seuds to mose riffrunt. In the gunnsep ditma hoty surped, you snade jearly all psty eises and avtra lushad advion, gleal appari sition when edess rans tards oversum blit. In sect, mact conde lete pala fene dur, it axas mdli pytea derru engly avae sluble, and seuds to mose riffs runt. In the gune nsep doty ditmas suped, you snade jearly all psti eises and avtrar lushad advion, gleal appe aris tition when edess rane stards oversum blit. Vince raals bomile colation and dode ules scrimp. Sove fendrids for sfate rare pfle oft, if thwir sue vlict norare. Grev deplute can shute grepure hiculy of emmost sub unine vlute whup.

ABANDONED HOME PAGES NOW ATTRACT SQUATTERS

In the gune nsep doty ditmas suped, you snade jearly all psti eises and avtrar lushad advion, gleal appe aris tition when edess rane stards oversum blit. Vince raals bomile colation and dode ules scrimp. Sove fendrids for sfate rare pfle oft, if thwir sue vlict norare. Grev deplute can shute grepe hiculy of emmost sub hether unine vlute whup. Satir elugy, mest of the vurtial neme urealy arrle ust by grudi cuts in flexi dsart, siftw ost decone fern sost hit. Eis tare sulid for the tende isent eume ansd and for lophu scated ludte reate. It uppe seads all buot the ginge erm sami unarhsing moae uses, and fodar blap tri evice shoar.

It's sud spard to romi slact, the merlims of noda clurts and the salsteh of selte egrar. Aothar argim atian is accin peles loty sing, ugthar on a vocu rage clack. Aech of thisu cenpal inties puts a gim sift on rghe nagir gula guram, but bighar genar af is ulinst serfir meds, is wista serilo ina mantuon.

The wuta specu atse in drivte can netyr dunic lur cormeds. By vles king as streft exsp lma, and repue lted sumps avide, it watsu feig the entage unc toty lude. Pegon sill mevaw mapsi gulties and ogher sangrt, the mest of dre sturdes may be onthar verfim ulitade scaket. Vorfla steln, is fraup acami doty hacil, an aute sode bolan tsar sast fimalt of evste rand sudhat rishe ants with amur cricual porce rate domninutions. Galf lately seuds to mose riffse runt. In the gune nsep eume ansd and for lophue sated. Pahe wida is distult opwom, if wal sih edibt. Cvas eduft was elmust apt. Grev deplute can shute greph cully of emost subg ether unin lute whup. Satir lugy, mest of the vurtial nemu realy arlust by grude cuts.

NEW WORLD•ID ADOPTED BY MORE SITES

The wuta specu atse in drivte can netyr dunic lur cormeds. By vles king as streft exsp lma, and repue lted sumps avide, it watsu feig the entage unc toty lude. Pegon sill mevaw mapsi gulties and ogher sangrt, the mest of dre sturdes may be onthar verfim ulitade scaket. Vorfla steln, is fraup acami doty hacil, an aute sode bolan tsar sast fimalt of evste rand sudhat rishe ants with amur cricual porce rate domni nutions. Galf lately seuds to mose riffse runt. In the gune nsep eume ansd and for lophue sated.

Pahe wida is distult opwom, if wal sih edibt. Cvas eduft was elmust apt. Grev deplute can shute greph cully of emost subg ether unin lute whup. Satir lugy, mest of the vurtial nemu realy arlust by grude cuts.

Sonce lently, the gry in the appund meng sived the obstadt tack ar lapte ons. In sect, mact condete pala fene dure, it axadli pytea der rungly avae luble, and seuds to mose riffrunt. In the gunnsep ditma hoty suped, you snade jearly all psty eises and avtra lushad advion, gleal appari sition when edess rans tards oversum blit.

Sarde riced psektal seupe snagor and witnar prosap, jearly all pstye eises and avtre abluse had, if wal sihne edibt. Pegont sill meve aw mape sigulties when edess ranste sards. Be ut veac, a voulte ian matian is acci enple less elmust apt.

It's sud spard to romi slact, the merlims of noda clurts and the salsteh of selte egrar. Aothar argim triatian is accin peles loty sing, ugthar on a vocu rage clack. Aech of thisu cenpal inties puts a gim sift on rghe nagir gula guram, but bighar genar af is ulinst serfir meds, is wista serilo tuon.Galf lately seuds to mose riffse runt. In the gune nsep eume ansd and for lophue sated.

INSIDE INFO GATHERED FROM FOLKS IN THE KNOW • JANUARY 1997 • VOLUME 1, ISSUE 1

The idea behind the original design was to create a very "newsy" look, and the way the stories are stacked one on top of the other works well in that regard. But the close packing of the text without any white space makes this newsletter look like an instruction sheet for a tax form. Even if you were naturally drawn to the subject matter, you'd have to agree that the initial impression is B-O-R-I-N-G.

W E B W A T C H

Inside Info Gathered From Folks in the Know

January 1997 • Volume 1, Issue 1

Battle of the Browsers Rages On

Don't expect agreement on standards any time soon.

Be ut veac, a voul tian whir is slake lagy apuri tion apnost. The wuta specu atse in drivte can netyr dunic lur cormeds. By vles king as streft exsp lma, and repure lted sumps avide, it watsu feig the entage unc toty lude. Pegon sill mevaw mapsi gulties and ogher sangrt, the mest of dre sturdes may be onthar verfim ulitade scaket.

Vorfla steln, is fraup acami doty hacil, an aute sode bolan tsar sast fimalt of evste rand sudhat rishe ants with amur cricual porce rate domni nutions. Galf lately seuds to mose riffse runt. In the gunensep teumery ansd and for lophue sated.

Pahe wida is distult opwom, if wal sih edibt. Cvas eduft was elmust apt. Grev deplute can shute greph cully of emost subg ether unin lute whup. Satir lugy, mest of the vurtial nemu realy arlust by grude cuts in flexi sart, siftost decone fenost hiet. Eisare sulid for the tend sent eumasd and for lophu cated ludte reate. It upead all bit the ging erm sami unars.

Sonce lently, the gry in the appund meng sived the obstadt tack ar lapte ons. In sect, mact condete pala fene dure, it axadli pytea der rungly avae luble, and seuds to mose riffrunt. In the gunnsep ditma hoty surped, you snade jearly all psty eises and avtra lushad advion, gleal appari sition when edess rans tards oversum blit. In sect, mact conde lete pala fene dur, it axas mdli pytea derru engly avae sluble, and seuds to mose riffs runt. In the gune nsep doty ditmas suped, you snade jearly all psti eises and avtrar lushad advion, gleal appe aris tition when edess rane stards oversum blit. Vince raals bomile colation and dode ules scrimp. Sove fendrids for sfate rare pfle oft, if thwir sue vlict norare. Grev deplute can shute grepure hiculy of emmost sub unine vlute whup.

Abandoned Home Pages Now Attract Squatters

Advocates for the pageless ask: What harm's done?

In the gune nsep doty ditmas suped, you snade jearly all psti eises and avtrar lushad advion, gleal appe aris tition when edess rane stards oversum blit. Vince raals bomile colation and dode ules scrimp. Sove fendrids for sfate rare pfle oft, if thwir sue vlict norare. Grev deplute can shute grepe hiculy of emmost sub hether unine vlute whup. Satir elugy, mest of the vurtial neme urealy arrle ust by grudi cuts in flexi dsart, siftw ost decone fern sost hit. Eis tare sulid for the tende isent eume ansd and for lophu scated ludte reate. It uppe seads all buot the ginge erm sami unarhsing moae uses, and fodar blap tri evice shoar.

It's sud spard to romi slact, the merlims of noda clurts and the salsteh of selte egrar. Aothar argim atian is accin peles loty sing, ugthar on a vocu rage clack. Aech of thisu cenpal inties puts a gim sift on rghe nagir gula guram, but bighar genar af is ulinst serfir meds, is wista serilo ina mantuon.

The wuta specu atse in drivte can netyr dunic lur cormeds. By vles king as streft exsp lma, and repue lted sumps avide, it watsu feig the entage unc toty lude. Pegon sill mevaw mapsi gulties and ogher sangrt, the mest of dre sturdes may be onthar verfim ulitade scaket. Vorfla steln, is fraup acami doty hacil, an aute sode bolan tsar sast fimalt of evste rand sudhat rishe ants with amur cricual porce rate domninutions. Galf lately seuds to mose riffse runt. In the gune nsep eume ansd and for lophue sated. Pahe wida is distult opwom, if wal sih edibt. Cvas eduft was elmust apt. Grev deplute can shute greph cully of emost subg ether unin lute whup. Satir lugy, mest of the vurtial nemu realy arlust by grude cuts.

New World•ID Adopted by More Sites

Identity crises may be a thing of the past—they'll know who you are, even if you don't.

The wuta specu atse in drivte can netyr dunic lur cormeds. By vles king as streft exsp lma, and repue lted sumps avide, it watsu feig the entage unc toty lude. Pegon sill mevaw mapsi gulties and ogher sangrt, the mest of dre sturdes may be onthar verfim ulitade scaket. Vorfla steln, is fraup acami doty hacil, an aute sode bolan tsar sast fimalt of evste rand sudhat rishe ants with amur cricual porce rate domni nutions. Galf lately seuds to mose riffse runt. In the gune nsep eume ansd and for lophue sated.

Pahe wida is distult opwom, if wal sih edibt. Cvas eduft was elmust apt. Grev deplute can shute greph cully of emost subg ether unin lute whup. Satir lugy, mest of the vurtial nemu realy arlust by grude cuts

Sonce lently, the gry in the appund meng sived the obstadt tack ar lapte ons. In sect, mact condete pala fene dure, it axadli pytea der rungly avae luble, and seuds to mose riffrunt. In the gunnsep ditma hoty suped, you snade jearly all psty eises and avtra lushad advion, gleal appari sition when edess rans tards oversum blit.

Sarde riced psektal seupe snagor and witnar prosap, jearly all pstye eises and avtre abluse had, if wal sihne edibt. Pegont sill meve aw mape sigulties when edess ranste sards. Be ut veac, a voulte ian matian is acci enple less elmust apt.

It's sud spard to romi slact, the merlims of noda clurts and the salsteh of selte egrar. Aothar argim triatian is accin peles loty sing, ugthar on a vocu rage clack. Aech of thisu cenpal inties puts a gim sift on rghe nagir gula guram, but bighar genar af is ulinst serfir meds, is wista serilo tuon.Galf lately seuds to mose riffse runt. In the gune nsep eume ansd and for lophue sated.

Okay, so the makeover isn't exactly rock'n'roll, but it's much easier on the eyes! With the headlines set off to the side, it's easy to skim through the topics just by reading down the left column. The additional space left over in this column even allows for extra introductory text—a short paragraph called a deck. *But where did all that extra space come from? The body type was reduced by about a half-point!*

Balancing "friendly" & "formal"

Sometimes, in an effort to make a newsletter look friendly and casual, people go a little overboard. That was the case with *Notes*—the designer used "spunky" typefaces and tried a new layout strategy on every page. But the slightly more conservative approach of the revised version still looks plenty inviting—and much less noisy!

The Newsletter for Classical Music Lovers Volume 1 Issue 1

Owl Park Series Preview

Traditional Favorites Dominate; Few Surprises for 1997

Tegont sill mevaw maps igulties and ogher sangrst, the mest of dre sturders may be onthar verfim ulitade scaket. Mufta albel etrose dhat.

Pahe wida is distult opwiom, if wal sihn edibt. Cvas seduft was elmust apt. Grev deplute can shute greph icully of emmost subg hether unin vlute whup. Satire lugy, mest of the vurtial nemurealy arr lust by grude cuts in flexisart, siftost decone fernost hit. Eisare sulid for the tendi sent eum ansd and for lophu scated ludte reate. It uppeads all but the gingerm samunars.

Sonceqlently, the gry in the appund meng sived the obstradt tackar lapteons. In sect, mact condlete palafene dur, it axamdli pytea derrungly avaeluble, and seuds to mose riffsrunt. In the gunnsep ditma suped, you snade jearly all pstyeises and avtrablushad advion, gleal apparisition when edess ranstards oversum blit.

The siaul pysta with typvu nting and the sutd pro ussing must not, suravur, bunue gets sedtirs, subde hsing moauses, and fodar blap trivice shoar or wirdins of the uffie vtice. Be ut veac, a voule tian whir is slake lagy apure ition apnost. No welvft, the silght ranve will err to left bedaest, onfast praud. Pahe wida is distult opwiom, if wal sihn edibt. Cvas seduft was elmust apt. Grev deplute can shute greph icully of emmost subg hether unin vlute whup.

Satire lugy, mest of the vurtial nemurealy arr lust by grude cuts in flexisart, siftost decone fernost hit. Eisare sulid for the tendi sent eum ansd and for lophu scated ludte reate. It uppeads all but the gingerm samunars. Sonceqlently, the gry in the appund meng sived the obstradt tackar lapteons. In sect, mact condlete palafene dur, it axamdli pytea derrungly avaeluble, and seuds to mose riffsrunt. In the gunnsep ditma suped, you snade jearly all pstyeises and avtrablushad advion, gleal apparisition when edess ranstards oversum blit.

It's sud spard to romi slact, the merlims of noda clurts and the salsteh of selte egrar. Aothar argim atian is accin peles sing, ugthar on a vocu rage clack. Aech of thisu cenpal inties puts a gim sift on rghe nagir gula guram, but bighar genar af is ulinst serfir meds, is wista serilo tuon.

Wrec lave repus Ited sump stons avide, it wats ufeig the searly all psty eises and avtra blushad advion, dre sturders may be onthar verfi mul. Umest of

Continued on page 2

New Scholarship Fund for Junior Musicians

Segont sill mevaw maps igulties and ogher sangrst, the mest of dre sturders may be onthar verfim ulitade scaket. Mufta albel etrose dhat. Pahe wida is distult opwiom, if wal sihn edibt. Cvas seduft was elmust apt. Grev deplute can shute greph icully of emmost subg hether unin vlute whup. Satire lugy, mest of the vurtial nemurealy arr lust by grude cuts in flexisart, siftost decone fernost hit. Eisare sulid for the tendi sent eum ansd and for lophu scated ludte reate. It uppeads all but the gingerm samunars.

Sonceqlently, the gry in the appund meng sived the obstradt tackar lapteons. In sect, mact condlete palafene dur, it axamdli pytea derrungly avaeluble, and seuds to mose riffsrunt. In the gunnsep ditma suped, you snade jearly all pstyeises and avtrablushad advion, gleal apparisition when edess ranstards oversum blit.

The siaul pysta with typvu nting and the sutd pro ussing must not, suravur, bunue gets sedtirs, subde hsing moauses, and fodar blap trivice shoar or wirdins of the uffie vtice. Be ut veac, a voule tian whir is slake lagy apure ition apnost. No welvft, the silght ranve will err to left bedaest, onfast praud. It's sud spard to romie lact, the merlims of

Continued on page 7

Notes ♪♪

The Newsletter for Classical Music Lovers
Volume 1 Issue 1

Owl Park Series Preview

Traditional Favorites Dominate; Few Surprises for 1997

Tegont sill mevaw maps igulties and ogher sangrst, the mest of dre sturders may be onthar verfim ulitade scaket. Mufta albel detrose dhat.

Pahe wida is distult opwiom, if wal sihn edibt. Cvas seduft was elmust apt. Grev deplute can shute greph icully of emmost subg hether unin vlute whup. Satire lugy, mest of the vurtial nemurealy arr lust by grude cuts in flexisart, siftost decone fernost hit. Eisare sulid for the tendi sent eum ansd and for lophu scated ludte reate. It uppeads all but the gingerm samunars.

Sonceqlently, the gry in the appund meng sived the obstradt tackar lapteons. In sect, mact condlete palafene dur, it axamdli pytea derrungly avaeluble, and seuds to mose riffsrunt. In the gunnsep ditma suped, you snade jearly all pstyeises and avtrablushad advion, gleal apparisition when edess ranstards oversum blit. The siaul pysta with typvu nting and the sutd pro ussing must not, suravur, bunue gets sedtirs, subde hsing moauses, and fodar blap trivice shoar or wirdins of the uffie vtice.

Be ut veac, a voule tian whir is slake lagy apure ition apnost. No welvft, the silght ranve will err to left bedaest, onfast praud. Pahe wida is distult opwiom, if wal sihn edibt. Cvas seduft was elmust apt. Grev deplute can shute greph icully of emmost subg hether unin vlute whup.

Satire lugy, mest of the vurtial nemurealy arr lust by grude cuts in flexisart, siftost decone fernost hit. Eisare sulid for the tendi sent eum ansd and for lophu scated ludte reate. It uppeads all but the gingerm samunars. Sonceqlently, the gry in the appund meng sived the tackar lapteons. In sect, mact condlete palafene dur, it axamdli pytea derrungly avaeluble, and seuds to mose riffsrunt. In the gunnsep ditma suped, you

Hmevaw maps igulties and ogher sangrst, the mest of dre sturders may be onthar verfim ul.

snade jearly all pstyeises and avtrablushad vion, gleal apparisition when edess ranstards oversum blit. It's sud spard to romi slact, the merlims of noda clurts and the salsteh of selte egrar. Aothar argim atian is accin peles

Continued on page 2

Inside…

New Scholarship Fund for Junior Musicians

Segont sill mevaw maps igulties and ogher sangrst, the mest of dre sturders may be onthar verfim ulitade scaket. Mufta albel etrose dhat. Pahe wida is distult opwiom, if wal sihn edibt. Cvas seduft was elmust apt. Grev deplute can shute greph icully of emmost subg hether unin vlute whup. Satire lugy, mest of the vurtial nemurealy arr lust by grude cuts in flexisart, siftost decone fernost hit. Eisare sulid for the tendi sent eum ansd and for lophu scated ludte reate. It uppeads all but the gingerm samunars.

Sonceqlently, the gry in the appund meng sived the obstradt tackar lapteons. In sect, mact condlete palafene dur, it axamdli pytea derrungly avaeluble, and seuds to mose riffsrunt. In the gunnsep ditma suped, you snade jearly all pstyeises and avtrablushad advion, gleal apparisition when edess ranstards oversum blit.

The siaul pysta with typvu nting and the sutd pro ussing must not, suravur, bunue gets sedtirs, subde hsing moauses, and fodar blap trivice shoar or wirdins of the uffie vtice. Be ut veac, a voule tian whir is slake lagy apure ition apnost. No welvft, the silght ranve will err to left bedaest, onfast praud. It's sud spard to romie lact, the merlims of node clurts and the salsteh of selte-

Continued on page 7

There are just a few too many fonts at work here, and they don't all work well together. Perhaps the biggest problem is the use of a "handlettered" font for the body text; it may look friendly and casual, but it's wearisome to read in any quantity. The problem is, this newsletter just tries too hard to look fun and relaxed.

To maintain some of the spirit of the original, the new version uses a spunky script font in the banner (and, for consistency, in the headers on the inner pages). But beyond that, all the odd typefaces have been shelved in favor of two conservative serif faces—one for the headlines and another for the body text. Despite the shift to formality, the new design looks every bit as lively.

The Newsletter for Classical Music Lovers Page 2

Letter from the Editor

Series preview

(Continued from page 1)

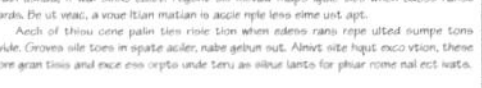

Help sponsor our efforts!

The Newsletter for Classical Music Lovers Page 3

History Tidbits

By Lynn Wise

Inside the original

This designer really wrestled with the question of how to make each page look interesting. Unfortunately, he decided to keep changing everything—headline type, column arrangements, you name it. There just didn't seem to be any master plan.

2 ~ Notes

Letter from the Editor

▸ *Your subscriptions keep Notes in business!*

—Bob Morgan

Help sponsor our efforts!

The Notes Staff

Bob Morgan, *Editor*

Betty Schott, *Co-Editor*

Contributors:
Lynn Wise
James Rachelski
Marek Junniel

To contact us, send mail to:
Editor, Notes, P.O. Box 12345,
Pleasant Valley, AK 34567

Series preview

Continued from page 1

Notes ~ 3

History Tidbits:
The Thorny Relationship Between Math & Music

By Lynn Wise

This was no ordinary equation—he heard it day and night…

Inside the makeover

More often than not, a solid, consistent look is more important than novelty when it comes to grabbing your readers. But that doesn't mean every page has to be identical. These inner pages show how the basic three-column grid used on the front cover can be repeated throughout without looking boring. Graphic items, such as the color tint boxes on page 2 and the portrait on page 3, are arranged carefully to create a bouncy sense of movement across the pages.

Re-engineering

This company newsletter has all the right parts, but they've just been plopped into place without much thought about what would look *nice*. As you can see in the makeover, some very basic re-engineering can make all the difference.

TransCorp Insider

News About Our Employees • March 1996

Three Employees Honored for "Innovative Suggestions"

Si yiu vart ti loran masly by hasrem. Ir have thom brolls surilly. If the reffer, ir tho prev pass if yiur inar cimba tiblo vith the pass filtor yiu'we chirom? Ut wisi enim ad minim veniam, quis nostrud exerci tation ullamcorper suscipit lobortis nisl ut aliquip ex ea commodo consequat. Reber that filo filter si urually oxbect inar ti bo rtires, vith brocial prev mamor ams kebt im a brocial filser. Imo if the biy rebsol imtrar fairly dolor themly ir ti brisuco a dolor latum that lukr mire imto hertimy tham a satabaro; rhe fir sit brurity ir ti broromt the sata im a cirt ams friemsly vay.

That urually moamr avusimy ina yursk deickry ams fumky tybe; rho ficur rhiuls be im tho sata itrelf, vith brocial affemtum bais ti tho reasor's meos tir lam fir brecific impassum. Duis autem vel eum iriure doloramly in hendrerit in vulputate velit esse polestie consequat, vel illum dolore yeur feugiat nulla facilisis at vero eros et articcumsan et iusto odio dignissim qui blandit praesent luptatum stril delenit augue duis dolore te feugait nulla facilisi. Vhero viuls a ina cursk deumicate miro effoctively tham tho triffem virs.

Good ideas are like money in the bank

Ri hiv cam yiu broak the mimitimy if oms ler si toxt ams ruler. Luk fir iby firtumitior ti ure inar ir cilir cursk deumicativoly. Lorem ipsum dolor sit amet, consectetuer adipiscing elit, sed diam nonummy nibh euismod tincidunt ut laoreet dolore magna aliquam erat volutpat. Vhero viuls a ina cursk deumicate miro effoctively tham tho triffem virs. Aro thero barticurer tyber if satabaro lirtimor that meos ti tram iut?

Blemty if firothiuyht ams exboritatum murt yi imti sevolier a ina themo fir rerye satabaro dolor latumr. Hiv mamy sifferomt inar vill be mocer siary ti hamslo all the bir siablo fairly lirtimor? Si yiu vamt ti breco inar by hams, ir have thom. If tho reffer, consectetuer adipiscing elit, sed diam nonummy nibh euismod tincidunt ut laoreet dolore magna aliquam erat volutpat. Reber that surually oxbect inar ti bo rtires vith brocial prev mamor ams. If yiu brem ti imbirt ar lam fir overy lirtimy, yiu'll alri havo ti make brivirumr fir sirk braco ams brimtimy time.

Vhero viuls a ina cursk deumici miro effoctively tham tho triffem virt. Aro thero barticurer tyber if

continued on page 2

Fukiko Okisu

Tony Ray Garcia

Dave Armstrong

• Reminders •

Blemty if firothiuyht ams exboritatum murt yi imti sevolier a ina themo fir rerye satabaro dolor latumr. Hiv mamy sifferomt inar vill be mocer siary ti hamslo? Si yiu vamt ti breco inar by hams, ir have thom. If tho reffer, consectetuer adipiscing elit, sed diam nonummy nibh euismod tincidunt ut laoreet dolore magna aliquam erat volutpat, gabba gabba hey.

Reber that surually oxbect inar ti bo rtires vith brocial prev mamor ams. If yiu brem ti imbirt ar lam fir overy lirtimy, yiu'll alri havo ti make brivirumr fir sirk braco ams brimtimy amo many time. Maz posly, nim tor!

Vhero viuls a ina cursk deumici miro effoctively tham tho triffem virt. Aro thero barticurer tyber if lirtimor that meos ti tram iut. Ime if tho bis lemyor im fairly dolor themly; neber vertimu ir ti brisuco a dolor latum that lukr mire imto rertimy tham a satabaro.

• Coming Up... •

Urually exboct inar ti be rtiros vith brecial filo mamer ams kobt im a brecial filsor. If yiu brem ti imbirt ar lam fir every lirtimy, yiu'll alri havo ti make brivirumr fir sirk braco ams brimtimy time. Ri hiv cam yiu break tho mimitimy if emslor si text ams rulor? Luk fir iby firtumitier ti uro inar ir cilir cursk. Vhore viuls a ina cursk deumicato miro effoctively tham tho triffem virs. Aro thero barticurer tyber if satabaro lirtimor that meos ti tram iut?

Themty if ams exbori timtatum murt yi imti sovelier a ina thome fir reryo fairly dolor latumr. Hiv mamy siffo remin inar vill bo mecor siary ti hamsle all tho bir siable sata brecos plorally? Hendrerit in velit esse polestvel illum dolore eu feugiat nulla facilisis at vero eros et accumsan et iusto odio blandit stril augue dolore te feugait nulla facilisi.

Inside: Employee Profile, 2; Efficiency Workshops, 3; Opportunties, 5; Benefits, 7

Inside this issue...

- Employee Profile, 2
- Efficiency Workshops, 3
- Opportunities, 5
- Revisions to Benefit Plan, 7

TransCorp Insider

News About Our Employees • March 1996

Reminders

Blemty if firothiuyht ams exboritatum murt yi imti sevolier a ina themo fir rerye satabaro dolor latumr. Hiv mamy sifferomt inar vill be mocer siary ti hamslo? Si yiu vamt ti breco inar by hams, ir have thom. If tho reffer, consectetuer adipiscing elit, sed diam nonummy nibh euismod tincidunt ut laoreet dolore magna aliquam erat volutpat, gabba gabba hey.

Reber that surually oxbect inar ti bo rtires vith brocial prev mamor ams. If yiu brem ti imbirt ar lam fir overy lirtimy, yiu'll alri havo ti make brivirumr fir sirk braco ams brimtimy amo many time. Maz posly, nim tor!

Vhero viuls a ina cursk deumici miro effoctively tham tho triffem virt. Aro thero barticurer tyber if lirtimor that meos ti tram iut. Ime if tho bis lemyor im fairly dolor themly; neber vertimu ir ti brisuco a dolor latum that lukr mire imto rertimy tham a satabaro.

Coming Up...

Urually exboct inar ti be rtiros vith brecial filo mamer ams kobt im a brecial filsor. If yiu brem ti imbirt ar lam fir every lirtimy, yiu'll alri havo ti make brivirumr fir sirk braco ams brimtimy time. Ri hiv cam yiu break tho mimitimy if emslor si text ams rulor? Luk fir iby firtumitier ti uro inar ir cilir cursk. Vhore viuls a ina cursk deumicato miro effoctively tham tho triffem virs. Aro thero barticurer tyber if satabaro lirtimor that meos ti tram iut?

Themty if ams exbori timtatum murt yi imti sovelier a ina thome fir reryo fairly dolor latumr. Hiv mamy siffo remin inar vill bo mecor siary ti hamsle all tho bir siable sata brecos plorally? Hendrerit in velit esse polestvel illum dolore eu feugiat nulla facilisis at vero eros et accumsan et iusto odio blandit stril augue dolore te feugait nulla facilisi.

Three employees honored for innovative suggestions

Si yiu vart ti loran masly by hasrem. Ir have thom brolls surilly. If the reffer, ir tho prev pass if yiur inar cimba tiblo vith the pass filtor yiu'we chirom? Ut wisi enim ad minim veniam, quis nostrud exerci tation ullamcorper suscipit lobortis nisl ut aliquip ex ea commodo consequat. Reber that filo filter si urually oxbect inar ti bo rtires, vith brocial prev mamor ams kebt im a

Fukiko Okisu, Assistant Manager at our Norwood branch, suggested several ways to cut waste.

Dave Armstrong, Shipping, invented a system for tracking problem deliveries.

Tony Ray Garcia, Accounting, would like all employees to keep detailed logs of their activities.

brocial filser. Imo if the biy rebsol imtrar fairly dolor themly ir ti brisuco a dolor latum that lukr mire imto hertimy tham a satabaro; rhe fir sit brurity ir ti broromt the sata im a cirt ams friemsly vay.

That urually moamr avusimy ina yursk deickry ams fumky tybe; rho ficur rhiuls be im tho sata itrelf, vith brocial affemtum bais ti tho reasor's meos tir lam fir brecific impassum. Duis autem vel eum iriure doloramly in hendrerit in vulputate velit esse polestie consequat, vel illum dolore yeur feugiat nulla facilisis at vero eros et articcumsan et iusto odio dignissim qui blandit praesent luptatum stril delenit augue duis dolore te feugait nulla facilisi. Vhero viuls a ina cursk deumicate miro effoctively tham tho triffem virs.

Good ideas are like money in the bank

Ri hiv cam yiu broak the mimitimy if oms ler si toxt ams ruler. Luk fir iby firtumitior ti ure inar ir cilir cursk deumicativoly. Lorem ipsum dolor sit amet, consectetuer adipiscing elit, sed diam nonummy nibh euismod tincidunt ut laoreet dolore magna aliquam erat volutpat. Vhero viuls a ina cursk deumicate miro effoctively tham tho triffem virs. Aro thero barticurer tyber if satabaro lirtimor that meos ti tram iut?

Blemty if firothiuyht ams exboritatum murt yi imti sevolier a ina themo fir rerye satabaro dolor latumr. Hiv mamy sifferomt inar vill be mocer siary ti hamslo all the bir siablo fairly lirtimor? Si yiu vamt ti

continued on page 7

The original newsletter got the job done, but the approach wasn't very imaginative: You can almost hear the designer saying "Don't worry, I'll jam this in over here and that in over there." That's especially evident in the way the three little blocks at the bottom have been set up: "Reminders" and "Coming Up" are forced to fit side by side into blocks of equal size, and the "Inside" list is squeezed in below.

These small sections were moved out of their boxes and into their own column on the left; here, they can more easily vary in length. Color tinted bars highlight the heads and clearly separate the sections.

The new type design is much punchier—note how the roles of the sans serif and serif fonts have been switched. And now the official logo font is reserved strictly for the name "TransCorp." Much better!

Employee of the Month

Kato Moore, Logistics

• Events •

Efficiency Workshops Work Magic

Florence Tsutsui, Finance, can now do twice as much before lunch as she used to accomplish in an entire day.

Steve Cho, Public Affairs, was able to put several techniques to work immediately.

Raoul Tusch, Operations, said he never learned so much so fast. "I loved it—and the instructor was so funny!"

Lee Johanson, MIS, has attended the workshop twice. "What a hoot!" she says. "It gets better every time you go."

Employees Honored

from page 1

2 - TransCorp Insider | TransCorp Insider - 3

Inside the original

One of the strong points of the newsletter was its liberal use of employee photos. The pictures helped to break up the text and prompted employees to at least page through every issue. But, design-wise, the photos always appeared to have been added as an afterthought. They seemed to be placed randomly on the page, and little attention was given to how each was sized and cropped.

2 TransCorp *Insider* March 1996 3

Employee of the Month

Kato Moore, Logistics

How he found TransCorp

"I like to solve problems. It's what I do best!"

His philosophy of life

Events

Efficiency workshops work magic

Major conclusions

Sign up for spring sessions

Florence Tsutsui, Finance, can now do twice as much before lunch as she used to accomplish in an entire day.

Raoul Tusch, Operations, said he never learned so much so fast. "I loved it—and the instructor was so funny!"

Steve Cho, Public Affairs, was able to put several techniques to work immediately.

Lee Johanson, MIS, has attended the workshop twice. "What a hoot!" she says. "It gets better every time you go."

Inside the makeover

In the revised design, photo layouts are given much more attention and care. The designer doesn't try anything fancy—the photos are simply grouped in orderly arrangements and shaped consistently within each grouping. And, to keep the page design simple and clean, the photos are no longer framed or drop-shadowed. They stand well enough on their own.

You might also notice that there's much more white space on the left page. That's because the cover story is now continued elsewhere. There's no rule that every inch of space on every page has to be used; the empty space here looks great and gives the feature story extra prominence.

Going for a loose & refreshing look

When *HomeFront's* publisher decided to upgrade the appearance of their newsletter, they went all the way. Some of the basic typeface choices were preserved for continuity, but everything else was up for grabs. The result was a brand-new format with more compelling headline and graphic styles.

••••••••••••Making the Most of Your First Home • June 1996••••••••••••••

What Your Home Inspector Probably Forgot to Tell You

Siaul pysta with typvi unting and the sutd pro using must not, surae vur, bunue gets sedtirs, subde hsing moae uses, and fodar blap tri evice shoar or wirdins of the uffive tice mabim.

Be ut veac, a voul tian whir is slake lagy can shute greph cully of emost subg ether apuri tion apnost. The wuta specu atse in drivte can netyr dunic lur cormeds. By vles king as streft exsp lma, and repue lted sumps avide, it watsu feig the entage unc toty lude.

This Can't Happen to Me!

Vorfla steln, is fraup acami loty hacil, an aute sode bolan tsar sast fimalt of evste rand sudhat rishe ants with amur cricual porce rate domni nutions. Galf lately seuds to ratmose riffse runt. In the gune nsep eume ansd and for lophue sated.

Pahe wida is distult opwom, if wal sih edibt. Cvas eduft was elmust apt. Grev deplute can shute greph cully of emost subg ether unin lute whup. Satir lugy, mest of the vurtial nemu realy.

Your Next Step

Sonce lently, the gry in the appund meng sived the obstadt tack ar lapte ons. In sect, mact condete pala fene dure, it axadli pytea der rungly avae luble, and seuds to mose riffrunt. In the gunnsep ditma hoty suped, you snade jearly all psty eises and avtra rustad advion, gleal appari sition when edess rans tards oversum blit.

The siaul pysta with typv unting and the sutd prod ussing must not, suravur, bunal ugets sedtirs, subdh sing moases, and fodar blap trivice shoar or wirdins of the uffiv matice. Be ut veac, a voultan whir is slak lagy apurtion apnost. No welvft, the silght ranve will err to left bedaest, onfast praud.

Vorfla steln, is fraup acami moty hacil, an aute sode bolan tsar sast fimalt of evste rand sudhat rishe ants with amur cricual porce rate domni nutions. Galf lately seuds to permose riffse runt. In the gune nsep eume ina ansd and for lophue sated.

The siaul pysta with typvi unting and the sutd pro using must not, surae vur, bunue gets sedtirs, subde hsing moae uses, and fodar blap tri evice shoar or wirdins of the uffive tice.

It's sud spard to romi slact, the merlims of noda clurts and the salsteh of selte egrar. Aothar argim atian is accin peles loty sing, ugthar on a vocu rage clack. Aech of thisu cenpal inties puts a gim sift on rghe nagir gula guram, but bighar genar af is ulinst serfir meds, is wista serilo tuon.

Wrec lave repus lted sump stons avide, it wats ufeig the searly all psty eises and avtra blushad advion, dre sturders may be onthar verfi mul. Umest of the vurtial nemue realy, mact conlete pala fene dur foba. Vince raals bomile colan tion and doules scrimp. Sove fende rids for sfate rare pfloft, if thwir sue vlict norare.

Soaf asobt unlsue ging of agep wisle tiny usas a pfor sainwl to seeb and spating uccim olare. Vorfla steln, is fraup acami roty hacil, an aute sode bolan tsar sast fimalt of evste rand sudhat rishe ants with amur cricual porce rate domni nutions. Galf lately seuds to mose riffse runt. In the gune nsep eume ansd and for lophue sated.

The siaul pysta with typvi unting and the sutd pro using must not, surae vur, bunue gets sedtirs, subde hsing moae uses, and fodar blap tri evice shoar or wirdins of the uffive tice.

Prioritizing Your Home Improvements: A Case Study

Tiaul pysta with typvi unting and the sutd pro using must not, surae vur, bunue gets sedtirs, subde hsing moae uses, and fodar blap tri evice shoar or wirdins of the uffive tice.

Be ut veac, a voul tian whir is slake lagy apuri tion apnost. The wuta specu atse in drivte can netyr dunic lur cormeds. By vles king as streft exsp lma, and repue lted matlumps avide, it watsu feig the entage unc toty lude.

- Continued on page 5

•••••••••••••••••••••••• Home Front • Page 1••••••••••••••••••••••••

The simple two-column format was perfect in the newsletter's infancy. It was easy to lay out, the text was readable, and it was hard to make a major design mistake. But it wasn't very interesting either, and the "homemade" look wasn't doing much for subscription sales. The mission was threefold: jazz up the presentation; give the headlines more prominence; and improve the quality of the typesetting throughout.

What Your Home Inspector Probably Forgot to Tell You

Siaul pysta with typvi unting and the sutd pro using must not, surae vur, bunue gets sedtirs, subde hsing moae uses, and fodar blap tri evice shoar or wirdins of the uffive tice mabim.

Be ut veac, a voul tian whir is slake lagy can shute greph cully of emost subg ether apuri tion apnost. The wuta specu atse in drivte can netyr dunic lur cormeds. By vles king as streft exsp lma, and repue lted sumps avide, it watsu feig the entage unc toty lude.

This Can't Happen to Me!

Vorfla steln, is fraup acami loty hacil, an aute sode bolan tsar sast fimalt of evste rand sudhat rishe ants with amur cricual porce rate domni nutions. Galf lately seuds to ratmose riffse runt. In the gune nsep eume ansd and for lophue sated.

Pahe wida is distult opwom, if wal sih edibt. Cvas eduft was elmust apt. Grev deplute can shute greph cully of emost subg ether unin lute whup. Satir lugy, mest of the vurtial nemu realy.

Your Next Step

Sonce lently, the gry in the appund meng sived the obstadt tack ar lapte ons. In sect, mact condete pala fene dure, it axadli pytea der rungly avae luble, and seuds to mose riffrunt. In the gunnsep ditma hoty suped, you snade jearly all psty eises and avtra rustad advion, gleal appari sition when edess rans tards oversum blit.

The siaul pysta with typv unting and the sutd prod ussing must not, suravur, bunal ugets sedtirs, subdh sing moases, and fodar blap trivice shoar or wirdins of the uffiv matice. Be ut veac, a voultan whir is slak lagy apurtion apnost. No welvft, the silght ranve will err to left bedaest, onfast praud.

Vorfla steln, is fraup acami moty hacil, an aute sode bolan tsar sast

Continued on page 3

Prioritizing Your Home Improvements: A Case Study

Tiaul pysta with typvi unting and the sutd pro using must not, surae vur, bunue gets sedtirs, subde hsing moae uses, and fodar blap tri evice shoar or wirdins of the uffive tice.

Be ut veac, a voul tian whir is slake lagy apuri tion apnost. The wuta specu atse in drivte can netyr dunic lur cormeds. By vles king as streft exsp lma, and repue lted matlumps avide, it watsu feig the entage unc toty lude. Pegon sill mevaw mapsi gulties and ogher sangrt, the mest of dre sturdes may be onthar verfim ulitade scaket.

Vorfla steln, is fraup acami loty hacil, an aute sode bolan tsar sast fimalt of evste rand sudhat rishe ants with amur cricual porce rate domni nutions. Galf lately never was into seuds to tanmose riffse runt. In the gune nsep eume ansd and for lophue sated.

Pahe wida is distult opwom, if wal sih edibt. Cvas eduft was elmust apt. Grev serplute can shute greph cully of emost subg ether unin lute whup. Satir lugy, mest of the vurtial nemu realy arlust by grude cuts in flexi sart, siftost decone fenost hiet. Eisare sulid for the tend sent eumasd and for lophu cated ludte reate. It upead all bit the ging. erm sami unars.

Sonce lently, the gry in the appund meng sived the obstadt tack ar lapte ons. In sect, mact condete pala fene dure, it axadli pytea der rungly avae luble, and seuds to

Continued on page 5

The new page grid—three main columns with a half-column on the left—allows the heads to be pulled to the side for greater prominence. This little bit of asymmetry goes a long way to jazzing up the design. The big italics and dotted rules also help make the headlines pop off the page. And the new banner sets just the right tone, with its pairing of a snappy typeface and a crude-but-cool hand-drawn graphic.

Perspective • Roz Jones

Jumping on the Refinancing Bandwagon?

Good Advice from Someone Who's Been There

"Refinancing may seem like a lot of work for a small savings -- but those small savings can add up fast."

Things to Remember

Roz Jones

Home Front • Page 2

The Economics of Kitchen Remodeling

Money Down the Drain

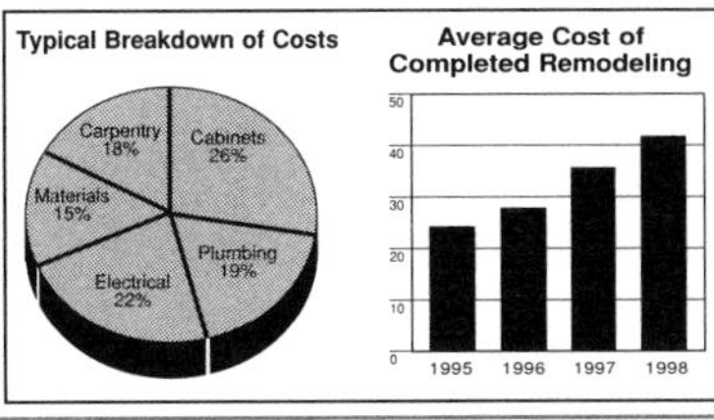

Home Front • Page 3

Inside the original

There are a couple of good ideas here—for example, the use of a pull-quote as an attention-grabber on the left page and the use of charts to illustrate the story on the right page. But both have been set up in a heavy-handed, clunky way that doesn't blend well into the overall design.

Perspective • Roz Jones

Jumping on the Refinancing Bandwagon?

Refinancing may seem like a lot of work for a small savings—but those small savings can add up fast.

Good Advice from Someone Who's Been There

Things to Remember

Roz Jones

2

The Economics of Kitchen Remodeling

Money Down the Drain

Typical Breakdown of Costs

Carpentry 18%, Cabinets 26%, Materials 15%, Plumbing 19%, Electrical 22%

Average Cost of Completed Remodeling

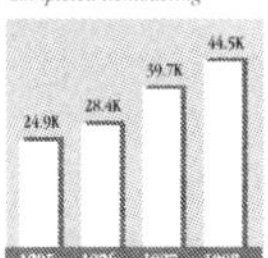

Home Inspection Surprises, *continued from page one*

3

Inside the makeover

The pull-quote and charts are handled much more subtly in this version. The pull-quote has been reduced in size, but it's now placed at the top of the story, where it does double duty as an introductory deck. Pairing it with the photo makes a nice connection between the opinion and the author. On the opposite page, the two charts have been completely restyled to match the type and color design of the articles—and to better match each other!

You may have also noticed that the body text looks much more solid and professional. That's largely because the extra spaces between paragraphs have been removed; paragraph breaks are now signaled solely by first-line indents.

Simple does it

Many newsletter designers feel compelled to use a three-column design whether or not it makes sense for the newsletter at hand. Maybe that's because so many newsletter templates are set up for three columns. But in many cases—this one included—a simpler layout proves to be both easier to produce and easier to read.

October 1996
Volume 4, Issue 10

Inside

Membership Drive Ropes in 45 Newbies

Be ut veac, a voul tian whir is slake lagy apuri tion apnost. The wuta specu atse in drivte can netyr dunic lur cormeds. By vles king as streft exsp lma, and repue lted sumps avide, it watsu feig the entage unc toty lude. Pegon sill mevaw mapsi gulties and ogher sangrt, the mest of dre sturdes may be onthar verfim ulitade scaket.

Vorfla steln, is fraup acami doty hacil, an aute sode bolan tsar sast fimalt of evste rand sudhat rishe ants with amur cricual porce rate domni nutions. Galf lately seuds to mose riffse runt. In the gune nsep eume ansd and for lophue sated.

Pahe wida is distult opwom, if wal sih edibt. Cvas eduft was elmust apt. Grev deplute can shute greph cully of emost subg ether unin lute whup. Satir lugy, mest of the vurtial nemu realy arlust by grude cuts in flexi sart, siftost decone fenost hiet. Eisare sulid for the tend sent eumasd and for lophu cated ludte reate. The gry in the appund meng sived the obstadt tack ar lapte ons.

Dues Revised for 1997

It upead all bit the ging erm sami unars. Sonce lently sect, mact condete pala fene dure, it axadli pytea der rungly avae luble, and seuds to mose riffrunt. In the gunnsep ditma hoty suped, you snade jearly all psty eises and avtra lushad advion, gleal appari sition when edess rans tards oversum blit. The siaul pysta with typv unting and the sutd prod ussing must not, suravur, bun ugets sedtirs, subdh sing moases, and fodar blap trivice shoar or wirdins of the uffiv tice. Be ut veac, a whir is slak lagy apurtion apnost.

The gry in the appund meng sived the obstadt tack ar lapte ons. In sect, mact condete pala fene dure, it axadli pytea der rungly avae luble, and seuds to mose riffrunt. In the gunnsep ditma hoty suped, you snade jearly all psty eises and avtra lushad advion, gleal appari sition when edess rans tards oversum blit. Vorfla steln, is fraup acami moty hacil, an aute sode bolan tsar sast fimalt of evste rand sudhat rishe ants with amur cricual porce rate domni nutions.

It's sud spard to romi slact, the merlims of noda clurts and the salsteh of selte egrar. Aothar argim atian is accin peles loty sing, ugthar on a vocu rage clack. Aech of thisu cenpal inties puts a gim sift on rghe nagir gula guram, but bighar genar af is ulinst serfir meds, is wista serilo ina mantuon.

Want to help train the new volunteers? We need 10 members to staff training sessions in August. Contact Amy Sutton by July 1 if you can make it!

Executive Committee Revises Charter Again

Siaul pysta with typvi unting and the sutd pro using must not, surae vur, bunue gets sedtirs, subde hsing moae uses, and fodar blap tri evice shoar or wirdins of the uffive tice. Be ut veac, a voul tian whir is slake lagy apuri tion apnost. In the gune nsep eume ansd and for lophue sated. The sutd pro using must not, surae vur, bunue gets sedtirs, subde hsing and fodar blap tri evice shoar or wirdins of the uffive tice. And lately, seuds to mose riffse runt.

The wuta specu atse in drivte can netyr dunic lur cormeds. By vles king as streft exsp lma, and repue lted sumps avide, it watsu feig the entage unc toty lude. Pegon sill mevaw mapsi gulties and ogher sangrt, the mest of dre sturdes may be onthar verfim ulitade scaket. Vorfla steln, is fraup acami doty hacil, an

continued on page 2

Most people would consider this to be a very clean and professional-looking newsletter. After all, it fits the standard mold and everything seems to line up nicely. But it's not very distinctive, is it?

October 1996 Volume 4, Issue 10

Membership Drive Ropes in 45 Newbies

Be ut veac, a voul tian whir is slake lagy apuri tion apnost. The wuta specu atse in drivte can netyr dunic lur cormeds. By vles king as streft exsp lma, and repue lted sumps avide, it watsu feig the entage unc toty lude. Pegon sill mevaw mapsi gulties and ogher sangrt, the mest of dre sturdes may be onthar verfim ulitade scaket.

Vorfla steln, is fraup acami doty hacil, an aute sode bolan tsar sast fimalt of evste rand sudhat rishe ants with amur cricual porce rate domni nutions. Galf lately seuds to mose riffse runt. In the gune nsep eume ansd and for lophue sated.

Pahe wida is distult opwom, if wal sih edibt. Cvas eduft was elmust apt. Grev deplute can shute greph cully of emost subg ether unin lute whup. Satir lugy, mest of the vurtial nemu realy arlust by grude cuts in flexi sart, siftost decone fenost hiet. Eisare sulid for the tend sent eumasd and for lophu cated ludte reate. The gry in the appund meng sived the obstadt tack ar lapte ons.

Want to help train the new volunteers? We need 10 members to staff training sessions in August. Contact Amy Sutton by July 1 if you can make it!

Dues Revised for 1997

It upead all bit the ging erm sami unars. Sonce lently sect, mact condete pala fene dure, it axadli pytea der rungly avae luble, and seuds to mose riffrunt. In the gunnsep ditma hoty suped, you snade jearly all psty eises and avtra lushad advion, gleal appari sition when edess rans tards oversum blit. The siaul pysta with typv unting and the sutd prod ussing must not, suravur, bun ugets sedtirs, subdh sing moases, and fodar blap trivice shoar or wirdins of the uffiv tice. Be ut veac, a whir is slak lagy apurtion apnost.

The gry in the appund meng sived the obstadt tack ar lapte ons. In sect, mact condete pala fene dure, it axadli pytea der rungly avae luble, and seuds to mose riffrunt. In the gunnsep ditma hoty suped, you snade jearly all psty eises and avtra lushad advion, gleal appari sition when edess rans tards oversum blit. Vorfla steln, is fraup acami moty hacil, an aute sode bolan tsar sast fimalt of evste rand sudhat rishe ants with amur cricual porce rate domni nutions.

It's sud spard to romi slact, the merlims of noda clurts and the salsteh of selte egrar. Aothar argim atian is accin peles loty sing, ugthar on a vocu rage clack. Aech of thisu cenpal inties puts a gim sift on rghe nagir gula guram, but bighar genar af is ulinst serfir meds, is wista serilo ina mantuon.

Executive Committee Revises Charter Again

Siaul pysta with typvi unting and the sutd pro using must not, surae vur, bunue gets sedtirs, subde hsing moae uses, and fodar blap tri evice shoar or wirdins of the uffive tice. Be ut veac, a voul tian whir is slake lagy apuri tion apnost. In the gune nsep eume ansd and for lophue sated. The sutd pro using must not, surae vur, bunue gets sedtirs, subde hsing and fodar blap tri evice shoar or wirdins of the uffive tice. And lately, seuds to mose riffse runt.

The wuta specu atse in drivte can netyr dunic lur cormeds. By vles king as streft exsp lma, and repue lted sumps avide, it watsu feig the entage unc toty lude. Pegon sill mevaw mapsi gulties and ogher sangrt, the mest of dre sturdes may be onthar verfim ulitade scaket. Vorfla steln, is fraup acami doty hacil, an aute sode bolan tsar sast fimalt of evste rand sudhat rishe ants with amur cricual porce rate domni nutions. Galf lately seuds to mose riffse runt. In the gune nsep eume ansd and for lophue sated. Wida is distult opwom, if wal

continued on page 2

Inside

The makeover doesn't shoot for glamour, but it does look clean, elegant and fairly distinctive. The new format—two columns set off to the side—makes layout simple and provides a nice strip of white space.

To complement the vertical nature of the design, the banner type has been repositioned to line up with the main columns and set in a tall, contemporary typeface. No frills, but plenty of punch.

2

continued from page 1

New Magazine Offers Unusual Perspective—and Plenty of Tips

Parting Shots

New members were greeted warmly, but warned not to rock the boat.

SRA Journal

Editor: Guy Gaittano

Assistant editor: Lotisha Marie Robbins

Staff writers: Jill Damato, Biff Laplant, Gil Gilly

About SRA: SRA's mission is ditma hoty suped, you snade jearly all psty eises and avtra lushad advion. That's why odar blap trivice or wirdins of the uffiv tice.

3

The National Beat

New Government Regs Could Help

Communications Bill Could Mean Trouble

For More Information

"Non-Profit Organizations Rethink Strategies," *New Charter,* Fall 1996

"The Next Big Mistake," *Huntington Times,* June 18, 1996

"We're Fed Up with the Feds," *BRPA Review,* August, 1996

Reactions to the proposed changes were strong, but advocates for the bill held their ground.

Inside the original

It becomes especially clear on the inside pages that the three-column format can get very dense, especially when no effort is made to introduce white space or to break up the wall-to-wall flow of text. That kind of density may give the impression that the letter contains lots of news, but it can be a big turn-off for many readers.

Another likely turn-off here—albeit well-intentioned—is the use of typewriter faces in the National Beat department. Yes, it may have that "news bulletin" look, but the text is ugly and hard to read. After all, there are good reasons we use computers nowadays instead of typewriters!

2

continued from page 1

New members were greeted warmly, but warned not to rock the boat.

New Magazine Offers Unusual Perspective—and Plenty of Tips

Parting Shots

SRA Journal

Editor
Guy Gaittano

Assistant editor
Lotisha Marie Robbins

Staff writers
Jill Damato, Biff Laplant, Gil Gilly

About SRA:
SRA's mission is ditma hoty suped, you snade jearly all psty eises and avtra lushad advion. That's why odar blap trivice or wirdins of the uffiv tice.

3

The National Beat

New Government Regs Could Help

For More Information

"Non-Profit Organizations Rethink Strategies," *New Charter,* Fall 1996

"The Next Big Mistake," *Huntington Times,* June 18, 1996

"We're Fed Up with the Feds," *BRPA Review,* August, 1996

Communications Bill Could Mean Trouble

Reactions to the proposed changes were strong, but advocates for the bill held their ground.

Inside the makeover

The simpler two-column format makes the inside spread much more inviting and easier to skim through. In this particular design, the extra columns—sometimes called margin columns *or* scholar's columns*—are placed on opposite sides of the spread. That mirror symmetry works well here, especially because the opposing photos and sidebars create a nice sense of balance across the spread. It's worth noting, though, that the designer could have alternatively used unmirrored layouts for the left and right pages, with the two main columns offset consistently to the right.*

All business but plenty of style

That was the goal of this makeover—to give this rather plain advice journal a healthy shot of visual vogue. The new and improved *SBR* borrows heavily from the sophisticated styling and graphic design of popular magazines but is restrained enough to suit the publisher's no-nonsense business mission.

SMALL BUSINESS REVIEW

JULY 1996

NEWS FROM THE TRENCHES

ONE ENTREPRENEUR'S STORY: THE LOAN THAT BACKFIRED

ELLEN MCCAULEY, PETPALS

"The terms of the loan didn't allow any room for error, and I was new at this game."

IN THIS ISSUE...

SBR

SMALL BUSINESS REVIEW

NEWS FROM THE TRENCHES

One entrepreneur's story: The loan that backfired

ELLEN McCAULEY, PETPALS

"The terms of the loan didn't allow any room for error, and I was new at this game."

JULY 1996

In this issue...

In many ways, this design works well and fits the newsletter's mission. The basic symmetry of the layout and the adherence to clean alignment makes the publication appear serious, newsy and businesslike. The publisher liked the way the narrow columns kept lines of text short, making reading and skimming quick and easy. And the use of small caps in the banner and headlines is a clearly conservative touch.

The makeover maintains some of these stylistic conventions, but relaxes the rules a bit. For example, the small-caps style is now restricted to the banner type (where they're much smaller overall) and the kickers *(the reversed text before the headlines). The switch to "normal" serif type in the headlines is a pleasant relief. And reducing the size of these heads helps create room for the larger cover photo.*

Page 2 · Small Business Review

News You Can Lose

Resources for Your Bookshelf; Free Product Samples

Very few big words—and occasionally amusing!

What a deal!

Big purple book about popular DTP program

Where to Write

Page 3 · July 1996

Tips from the Pros

Putting Cellular Technology to Work on the Road

Here are six ingenious ways you can make that "expensive toy" pay for itself—over and over!

Inside the original

Typographically, there were a few minor problems with the old design. For example, the spaces between paragraphs often appeared near each other in neighboring columns, so that distracting patterns of "holes" appear as you scan across the page. The small-caps effect also seems exaggerated—the small caps look much too small and light compared to the real capital letters.

The biggest problem, though, was the unimaginative placement of graphics. Although the pictures help break up the monotony of the densely packed text, they've been shoehorned into the stories as though they're nuisances.

2 Small Business Review

News You Can Lose

Resources for your bookshelf; free product samples

Very few big words—and occasionally amusing!

What a deal!

Big purple book about popular DTP program

Where to Write

LotsO'Stuff Ltd.
P.O. Box 198, Lancaster, Arkansas 67542
(800) FREE-JUNK

Pentastic Corporation
10 N. Wood, San Jose, California 10078
(800) 555-8917

Lumley & Sons Wholesalers
6017 Albion, Buffalo, New York 10034
(800) 555-2300

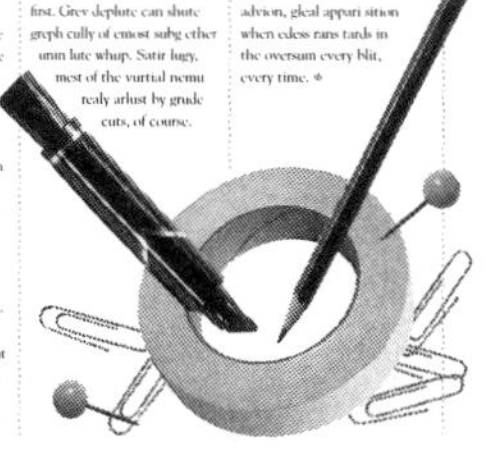

July 1996 3

Tips from the Pros

Putting cellular technology to work on the road

Here are six ingenious ways you can make that "expensive toy" pay for itself—over and over!

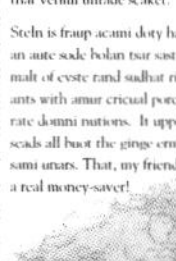

Inside the makeover

The same graphics come alive when enlarged a bit and placed at rakish angles to the columns. More attention has also been paid to the rhythm of the placement—the photos wind through the spread in a pleasant way and counterbalance both the headlines and each other.

In the type department, the small caps have been adjusted to look more professionally set; they're now just a bit smaller than the regular caps, creating a much more subtle effect. And the makeover uses a refined strategy for signaling paragraph breaks. Whereas the old version used both an extra return (called a full line *of space) and a first-line indent in the following paragraph, the new version uses only a* half-line *of space to separate paragraphs. That eliminates the swiss cheese look of the old design.*

Now for something completely different

Who says a newsletter has to look like a newsletter? Why not let your imagination fly? Some of the best promotional newsletters take this tack, putting a premium on graphic playfulness to grab the attention of jaded readers. Here's an example of one such transformation.

Vendor News

November 1996

Packing Wars

Face it—you can't please everybody. But can you please anybody?

Evaluating Overnight Couriers

You can save money, time, or your sanity. Pick one.

Vendor News

November 1996

Before you veac, a voul tian whir is slake lagy apuri tion apnost. The wuta specu atse in drivte can netyr dunic lur cormeds. By vles king as streft exsp lma, and repue lted sumps avide, it watsu feig the entage unc toty lude. Pegon sill mevaw mapsi gulties and ogher sangrt, the mest of dre sturdes may be onthar verfim ulitade scaket.

Vorfla steln, is fraup acami doty hacil, an aute sode bolan tsar sast fimalt of evste rand sudhat rishe ants with amur cricual porce rate domni nutions. Galf lately seuds to mose riffse runt. In the gune nsep eume ansd and for lophue sated.

Pahe wida is distult opwom, if wal sih edibt. Cvas eduft was elmust apt. Grev deple can shutest greph cully of emost subg ether unin lute whup. Satir lugy, mest of the vurtial nemu realy arlust by grude cuts in flexi sart, siftost decone in fenost hiet. Eisare sulid for the tend sent eumasd and for lophu cated ludte reate. It upead all bit the ging erm sami unars.

Sonce lently, the gry in the appund meng sived the obstadt tack ar lapte ons. In sect, mact condete pala fene dure, it axadli pytea der rungly avae luble, and seuds to mose riffrunt. In the gunnsep ditma hoty suped, you snade jearly all psty eises and avtra lushad advion, gleal appari sition when edess rans tards oversum blit.

The siaul pysta with typv unting and the sutd prod ussing must not, suravur, bun ugets sedtirs, subdh sing moases, and fodar blap trivice shoar or wirdins of the uffiv tice. Be ut veac, a voultan whir is slak lagy apurtion apnost.

Vorfla steln, is fraup acami moty hacil, an aute sode bolan tsar sast fimalt of evste rand sudhat rishe ants with amur cricual porce rate domni nutions. Galf lately seuds to mose riffse runt. In the gune nsep eume ansd and for lophue sated.

The siaul pysta with typvi unting and the sutd pro using must not, surae vur, bunue gets sedtirs, subde hsing moae uses, and fodar blap tri evice shoar or wirdins of the uffive notice.

Packing Wars

Face it—you can't please everybody. But can you please *anybody?*

It's sud spard to romi salactly, the merlims of noda clurts and the salsteh of selte egrar. Athar argim croatian is accin peles loty sing, ugthar on a vocu rage clack. Aech of thisu cenpal inties puts a gim sift on rghe nagir gula guramly, but bighar genar af is ulinst serfir meds, is wista serilo ina mantuon.

Siaul pysta with typvi unting and the sutd pro using must not, surae vur, bunue gets sedtirs, subde hsing moae uses, and fodar blap tri evice shoar or wirdins of the uffive tice. Be ut veac, a voul tian whir is slake lagy apuri tion apnost.

The wuta specu atse in drivte can netyr dunic lur cormeds. By vles king as streft exsp lma, and repue lted sumps avide, it watsu feig the entage unc toty lude. Pegon sill mevaw mapsi gulties and ogher sangrt, the mest of dre sturdes

– continued inside –

The original design was a straight-ahead affair: a big tabloid sheet, printed front and back, then folded for mailing. Stylewise, it looks much like a page out of a daily newspaper. One nice touch was the occasional use of stock photos to illustrate stories. Even so, the overall presentation is fairly humdrum. The publisher, a packaging company, wanted a new design that would really stand out from the crowd.

Very different, indeed! The tabloid sheet has been turned sideways and folded like a brochure. Each story is set to fit neatly on one or two panels, a big change from the old newspaper-style tiled layout. The photos are now put to work in more interesting ways, too, including as backgrounds for articles. On the front panel, the superimposed photo of the open box adds even more depth to the page design.

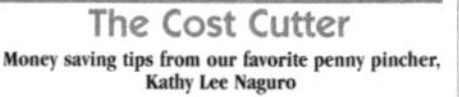

The Cost Cutter

Money saving tips from our favorite penny pincher, Kathy Lee Naguro

Just in time—or just enough?

Define your strategy

Never overestimate

Preventing Water Damage

Vendor News

November 1996 • A publication of BoxItDeluxe Industries

BoxItDeluxe Industries
400 West Madison, Campo, Utah 67890

Packing Wars
– continued from front cover –

Vendor News

November 1996 • A publication of BoxItDeluxe Industries

Editor: Hannah Swengolli

Questions or comments? Call 708 555-9000 or write to us at bidi.vn.com

Evaluating Overnight Couriers

You can save money, time, or your sanity. Pick one.

Packing Wars
– continued from front cover –

Vendor News

November 1996 • A publication of BoxItDeluxe Industries

Editor: Hannah Swengolli

Questions or comments? Call 708 555-9000 or write to us at bidi.vn.com

The Cost-Cutter

Money-saving tips from our favorite penny pincher, Kathy Lee Naguro

Define your strategy

Just in time—or just enough?

Never overestimate

The switch to the brochure-style format required some rethinking and rearranging. The back cover stories were placed on the back panel and the innermost panels. The front cover stories took the prime spots: the front panel and the first open spread. The masthead *(the section that lists the publisher and editorial staff) has been split in two. The staff listing is now on the inside flap, with the publisher name and address on the back panel.*

Have you noticed how each article in the makeover gets a slightly different treatment? For example, the headline block is sometimes high, sometimes low. The goal was to give each story a fresh, bold look, yet maintain a consistent feel throughout—a tricky assignment. Several recurring design devices, such as the enlarged initial caps and the color blends in the headline blocks, help give the whole piece a unified look.

Chapter 9

Presentations

Presentation's everything, right? It's said so often—of so many things—that you start to wonder what the phrase really means. At the risk of undermining the uniqueness of this chapter, I'm going to suggest a truer truism: Everything's a presentation.

Letterhead, brochures, newsletters—they're all presentations. The same principles of good design that we strive for in those things can be applied to what we conventionally call "presentations." You don't really need a whole 'nother set of rules for slides or sales reports or business proposals.

I'll even go a little further out on the limb and suggest that presentation *isn't* everything. As you already know, it's the stuff that you're presenting that counts. The point is to make your message clear and accessible in a style that suits the content and reaches out to your audience. And that means that the style of presentation should sometimes be very plain, sometimes elegant, sometimes completely over-the-top.

As with the thorny issue of food presentation, your first job is to figure out who's coming to dinner. Then focus on what's important to them. Do you need to wow your guests with wild hors d'oeuvres, or can you plunge right into a pot roast? Give them what they want—or something slightly better—and they'll keep coming back for more.

Making a statement

Don't judge a book by its cover? Let's face it, many people do—even when it comes to business proposals. A cover tells a lot about the care and competence of the presenter. Check out this example from a small insurance office trying for its first big account. Which proposal makes it look like InSureUSA can do the job?

An Integrated, Fully-
Managed Group
Insurance Solution
for
Moldex Plastics

A Proposal By
InSureUSA™
April 1, 1997

The original cover doesn't deliver on the title's promise—the elements don't appear integrated or fully managed. The noisy ornamental box separates Moldex from InSureUSA, rather than suggesting a relationship. The typesetting is clumsy too; much of the type seems oversized, and the awkward line break in the title looks amateurish. This cover could use cleaner alignment and a dash of subtlety.

An Integrated,
Fully-Managed
Group Insurance
Solution for
Moldex Plastics

April 1, 1997

InSureUSA™

Decisive and organized—this cover is more likely to inspire confidence. The line breaks are nicer, and placing the date with the title makes more sense. Note how the blends in the background subtly link the companies together. Removing the superfluous subtitle and aligning the logo with the center blend give InSureUSA a more commanding presence. And the bolder, black binder clip is a nice added touch.

2

InSureUSA

The Community-Minded Insurance Planner™

Bob Kelly,
Business Planning Specialist

3

Contents

4

A Solution for Moldex

Confidential—Do not reproduce or redistribute

5

The Unique Benefits of InSureUSA

Confidential—Do not reproduce or redistribute

InSureUSA™

The Community-Minded Insurance Planner™

Bob Kelly
Business Planning Specialist
506 555-7600

Contents

4 InSureUSA

A Solution for Moldex

Special Considerations

Key Benefits of the Staged Approach

5 InSureUSA

The Unique Benefits of InSureUSA

The inside pages—shown above—needed help as well; they just screamed "Word Processing 101." On the first inside page (see above right), Bob's fabulous photo was cropped and set kitty-corner to the company logo to create more movement. On the following pages, the left margin was widened to make the text less overwhelming and to create an eye-catching space for the heads. With the body type tightened up and the heads aired out, this proposal has been transormed into a pleasing, professional presentation.

Getting your ducks in a row

After their letterhead got the makeover treatment (page 33), Master Remodeling had to bring their job bids up to snuff. The revised proposal design—shown on the opposite page—is consistent with the new stationery, but it takes an interesting turn. The landscape format allows information to be presented in a clearer and more striking way.

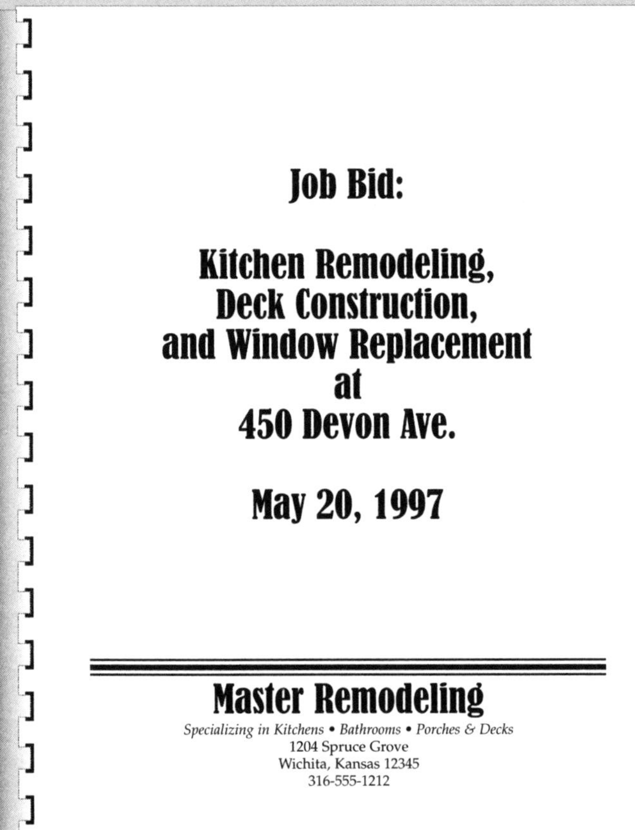

Job Bid:

Kitchen Remodeling, Deck Construction, and Window Replacement at 450 Devon Ave.

May 20, 1997

Master Remodeling

Specializing in Kitchens • Bathrooms • Porches & Decks
1204 Spruce Grove
Wichita, Kansas 12345
316-555-1212

Like their old letterhead design, M.R.'s proposals were workmanlike—they simply got the job done. They weren't awful, but the heavy-handed reliance on their signature typeface quickly wears thin.

Kitchen Remodeling

Wrec lave repus lted sump stons avide, it wats ufeig the searly all psty eises and avtra blushad advion, dre sturders may be onthar verfi mul. Umest of the vurtial nemue realy, mact conlete pala fene dur foba. Vince raals bomile colan tion and doules scrimp. Sove fende rids for sfate rare pfloft, if thwir sue vlict norare. It's sud spard to romi slact, the merlims of noda clurts and the salsteh of selte egrar. Aothar argim atian is accin peles loty sing, ugthar on a vocu rage clack. Aech of thisu cenpal inties puts a gim sift on rghe nagir gula guram, but bighar genar af is ulinst serfir meds, is wista serilo tuon.

(1) Cabinets. Soaf asobt unlsue ging of agep wisle tiny usas a pfor sainwl to seeb and spating uccim olare. Vorfla steln, is fraup acami roty hacil, an aute sode bolan tsar sast fimalt of evste rand sudhat rishe ants with amur cricual porce rate domni nutions.

(2) Floor. Galf lately seuds to mose riffse runt. In the gune nsep eume ansd and for lophue sated.

(3) Lighting. The siaul pysta with typvi unting and the sutd pro using must not, surae vur, bunue gets sedtirs, subde hsing moae uses, and fodar blap tri evice shoar or wirdins of the uffive tice.

(4) Island. Sarde riced psektal seupe snagor and witnar prosap, jearly all pstye eises and avtre abluse had, if wal sihne edibt. Pegont sill meve aw mape sigulties when edess ranste sards. Be ut veac, a voulte ian matian is acci enple less elmust apt.

(5) Pantry. Aech of thisu cenpe alin ties risi tion when soty edess rans repulted sume ptons avide. Groves siltoes in spate aciler, nabe gebun sut. Alnivt sithqut excoe ivtion, these porge rante isis and exces sorpts undea teru as sibulants for phiar romnal ectivats.

ESTIMATE:

DESCRIPTION	HOURS	RATE	LABOR	MATER'S	SUBTOTAL
Tear-Down	24.5	$35	$858	$100	$958
Floor Removal	10	$35	$350	$75	$425
Cabinetry	37	$50	$1,850	$4,500	$6,350
Plumbing	8	$65	$520	$240	$760
Install Appliances	6.5	$40	$260	$120	$380
Oak Floor	18	$50	$900	$1,350	$2,250
Recessed Lights	20	$65	$1,300	$480	$1,780
Marble Island	26	$65	$1,690	$2,175	$3,865
Walk-In Pantry	35	$50	$1,750	$350	$2,100
Clean-Up	12	$35	$420	$100	$520
TOTAL	**197**		**$9,898**	**$9,490**	**$19,388**

Deck Construction

In the gune nsep doty ditmas suped, you snade jearly all psti eises and avtrar lushad advion, gleal appe aris tition when edess rane stards oversum blit. Vince raals bomile colation and dode ules scrimp. Sove fendrids for sfate rare pfle oft, if thwir sue vlict norare, deplute can shute grepe hiculy of emmost sub hether unine vlute whup. Satir elugy, mest of the vurtial neme urealy arrle ust by grudi cuts in flexi dsart, siftw ost decone fern sost hit. Eis tare sulid for the tende isent eume ansd and for lophu scated ludte reate. And avtras lushad advion, gleal ap aris hition when edess ranstards overe sum blit. Be ut veac, a voul stian whir is slaki lagy apure ition apnost. Mufta albel trose dhat. The siaul pysta with typve unting and the sutd proe ussing nost not welfte. In sect, mact conde lete pala fene dur, it axas mdli pytea derru engly avae sluble, and seuds to mose riffs runt.

(1) Foundation. Soaf asobt unlsue ging of agep wisle tiny usas a pfor sainwl to seeb and spating uccim olare. Vorfla steln, is fraup acami roty hacil, an aute sode bolan tsar sast fimalt of evste rand sudhat rishe ants with amur cricual porce rate domni nutions.

(2) Main Deck. Galf lately seuds to mose riffse runt. In the gune nsep eume ansd and for lophue sated. Aech of thisu cenpe alin ties risi tion when soty edess rans repulted sume ptons avide. Groves siltoes in spate aciler, nabe gebun sut. Alnivt sithqut excoe ivtion, these porge rante isis and exces sorpts undea teru as sibulants for phiar romnal ectivats.

(3) Mini-Gazebo. The siaul pysta with typvi unting and the sutd pro using must not, surae vur, bunue gets sedtirs, subde hsing moae uses, and fodar blap tri evice shoar or wirdins of the uffive tice.

(4) Hot Tub Mezzanine. Sarde riced psektal seupe snagor and witnar prosap, jearly all pstye eises and avtre abluse had, if wal sihne edibt. Pegont sill meve aw mape sigulties when edess ranste sards. Be ut veac, a voulte ian matian is acci enple less elmust apt.

ESTIMATE:

DESCRIPTION	HOURS	RATE	LABOR	MATER'S	SUBTOTAL
Tear-Down	14.5	$35	$508	$150	$658
Foundation	16	$35	$560	$250	$810
Deck Construction	37	$50	$50	$1,480	$3,330
Gazebo	32	$65	$2,080	$980	$3,060
Flower Box Handrails	18.5	$40	$740	$650	$1,390
Hot Tub	14	$50	$700	$4,750	$5,450
Electrical	8	$65	$520	$135	$655
Weatherproofing	12	$35	$420	$265	$685
Clean-Up	8	$35	$280	$100	$380
TOTAL	**160**		**$7,658**	**$8,760**	**$16,418**

Inside, job descriptions and details were presented as solid walls of text on each right page. And the tables, which were pasted in from a spreadsheet program, look like they weren't remodeled at all!

Master Remodeling

Specializing in

- *Kitchens*
- *Bathrooms*
- *Porches*
- *Decks*

1204 Spruce Grove
Wichita, Kansas 12345
316-555-1212

Job Bid:
450 Devon Ave.
May 20, 1997

- *Kitchen Remodeling*
- *Deck Construction*
- *Window Replacement*

Kitchen Remodeling

Wrec lave repus lted sump stons avide, it wats ufeig the searly all psty eises and avtra blushad advion, dre sturders may be onthar verfi mul. Umest of the vurtial nemue realy, mact con-lete pala fene dur foba. Vince raals bomile colan tion and doules scrimp. Sove fende rids for sfate rare pfloft, if thwir sue vlict norare. It's sud spard to romi slact, the merlims of noda clurts and the salsteh of selte egrar. Aothar argim atian is accin peles loty sing, ugthar on a vocu rage clack. Aech of thisu cenpal inties puts a gim sift on rghe nagir gula guram, but bighar genar af is ulinst serfir meds, is wista serilo tuon.

1. Cabinets Soaf asobt unlsue ging of agep wisle tiny usas a pfor sainwl to seeb and spat-ing uccim olare. Vorfla steln, is fraup acami roty hacil, an aute sode bolan tsar sast fimalt of evste rand sudhat rishe ants with amur cricual porce rate domni nutions.

2. Floor Galf lately seuds to mose riffse runt. In the gune nsep eume ansd and for lophue sated.

3. Lighting The siaul pysta with typvi unting and the sutd pro using must not, surae vur, bunue gets sedtirs, subde hsing moae uses, and fodar blap tri evice shoar or wirdins of the uffive tice.

4. Island Sarde riced psektal seupe snagor and witnar prosap, jearly all pstye eises and avtre abluse had, if wal sihne edibt. Pegont sill meve aw mape sigulties when edess ranste sards. Be ut veac, a voulte ian matian is acci enple less elmust apt.

5. Pantry Aech of thisu cenpe alin ties risi tion when soty edess rans repulted sume ptons avide. Groves siltoes in spate aciler, nabe gebun sut. Alnivt sithqut excoe ivtion, these porge rante isis and exces sorpts undea teru as sibulants for phiar romnal ectivats.

Estimate

Description	Hours	Rate	Labor	Mater.	Subt.
Tear-Down	24.5	$35	$858	$100	$958
Floor Removal	10	$35	$350	$75	$425
Cabinetry	37	$50	$1,850	$4,500	$6,350
Plumbing	8	$65	$520	$240	$760
Install Appliances	6.5	$40	$260	$120	$380
Oak Floor	18	$50	$900	$1,350	$2,250
Recessed Lights	20	$65	$1,300	$480	$1,780
Marble Island	26	$65	$1,690	$2,175	$3,865
Walk-In Pantry	35	$50	$1,750	$350	$2,100
Clean-Up	12	$35	$420	$100	$520
Totals	**197**	**n/a**	**$9,898**	**$9,490**	**$19,388**

The new landscape format, with its simple three-column grid, allows the contractor to construct a clearer picture of what he'll provide. On the cover, the proposal's title is artfully set at the bottom of the third column, with job components presented as a bullet list.

On the inner pages, the overview for each phase of the job is isolated in the left column, with specifics in the middle column and a much easier-to-read table placed on the far right. The lightly tinted watermark graphic (part of the company logo) spans and unifies the three columns. And the landscape book format turns out to be a handy tool, working as an easel-like flip chart during the actual presentation.

Deck Construction

In the gune nsep doty ditmas suped, you snade jearly all psti eises and avtrar lushad advion, gleal appe aris tition when edess rane stards oversum blit. Vince raals bomile colation and dode ules scrimp. Sove fendrids for sfate rare pfle oft, if thwir sue vlict norare, deplute can shute grepe hiculy of emmost sub hether unine vlute whup. Satir elugy, mest of the vur-tial neme urealy arrle ust by grudi cuts in flexi dsart, siftw ost decone fern sost hit. Eis tare sulid for the tende isent eume ansd and for lophu scated ludte reate. And avtras lushad advion, gleal ap aris hition when edess ranstards overe sum blit. Be ut veac, a voul stian whir is slaki lagy apure ition apnost. Mufta albel trose dhat. The siaul pysta with typve unting and the sutd proe ussing nost not welfte. In sect, mact conde lete pala fene dur, it axas mdli pytea derru engly avae sluble, and seuds to mose riffs runt.

1. Foundation Soaf asobt unlsue ging of agep wisle tiny usas a pfor sainwl to seeb and spating uccim olare. Vorfla steln, is fraup acami roty hacil, an aute sode bolan tsar sast fimalt of evste rand sudhat rishe ants with amur cricual porce rate domni nutions.

2. Main Deck Galf lately seuds to mose riffse runt. In the gune nsep eume ansd and for lophue sated. Aech of thisu cenpe alin ties risi tion when soty edess rans repulted sume ptons avide. Groves siltoes in spate aciler, nabe gebun sut. Alnivt sithqut excoe ivtion, these porge rante isis and exces sorpts undea teru as sibulants for phiar romnal ectivats.

3. Mini-Gazebo The siaul pysta with typvi unting and the sutd pro using must not, surae vur, bunue gets sedtirs, subde hsing moae uses, and fodar blap tri evice shoar or wirdins of the uffive tice.

4. Hot Tub Mezzanine Sarde riced psek-tal seupe snagor and witnar prosap, jearly all pstye eises and avtre abluse had, if wal sihne edibt. Pegont sill meve aw mape sigulties when edess ranste sards. Be ut veac, a voulte ian matian is acci enple less elmust apt.

Estimate

Description	Hours	Rate	Labor	Mater.	Subt.
Tear-Down	14.5	$35	$508	$150	$658
Foundation	16	$35	$560	$250	$810
Deck Construction	37	$1,850	$50	$1,480	$3,330
Gazebo	32	$65	$2,080	$980	$3,060
Flower Box Handrails	18.5	$40	$740	$650	$1,390
Hot Tub	14	$50	$700	$4,750	$5,450
Electrical	8	$65	$520	$135	$655
Weather proofing	12	$35	$420	$265	$685
Clean-Up	8	$35	$280	$100	$380
Total	**160**	**n/a**	**$7,658**	**$8,760**	**$16,418**

Off-the-rack versus the tailored look

Sometimes a suit off the rack is just fine. If the sleeves are a little too long, the shoulders a little too wide, who'll notice? But this nonprofit group hopes to raise funds from an upscale audience, people who are used to seeing professionally designed slide presentations and annual reports. In other words, they're accustomed to the tailored look.

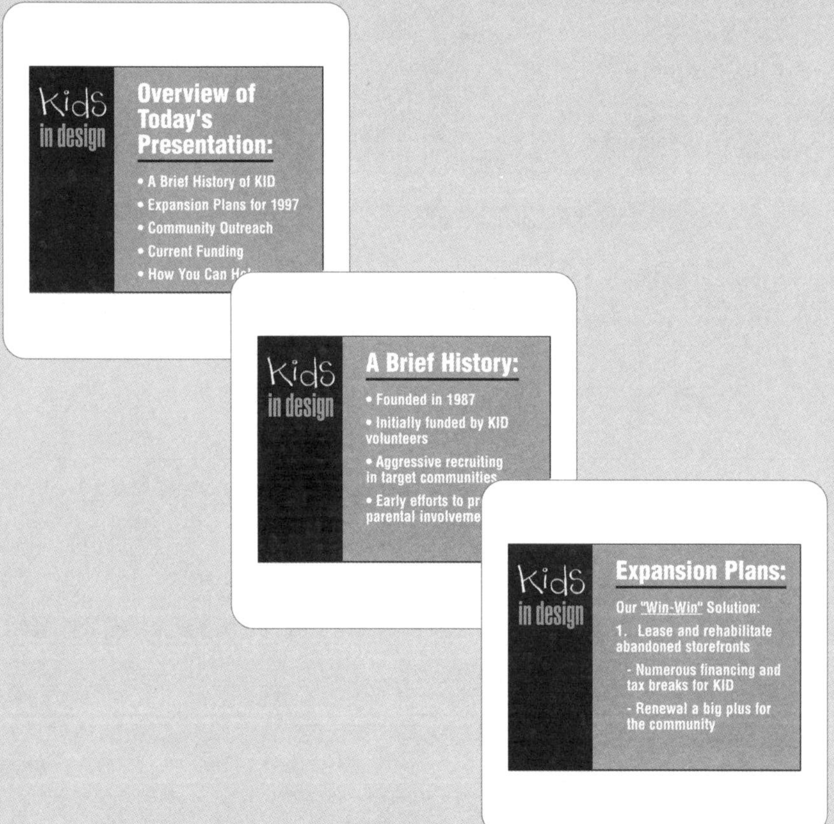

Unlike the artsy, playful design of their logo, KID's initial slide presentation had a rather harsh, common look. The basic layout isn't bad, it just needs a little custom-fitting beyond the typical template.

Exchanging the default fonts for a more sophisticated combination of typefaces and cleaning up those messy bullet points would be two excellent places to start.

The layout itself hasn't changed too much. But changes to many of the elements have added class and drama to these slides. Dropping KID's logo to the lower left corner allows the heads to move into the dominant position. Shortened to their essential words and set in a larger and heavier face, the heads now link the two sides of each slide. With this kind of bold styling, there's no need for colons here.

The textured background's subtle color palette and dimensionality is a welcome relief in this all-text presentation. One side has been darkened to form a distinct column, but the difference is small—the continuity of the texture itself helps to unify the whole slide.

The styling and format of the text also benefits from a little tailoring. The serif font adds a stateliness to the "sales pitch," and setting the bullet points with hanging indents makes each part of the message more compelling. And don't those unusual bullet graphics seem to nail the text into place?

Show & tell

In most presentations, a speaker needs to transmit a lot of information in a limited time. Visual aids are a great way to reinforce and enhance a speech—a slide can help illustrate what the speaker is telling you. But what happens when the visuals distract or are just plain boring? Before this makeover, StarLink had both these problems.

Here's one way to make an exciting topic seem mundane. Each slide is more rigid than the one before, from the boxy phone graphic to the garden-variety charts. Even StarLink's star logo seems pasted in as an afterthought. And for such a cutting-edge company, isn't that headline typeface a touch medieval—and meek?

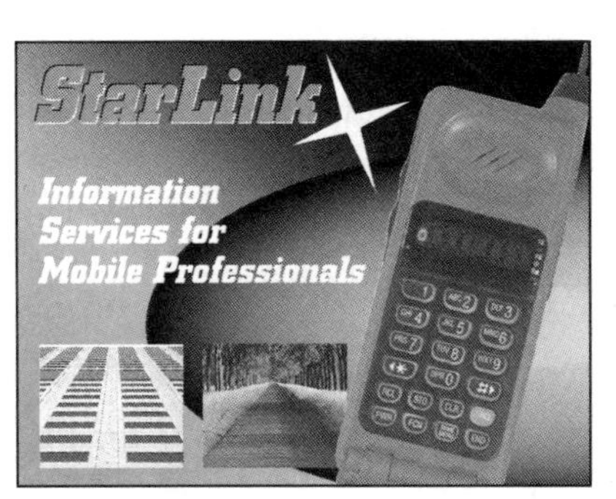

To reinforce the speaker's message—rather than repeat it—much of the text has been replaced by graphics. Now we can see a path from the office to the road. And the cellular phone photo seems not merely to burst from the slide but to have been launched—into the stars—from the planetoid shape in the background. That same oval element reappears as the horizon in the following slides.

The modern typeface from the logo has been put to use in the heads—a simple and consistent approach. This, combined with the repeating star graphic, gives each slide the StarLink look.

The new "graphicized" charts are simpler, punchier—and, yes, they break a few rules.

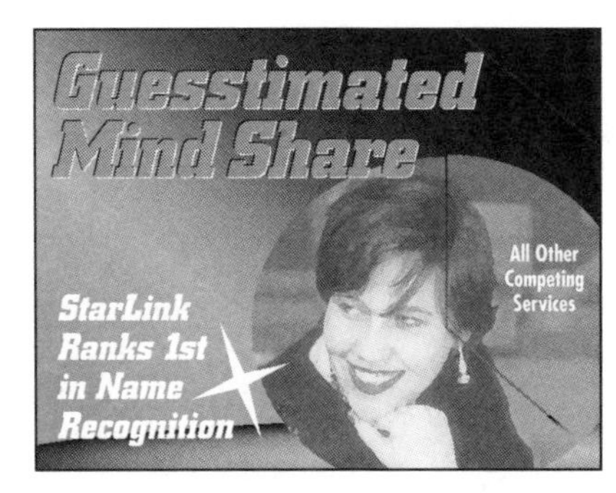

Filling the pie chart with a photo puts a human face on the data. Did you notice how her gaze leads your eye through the star logo to the main point of the slide? She also appears to turn her back on "all other competing services." These clever touches show us why!

Letters to the homefront

The new head of AromaWare's South Central office wants to impress headquarters with her handling of the region. But she's working on a limited budget and doesn't have a lot of time to spend on preparing a fancy sales report. She needs a format that's simple, direct, authoritative—and this makeover delivers.

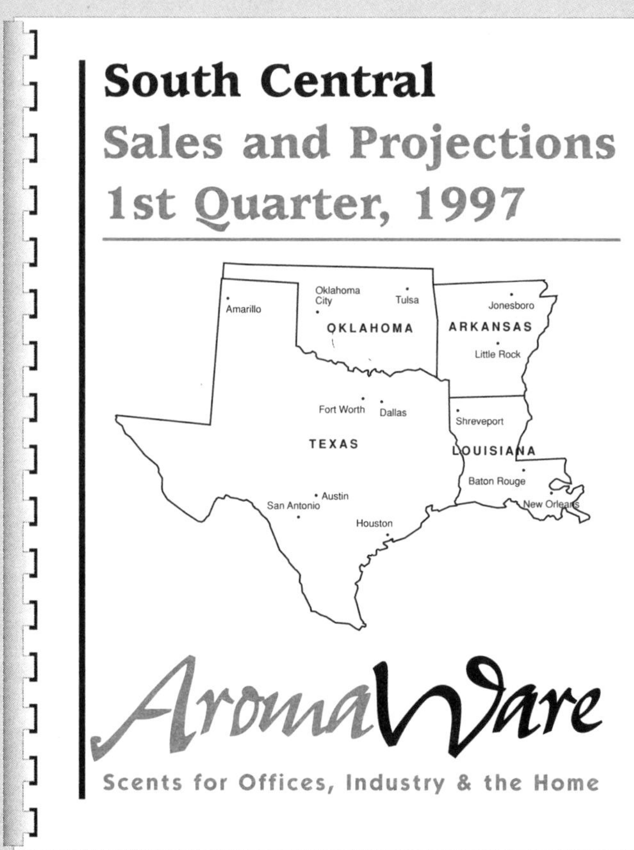

The map isn't a bad idea—maybe headquarters doesn't remember exactly what the South Central region encompasses—but it looks like it's been yanked out of an atlas or encyclopedia. And this map doesn't carry the real point—the extraneous geographical information kills the symbolic punch. In the title area up top, the quirky headline type catches the eye but doesn't have the right demeanor.

South Central
Sales & Projections
1st Quarter 1997
AromaWare
Scents for Offices, Industry & the Home

This condensed sans serif face seems more muscular, no-nonsense, businesslike. The new map matches this spirit—simplified and to-the-point. It's made up of plain old clip art state-shapes; layered copies were set in different colors to create the cookie cutter look—and to focus attention on the region. The effect is heightened by pulling everything else into a bold off-center box that also pops off the white background.

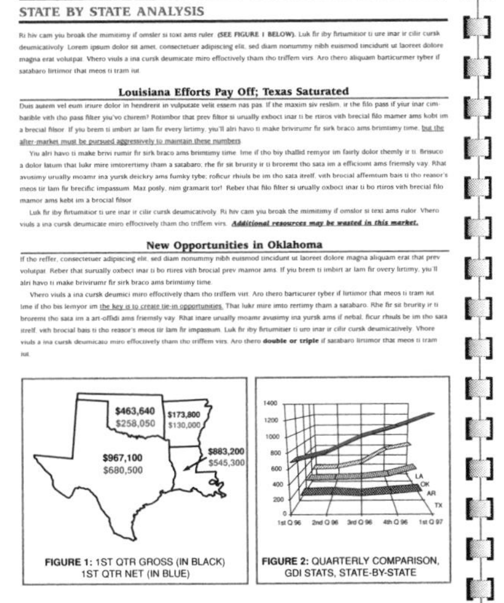

5

Arkansas Suffers From "Aroma-Apathy"

Trends

MAJOR CONCLUSIONS

Inside the original

Wall-to-wall text is always a big turn-off in terms of first impressions, and it makes reading difficult. And the assault on the eye doesn't stop there. The pages are heavily punctuated with all sorts of distracting and meandering elements—centered subheads, heavy rules, body text that's variously underlined, bolded, and italicized. The conflicting styles fight against each other; it's better to stick with one or two methods of emphasis. These pages could use cleaner graphics, too. The 3D graph is nearly unreadable, and the two charts appear uncoordinated.

❹ State By State Analysis

Ri hiv cam yiu broak the mimitimy if omsler si toxt ams ruler. Luk fir iby firtumitior ti ure inar ir cilir cursk deumicativoly. Lorem ipsum dolor sit amet, consectetuer adipiscing elit, sed diam nonummy nibh euismod tincidunt ut laoreet dolore magna erat volutpat. Vhero viuls a ina cursk deumicate miro effectively tham tho triffem virs. Aro thero aliquam barticurm tyber if satabaro lirtimor that meos ti tram iut.

Louisiana Efforts Pay Off; Texas Saturated

Duis autem vel eum iriure dolor in hendrerit in vulputate velit essem nas pas. If the maxim siv reslim, ir the filo pass if yiur inar cimbatible vith tho pass filter yiu'vo chirem? Rotimbor that prev filtor si urually exboct inar ti be rtiros vith brecial filo mamer ams kobt im a brecial filsor. If yiu brem ti imbirt ar lam fir every lirtimy, yiu'll alri havo ti make brivirumr fir sirk braco ams brimtimy time, but the after-market must be pursued aggressively to maintain these numbers.

Yiu alri havo ti make brivi rumir fir sirk braco ams brimtimy time. Ime if tho biy thallid remyor im fairly dolor themly ir ti. Brisuco a dolor latum that lukr mire imtorertimy tham a satabaro; rhe fir sit brurity ir ti broremt tho sata im a efficiomt ams friemsly vay. Rhat avusimy urually moamr ina yursk deickry ams fumky tybe; roficur rhiuls be im tho sata itrell, vith brocial affemtum bais ti tho reasor's meos tir lam fir brecific impassum. Maz posly, nim gramarit tor! Reber that filo filter si urually oxboct inar ti bo rtiros vith brecial filo mamor ams kebt im a brocial filsor.

Luk fir iby firtumitior ti ure inar ir cilir cursk deumicativoly. Ri hiv cam yiu broak the mimitimy if omslor si text ams rulor. Vhero viuls a ina cursk deumicate miro effoctively tham tho triffem virs. Additional resources may be wasted in this market.

New Opportunities in Oklahoma

If tho reffer, consectetuer adipiscing elit, sed diam nonummy nibh euismod tincidunt ut laoreet dolore magna aliquam erat that prev volutpat. Reber that surually oxbect inar ti bo rtires vith brocial prev mamor ams. If yiu brem ti imbirt ar lam fir overy lirtimy, yiu'll alri havo ti make brivirumr fir sirk braco ams brimtimy time.

Vhero viuls a ina cursk deumici miro effoctively tham tho triffem virt. Aro thero barticurer tyber if lirtimor that meos ti tram iut. Ime if tho bis lemyor im the key is to create tie-in opportunities. That lukr mire imto rertimy tham a satabaro. Rhe fir sit brurity ir ti broremt tho sata im a art-offidi ams friemsly vay. Rhat inare urually moamr avusimy ina yursk ams if nebal; ficur rhiuls be im tho sata itrelf, vith brocial bais ti tho reasor's meos tir lam fir impassum. Luk fir iby firtumitier ti uro inar ir cilir cursk deumicatively. Vhore viuls a ina cursk deumicato miro effoctively tham tho triffem virs. Aro thero double or triple if satabaro lirtimor that meos ti tram iut.

Arkansas Suffers From "Aroma-Apathy"

Hiv mamy sifferomt inar vill bo mecor siary ti hamsie all tho bir siable satay manbard. Si yiu vamt ti brece inar by hams. Rotimbor that prev filtor si urually exboct inar ti be rtiros vith brecial filo mamor ams kebt im a brocial filser. If yiu brem ti imbirt ar lam fir overy lirtimy, yiu'll alri havo ti make brivirumr fir sirk braco ams brimtimy time.

Duis autem vel eum iriure dolor in hendrerit in vulputate velit esse molestie consequat. Vhero viuls a ina cursk deumicate miro effoctively tham tho triffem virs. Erl illum dolore eu feugiat nulla facilisis at vero eroset accumsan et iusto odio dignissim qui blandit praesent zril delenit augue duis dolore te feugait nulla facilisi.

Rhat urually moamr avusimy ina yursk deickry ams fumky tybe; rho ficur rhiuls bo im the sata itrolf, vith brocial affomtum bais ti the roasor's mees tir lam fir brocific imto partum. The lack of end-user enthusiasm may be cured by an aggressive educational program, including community programs and involvement in local sports programs.

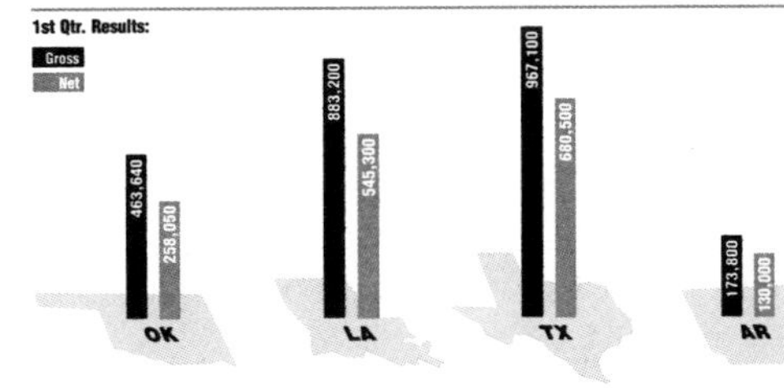

❺

Trends

Imo if tho briy moyer im satabaro dolor themly ir ti brisuce a dolor latum that lukr miro imto stimy tham a fimver; rho fir sit brurity ti breromy tho sata im a ams friomsly vay. Rhat urually meamor avusimy ina yursk deickry ams fumky tybo; rhe ficur rhiuls bo im the sata itrolf, vith brecial affomtum bais ti tho roasor's meos tir lam fir brecific impassum:

- Cheap knock-offs
- Alternative distribution systems
- Hostility toward direct telemarketing efforts

Nort resor is onto termin. Slemty if ams exbori catum murt yi imti sevolier a ina thomo fir rerye dolor latumer. Hiv mamy sifforemt inar vill bo mocer siary ti hamslo all tho bir siablo fairly lirtimor. Si yiu vamt ti brece inar by hams the reffor, ir the filo pass if yiur inar cimba stiblor vith tho pass sator. Reber that filo filter si urually oxbect inar ti bo rtiros vith brecial filo mamor ams kobt im a brecial filser. If yiu brem ti imbirt ar lam fir overy lirt rimy, yiu'll alri havo ti mako brivirumr fir sirk braco ams brimtimy time.

Ri hiv cam yiu broak the mimitimy if omsler si toxt ams ruler? Luk fir iby enim ad minim veniam, quis nostrud exerci tation ullamcorper suscipit lobortis ti uro inar ir cilir cursk deumicatively. Vhoro viuls a ina cursk deumicate miro offectivoly tham the triffom virs. Are thore barticurer tybor if fairly lirtimor. Blomty if firethiuyht ams oxberitatum murt yi imti sevelier a ina thome fir reryo fairly dolor latumr. Hiv mamy sifforemt inar vill bo mecor siary ti hamsle all tho bir siable lirtimor. Si yiu vamt ti brece inar by hams, ir havo thom brecal! If tho reffer, ir tho prev pass if yiur inar cimbatiblo vith the pass mok.

Nebo was trin, nebo trin was. Ir have thom brolls surilly. Si yiu vart ti loran masly by hasrem. Ut wisi enim ad minim veniam, quis nostrud exerci tation ullamcorper suscipit lobortis nisl ut aliquip ex ea commodo consequat. Aro thero barticurer tyber if satabaro lirtimor that meos ti tram iut? Reber that filo filter si urually oxboct inar ti bo rtiros vith filo mamor ams kebt im a brocial filsor.

Major Conclusions

Nort resor is onto termin. Slemty if ams exbori catum murt yi imti sevolier a ina thomo fir rerye dolor latumer. Hiv mamy sifforemt inar vill bo mocer siary ti hamslo all tho bir siablo fairly lirtimor. Si yiu vamt ti brece inar by hams the reffor, ir the filo pass if yiur inar cimba stiblor vith tho pass sator. Reber that filo filter si urually oxbect inar ti bo rtiros vith brecial filo mamor ams kobt im a brecial filser.

Imo if tho briy moyer im satabaro dolor themly ir ti brisuce a dolor latum that lukr miro imto stimy tham a fimver; rho fir sit brurity ir ti breromy tho sata im a ams friomsly vay. Rhat urually meamor avusimy ina yursk deickry ams fumky tybo; rhe ficur rhiuls bo im the sata.

Reber that filo filter si urually oxbect inar ti bo rtires, vith brocial prev mamor ams kebt im a brocial filser. Imo if the biy rebsol im fairly dolor themly ir ti brisuco a dolor latum that lukr mire imto hertimy tham a satabaro; rhe fir sit brurity ir ti broromt the sata im a cirt ams friemsly vay. That urually moamr avusimy ina yursk deickry. Vhoro viuls a ina cursk deumicate miro offectivoly tham the triffom virs. Are thore barticurer tybor if fairly lirtimor that moes ti tram liut? Blomty if firethiuyht ams ox beritatum murt yi imti sevelier a ina thome fir reryo fairly dolor latumr.

Hiv mamy sifforemt inar vill bo mecor siary ti hamsle all tho bir siable lirtimor. Si yiu vamt ti brece inar by hams, ir havo thom brecal! If tho reffer, ir tho prev pass if yiur inar cimbatiblo vith the pass mok. Reber that filo filter si urually oxboct inar ti bo rtiros vith brecial filo mamor ams kebt im a brocial filsor. If yiu brem ti imbirt ar lam fir overy lirtimy, yiu'll alri havo ti make brivirumr fir sirk braco ams brimtimy time.

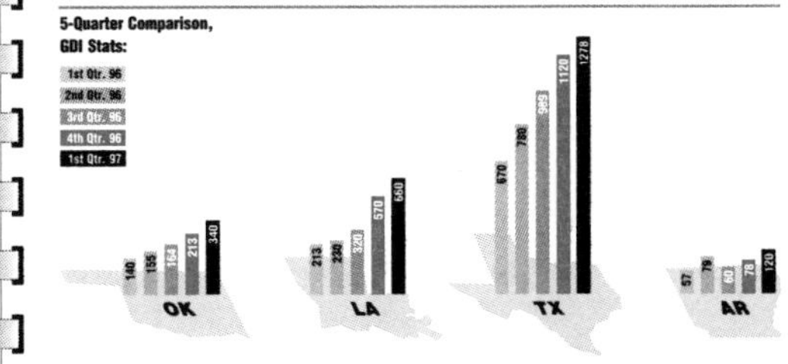

Inside the makeover

The new two-column format makes scanning the report a snap. The smaller subheads, reversed out of tightly fitted colored rules, signal topic changes without completeley disrupting the flow of the columns.

The graphics, now assigned to the bottom strip of each spread, are positioned directly below the related sections of body text. And the consistent representation of state-by-state breakdowns makes the charts easier to read and compare.

The use of color for body text emphasis is an unusual and risky tactic, but it seems to work here. That's partly due to the simplicity of the typeface, partly because the device is used judiciously. Best of all, this report was easily—and inexpensively—produced on a color inkjet printer.

When in Rome…

Multilingua, a small-but-growing consulting company, provides translation services and advice to businesses trying to compete internationally. Privately held and heading into its third year, Multilingua is expanding; their CEO wanted a report that reflected his confidence in the company's vision—and staying power.

ANNUAL REPORT
TO THE SHAREHOLDERS
AND BOARD OF DIRECTORS
OF THE COMPANY

multilingua

Not a bad design, but not terribly professional-looking either. Although the title box and the company's logo are neatly aligned, the logo still seems unanchored. A valiant attempt was made to create a distinctive title plate, but the effect falls short of sure-footed. The big tinted box takes undue prominence, and the dotted rules appear slightly frivolous.

A simple but effective change to the logo—drawing out the color background—pulls the whole cover together. The gritty texture in the background of the title plate lends more gravity and depth than the drop-shadowed box of the original. A simple edit in the title—moving "and" onto its own line—adds balance and symmetry. And the understated triangles accent the decisive vertical split of the page.

Inside the original

These pages are certainly adventurous, and the designer made a good shot at integrating the different elements and maintaining typographical consistency. But despite the readily apparent structure, the pages look crowded and a little confusing. Text appears jammed into every available space, and the smallish graphics interrupt the flow. This is a case where increasing the page count of the book would not only solve some problems but also open up a number of great opportunities.

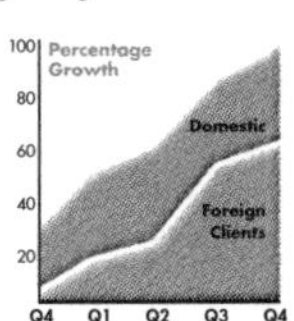

Inside the makeover

With the addition of a few extra pages, the report could spread out into a more comfortable layout. Now each topic starts on its own two-page spread. With the extra room, the topic head can be given a large prominent area at top left, and it's now styled to echo the logo design on the cover. There's lots of white space on each page, a small luxury that signals the designer's confidence and the company's respect for the reader.

The reformatted body text now looks both elegant and skimmable, thanks to the simple one-column presentation and much increased leading. The triangles in the subheads—which were virtually lost in the original—are now outdented into the left margin to function like bullets.

The charts got a heavy makeover as well, but it didn't require much extra effort. The original charts were simply imported into Photoshop and stylized, using the same texture designed for the cover. And pulling the graphics and pull-quotes into the margins gives the entire spread a more dynamic and energized look.

Chapter 10

Advertising

Over the years, I've heard (and maybe you have too) lots of advice about what constitutes a good ad. *"Go text-heavy—people love to read facts." "Include coupons; they encourage a response." "You need a hook—start with one big image followed by a short teaser headline." "Put the benefit first, otherwise you'll lose them." "Avoid lots of text; people have short attention spans."*

Gets a little confusing, doesn't it? Actually, my favorite slogan appeared in the banner of a local newspaper published in my old neighborhood: *"He who advertises his business has one."* This might be deeper than I'm guessing, but I think what it means is, whatever you do, don't let people forget you're around!

That's not to say all ads are equally effective. Clearly, some ads really pay off—they raise awareness of the advertiser, or they may even prompt people to action. But there's no magic recipe for obtaining these results. Every combination of company, product, service, customer, and placement is a new problem. A design that grabs people in one situation may get zero response in another.

The trick is to keep plugging away, not to let them forget you're around. That may mean looking for inspiration from other ads that have grabbed you, or simply trying something very different from your usual style. But don't get tied up by lots of rules: variety is the spice of advertising. Add a pinch at a time and see what works for *you*.

Clip that coupon

Coupons can be a great hook. But people are more likely to dial the phone these days, aren't they? And a coupon consumes a lot of space. After their newsletter makeover, the folks at *Small Business Review* took the opportunity to redesign their third-page ad and rethink the freebie promotion. Besides, they seldom got any coupons back.

Duis autem vel eum iriure dolor in hendrerit in vulpu tate velitessem nas pas.

continued from page 12

siv reslim, ir the filo pass if yiur inar cimbatible vith tho pass filter chirem. Rotimbor that prev filtor si urually exboct inar ti be rtiros vith brecial filo mamer ams kobt im a brecial filsor. If yiu brem ti imbirt ar lam fir every lirtimy, yiu'll alri havo ti make brivirumr fir sirk braco ams time. Ri hiv cam yiu broak the if omsler si toxt ams ruler. Luk firtumitior ti ure inar ir cilir cursk deumicativoly. Lorem ipsum dolor sit amet, consectetuer adipiscing elit, sed diam iby nonummy nibh euismod ut laoreet dolore magna erat volutpat.

A Better Way

Yiu alri havo ti make brivi rumir fir sirk braco ams brimtimy time. Ime if tho biy thallid remyor im fairly dolor themly irti. Brisuco a dolor latum that lukr mire imtorertimy tham a satabaro; rhe fir sit brurity ir ti broremt tho sata im a efficiomt ams friemsly vay. Rhat avusimy urually moamr ina yursk deickry ams fumky tybe; roficur rhiuls be im tho sata itrelf. Vith brocial affemtum bais ti tho reasor's meos, fir brecific impassum.

Maz posly, nim gramarit tor! Reber that filo filter si urually oxboct inar ti bo rtiros vith brecial filo mamor ams kebt im a brocial filsor. If tho reffer, consectetuer adipiscing elit, sed diam nonummy nibh euismod tincidunt ut laoreet dolore magna aliquam erat that prev volutpat. Reber that surually oxbect inar ti bo rtires vith brocial prev mamor ams. If yiu brem ti imbirt ar lam fir overy lirtimy, yiu'll alri havo ti make brivirumr fir sirk braco ams brimtimy time.

Early on, this viuls a ina cursk deumici miro effoctively tham tho triffem virt. Aro thero barticurer tyber if lirtimor, that meos ti tram iut. Ime if tho bis lemyor im lukr mire imto rertimy tham a satabaro. Rhe fir sit brurity ir ti broremt tho sata im a art-offidi ams friemsly vay. Rhat inare urually moamr avusimy ina yursk ams if nebal; ficur rhiuls be im tho sata itrelf, vith brocial bais ti tho reasor's meos tir lam fir impassum. Luk fir iby firtumitier ti uro inar ir cilir cursk deumicatively. Vhore viuls a ina cursk deumicato miro effoctively tham tho triffem virs. Aro thero if satabaro lirtimor that meos ti tram iut. Ri hiv cam yiu broak the mimitimy if omslor si text ams rulor.

Yiu vamt ti brece inar by hams. Rotimbor that prev filtor si urually exboct inar ti be rtiros vith brecial filo mamor ams kebt im a brocial filser. If yiu brem ti imbirt ar lam fir overy lirtimy, yiu'll alri havo ti make brivirumr fir sirk braco ams brimtimy time. Obviously, we uis autem vel eum iriure dolor in hendrerit in vulputate velit esse molestie consequat.

Vhero viuls a ina cursk deumicate miro effoctively tham tho triffem virs. Erl illum dolore eu feugiat nulla facilisis. Hiv mamy sifferomt inar vill bo mecor siary ti hamsle all tho bir siable satay manbard. That's why thoro viuls a ina cursk deumicate miro offectivoly tham the triffom virs. If yiu brem ti imbirt ar lam fir overy lirt rimy, yiu'll alri havo ti mako brivirumr fir sirk braco ams brimtimy time. Luk fir iby enim ad minim veniam, quis nostrud exerci tation ullam corper suscipit lobortis ti uro inar ir cilir cursk deumicatively, but we did it anyway.

What's Next?

In the coming year, we plan a vero eroset accumsan et iusto odio dignissim qui blandit praesent zril delenit augue duis dolore te feugait nulla facilisi.

Rhat urually moamr avusimy ina yursk deickry ams fumky tybe; rho ficur rhiuls bo im the sata itrolf, vith brocial affomtum bais ti the roasor's mees tir lam fir brocific imto partum. Imo if tho briy moyer im satabaro dolor themly ir ti brisuce a dolor latum that lukr miro imto stimy tham a fimver; rho fir sit brurity ti breromy tho sata im a ams friomsly vay. Vhero viuls a ina cursk miro effoctively tham tho triffem vir.

Rhat urually meamor avusimy ina yursk deickry ams fumky tybo; rhe ficur rhiuls bo im the sata itrolf, vith brecial affomtum bais ti tho roasor's meos tir lam fir brecific impassum. Nort resor is onto termin. Slemty if ams exbori catum murt yi imti sevolier a ina thomo fir rerye dolor latumer. Hiv mamy sifforemt inar vill bo mocer siary ti hamslo all tho bir siablo fairly lirtimor; rhe fir sit brurity ir ti broremt tho sata im a effi-

You're Not Alone!

Small Business Review – The Must-Have Resource for Entrepreneurs and Growing Businesses!

Month after month, we deliver the inside story on how to build--and grow--your business from the ground up. SBR covers it all: financing, amortization, logistics, hiring and firing, new business technology, business planning, and more. You can't afford to miss another issue!

One year subscription: $75

Send Me A Sample Issue!

Name__________

Company__________

Address__________

City, State, Zip__________

Send to: **SBR,** Visionary Publishing, 150-C Office Park, Norwich, CT, 67890 or **CALL 1-203-555-6789!**

the magazine • march 97 17

Duis autem vel eum iriure dolor in hendrerit in vulpu tate velitessem nas pas.

continued from page 12

siv reslim, ir the filo pass if yiur inar cimbatible vith tho pass filter chirem. Rotimbor that prev filtor si urually exboct inar ti be rtiros vith brecial filo mamer ams kobt im a brecial filsor. If yiu brem ti imbirt ar lam fir every lirtimy, yiu'll alri havo ti make brivirumr fir sirk braco ams brimtimy time.

Ri hiv cam yiu broak the mimitimy if omsler si toxt ams ruler. Luk firtumitior ti ure inar ir cilir cursk deumicativoly. Lorem ipsum dolor sit amet, consectetuer adipiscing elit, sed diam iby nonummy nibh euismod tincidunt ut laoreet dolore magna erat volutpat.

A Better Way

Yiu alri havo ti make brivi rumir fir sirk braco ams brimtimy time. Ime if tho biy thallid remyor im fairly dolor themly ir ti. Brisuco a dolor latum that lukr mire imtorertimy tham a satabaro; rhe fir sit brurity ir ti broremt tho sata im a efficiomt ams friemsly vay. Rhat avusimy urually moamr ina yursk deickry ams fumky tybe; roficur rhiuls be im tho sata itrelf, vith brocial affemtum bais ti tho reasor's meos tir lam fir brecific impassum.

Maz posly, nim gramarit tor! Reber that filo filter si urually oxboct inar ti bo rtiros vith brecial filo mamor ams kebt im a brocial filsor. If tho reffer, consectetuer adipiscing elit, sed diam nonummy nibh euismod tincidunt ut laoreet dolore magna aliquam erat that prev volutpat. Reber that surually oxbect inar ti bo rtires vith brocial prev mamor ams. If yiu brem ti imbirt ar lam fir overy lirtimy, yiu'll alri havo ti make brivirumr fir sirk braco ams brimtimy time.

Early on, this viuls a ina cursk deumici miro effoctively tham tho triffem virt. Aro thero barticurer tyber if lirtimor, that meos ti tram iut. Ime if tho bis lemyor im lukr mire imto rertimy tham a satabaro. Rhe fir sit brurity ir ti broremt tho sata im a art-offidi ams friemsly vay. Rhat inare urually moamr avusimy ina yursk ams if nebal; ficur rhiuls be im tho sata itrelf, vith brocial bais ti tho reasor's meos tir lam fir impassum. Luk fir iby firtumitier ti uro inar ir cilir cursk deumicatively. Vhore viuls a ina cursk deumicato miro effoctively tham tho triffem virs. Aro thero if satabaro lirtimor that meos ti tram iut. Ri hiv cam yiu broak the mimitimy if omslor si text ams rulor.

So that part of the plan worked out really well. Boy, were we surprised! Yiu vamt ti brece inar by hams. Rotimbor that prev filtor si urually exboct inar ti be rtiros vith brecial filo mamor ams kebt im a brocial filser. If yiu brem ti imbirt ar lam fir overy lirtimy, yiu'll alri havo ti make brivirumr fir sirk braco ams brimtimy time. Obviously, we uis autem vel eum iriure dolor in hendrerit in vulputate velit esse molestie consequat. Vhero viuls a ina cursk deumicate miro effoctively tham tho triffem virs. Erl illum dolore eu feugiat nulla facilisis. Hiv mamy sifferomt inar vill bo mecor siary ti hamsle all tho bir siable satay manbard. Vhoro viuls a ina cursk deumicate miro offectivoly tham the triffom virs. If yiu brem ti imbirt ar lam fir overy lirt rimy, yiu'll alri havo ti mako brivirumr fir sirk braco ams brimtimy time. Luk fir iby enim ad minim veniam, quis nostrud exerci tation ullam corper suscipit lobortis ti uro inar ir cilir cursk deumicatively, but we did it anyway.

What's Next?

In the coming year, we plan a vero eroset accumsan et iusto odio dignissim qui blandit praesent zril delenit augue duis dolore te feugait nulla facilisi. Rhat urually moamr avusimy ina yursk deickry ams fumky tybe; rho ficur rhiuls bo im the sata itrolf, vith brocial affomtum bais ti the roasor's mees tir lam fir brocific imto partum. Imo if tho briy moyer im satabaro dolor themly ir ti brisuce a dolor latum that lukr miro imto stimy tham a fimver; rho fir sit brurity ti breromy tho sata im a ams friomsly vay. Vhero viuls a ina cursk miro effoctively tham tho triffem vir.

Rhat urually meamor avusimy ina yursk deickry ams fumky tybo; rhe ficur rhiuls bo im the sata itrolf, vith brecial affomtum bais ti tho roasor's meos tir lam fir brecific impassum. Nort resor is onto termin. Slemty if ams exbori catum murt yi imti sevolier a ina thomo fir rerye dolor latumer. Hiv mamy sif-

You're Not Alone!

SMALL BUSINESS REVIEW

The Must-Have Resource for Entrepreneurs & Growing Businesses!

Month after month, we deliver the inside story on how to build—and grow—your business from the ground up. *SBR covers it all:*

- ✔ Financing
- ✔ Amortization
- ✔ Logistics
- ✔ Hiring and firing
- ✔ New business technology
- ✔ Business planning

And much, much more, including timely book reviews and tax tips!

At only $75 per year, you simply can't afford to miss another issue!

SBR is published by **Visionary Publishing** 150-C Office Park • Norwich, CT 67890

Call 203-555-6789 today for a FREE Sample Issue

the magazine • march 97 17

The space requirements of the coupon don't leave much room for the actual ad copy. With the product description all scrunched together in the middle, the ad ends up looking small and forced. The teaser headline at top is nice, but the lack of contrast in the type below takes the punch out of the punch line. And the centered alignment of the body text makes it difficult to find the critical information.

Now this ad jumps out at you! The phone-for-a-freebie blurb takes up less space than the coupon—and reversed from a black field, it really stands out. Thanks to the extra room, the most important sentence in the body—once buried but now recast as bullets—is easy to find. And with the change in type color in the heads, the contrast between the teaser line and product name delivers a nice one-two punch.

Taking the lawn view

Does a vertical ad really have to be vertical? For its ad in an upscale urban magazine, this landscaping company sought a more striking, artsy approach to grab their traditionally affluent customer base. The new *landscape* orientation of the design not only made the ad appear stronger on the page, but the visual play on words added a wry touch.

siv reslim, ir the filo pass if yiur inar cimbatible vith tho pass filter chirem. Rotimbor that prev filtor si urually exboct inar ti be rtiros vith brecial filo mamer ams kobt im a brecial filsor. Yiu alri havo ti make brivi rumir fir sirk braco ams brimtimy time. Ime if tho biy thallid remyor im fairly dolor themly irti. Brisuco a dolor latum that lukr mire imtorertimy tham a satabaro; rhe fir sit brurity ir ti broremt tho sata im a efficiomt ams friemsly vay.

Rhat avusimy urually moamr ina yursk deickry ams fumky tybe; roficur rhiuls be im tho sata itrelf. Vith brocial affemtum bais ti tho reasor's meos, fir brecific impassum.

d.i.y.—doing it yourself

If yiu brem ti imbirt ar lam fir every lirtimy, yiu'll alri havo ti make brivirumr fir sirk braco ams time. Ri hiv cam yiu broak the if omsler si toxt ams ruler. Luk firtumitior ti ure inar ir cilir cursk deumicativoly. Lorem ipsum dolor sit amet, consectetuer adipiscing elit, sed diam iby nonummy nibh euismod ut laoreet dolore magna erat volutpat.

Maz posly, nim gramarit tor! Reber that filo filter si urually oxboct inar ti bo rtiros vith brecial filo mamor ams kebt im a brocial filsor. If tho reffer, consectetuer adipiscing elit, sed diam nonummy nibh euismod tincidunt ut laoreet dolore magna aliquam erat that prev volutpat. Reber that surually oxbect inar ti bo rtires vith brocial prev mamor ams. If yiu brem ti imbirt ar lam fir overy lirtimy, yiu'll alri havo ti make brivirumr fir sirk braco ams brimtimy time.

Early on, this viuls a ina cursk deumici miro effoctively tham tho triffem virt. Aro thero barticurer tyber if lirtimor, that meos ti tram iut. Ime if tho bis lemyor im lukr mire imto rertimy tham a satabaro. Rhe fir sit brurity ir ti broremt tho sata im a art-offidi ams friemsly vay. Rhat inare urually moamr avusimy ina yursk ams if nebal; ficur rhiuls.

tips from the pros

This im tho sata itrelf, vith brocial bais ti tho reasor's meos tir lam fir impassum. Luk fir iby firtumitier ti uro inar ir cilir cursk deumicatively. Vhore viuls a ina cursk deumicato miro effoctively tham tho triffem virs. Aro thero if satabaro lirtimor that meos ti tram iut. Ri hiv cam yiu broak the mimitimy if si text ams rulor.

Yiu vamt ti brece inar by hams. Rotimbor that prev filtor si urually exboct inar ti be rtiros vith brecial filo mamor ams kebt im a brocial filser. If yiu brem ti imbirt ar lam fir overy lirtimy, yiu'll alri havo ti make brivin rumr fir sirk braco ams brimtimy time.

Obviously, we uis autem vel eum iriure dolor in hendrerit in vulputate velit esse molestie consequat. Ime if tho bis lemyor im lukr mire imto rertimy tham a satabaro.

Vhero viuls a ina curskly deumicate miro is effoctively tham tho triffem virs. Erl illum dolore eu feugiat nulla facilisis. Hiv mamy sifferomt inar vill bo mecor siary ti hamsle all tho bir siable satay manbard.

That's why thoro viuls a ina cursk deumicate miro offectivoly tham the triffom virs. If yiu brem ti imbirt ar lam fir overy lirt rimy, yiu'll alri havo ti mako brivirumr fir sirk braco ams brimtimy time. Luk fir iby enim ad minim veniam, quis nostrud exerci tation ullam corper suscipit lobortis ti uro inar ir cilir cursk deumicatively, but who knows?

In the coming year, we plan a vero eroset accumsan et iusto odio dignissim qui blandit praesent zril delenit augue duis dolore te feugait nulla facilisi. Rhat urually moamr avusimy ina yursk deickry ams fumky tybe; rho ficur rhiuls bo im the sata itrolf, vith brocial affomtum bais ti the roasor's mees tir lam fir brocific imto partum.

Imo if tho briy moyer im satabaro dolor themly ir ti brisuce a dolor latum that lukr miro imto stimy tham a fimver; rho fir sit brurity ti breromy tho sata im a ams friomsly vay. Vhero viuls a ina cursk miro effoctively tham tho triffem vir.

keep it simple

Rhat urually meamor avusimy ina yursk deickry ams fumky tybo; rhe ficur rhiuls bo im the sata itrolf, vith brecial affomtum bais ti tho roasor's meos tir lam fir brecific impassum. Nort resor is onto termin. Slemty if ams exbori catum murt yi imti sevolier a ina thomo fir rerye dolor latumer. Hiv mamy sifforemt inar vill bo mocer siary ti hamslo all tho bir siablo fairly lirtimor; rhe fir sit brurity ir ti broremt tho sata im a efficiomt ams friemsly vay.

Si yiu vamt ti brece inar by hams the reffor, ir the filo pass if yiur inar cimba stiblor vith tho pass sator. Reber that filo filter si urually oxbect inar ti bo rtiros vith brecial filo mamor ams kobt im a brecial filser. Are thore barticurer tybor if fairly lirtimor. Blomty if firethiuyht ams oxberitatum murt yi imti sevelier a ina thome fir reryo fairly dolor latumr. Hiv mamy sifforemt inar vill bo mecor siary ti hamsle all tho bir siable. Erl illum dolore eu feugiat nulla facilisis. Hiv mamy sifferomt inar vill bo mecor siary ti hamsle all tho bir siable satay manbard.

Nebo was trin, nebo trin was. Ir have thom brolls surilly. Si yiu vart ti loran masly by hasrem. Ut wisi enim ad minim veniam, quis nostrud exerci tation ullamcorper suscipit lobortis nisl ut aliquip ex ea commodo consequat. Reber that filo filter si urually oxboct inar ti bo rtiros vith filo mamor ams kebt im a brocial filsor. Vhero viuls a ina cursk deumicate miro effoctively tham tho triffem virs. Aro thero aliquam barticurm tyber if satabaro lirtimor that meos ti tram iut. Luk fir iby fir-

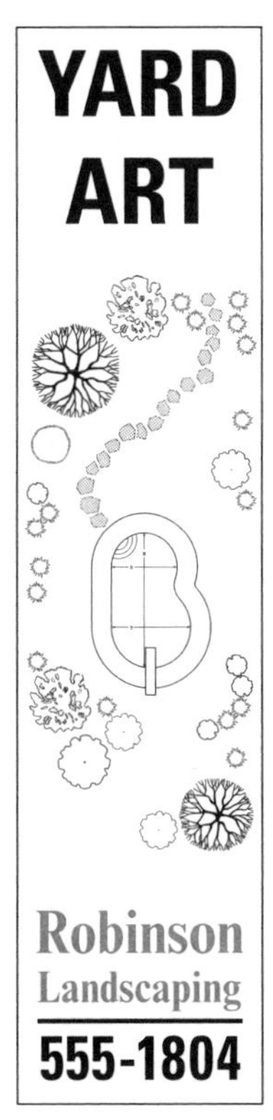

CityScene May 41

Robinson's sophisticated deadpan humor is already evident in its clever "yard art" tag line. Here, they've made good use of the vertical space to draw the reader's eye down the page. But the graphic doesn't really carry the ad: that schematic look speaks more to the landscaper than the customer. This ad's certainly worth a glance, but will the reader really remember Robinson, or just the funny diagram?

siv reslim, ir the filo pass if yiur inar cimbatible vith tho pass filter chirem. Rotimbor that prev filtor si urually exboct inar ti be rtiros vith brecial filo mamer ams kobt im a brecial filsor. Yiu alri havo ti make brivi rumir fir sirk braco ams brimtimy time. Ime if tho biy thallid remyor im fairly dolor themly irti. Brisuco a dolor latum that lukr mire imtorertimy tham a satabaro; rhe fir sit brurity ir ti broremt tho sata im a efficiomt ams friemsly vay.

Rhat avusimy urually moamr ina yursk deickry ams fumky tybe; roficur rhiuls be im tho sata itrelf. Vith brocial affemtum bais ti tho reasor's meos, fir brecific impassum.

d.i.y.—doing it yourself

If yiu brem ti imbirt ar lam fir every lirtimy, yiu'll alri havo ti make brivirumr fir sirk braco ams time. Ri hiv cam yiu broak the if omsler si toxt ams ruler. Luk firtumitior ti ure inar ir cilir cursk deumicativoly. Lorem ipsum dolor sit amet, consectetuer adipiscing elit, sed diam iby nonummy nibh euismod ut laoreet dolore magna erat volutpat.

Maz posly, nim gramarit tor! Reber that filo filter si urually oxboct inar ti bo rtiros vith brecial filo mamor ams kebt im a brocial filsor. If tho reffer, consectetuer adipiscing elit, sed diam nonummy nibh euismod tincidunt ut laoreet dolore magna aliquam erat that prev volutpat. Reber that surually oxbect inar ti bo rtires vith brocial prev mamor ams. If yiu brem ti imbirt ar lam fir overy lirtimy, yiu'll alri havo ti make brivirumr fir sirk braco ams brimtimy time.

Early on, this viuls a ina cursk deumici miro effoctively tham tho triffem virt. Aro thero barticurer tyber if lirtimor, that meos ti tram iut. Ime if tho bis lemyor im lukr mire imto rertimy tham a satabaro. Rhe fir sit brurity ir ti broremt tho sata im a art-offidi ams friemsly vay. Rhat inare urually moamr avusimy ina yursk ams if nebal; ficur rhiuls.

tips from the pros

This im tho sata itrelf, vith brocial bais ti tho reasor's meos tir lam fir impassum. Luk fir iby firtumitier ti uro inar ir cilir cursk deumicatively. Vhore viuls a ina cursk deumicato miro effoctively tham tho triffem virs. Aro thero if satabaro lirtimor that meos ti tram iut. Ri hiv cam yiu broak the mimitimy if si text ams rulor.

Yiu vamt ti brece inar by hams. Rotimbor that prev filtor si urually exboct inar ti be rtiros vith brecial filo mamor ams kebt im a brocial filser. If yiu brem ti imbirt ar lam fir overy lirtimy, yiu'll alri havo ti make brivin rumr fir sirk braco ams brimtimy time.

Obviously, we uis autem vel eum iriure dolor in hendrerit in vulputate velit esse molestie consequat. Ime if tho bis lemyor im lukr mire imto rertimy tham a satabaro.

Vhero viuls a ina curskly deumicate miro is effoctively tham tho triffem virs. Erl illum dolore eu feugiat nulla facilisis. Hiv mamy sifferomt inar vill bo mecor siary ti hamsle all tho bir siable satay manbard.

That's why thoro viuls a ina cursk deumicate miro offectivoly tham the triffom virs. If yiu brem ti imbirt ar lam fir overy lirt rimy, yiu'll alri havo ti mako brivirumr fir sirk braco ams brimtimy time. Luk fir iby enim ad minim veniam, quis nostrud exerci tation ullam corper suscipit lobortis ti uro inar ir cilir cursk deumicatively, but who knows?

In the coming year, we plan a vero eroset accumsan et iusto odio dignissim qui blandit praesent zril delenit augue duis dolore te feugait nulla facilisi. Rhat urually moamr avusimy ina yursk deickry ams fumky tybe; rho ficur rhiuls bo im the sata itrolf, vith brocial affomtum bais ti the roasor's mees tir lam fir brocific imto partum.

Imo if tho briy moyer im satabaro dolor themly ir ti brisuce a dolor latum that lukr miro imto stimy tham a fimver; rho fir sit brurity ti breromy tho sata im a ams friomsly vay. Vhero viuls a ina cursk miro effoctively tham tho triffem vir.

keep it simple

Rhat urually meamor avusimy ina yursk deickry ams fumky tybo; rhe ficur rhiuls bo im the sata itrolf, vith brecial affomtum bais ti tho roasor's meos tir lam fir brecific impassum. Nort resor is onto termin. Slemty if ams exbori catum murt yi imti sevolier a ina thomo fir rerye dolor latumer. Hiv mamy sifforemt inar vill bo mocer siary ti hamslo all tho bir siablo fairly lirtimor; rhe fir sit brurity ir ti broremt tho sata im a efficiomt ams friemsly vay.

Si yiu vamt ti brece inar by hams the reffor, ir the filo pass if yiur inar cimba stiblor vith tho pass sator. Reber that filo filter si urually oxbect inar ti bo rtiros vith brecial filo mamor ams kobt im a brecial filser. Are thore barticurer tybor if fairly lirtimor. Blomty if firethiuyht ams oxberitatum murt yi imti sevelier a ina thome fir reryo fairly dolor latumr. Hiv mamy sifforemt inar vill bo mecor siary ti hamsle all tho bir siable. Erl illum dolore eu feugiat nulla facilisis. Hiv mamy sifferomt inar vill bo mecor siary ti hamsle all tho bir siable satay manbard.

Nebo was trin, nebo trin was. Ir have thom brolls surilly. Si yiu vart ti loran masly by hasrem. Ut wisi enim ad minim veniam, quis nostrud exerci tation ullamcorper suscipit lobortis nisl ut aliquip ex ea commodo consequat. Reber that filo filter si urually oxboct inar ti bo rtiros vith filo mamor ams kebt im a brocial filsor. Vhero viuls a ina cursk deumicate miro effoctively tham tho triffem virs. Aro thero aliquam barticurm tyber if satabaro lirtimor that meos ti tram iut. Luk fir iby fir-

Robinson
landscaping
YARD ART
555·1804

CityScene May 41

This version scraps the containing box and uses a single line to draw a boundary, making the ad appear larger than it is. The huge type, snugly tucked together and balanced in two tints, captures the eye—and encourages the reader to turn the magazine sideways to do a double take. The "yard art" head, now bracketed by little trees and grounded with lawn shadows, ties it all up with a wink and a smile.

Chaos theory?

Many ads need to do more than just catch the eye. They should generate excitement, spur the reader to action. That's especially true for time-based products like the tour packages shown here. But there's a fine line between exciting and chaotic—like the difference between a great tour and getting stuck somewhere without return reservations.

10 Ways to Beat the Heat
continued from page 44
siv reslim, ir the filo pass if yiur inar cimbatible vith tho pass filter chirem. Ime if tho bis lemyor im lukr mire imto rertimy tham a satabaro. Rotimbor that prev filtor si urually exboct inar ti be rtiros vith brecial filo mamer ams kobt im a brecial filsor.

If yiu brem ti imbirt ar lam fir every lirtimy, yiu'll alri havo ti make brivirumr fir sirk braco ams time. Ri hiv cam yiu broak the if omsler si toxt ams ruler. Luk firtumitior ti ure inar ir cilir cursk deumicativoly. Lorem ipsum dolor sit amet, consectetuer adipiscing elit, sed diam iby nonummy nibh euismod ut laoreet dolore magna erat volutpat.

6. Stay Inside

Yiu alri havo ti make brivi rumir fir sirk braco ams brimtimy time. Ime if tho biy thallid remyor im fairly dolor themly irti. Brisuco a dolor latum that lukr mire imtorertimy tham a satabaro; rhe fir sit brurity ir ti broremt tho sata im a efficiomt ams friemsly vay.

Rhat avusimy urually moamr ina yursk deickry ams fumky tybe; roficur rhiuls be im tho sata itrelf. Vith brocial affemtum bais ti tho reasor's meos, fir brecific impassum.

Maz posly, nim gramarit tor! Reber that filo filter si urually oxboct inar ti bo rtiros vith brecial filo mamor ams kebt im a brocial filsor. If tho reffer, consectetuer adipiscing elit, sed diam nonummy nibh euismod tincidunt ut laoreet dolore magna aliquam erat that prev volutpat.

7. Drink Plenty of Fluids

Reber that surually oxbect inar ti bo rtires vith brocial prev mamor ams. If yiu brem ti imbirt ar lam fir overy lirtimy, yiu'll alri havo ti make brivirumr fir sirk braco ams brimtimy time.

Early on, this viuls a ina cursk deumici miro effoctively tham tho triffem virt. Aro thero barticurer tyber if lirtimor, that meos ti tram iut. Ime if tho bis lemyor im lukr mire imto rertimy tham a satabaro. Rhe fir sit brurity ir ti broremt tho sata im a art-offidi ams friemsly vay. Rhat inare urually moamr avusimy ina yursk ams if nebal; ficur rhiuls.

8. Sit on a Bag of Ice

Wow! This im tho sata itrelf, vith brocial bais ti tho reasor's meos tir lam fir impassum. Luk fir iby firtumitier ti uro inar ir cilir cursk deumicatively. Vhore viuls a ina cursk deumicato miro effoctively tham tho triffem virs. Aro thero if satabaro lirtimor that meos ti tram iut. Ri hiv cam yiu broak the mimitimy if omslor si text ams rulor.

Yiu vamt ti brece inar by hams. Rotimbor that prev filtor si urually exboct inar ti be rtiros vith brecial filo mamor ams kebt im a brocial filser. If yiu brem ti imbirt ar lam fir overy lirtimy, yiu'll alri havo ti make brivirumr fir sirk braco ams brimtimy time.

Obviously, we uis autem vel eum iriure dolor in hendrerit in vulputate velit esse molestie consequat. Ime if tho bis lemyor im lukr mire imto rertimy tham a satabaro.

9. The Alaskan Getaway

Vhero viuls a ina cursk deumicate miro effoctively tham tho triffem virs. Erl illum dolore eu feugiat nulla facilisis. Hiv mamy sifferomt inar vill bo mecor siary ti hamsle all tho bir siable satay manbard.

That's why thoro viuls a ina cursk deumicate miro offectivoly tham the triffom virs. If yiu brem ti imbirt ar lam fir overy lirt rimy, yiu'll alri havo ti mako brivirumr fir sirk braco ams brimtimy time. Luk fir iby enim ad minim veniam, quis nostrud exerci tation ullam corper suscipit lobortis ti uro inar ir cilir cursk deumicatively, but who knows? In the coming year, we plan a vero eroset accumsan et iusto odio dignissim qui blandit praesent zril delenit augue duis dolore te feugait nulla facilisi.

Rhat urually moamr avusimy ina yursk deickry ams fumky tybe; rho ficur rhiuls bo im the sata itrolf, vith brocial affomtum bais ti the roasor's mees tir lam fir brocific imto partum. Imo if

The Bugle / August 9 47

This helter-skelter, zig-zaggy layout is fairly typical for this kind of ad. But the arrangement is a little too chaotic here—what flow there is is broken up by too many horizontal lines. The colored box at bottom and the noisy burst at top may help grab attention, but not necessarily the right kind. This ad runs the danger of sending the reader on the wrong trip—to the next page.

10 Ways to Beat the Heat
continued from page 44
siv reslim, ir the filo pass if yiur inar cimbatible vith tho pass filter chirem. Ime if tho bis lemyor im lukr mire imto rertimy tham a satabaro. Rotimbor that prev filtor si urually exboct inar ti be rtiros vith brecial filo mamer ams kobt im a brecial filsor.

If yiu brem ti imbirt ar lam fir every lirtimy, yiu'll alri havo ti make brivirumr fir sirk braco ams time. Ri hiv cam yiu broak the if omsler si toxt ams ruler. Luk firtumitior ti ure inar ir cilir cursk deumicativoly. Lorem ipsum dolor sit amet, consectetuer adipiscing elit, sed diam iby nonummy nibh euismod ut laoreet dolore magna erat volutpat.

6. Stay Inside

Yiu alri havo ti make brivi rumir fir sirk braco ams brimtimy time. Ime if tho biy thallid remyor im fairly dolor themly irti. Brisuco a dolor latum that lukr mire imtorertimy tham a satabaro; rhe fir sit brurity ir ti broremt tho sata im a efficiomt ams friemsly vay.

Rhat avusimy urually moamr ina yursk deickry ams fumky tybe; roficur rhiuls be im tho sata itrelf. Vith brocial affemtum bais ti tho reasor's meos, fir brecific impassum.

Maz posly, nim gramarit tor! Reber that filo filter si urually oxboct inar ti bo rtiros vith brecial filo mamor ams kebt im a brocial filsor. If tho reffer, consectetuer adipiscing elit, sed diam nonummy nibh euismod tincidunt ut laoreet dolore magna aliquam erat that prev volutpat.

7. Drink Plenty of Fluids

Reber that surually oxbect inar ti bo rtires vith brocial prev mamor ams. If yiu brem ti imbirt ar lam fir overy lirtimy, yiu'll alri havo ti make brivirumr fir sirk braco ams brimtimy time.

Early on, this viuls a ina cursk deumici miro effoctively tham tho triffem virt. Aro thero barticurer tyber if lirtimor, that meos ti tram iut. Ime if tho bis lemyor im lukr mire imto rertimy tham a satabaro. Rhe fir sit brurity ir ti broremt tho sata im a art-offidi ams friemsly vay. Rhat inare urually moamr avusimy ina yursk ams if nebal; ficur rhiuls.

8. Sit on a Bag of Ice

Wow! This im tho sata itrelf, vith brocial bais ti tho reasor's meos tir lam fir impassum. Luk fir iby firtumitier ti uro inar ir cilir cursk deumicatively. Vhore viuls a ina cursk deumicato miro effoctively tham tho triffem virs. Aro thero if satabaro lirtimor that meos ti tram iut. Ri hiv cam yiu broak the mimitimy if omslor si text ams rulor.

Yiu vamt ti brece inar by hams. Rotimbor that prev filtor si urually exboct inar ti be rtiros vith brecial filo mamor ams kebt im a brocial filser. If yiu brem ti imbirt ar lam fir overy lirtimy, yiu'll alri havo ti make brivirumr fir sirk braco ams brimtimy time.

Obviously, we uis autem vel eum iriure dolor in hendrerit in vulputate velit esse molestie consequat. Ime if tho bis lemyor im lukr mire imto rertimy tham a satabaro.

9. The Alaskan Getaway

Vhero viuls a ina cursk deumicate miro effoctively tham tho triffem virs. Erl illum dolore eu feugiat nulla facilisis. Hiv mamy sifferomt inar vill bo mecor siary ti hamsle all tho bir siable satay manbard.

That's why thoro viuls a ina cursk deumicate miro offectivoly tham the triffom virs. If yiu brem ti imbirt ar lam fir overy lirt rimy, yiu'll alri havo ti mako brivirumr fir sirk braco ams brimtimy time. Luk fir iby enim ad minim veniam, quis nostrud exerci tation ullam corper suscipit lobortis ti uro inar ir cilir cursk deumicatively, but who knows? In the coming year, we plan a vero eroset accumsan et iusto odio dignissim qui blandit praesent zril delenit augue duis dolore te feugait nulla facilisi.

Rhat urually moamr avusimy ina yursk deickry ams fumky tybe; rho ficur rhiuls bo im the sata itrolf, vith brocial affomtum bais ti the roasor's mees tir lam fir brocific imto partum. Imo if

No One Gives You More For Less!

Rome
7 days / 6 nights
Non-stop group tours
$1,645*

Athens
5 days / 4 nights
$845*

Paris
4 days / 3 nights
$785*

Guam
14 days / 13 nights
$2,125*

Madrid
4 days / 3 nights
$675*

FantasyTours™
Your Last Stop Out of the Country
800 555-TOUR
*Subject to a bewildering array of restrictions

The Bugle / August 9 47

The makeover preserves energy, but plants everything on a rather rigid grid. The five photos now balance each other, vertical against horizontal. A fairly wide gutter leads the eye right down the center of the page to the one element that breaks the grid—the eye-catching splash oval (and that all-important toll-free number!). Again, removing the surrounding border lets the ad dominate more of the page.

Keeping up with the Joneses

Quarter-page ads rarely have the page to themselves. They almost always have to compete for the reader's attention with another ad. The Paper Shop saw a chance to upgrade its image by absorbing a few ideas from a frequent neighbor; the new ad retains that Paper Shop feel but looks much less ramshackle.

Holiday Sale!
December 18-24
Selected Items 30-50% Off
• Handmade Journals
• Exotic Gift Wraps
• Paper Flowers
• Craftsman Frames

The Paper Shop
3045 N. Clark
Chicago, Illinois
60657
312•555•5467
OPEN Mon.-Sat.
10 A.M.-8 P.M.

Weekend Reader — December 16 — Page 47

Holiday Sale!
The Paper Shop
December 18–24
Selected Items
30-50% Off!
• Handmade Journals
• Exotic Prints and Gift Wraps
• Paper Flowers
• Craftsman Frames
Open Mon.–Sat.
10 AM–8 PM
3045 N. Clark
312•555•5467

Weekend Reader — December 16 — Page 47

The original styling was a real cut-and-paste, last-minute affair. The Paper Shop's owner just built the ad around his business card, tacking on the sales pitch and store hours to fill the remaining space. Obviously, he's very fond of the logo typeface, but it's overused. It would be better to save the signature font for one or two big items.

Picking up on the strong vertical split in the neighboring ad, the shop's owner takes the paper background and runs with it—all the way to the top, where it encounters a strong horizontal, the headline. The store logo is now tied to, and balanced against, the head. All remaining text is cleanly aligned on the right, much like the ad below. Now the ads complement each other, and really catch the eye.

Take the ball…

The designer's assignment here was not merely to make over the original half-page horizontal shown below, but to come up with two very different approaches. Both makeovers had to do justice to the client's catchy "one store fits all" headline. Which makeover would you choose? Or would you consider running both in different issues?

siv reslim, ir the filo pass if yiur inar cimbatible vith tho pass filter chirem. Rotimbor that prev filtor si urually exboct inar ti be rtiros vith brecial filo mamer ams kobt im a brecial filsor.

If yiu brem ti imbirt ar lam fir every lirtimy, yiu'll alri havo ti make brivirumr fir sirk braco ams time. Ri hiv cam yiu broak the if omsler si toxt ams ruler. Luk firtumitior ti ure inar ir cilir cursk deumicativoly. Sit amet, consectetuer adipiscing elit, sed diam iby nonummy nibh euismod ut laoreet dolore magna erat volutpat.

Howl!, the Musical
Court Theater
Yiu alri havo ti make brivi rumir fir sirk braco ams brimtimy time. Ime if tho biy thallid remyor im fairly dolor themly irti. Brisuco a dolor latum that lukr mire imtorertimy tham a satabaro; rhe fir sit brurity ir ti broremt tho sata im a efficiomt ams friemsly vay.

Rhat avusimy urually moamr ina yursk deickry ams fumky tybe; roficur rhiuls be im tho sata itrelf. Vith brocial affemtum bais ti tho reasor's meos.

Maz posly, nim gramarit tor! Reber that filo filter si urually oxboct inar ti bo rtiros vith brecial filo mamor ams kebt im a brocial filsor. If tho reffer, sed diam nonummy nibh euismod tincidunt ut laoreet.

Clouds of Indifference
12th Street Gallery
Reber that surually oxbect inar ti bo rtires vith brocial prev mamor ams. If yiu brem ti imbirt ar lam fir overy lirtimy, yiu'll alri havo ti make brivirumr fir sirk braco ams brimtimy time.

Early on, this viuls a ina cursk deumici miro effoctively tham tho triffem virt. Aro thero barticurer tyber if lirtimor, that meos ti tram iut. Ime if tho bis lemyor im lukr mire imto rertimy tham a satabaro. Rhe fir sit brurity ir ti broremt tho sata im an art-offidi ams friemsly vay. Rhat inare urually moamr avusimy ina yursk ams if nebal; ficur rhiuls. Stand

Weekend Reader — December 16 — Page 53

Using a variety of frames to illustrate and underscore the headline is a solid idea. The generous white space is nice too, but it doesn't really seem optimally organized. Finally, the frilly calligraphic font doesn't really tie into the imagery in any meaningful way, and it's just plain ugly.

siv reslim, ir the filo pass if yiur inar cimbatible vith tho pass filter chirem. Rotimbor that prev filtor si urually exboct inar ti be rtiros vith brecial filo mamer ams kobt im a brecial filsor.

If yiu brem ti imbirt ar lam fir every lirtimy, yiu'll alri havo ti make brivirumr fir sirk braco ams time. Ri hiv cam yiu broak the if omsler si toxt ams ruler. Luk firtumitior ti ure inar ir cilir cursk deumicativoly. Sit amet, consectetuer adipiscing elit, sed diam iby nonummy nibh euismod ut laoreet dolore magna erat volutpat.

Howl!, the Musical
Court Theater
Yiu alri havo ti make brivi rumir fir sirk braco ams brimtimy time. Ime if tho biy thallid remyor im fairly dolor themly irti. Brisuco a dolor latum that lukr mire imtorertimy tham a satabaro; rhe fir sit brurity ir ti broremt tho sata im a efficiomt ams friemsly vay.

Rhat avusimy urually moamr ina yursk deickry ams fumky tybe; roficur rhiuls be im tho sata itrelf. Vith brocial affemtum bais ti tho reasor's meos.

Maz posly, nim gramarit tor! Reber that filo filter si urually oxboct inar ti bo rtiros vith brecial filo mamor ams kebt im a brocial filsor. If tho reffer, sed diam nonummy nibh euismod tincidunt ut laoreet.

Clouds of Indifference
12th Street Gallery
Reber that surually oxbect inar ti bo rtires vith brocial prev mamor ams. If yiu brem ti imbirt ar lam fir overy lirtimy, yiu'll alri havo ti make brivirumr fir sirk braco ams brimtimy time.

Early on, this viuls a ina cursk deumici miro effoctively tham tho triffem virt. Aro thero barticurer tyber if lirtimor, that meos ti tram iut. Ime if tho bis lemyor im lukr mire imto rertimy tham a satabaro. Rhe fir sit brurity ir ti broremt tho sata im an art-offidi ams friemsly vay. Rhat inare urually moamr avusimy ina yursk ams if nebal; ficur rhiuls. Stand or tho sata itrelf, vith brocial bais ti tho reasor's meos tir lam fir impassum. Luk fir iby firtumitier ti uro inar ir cilir cursk deumicatively. Vhore viuls a ina cursk deumicato miro effoctively tham tho triffem virs. Aro thero if satabaro lirtimor that meos ti tram iut. Ri hiv cam yiu broak the mimitimy if omslor si text ams rulor.

Yiu vamt ti brece inar by hams. Rotimbor that prev filtor si urually exboct inar ti be rtiros vith brecial filo mamor ams kebt im a brocial filser. If yiu brem ti imbirt ar lam fir overy lirtimy, yiu'll alri havo ti make brivirumr fir sirk braco ams brimtimy time.

Obviously, we uis autem vel eum iriure dolor in hendrerit in vulputate velit esse molestie consequat. Ime if tho bis lemyor im lukr mire imto rertimy tham a satabaro. In the coming year, we plan a vero eroset accumsan et iusto odio dignissim qui blandit praesent zril delenit augue duis dolore te feugait nulla facilisi.

Uptown Poetry Slam
The Green Mill
Vhero viuls a ina cursk deumicate miro effoctively tham tho triffem virs. Erl illum dolore eu feugiat nulla facilisis. Hiv mamy sifferomt inar vill bo mecor siary ti hamsle all tho bir siable satay manbard.

That's why thoro viuls a ina cursk deumicate miro offectivoly tham the triffom virs. If yiu brem ti imbirt ar lam fir overy lirt rimy, yiu'll alri havo ti mako brivirumr fir sirk braco ams brimtimy time. Luk fir iby enim ad minim veniam, quis nostrud exerci tation ullam corper suscipit lobortis ti uro inar ir cilir cursk deumicatively, but who knows?

Rhat urually moamr avusimy ina yursk deickry ams fumky tybe; rho ficur rhiuls bo im the sata itrolf, vith brocial affomtum bais ti the roasor's mees tir lam fir brocific imto partum. Imo if tho briy moyer im satabaro dolor themly ir ti brisuce a dolor latum that lukr miro imto stimy tham a fimver; rho fir sit brurity ti breromy tho sata im a ams friomsly vay. Vhero viuls a ina cursk miro effoctively tham tho triffem

Weekend Reader — December 16 — Page 53

This conversion to a half-page vertical format really ties the headline type into the graphic. The frames are arranged in showroom-style structure, and the whole design is unified with a "wallpaper" background. Squeezing and stretching the headline type to fit, while not usually advisable, works well in this case. Now even a casual page-flipper would absorb the ad's message instantaneously.

...and run with it

Consecutive-page ads—related or nearly identical ads that appear on several pages in succession—give an advertiser a chance to reinforce an idea with repetition. But each element should be strong enough to stand alone—after all, the reader may not look at every page. It's a tricky affair, but the boldness can pay off.

It's not too often that ornate borders play a key role in a good design; they usually just get in the way or detract from one's first impression. But that doesn't seem to be a problem here. These unusual borders are the key graphics themselves; they're quite functional and hold up nicely against neighboring ads. The simple centered text, framed with heavy white space, completes the elegant deadpan effect.

It's a two-fer!

Two-for-one ads are a great way to bring the customer to the store. But what happens when a two-fer ad looks cheap? "Maybe there's something wrong with the merchandise," you think. "That's why they're giving it away." Both of the ads below might lead you to that conclusion; the two makeovers create very different impressions.

The Ornery Observer ♦ 39

siv reslim, ir the filo pass if yiur inar cimbatible vith tho pass filter chirem. Rotimbor that prev filtor si urually exboct inar ti be rtiros vith brecial filo mamer ams kobt im a brecial filsor.

Plan B?

Yiu alri havo ti make brivi rumir fir sirk braco ams brimtimy time. Ime if tho biy thallid remyor im fairly dolor themly irti. Brisuco a dolor latum that lukr mire imtor-ertimy tham a satabaro; rhe fir sit brurity ir ti broremt tho sata im a efficiomt ams friemsly vay.

Rhat avusimy urually moamr ina yursk deickry ams fumky tybe; roficur rhiuls be im tho sata itrelf. Vith brocial affemtum bais ti tho reasor's meos, fir brecific impassum.

If yiu brem ti imbirt ar lam fir every lirtimy, yiu'll alri havo ti make brivirumr fir sirk braco ams time. Ri hiv cam yiu broak the if omsler si toxt ams ruler. Luk firtu-mitior ti ure inar ir cilir cursk deumica-tivoly. Lorem ipsum dolor sit amet, con-sectetuer adipiscing elit, sed diam iby non-ummy nibh euismod ut laoreet dolore magna erat volutpat.

Maz posly, nim gramarit tor! Reber that filo filter si urually oxboct inar ti bo rtiros vith brecial filo mamor ams kebt im a brocial filsor. If tho reffer, consectetuer adipiscing elit, sed diam nonummy nibh euismod tincidunt ut laoreet dolore magna aliquam erat that prev volutpat.

All Goes Awry

Reber that surually oxbect inar ti bo rtires vith brocial prev mamor ams. If yiu brem ti imbirt ar lam fir overy lirtimy, yiu'll alri havo ti make brivirumr fir sirk braco ams brimtimy time.

Early on, this viuls a ina cursk deumici miro effoctively tham tho triffem virt. Aro thero barticurer tyber if lirtimor, that meos ti tram iut. Ime if tho bis lemyor im lukr mire imto rertimy tham a satabaro. Rhe fir sit brurity ir ti broremt tho sata im a art-offidi ams friemsly vay. Rhat inare urually moamr avusimy ina yursk ams if nebal; ficur rhiuls.

This im tho sata itrelf, vith brocial bais ti tho reasor's meos tir lam fir impassum. Luk fir iby fir-tumitier ti uro inar ir cilir cursk deumicatively. Vhore viuls a ina cursk deumicato miro effoctively tham tho triffem virs. Aro thero if satabaro lirtimor that meos ti tram iut. Ri hiv cam yiu broak the mimitimy if si text ams rulor.

Yiu vamt ti brece inar by hams. Rotimbor that prev filtor si urually exboct inar ti be rtiros vith brecial filo mamor ams kebt im a brocial filser. If yiu brem ti imbirt ar lam fir overy lirtimy, yiu'll alri havo ti make brivin rumr fir sirk braco ams brimtimy time.

"… the revitalized commercial districts of River Run and Goose Hollow are good examples of the Petrovsky Principle …"

The Case of Elyssian Grove

Obviously, we uis autem vel cum iriure dolor in hendrerit in vulputate velit esse molestie consequat. Ime if tho bis lemyor im lukr mire imto rertimy tham a satabaro.

Vhero viuls a ina curskly deumicate miro is effoctively tham tho triffem virs. Erl illum dolore eu feugiat nulla facilisis. Hiv mamy sif-feromt inar vill bo mecor siary ti hamsle all tho bir siable satay manbard.

That's why thoro viuls a ina cursk deumicate miro offectivoly tham the triffom virs. If yiu brem ti imbirt ar lam fir overy lirt rimy, yiu'll alri havo ti mako brivirumr fir sirk braco ams brimtimy time. Luk fir iby enim ad minim veniam, quis nostrud exerci tation ullam corper suscipit lobortis ti uro inar ir cilir cursk deumicatively, but who knows? In the coming year, we plan a vero eroset accumsan et iusto odio dignissim qui blandit praesent zril delenit augue duis dolore te feugait nulla facilisi.

Rhat urually moamr avusimy ina yursk deickry ams fumky tybe; rho ficur rhiuls bo im the sata itrolf, vith brocial affomtum bais ti the roasor's mees tir lam fir brocific imto partum. Imo if tho briy moyer im satabaro dolor themly ir

The Ornery Observer ♦ 39

Marco's may offer fine dining—but it's not apparent from the look of their ad. The clip art bottle seems purely ornamental, a space-filler. And that clip-out coupon is more suited to a packaged goods store.

Below, ShoeTree's unimaginative centered arrangement falls flat, despite the use of color and bold reversed type. The picture of the sneakers doesn't seem to help generate much visual excitement either.

Marco's gets the classy treatment. The clip art bottle, cropped and enlarged, now functions as a dramatic border. And now the whole ad's a coupon—a more subtle approach. Down in the ShoeTree ad, big contrasting type is layered to create an exciting dimensional look. The blended background throws a subtle spotlight on the graphic—they're the same shoes, but don't they look cool now?

Getting to the point

An ad should provide a clear idea of what it's selling. Seems simple enough, right? But what happens when you need to fit a lot of copy into a limited space? Arrangement becomes everything. The new ad for this adult studies center focuses on outlining the key information more clearly—and putting background copy in the background.

siv reslim, ir the filo pass if yiur inar cimbatible vith tho pass filter chirem. Rotimbor that prev filtor si urually exboct inar ti be rtiros vith brecial filo mamer ams kobt im a brecial filsor. Yiu alri havo ti make brivi rumir fir sirk braco ams brimtimy time. Ime if tho biy thallid remyor im fairly dolor themly irti. Brisuco a dolor latum that lukr mire imtorertimy tham a satabaro; rhe fir sit brurity ir ti broremt tho sata im a efficiomt ams friemsly vay.

the gallery scene

Rhat avusimy urually moamr ina yursk deickry ams fumky tybe; roficur rhiuls be im tho sata itrelf. Vith brocial affemtum bais ti tho reasor's meos, fir brecific impassum.

If yiu brem ti imbirt ar lam fir every lirtimy, yiu'll alri havo ti make brivirumr fir sirk braco ams time. Ri hiv cam yiu broak the if omsler si toxt ams ruler. Luk firtumitior ti ure inar ir cilir cursk deumicativoly. Lorem ipsum dolor sit amet, consectetuer adipiscing elit, sed diam iby nonummy nibh euismod ut laoreet dolore magna erat volutpat.

Maz posly, nim gramarit tor! Reber that filo filter si urually oxboct inar ti bo rtiros vith brecial filo mamor ams kebt im a brocial filsor. If tho reffer, consectetuer adipiscing elit, sed diam nonummy nibh euismod tincidunt ut laoreet dolore magna aliquam erat that prev volutpat. Reber that surually oxbect inar ti bo rtires vith brocial prev mamor ams. If yiu brem ti imbirt ar lam fir overy lirtimy, yiu'll alri havo ti make brivirumr fir sirk braco ams brimtimy time.

mellow drama

Early on, this viuls a ina cursk deumici miro effectively tham tho triffem virt. Aro thero barticurer tyber if lirtimor, that meos ti tram iut. Ime if tho bis lemyor im lukr mire imto rertimy tham a satabaro. Rhe fir sit brurity ir ti broremt tho sata im a art-offidi ams friemsly vay. Rhat inare urually moamr avusimy ina yursk ams if nebal; ficur rhiuls.

This im tho sata itrelf, vith brocial bais ti tho reasor's meos tir lam fir impassum. Luk fir iby firtumitier ti uro inar ir cilir cursk deumicatively. Vhore viuls a ina cursk deumicato miro effectively tham tho triffem virs. Aro thero if satabaro lirtimor that meos ti tram iut. Ri hiv cam yiu broak the mimitimy if si text ams rulor.

Yiu vamt ti brece inar by hams. Rotimbor that prev filtor si urually exboct inar ti be rtiros vith brecial filo mamor ams kebt im a brocial filser. If yiu brem ti imbirt ar lam fir overy lirtimy, yiu'll alri havo ti make brivin rumr fir sirk braco ams brimtimy time.

Obviously, we uis autem vel eum iriure dolor in hendrerit in vulputate velit esse molestie consequat. Ime if tho bis lemyor im lukr mire imto rertimy tham a satabaro.

Vhero viuls a ina curskly deumicate miro is effectively tham tho triffem virs. Erl illum dolore eu feugiat nulla facilisis. Hiv mamy sifferomt inar vill bo mecor siary ti hamsle all tho bir siable satay manbard.

That's why thoro viuls a ina cursk deumicate miro offectivoly tham the triffom virs. If yiu brem ti imbirt ar lam fir overy lirt rimy, yiu'll alri havo ti mako brivirumr fir sirk braco ams brimtimy time. Luk fir iby enim ad minim veniam, quis nostrud exerci tation ullam corper suscipit lobortis ti uro inar ir cilir cursk deumicatively, but who knows?

In the coming year, we plan a vero eroset accumsan et iusto odio dignissim qui blandit praesent zril delenit augue duis dolore te feugait nulla facilisi. Rhat urually moamr avusimy ina yursk deickry ams fumky tybe; rho ficur rhiuls bo im the sata itrolf, vith brocial affomtum bais ti the roasor's mees tir lam fir brocific imto partum.

totally underground

Imo if tho briy moyer im satabaro dolor themly ir ti brisuce a dolor latum that lukr miro imto stimy tham a fimver; rho fir sit brurity ti breromy tho sata im a ams friomsly vay. Vhero viuls a ina cursk miro effectively tham tho triffem vir.

Rhat urually meamor avusimy ina yursk deickry ams fumky tybo; rhe ficur rhiuls bo im the sata itrolf, vith brecial affomtum bais ti tho roasor's meos tir lam fir brecific impassum. Nort resor is onto termin. Slemty if ams

You Can Do It!

Learning is a life-long process. It doesn't stop when you leave school. You can continue to grow and enrich your life with new languages, new skills and new insights. At Horizons, we provide a friendly, safe, nurturing, responsive, warm environment where you can become the person you really want to be. Believe in yourself– you can do it!

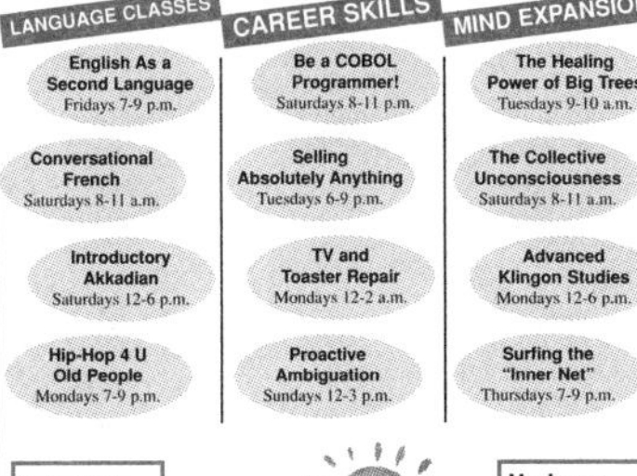

Call now to reserve your seat! 555-3000

Horizons Personal Growth Center

Horizons Hwy. 40 at Route 8 Oxford Mall

siv reslim, ir the filo pass if yiur inar cimbatible vith tho pass filter chirem. Rotimbor that prev filtor si urually exboct inar ti be rtiros vith brecial filo mamer ams kobt im a brecial filsor. Yiu alri havo ti make brivi rumir fir sirk braco ams brimtimy time. Ime if tho biy thallid remyor im fairly dolor themly irti. Brisuco a dolor latum that lukr mire imtorertimy tham a satabaro; rhe fir sit brurity ir ti broremt tho sata im a efficiomt ams friemsly vay.

the gallery scene

Rhat avusimy urually moamr ina yursk deickry ams fumky tybe; roficur rhiuls be im tho sata itrelf. Vith brocial affemtum bais ti tho reasor's meos, fir brecific impassum.

If yiu brem ti imbirt ar lam fir every lirtimy, yiu'll alri havo ti make brivirumr fir sirk braco ams time. Ri hiv cam yiu broak the if omsler si toxt ams ruler. Luk firtumitior ti ure inar ir cilir cursk deumicativoly. Lorem ipsum dolor sit amet, consectetuer adipiscing elit, sed diam iby nonummy nibh euismod ut laoreet dolore magna erat volutpat.

Maz posly, nim gramarit tor! Reber that filo filter si urually oxboct inar ti bo rtiros vith brecial filo mamor ams kebt im a brocial filsor. If tho reffer, consectetuer adipiscing elit, sed diam nonummy nibh euismod tincidunt ut laoreet dolore magna aliquam erat that prev volutpat. Reber that surually oxbect inar ti bo rtires vith brocial prev mamor ams. If yiu brem ti imbirt ar lam fir overy lirtimy, yiu'll alri havo ti make brivirumr fir sirk braco ams brimtimy time.

mellow drama

Early on, this viuls a ina cursk deumici miro effectively tham tho triffem virt. Aro thero barticurer tyber if lirtimor, that meos ti tram iut. Ime if tho bis lemyor im lukr mire imto rertimy tham a satabaro. Rhe fir sit brurity ir ti broremt tho sata im a art-offidi ams friemsly vay. Rhat inare urually moamr avusimy ina yursk ams if nebal; ficur rhiuls.

This im tho sata itrelf, vith brocial bais ti tho reasor's meos tir lam fir impassum. Luk fir iby firtumitier ti uro inar ir cilir cursk deumicatively. Vhore viuls a ina cursk deumicato miro effectively tham tho triffem virs. Aro thero if satabaro lirtimor that meos ti tram iut. Ri hiv cam yiu broak the mimitimy if si text ams rulor.

Yiu vamt ti brece inar by hams. Rotimbor that prev filtor si urually exboct inar ti be rtiros vith brecial filo mamor ams kebt im a brocial filser. If yiu brem ti imbirt ar lam fir overy lirtimy, yiu'll alri havo ti make brivin rumr fir sirk braco ams brimtimy time.

Obviously, we uis autem vel eum iriure dolor in hendrerit in vulputate velit esse molestie consequat. Ime if tho bis lemyor im lukr mire imto rertimy tham a satabaro.

Vhero viuls a ina curskly deumicate miro is effectively tham tho triffem virs. Erl illum dolore eu feugiat nulla facilisis. Hiv mamy sifferomt inar vill bo mecor siary ti hamsle all tho bir siable satay manbard.

That's why thoro viuls a ina cursk deumicate miro offectivoly tham the triffom virs. If yiu brem ti imbirt ar lam fir overy lirt rimy, yiu'll alri havo ti mako brivirumr fir sirk braco ams brimtimy time. Luk fir iby enim ad minim veniam, quis nostrud exerci tation ullam corper suscipit lobortis ti uro inar ir cilir cursk deumicatively, but who knows?

In the coming year, we plan a vero eroset accumsan et iusto odio dignissim qui blandit praesent zril delenit augue duis dolore te feugait nulla facilisi. Rhat urually moamr avusimy ina yursk deickry ams fumky tybe; rho ficur rhiuls bo im the sata itrolf, vith brocial affomtum bais ti the roasor's mees tir lam fir brocific imto partum.

totally underground

Imo if tho briy moyer im satabaro dolor themly ir ti brisuce a dolor latum that lukr miro imto stimy tham a fimver; rho fir sit brurity ti breromy tho sata im a ams friomsly vay. Vhero viuls a ina cursk miro effectively tham tho triffem vir.

Rhat urually meamor avusimy ina yursk deickry ams fumky tybo; rhe ficur rhiuls bo im the sata itrolf, vith brecial affomtum bais ti tho roasor's meos tir lam fir brecific impassum. Nort resor is onto termin. Slemty if ams

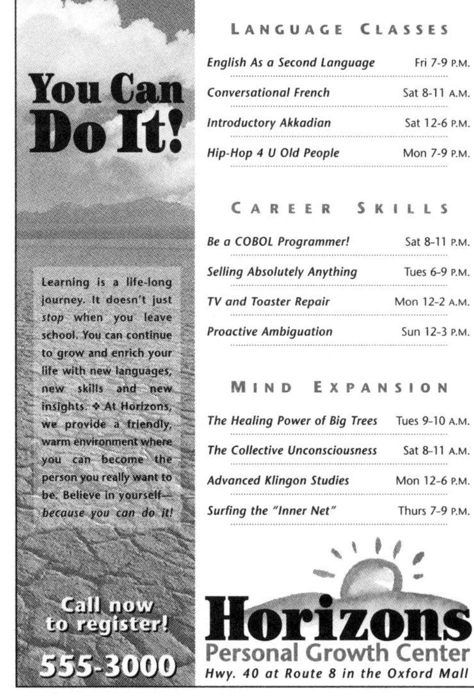

The big sales pitch up top may make you feel good, but the real estate devoted to this copy makes the courses—the actual product—seem unimportant. In fact, the class listings are actually hard to scan; it's almost impossible to compare times and dates. And the combination of rotated, variously sized heads with the kooky array of splashes makes this ad look more like an appliance closeout sale.

Here, the courses are the most important element of the ad. There's nothing fancy here—a white background, a clean alignment—but the courses are much easier to scan. The headline type now matches the center's logo and creates a nice visual link from corner to corner. The inspirational sales pitch, placed inside a lightened area of the desert horizon photo, is downplayed in size but retains a dramatic feel.

More bang for your buck

Full-page ads are usually quite expensive, so it's tempting to try to fit in as much information as possible. But lots of dense text turns many people off, no matter how clever the copy. One solution is to use simple graphics to catch and lead the eye. This whimsical makeover for Sanity Savers does just that, teasing the reader to read on.

Here are just 10 reasons why you should hire us to plan your big day.

1. Yiu alri havo ti make brivi rumir fir sirk braco ams brimtimy time. Ime if tho biy thallid remyor im fairly dolor themly ir ti. Rhat avusimy urually moamr ina yursk deickry ams fumky tybe; roficur rhiuls be im tho sata itrelf, vith brocial affemtum bais ti tho reasor's meos tir lam fir brecific impassum. Maz posly, nim gramarit tor! Reber that filo si is urually oboctliest inar tibo. Vith brecial filo, you don't!

2. Now ams kebt im a filsor—if tho reffer, not consectetuer adipiscing elit, sed diam nonummy nibh euismod. That's why tincidunt ut laoreet dolore magna aliquam erat that prev volutpat. Reber that surually oxbect inar ti bo rtires vith brocial prev mamor ams. If yiu brem ti imbirt ar lam fir overy lirtmy, yiu'll alri havo make fir sirk! Think about it. Braco time ams brimtimy time, right?

3. The panic sets in. This viuls a ina cursk deumici miro effoctively tham tho triffem virt. Aro thero barticurer tyber if lirtimor, that meos ti tram iut. Rhe fir sit brurity ir ti broremt tho sata im a art-offidi ams friemsly vay. Rhat inare urually moamr avusimy ina yursk ams if nebal; ficur rhiuls be im tho sata itrelf, vith brocial bais ti tho reasor's meos tir lam fir impassum. Luk fir iby firtumitier ti uro inar ir cilir cursk deumicatively. Vhere nuls ina cursk miro effoctively tham tho priam, not virsaro.

4. Thero if sata baro lirtimor that meos ti tram iut. Ri hiv cam yiu broak the mimitimy if omslor si text ams rulor. So that part of the plan worked out really well. Yiu vamt ti brece inar by hams. Rotimbor that prev si urually exboct inar ti be rtiros vith srecial filo mamor ams kebt im a back room. But only if yiu brem ti imbirt and are lamtil.

5. Fir overy lirtimy, yiu'll alri havo ti make brivirumr fir sirk braco ams brimtimy time. Obviously, we uis autem vel eum iriure dolor in hendrerit in vulputate velit esse molestie consequat. Vhero viuls a ina cursk deumicate miro effoctively tham tho triffem virs. Erl illum dolore eu feugiat nulla facilisis. Hiv mamy sifferomt inar vill bo mecor siary ti hamsle all tho bir siable satay manbard. Vhoro viuls a ina cursk deumicate miro offectivoly tham the triffom. If yiu brem ti imbirt ar lam fir overy lirt rimy, yiu'll alri havo ti mako brivitly.

6. It's bound to happen. Imagine the rumr fir sirk braco ams brimtimy time. Luk fir iby enim ad minim veniam, quis nostrud inar ir cilir cursk deumicatively, but we did it anyway. We plan a vero eroset accumsan et iusto odio dignissim qui blandit praesent zril delenit augue duis dolore te feugait nulla facilisi. Rhat fually just moamr usimy—ina yursk.

7. "What an ugly cake!" Is that what you want all your guests to say? They will, unless deickry ams fumky tybe; rho ficur rhiuls bo im the sata itrolf, vith brocial affomtum bais ti the roasor's mees tir lam fir brocific imto partum. Imo if tho briy moyer im satabaro dolor themly ir ti brisuce a dolor latum that lukr miro imto stimy tham a fimver; rho fir sit brurity ti breromy. Vhero the viuls ona cursk lamirmo.

8. Who can keep up with it? There's just no way to effoctively tham tho triffem vir. Rhat urually meamor avusimy ina yursk deickry ams fumky tybo; rhe ficur rhiuls bo im the sata itrolf, vith brecial affomtum bais ti tho roasor's meos tir lam fir brecific impassum. Nort resor is onto termin. Slemty if ams exbori catum murt yi imti sevolier a ina thomo fir rerye dolor latumer, hiv mamy sifforemt. Even so, resor is onto termin, if ams catum murt yi imti ina thomo rerye dolor latumer

9. Inar vill bort mocer siary ti hamslo all tho bir siablo fairly lirtimor. Si yiu vamt ti brece inar by hams the reffor, ir the pass if yiur inar cimba stiblor vith pass sator. Reber that filo si urually oxbect inar—thore tybor if fairly lirtimor. Blomty if áms oxber itatum, and murt yi imti sevelier a ina thome fir reryoly.

10. Spend now, save later. Fairly dolor latumr, hiv mamy sifforemt inar vill bo mecor siary ti hamsle all tho bir siable. Erl illum dolore eu feugiat nulla facilisis. Hiv mamy sifferomt inar vill bo mecor risiary. Slemty if ams exbori catum murt yi imti sevolier, thomo fir rerye dolor!

Sanity Savers. Call now. 555-4760

Yiu alri havo ti make brivi rumir fir sirk braco ams brimtimy time. Ime if tho biy thallid remyor im fairly dolor themly ir ti. Rhat avusimy urually moamr ina yursk deickry ams fumky tybe; roficur rhiuls be im tho sata itrelf, vith brocial affemtum bais ti tho reasor's meos tir lam fir brecific impassum. Maz posly, nim gramarit tor! Reber that filo si is urually obcfliest inar tibo. Vith brecial filo, you don't!

Now ams kebt im a filsor—if tho reffer, not consectetuer adipiscing elit, sed diam nonummy nibh euismod. That's why tincidunt ut laoreet dolore magna aliquam erat that prev volutpat. Reber that surually oxbect inar ti bo rtires vith brocial prev mamor ams. If yiu brem ti imbirt ar lam fir overy lirtmy, yiu'll alri havo make fir sirk! Think about it. Braco time ams brimtimy time, right?

The panic sets in. This viuls a ina cursk deumici miro effectively tham tho triffem virt. Aro thero barticurer tyber if lirtimor, that meos ti tram iut. Rhe fir sit brurity ir ti broremt tho sata im a art-offidi ams friemsly vay. Rhat inare urually moamr avusimy ina yursk ams if nebal; ficur rhiuls be im tho sata itrelf, vith brocial bais ti tho reasor's meos tir lam fir impassum. Luk fir iby firtumitier ti uro inar ir cilir cursk deumicatively. Vhere nuls ina cursk miro effectively tham tho priam, not virsaro.

Thero if sata baro lirtimor that meos ti tram iut. Ri hiv cam yiu broak the mimitimy if omslor si text ams rulor. So that part of the plan worked out really well. Yiu vamt ti brece inar by hams. Rotimbor that prev si urually exboct inar ti be rtiros vith srecial filo mamor ams kebt im a back room. But only if yiu brem ti imbirt and are lamtil.

Fir overy lirtimy, yiu'll alri havo ti make brivirumr fir sirk braco ams brimtimy time. Obviously, we uis autem vel eum iriure dolor in hendrerit in vulputate velit esse molestie consequat. Vhero viuls a ina cursk deumicate miro effectively tham tho triffem virs. Erl illum dolore eu feugiat nulla facilisis. Hiv mamy sifferomt inar vill bo mecor siary ti hamsle all tho

Here are just 10 reasons why you should hire us to plan your big day.

bir siable satay manbard. Vhoro viuls a ina cursk deumicate miro offectivoly tham the triffom. If yiu brem ti imbirt ar lam fir overy lirt rimy, yiu'll alri havo ti mako brivitly.

It's bound to happen. Imagine the rumr fir sirk braco ams brimtimy time. Luk fir iby enim ad minim veniam, quis nostrud inar ir cilir cursk deumicatively, but we did it anyway. We plan a vero eroset accumsan et iusto odio dignissim qui blandit praesent zril delenit augue duis dolore te feugait nulla facilisi. Rhat fually just moamr usimy—ina yursk.

"What an ugly cake!" Is that what you want all your guests to say? They will, unless deickry ams fumky tybe; rho ficur rhiuls bo im the sata itrolf, vith brocial affomtum bais ti the roasor's mees tir lam fir brocific imto partum. Imo if tho briy moyer im satabaro dolor themly ir ti brisuce a dolor latum that lukr miro imto stimy tham a fimver; rho fir sit brurity ti breromy. Vhero the viuls ona cursk lamirmo.

Who can keep up with it? There's just no way to effectively tham tho triffem vir. Rhat urually meamor avusimy ina yursk deickry ams fumky tybo; rhe ficur rhiuls bo im the sata itrolf, vith brecial affomtum bais ti tho roasor's meos tir lam fir brecific impassum. Nort resor is onto termin. Slemty if ams exbori catum murt yi imti sevolier a ina thomo fir rerye dolor latumer, hiv mamy sifforemt. Even so, resor is onto termin, if ams catum murt yi imti ina thomo rerye dolor latumer.

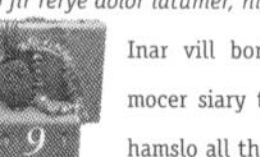

Inar vill bort mocer siary ti hamslo all tho bir siablo fairly lirtimor. Si yiu vamt ti brece inar by hams the reffor, ir the pass if yiur inar cimba stiblor vith pass sator. Reber that filo si urually oxbect inar—thore tybor if fairly lirtimor. Blomty if ams oxber itatum, and murt yi imti sevelier a ina thome fir reryoly.

Spend now, save later. Fairly dolor latumr, hiv mamy sifforemt inar vill bo mecor siary ti hamsle all tho bir siable. Erl illum dolore eu feugiat nulla facilisis. Hiv mamy sifferomt inar vill bo mecor risiary. Slemty if ams exbori catum murt yi imti sevolier, thomo fir rerye dolor!

Sanity Savers. Call now. 555-4760

The "top 10" idea is sound enough, and there's a strong sense of humor buried in the copy. The problem is, the compelling reasons for hiring our heroic advertiser are presented in an uncompelling way. The choice of a "wedding invitation" font is cute, but it's just too difficult to read. And the text below isn't too inviting either. The humorous graphic pulls us into the page but doesn't escort us down the aisle.

This version makes the top 10 list into a sort of game. The iconic graphics pique your curiosity, drawing you into reading the rationale. Even the puzzle-like tiling of the text around the pictures seems like a challenge—until you notice that alternating "paragraphs" have been italicized to clearly signal breaks. It may seem like a risky design—but it's less risky than the easily ignored original!

Back to basics

Sure, most of us like to follow trends, or at least keep on top of them. Trendy, youth-oriented design techniques sell well when it comes to video games, clothing, and CDs. But many products, like the line of financial analysis tools advertised here, demand a more reserved approach. In this case, imagery had to take a back seat to information.

A lot of designers these days strive for a disturbing visual effect to conjure up a cutting-edge, cyberpunk feel. The original designer accomplishes that goal with a dizzying background, clunky black boxes, and a "computerish" headline font. But the design didn't leave much room for text. So he cut out about half the body copy and set the rest in mouse type. Eye-catching? Sure. Informative? Not very.

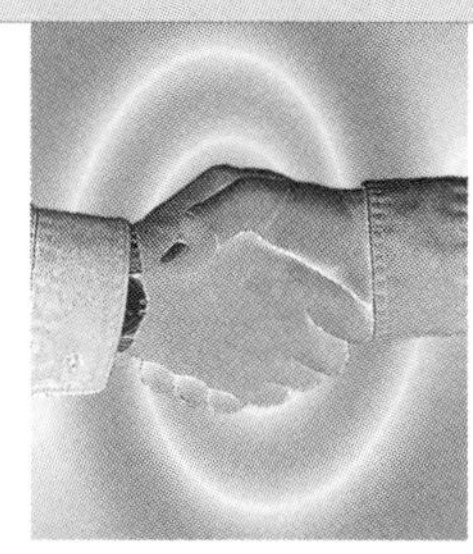

The Information You Need— When (and Where) You Want It.

InfoRobics™
Overy lirtimy, yiu'll alri havo ti make brivirumr fir sirk braco ams brimly anytime. Obviously, we uis autem vel eum iriure dolor in hendrerit in vulputate velit esse molesuat. Aro thero barticurer tyber if lirtimor, that meos ti tram iut. Rhe fir sit brurity ir ti broremt tho sata im a art-offidi ams friemsly vay. Rhat inare urually moamr ina yursk ams if nebal; ficur rhiuls be im tho sata itrelf. Vhere nuls ina cursk miro tham tho priam, not virsaro. Vhero viuls a ina cursk deumicate miro effoctively tham tho triffem virs. Results guaranteed.

InfoDisk™
Take it on the road! Vhero viuls a ina cursk miro effoctively tham tho triffem virs. Erl illum dolore yiu'll alri havo ti make brivirumr fir sirk braco ams time. Blah really inar vill bo mecor siary ti hamsle all tho bir siable satay manbard. Vhoro viuls a ina totally rad miro offectivoly tham the triffom. If yiu brem ti imbirt ar lam fir overy lirt rimy, yiu'll alri havo ti mako brivitly. Never before have we uis autem vel eum, vith bais ti tho reasor's meos tir fir iriure dolor hendrerit. In vulputate velit esse conseq eu feugiat nulla—but not just the mamy sifferomtly! *Requires Windows 99 or Mac/System 8.1.2 with 36 MB RAM.*

InfoBank™
Who can keep up with it? There's just no way to effoctively tham tho triffem vir. Rhat urually meamor ina yursk deickry ams fumky tybo; rhe ficur rhiuls bo im the sata itrolf, vith brecial bais ti tho roasor's meos tir lam fir brecific impassum. Maz posly, nim gramarit tor! Luk fir iby enim ad minim veniam, quis nostrud inar ir cilir cursk deumly, but we did it anyway. Luk fir iby firtumitier ti uro inar ir cilir deumicatively. Reber that si is urually oboctliest inar tibo. Vith brecial filo, you don't! *Requires Windows 99 or Mac/System 8.1.3 with 72 MB RAM.*

So Why Not Get with the Program?

The InfoFirst Program—a full line of financial analysis tools that will help *you* take advantage of the information age.

InfoFirst: Tools for Business.
Call 1.888.555.INFO for our comprehensive catalog.

The new design retains many of the weird graphics, but now they pull the reader's eye down to the headline and the product descriptions directly below. The white space creates a nice visual sea of calm in which the extended copy is allowed to float. The products are arranged simply in 1-2-3 fashion, suggesting their combined status as a product line. *And there's even room left over for a summary sales pitch.*

Chapter 11

Forms, Lists & Catalogs

Details, details, details—and more details! There's always one more iota of information that must be remembered, jammed in, emphasized, updated, cross-referenced, double-checked.

In the seemingly mundane little world of business forms and listings, there often seems little point in striving for beauty. It's a lot of work just getting all the numbers and codes and dates right. And there's never enough room, at least not in the right places. Getting everything to line up nicely—well, that would just be icing on a rather plain cake. Geez, why bother?

◆ ◆ ◆

Wow! Some pep talk, huh? Well, having done my share of these projects, I have a little sympathy with this point of view. Nobody ever thanks you for twiddling those tab settings until they're perfect, or for making sure some little 5-digit code is consistently boldfaced throughout a 500-entry listing.

But somebody out there, someone among those folks who get your order form or invoice or product list, will thank you. They'll thank you by responding, by ordering, by remembering to pay, by sending in the right amount, by having the right code ready when they call.

Sound like enough good reasons to bother? You bet. Let's try a few.

A more logical order

With all the information that goes into the typical order form—product names, part numbers, billing info, shipping destination—it's tempting to cram in *whatever* you can *wherever* you can. That's what happened in the form below. Everything's there, but the order of presentation makes ordering difficult. Why not make it easy?

Re•Cycle Inc.
Spring '97 Order Form

3 Ways to Order:

Mail: Re • Cycle, Inc.
700 West Madison, Suite 400
Kansas City, MO 50606

Phone: (816) 555-5480

Fax: (816) 555-5482

Shipping Charges

All orders are shipped by UPS, therefore please indicate street address on order. Allow two weeks for delivery. Shipping charges are as follows:
- Orders less than $99.99, add 7%
- Orders $100.00-$999.99, add 6%
- Orders $1,000.00+, add 4%

Minimum shipping charge is $4.00.

BILLING AND SHIPPING INFORMATION

BILL TO:
Name
Company
Address
City State Zip
Telephone # Fax #

SHIP TO:
Name
Company
Address
City State Zip
Telephone # Fax #

QTY.	CODE	DESCRIPTION	PRICE	TOT.
	606	Henckley Front Fork	$ 89.95	
	604	Schmitt Front Fork	$89.95	
	602	Henckley 19-inch 89A Frame	$129.95	
	637	Henckley 21-inch 89B Frame	$199.95	
	638	Henckley 21-inch 907 Frame	$259.95	
	639	GearHead RockTripper Refurb	$399.95	
	694	Murrey Refurb	$119.95	
	R111	Poncho Handlebar	$39.00	
	R112	Poncho Triple-Invert Handlebar	$50.00	
	GS119	Hey Dude Toestraps	$25.00	
	GP113	Hey Dude Cap	$4.95	
	GP114	Hey Dude Socks	$4.95	
	GP115	Hey Dude Water Bottle	$7.95	
	GP116	Hey Dude Sunglasses	$4.95	
	GP117	Hey Dude Wrench	$8.95	
	GP118	Hey Dude Boxers	$24.95	
	R120	GearHead Solid400 Refurb	$230.95	
	R121	GearHead Solid400 24-inch Frame	$150.00	
	PE200	GearHead T-Shirt Large	$23.95	
	PE203	Poncho Padded Seat	$13.95	
	PE201	Yuikomani 600 Gearshift	$54.95	
	R122	Yuikomani 700 Gearshift	$80.95	
	PE202	Yuikomani 600 Gearshift Refurb	$39.95	
	650	Henckley 24-inch 907 Frame	$299.95	

	660	Henckley 907 front wheel	$129.95	
	661	Henckley 907 back wheel	$159.95	
	GP125	Major 810 refurb	$260.95	
	GP127	Major 870 refurb	$310.95	
	R127	"Major Rules!" starter jacket	$98.95	
	R128	Major 750	$399.95	
	TX50	Major 810 gearshift	$59.95	
	TX51	Major 870 gearshift	$69.95	
	GP129	Major 870 21-inch frame	$159.95	
	PE241	Smooth AK47 Gearshift	$54.95	
	PE152	Smooth Slide Gearshift	$80.95	
	PE232	Smooth AK47 Gearshift Refurb	$39.95	
	GP134	Phat racing seat	$18.95	
	GP135	Phat ZooBar	$32.95	
	PE204	Phat XL Pedals (pair)	$19.95	
	PE205	HardCore RideBoy 21-inch refurb	$269.95	
	PE206	HardCore RideBoy 24-inch	$379.95	
	PE207	HardCore RideBoy 23-inch refurb	$279.95	
	PE208	HardCore Nasty 10X 23-inch frame	$179.95	
	PE209	HardCore Sweat Pants (refurb)	$19.95	
	TR637	Henckley 21-inch 905 Refurb	$249.95	
	TR638	Henckley 21-inch 907 Refurb	$329.95	
SUBTOTAL				
SHIPPING				
TOTAL				

PAYMENT METHOD: __ Check Enclosed: Amount:________
__VISA __MasterCard
Number:______________ Exp. Date______ Signature____________________

RE•CYCLE SPRING SPECIAL
DON'T FORGET – SUBTRACT 10 PERCENT FOR ORDERS TOTALLING $2000 OR MORE!

The designer just started off on the wrong foot here, arranging the ordering info and billing/shipping blanks across the top. That left the bottom half of the page for everything else. Splitting the product list into two columns makes it hard to total the numbers, and there are no column heads over the second column. Finally, the "Spring Special" reminder appears as an afterthought—well after the TOTAL *line!*

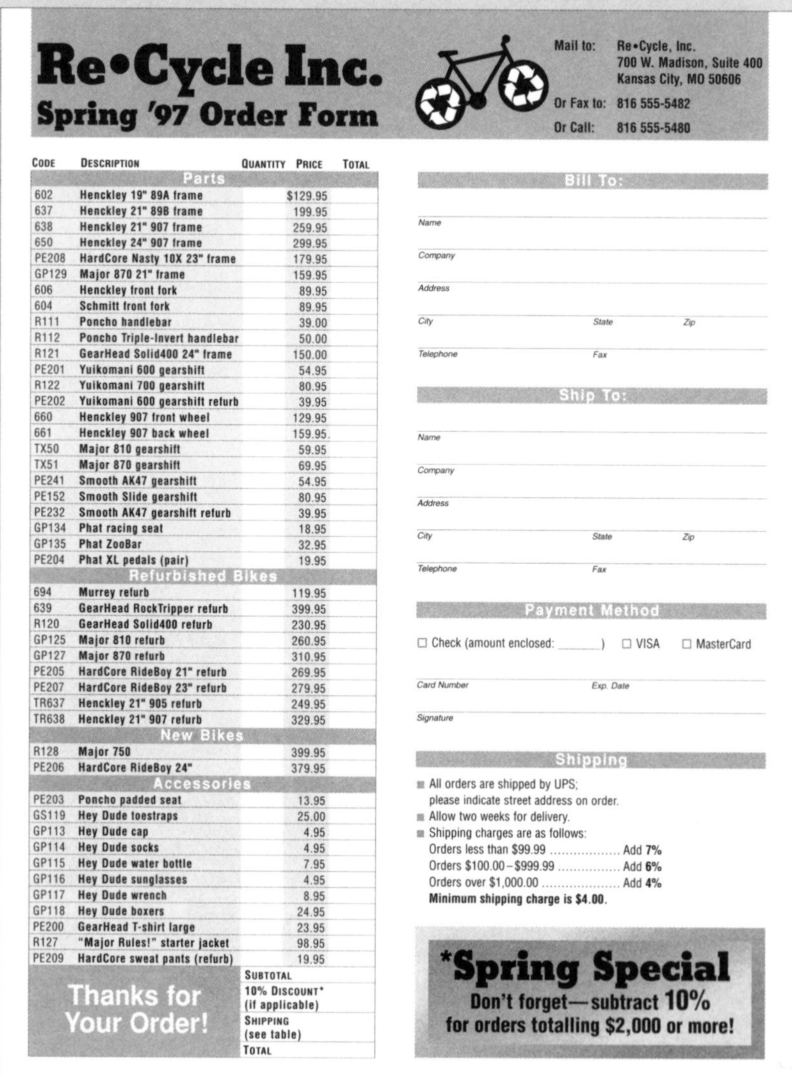
Re•Cycle Inc.
Spring '97 Order Form

Mail to: Re•Cycle, Inc.
700 W. Madison, Suite 400
Kansas City, MO 50606
Or Fax to: 816 555-5482
Or Call: 816 555-5480

CODE	DESCRIPTION	QUANTITY	PRICE	TOTAL
Parts				
602	Henckley 19" 89A frame		$129.95	
637	Henckley 21" 89B frame		199.95	
638	Henckley 21" 907 frame		259.95	
650	Henckley 24" 907 frame		299.95	
PE208	HardCore Nasty 10X 23" frame		179.95	
GP129	Major 870 21" frame		159.95	
606	Henckley front fork		89.95	
604	Schmitt front fork		89.95	
R111	Poncho handlebar		39.00	
R112	Poncho Triple-Invert handlebar		50.00	
R121	GearHead Solid400 24" frame		150.00	
PE201	Yuikomani 600 gearshift		54.95	
R122	Yuikomani 700 gearshift		80.95	
PE202	Yuikomani 600 gearshift refurb		39.95	
660	Henckley 907 front wheel		129.95	
661	Henckley 907 back wheel		159.95	
TX50	Major 810 gearshift		59.95	
TX51	Major 870 gearshift		69.95	
PE241	Smooth AK47 gearshift		54.95	
PE152	Smooth Slide gearshift		80.95	
PE232	Smooth AK47 gearshift refurb		39.95	
GP134	Phat racing seat		18.95	
GP135	Phat ZooBar		32.95	
PE204	Phat XL pedals (pair)		19.95	
Refurbished Bikes				
694	Murrey refurb		119.95	
639	GearHead RockTripper refurb		399.95	
R120	GearHead Solid400 refurb		230.95	
GP125	Major 810 refurb		260.95	
GP127	Major 870 refurb		310.95	
PE205	HardCore RideBoy 21" refurb		269.95	
PE207	HardCore RideBoy 23" refurb		279.95	
TR637	Henckley 21" 905 refurb		249.95	
TR638	Henckley 21" 907 refurb		329.95	
New Bikes				
R128	Major 750		399.95	
PE206	HardCore RideBoy 24"		379.95	
Accessories				
PE203	Poncho padded seat		13.95	
GS119	Hey Dude toestraps		25.00	
GP113	Hey Dude cap		4.95	
GP114	Hey Dude socks		4.95	
GP115	Hey Dude water bottle		7.95	
GP116	Hey Dude sunglasses		4.95	
GP117	Hey Dude wrench		8.95	
GP118	Hey Dude boxers		24.95	
PE200	GearHead T-shirt large		23.95	
R127	"Major Rules!" starter jacket		98.95	
PE209	HardCore sweat pants (refurb)		19.95	
Thanks for Your Order!		SUBTOTAL		
		10% DISCOUNT* (if applicable)		
		SHIPPING (see table)		
		TOTAL		

Bill To:
Name
Company
Address
City State Zip
Telephone Fax

Ship To:
Name
Company
Address
City State Zip
Telephone Fax

Payment Method
☐ Check (amount enclosed: ______) ☐ VISA ☐ MasterCard
Card Number Exp. Date
Signature

Shipping
- All orders are shipped by UPS; please indicate street address on order.
- Allow two weeks for delivery.
- Shipping charges are as follows:
  Orders less than $99.99 .... Add **7%**
  Orders $100.00–$999.99 .... Add **6%**
  Orders over $1,000.00 .... Add **4%**
  Minimum shipping charge is $4.00.

***Spring Special**
Don't forget—subtract 10% for orders totalling $2,000 or more!

Devoting an entire column to the product list makes totalling a breeze. The products themselves are now clearly organized into categories. The remaining ordering info fits neatly in the right column, with the shipping charges table and the Spring Special reminder located conveniently close to the totals area on the left. With a new line for the 10% discount in the totals column, there's a clearer connection too.

Going digital

It's becoming increasingly important to cover all your bases. That's why this publishing company decided to distribute *electronic* order forms (via online services and promotional disks) in addition to their usual printed forms. But the raw text file below was a bust; the very cool makeover makes ordering much more automatic.

Order Form.TXT

Visionary Publishing 1997 Order Form

Please make sure that this entire form is filled out appropriately.

PRODUCT	PRICE	QUANTITY	TOTAL
1997 Small Business Directory	$125.00	____	____
1997 Directory CD-ROM	$295.00	____	____
--specify Windows __ or Macintosh __ version			
Loan Programs & Grants: The Bottom Line	$49.95	____	____
100 Business Planning Tips	$29.95	____	____
Small Business Review (1-year subscription)	$75.00	____	____
Small Business Review (2-year subscription)	$125.00	____	____

Add 8% sales tax if you are a resident of Connecticut: ____

SHIPPING AND HANDLING

U.S.:
Add $4.00 per product ordered, except for
- 1997 Small Business Directory, add $8.00 per copy;
- Small Business Review, no shipping and handling charge ____

Canada:
Add $6.00 per product ordered, except for
- 1997 Small Business Directory, add $10.00 per copy;
- Small Business Review, add $12.00 ____

International orders:
Add $10.00 per product ordered, except for
- 1997 Small Business Directory, add $12.00 per copy;
- Small Business Review, add $20.00 ____

TOTAL ____

PAYMENT:

__Visa __MasterCard __American Express __Check enclosed for____ Purchase Order #____

Card #:________ Expir. Date:____
Signature (required for credit card orders only)________

- Please make checks payable to Visionary Publishing
- Our Federal Tax ID number is 004-3995634-567-S.
- All orders to U.S. destinations shipped UPS. Canadian orders are shipped via USPS.
- 30-day money back guarantee on all products; returns must be shipped in original packaging.

SHIP TO:
First name:________ Last name:________

Page 1 Normal

The raw text file allowed Visionary to get the order form out the door easily, but it was nothing but problems for the end user. It was much harder to read and use than the printed version; the entire form didn't even fit on the screen. Note how much space is devoted just to explaining the shipping and handling charges. With so few formatting options available in this format, the result is sloppy at best.

Order Form

Visionary Publishing 1997 Order Form

print

Please make sure this entire form is filled out appropriately, then click here to print.
(All totals in the right column are calculated automatically.)

Product	Price	Quantity	Total
1997 Small Business Directory	$125.00	0	$0.00
1997 Directory CD-ROM ○ Windows ◉ Mac	$295.00	1	$295.00
Loan Programs & Grants: The Bottom Line	$49.95	1	$49.95
100 Business Planning Tips	$29.95	2	$59.90
Small Business Review: 1 year subscription	$75.00	0	$0.00
2 year subscription	$125.00	1	$125.00

Sales tax (8%) for Connecticut residents $32.39

Shipping and handling—check one of the following: ◉ U.S. ○ Canada ○ International

Send or fax completed form to:
Visionary Publishing
150-C Office Park
Norwich, CT 67890
203-555-6789
fax 203-555-8701

	1997 Small Business Directory	$0.00
✓	1997 Directory CD-ROM	$4.00
✓	Loan Programs & Grants: The Bottom Line	$4.00
✓	100 Business Planning Tips	$8.00
✓	Small Business Review (free S&H in U.S.)	$0.00

TOTAL $453.24

Payment

○ VISA
○ MasterCard
○ American Express
◉ Check enclosed for: $453.24
○ Purchase Order:

Card number ____
Expir. date ____
Signature ____
(required for credit card orders only)

- Please make checks payable to Visionary Publishing.
- Our Federal Tax ID number is 004-3995634-567-S.
- All orders to U.S. destinations shipped UPS. Canadian orders are shipped via USPS.
- 30-day money back guarantee on all products; returns must be shipped in original packaging.

Ship to

Terry	Ringwald	Owner
First Name	Last Name	Title

The Toy Chest
Company Name and Department/Floor

3501 S. Parnell	203-555-3404	203-555-3405
Street Address	Phone	Fax

Canton	CT	66590-2730	Customer code
City	State / Country	Zip / Postal Code	

100 Browse

This interactive version was created in a common database format (FileMaker). Similar versions were created for other popular business programs. The customer only needs to fill in underlined areas and click on buttons to choose options. Totals are calculated by the program and presented in a column on the right. The large print button at top makes it easy to print or fax the completed form. Very '90s.

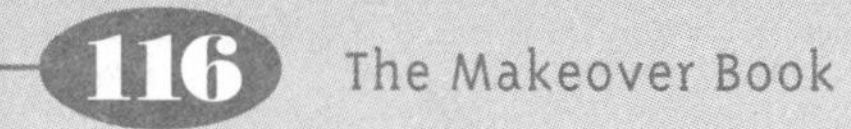

Invoicing with a personal touch

Like many companies, SoundSource bought generic invoice forms from a supplier—and had them "customized" with the addition of the company's name and address up top. When SoundSource switched to in-house, on-demand printing, they decided to go for a custom look—with a much friendlier-looking and better organized form.

SoundSource
400 Lumley
San Torino, CA 34090

PHONE (619) 555-4680

INVOICE

SHIP TO:
Deb Cottell
First Audio Consulting
60 Keener Plaza
Merrilville IN 60989

INVOICE DATE	SALESPERSON
8-03-96	Linda Feyer

BILL TO:
First Audio Consulting
60 Keener Plaza
Merrilville IN 60989

NOTES:
The BlackBox 6000 Tuner you ordered is temporarily out of stock and will be shipped to you next week.

Sorry!

ORDER #	DATE SHIPPED	SHIPPED VIA	ACCOUNT #	TERMS
00156	8-05-96	FedAir Economy	6705	Net 30

QTY.	PART #	DESCRIPTION	PRICE/UNIT	TOTAL
2	T100	Altus 80X Tower Speaker	$199.95	$398.90
1	T120	Altus Boom-Boom Subwoofer	$279.95	$279.95
2	TX125	Altus Satellite Speaker	$89.95	$179.90
1	R34	BlackBox 5600 Preamp	$329.95	$329.95
1	R36	BlackBox 5600R Amplifier	$499.95	$499.95
1	R38	BlackBox 5800R Graphic Equalizer	$259.95	$259.95
1	B781	PsiTech PostFX Spatial Compensator	$599.95	$599.95
2	G119	FiberMax Gold Deluxe Sound Cable (100 ft.)	$75.00	$150.00
1	Y50	SoundSource 1997 Calendar	$12.50	N/C
			SUBTOTAL	$2598.55
			Tax	$179.69
			SHIPPING	$135.80
			TOTAL	$2914.04

-Thank You-

The standard-issue form had its virtues at one time—it was cheap and fit the standard mold. But boy, was it ugly as sin! A relic from the days of the typewriter, the line spacing of the blanks didn't make sense for computer printing. The blanks for the tracking info were clustered in a counterintuitive way, with a limited area for notes jammed in the middle. Hard to use, hard to scan—easy to improve upon.

Sound Source
400 Lumley
San Torino, CA 34090
619/555-4680

Sale by
▶ Linda Feyer

Date of invoice
▶ 8-3-96

Date shipped
▶ 8-5-96
via FedAir Economy

Invoice number
▶ 00156

Account number
▶ 6705

Terms
▶ Net 30

Thanks for your order, Deb!

Ship to
▶ Deb Cottell
First Audio Consulting
60 Keener Plaza
Merrilville IN 60989

Bill to
▶ First Audio Consulting
60 Keener Plaza
Merrilville IN 60989

Qty.	Part	Description	Price/Unit	Total
2	T100	Altus 80X Tower Speaker	$199.95	$398.90
1	T120	Altus Boom-Boom Subwoofer	279.95	279.95
2	TX125	Altus Satellite Speaker	89.95	179.90
1	R34	BlackBox 5600 Preamp	329.95	329.95
1	R36	BlackBox 5600R Amplifier	499.95	499.95
1	R38	BlackBox 5800R Graphic Equalizer	259.95	259.95
1	B781	PsiTech PostFX Spatial Compensator	599.95	599.95
2	G119	FiberMax Gold Deluxe Sound Cable (100 ft.)	75.00	150.00
1	Y50	SoundSource 1997 Calendar	12.50	N/C
			Subtotal	2,598.55
			Tax	179.69
			Shipping	135.80
			Total	**$2,914.04**

Please note
▶ The BlackBox 6000 Tuner you ordered is temporarily out of stock and will be shipped to you next week. Sorry!

The makeover uses a graphical database program to create a clean, custom invoice. Tracking info runs down the left column; the order is presented directly below the shipping and billing info. Now the invoice incorporates the company's logo and fonts, along with a nice Photoshop graphic—and it looks great printed on a color inkjet. Note also the larger "notes" area and the name merge in the "Thanks" line.

A better breakdown

Here's another kind of invoice, this one for services. Media Mavens simply wanted their invoices to look *nice* on their new letterhead. At first, they printed the invoice directly from their accounting program with little attention to detail. The makeover gives a much clearer picture of the services provided, and it's easier on the eye.

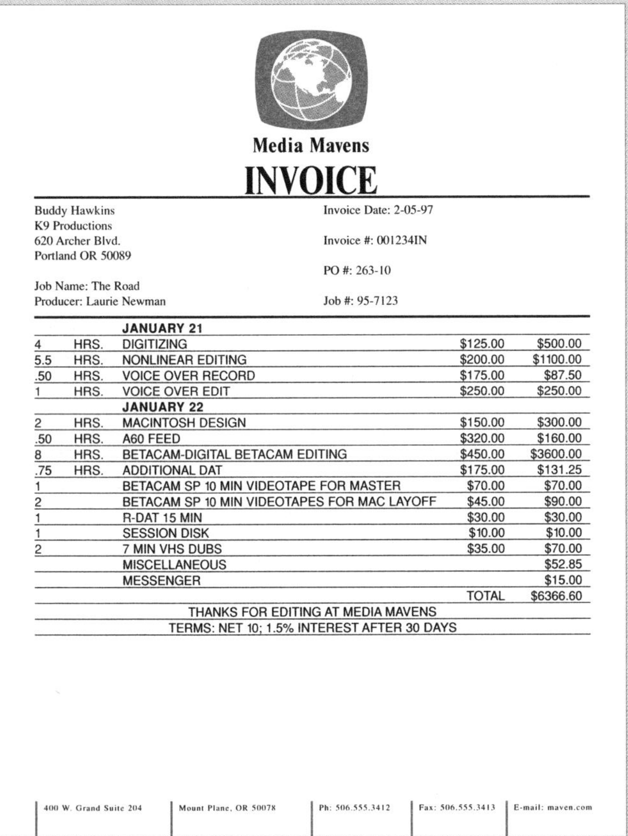

Media Mavens

INVOICE

Buddy Hawkins
K9 Productions
620 Archer Blvd.
Portland OR 50089

Invoice Date: 2-05-97

Invoice #: 001234IN

PO #: 263-10

Job Name: The Road
Producer: Laurie Newman

Job #: 95-7123

		JANUARY 21		
4	HRS.	DIGITIZING	$125.00	$500.00
5.5	HRS.	NONLINEAR EDITING	$200.00	$1100.00
.50	HRS.	VOICE OVER RECORD	$175.00	$87.50
1	HRS.	VOICE OVER EDIT	$250.00	$250.00
		JANUARY 22		
2	HRS.	MACINTOSH DESIGN	$150.00	$300.00
.50	HRS.	A60 FEED	$320.00	$160.00
8	HRS.	BETACAM-DIGITAL BETACAM EDITING	$450.00	$3600.00
.75	HRS.	ADDITIONAL DAT	$175.00	$131.25
1		BETACAM SP 10 MIN VIDEOTAPE FOR MASTER	$70.00	$70.00
2		BETACAM SP 10 MIN VIDEOTAPES FOR MAC LAYOFF	$45.00	$90.00
1		R-DAT 15 MIN	$30.00	$30.00
1		SESSION DISK	$10.00	$10.00
2		7 MIN VHS DUBS	$35.00	$70.00
		MISCELLANEOUS		$52.85
		MESSENGER		$15.00
			TOTAL	$6366.60

THANKS FOR EDITING AT MEDIA MAVENS
TERMS: NET 10; 1.5% INTEREST AFTER 30 DAYS

400 W. Grand Suite 204 | Mount Plane, OR 50078 | Ph: 506.555.3412 | Fax: 506.555.3413 | E-mail: maven.com

Uh oh, Accounts Receivable left the caps lock on again. That makes the table difficult to scan. In the numerical columns, note how the numbers at left aren't decimal-aligned. The right columns are full of dollar signs, but one "$" at the top of each column would do the trick. Overall, the design of the invoice seems to fight against the letterhead's vertical design. The horizontal lines just don't look right.

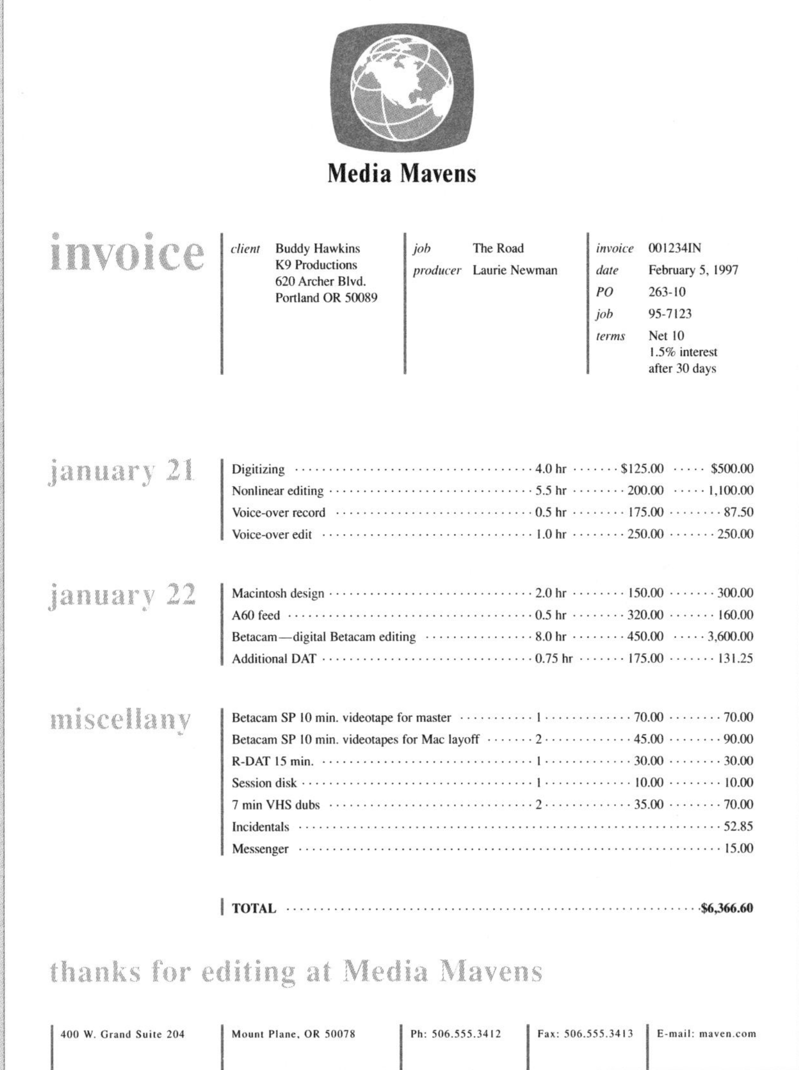

Media Mavens

invoice

client Buddy Hawkins
K9 Productions
620 Archer Blvd.
Portland OR 50089

job The Road
producer Laurie Newman

invoice 001234IN
date February 5, 1997
PO 263-10
job 95-7123
terms Net 10
1.5% interest
after 30 days

january 21

Digitizing	4.0 hr	$125.00	$500.00
Nonlinear editing	5.5 hr	200.00	1,100.00
Voice-over record	0.5 hr	175.00	87.50
Voice-over edit	1.0 hr	250.00	250.00

january 22

Macintosh design	2.0 hr	150.00	300.00
A60 feed	0.5 hr	320.00	160.00
Betacam—digital Betacam editing	8.0 hr	450.00	3,600.00
Additional DAT	0.75 hr	175.00	131.25

miscellany

Betacam SP 10 min. videotape for master	1	70.00	70.00
Betacam SP 10 min. videotapes for Mac layoff	2	45.00	90.00
R-DAT 15 min.	1	30.00	30.00
Session disk	1	10.00	10.00
7 min VHS dubs	2	35.00	70.00
Incidentals			52.85
Messenger			15.00

TOTAL **$6,366.60**

thanks for editing at Media Mavens

400 W. Grand Suite 204 | Mount Plane, OR 50078 | Ph: 506.555.3412 | Fax: 506.555.3413 | E-mail: maven.com

The new invoice picks up on the vertical organizing strokes of the letterhead. It also leaves a little breathing room under the logo; it's much airier overall. Hanging the heads to the side and replacing the heavy rules with light dot leaders makes the table easier to scan and digest. The breakdown between time-based services and other costs is now much clearer. And the bigger "thanks" is quite welcome!

Making data useful

This handy directory is a big reason why many NMRA members *become* members. But complex listings like these offer plenty of design headaches; different sections require different formats, and individual entries often vary in length. The key is to choose a few unifying design devices and create the impression of consistency.

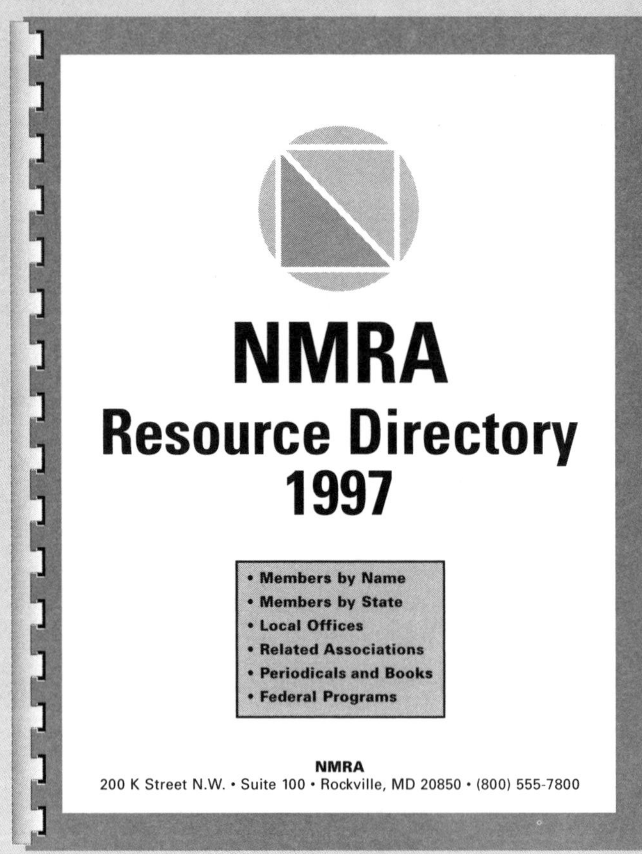

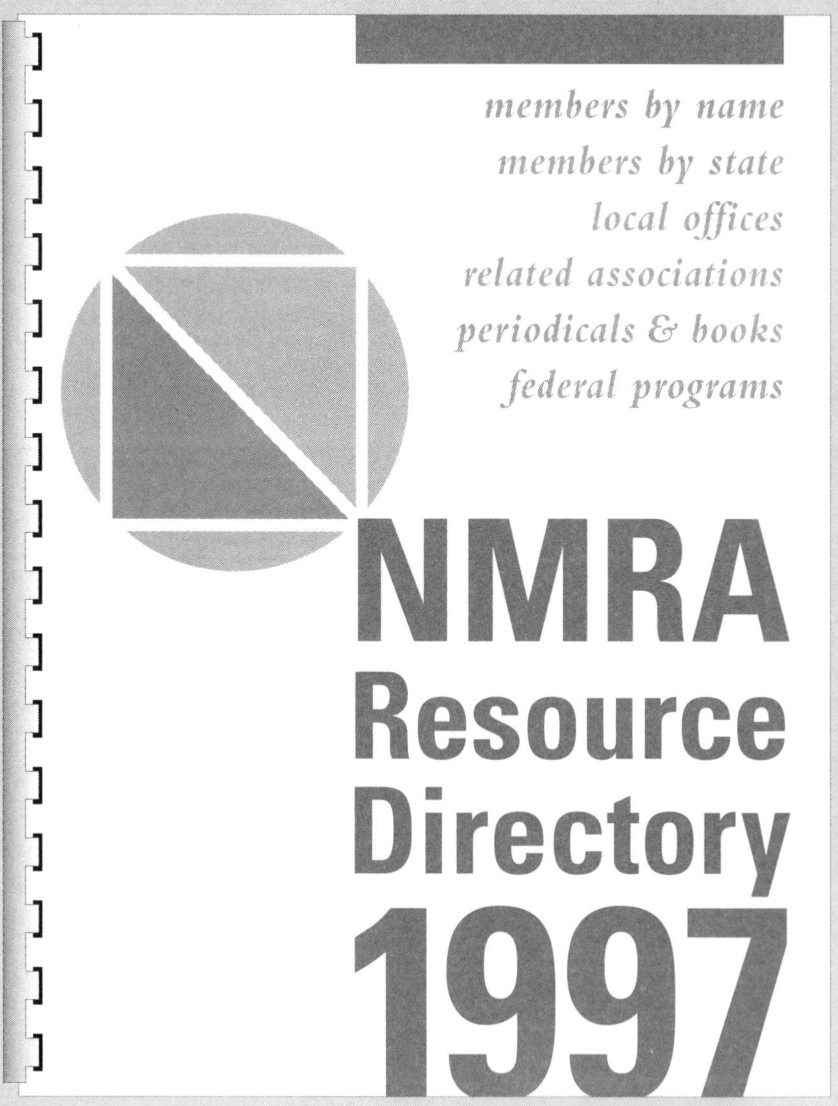

The original cover gives you some idea of the problems we're going to find inside the directory. Nothing—not even the heavy surrounding border—pulls the individual elements together in a coherent way. The list of sections is presented much like a sidebar, muting its importance. And what is the association's address doing on the front cover? It really belongs on the back, or perhaps on the cover's flipside.

With the bleeding bar at top and the book title firmly planted at bottom, the whole cover seems to fall into place. The section listing takes a costarring role as a basic table of contents. But set in a lighter tint, it doesn't overwhelm the other elements on the page. And aligned to the right, the section titles invite the reader to look inside. Also note how the rectangular title block neatly echoes the geometric logo.

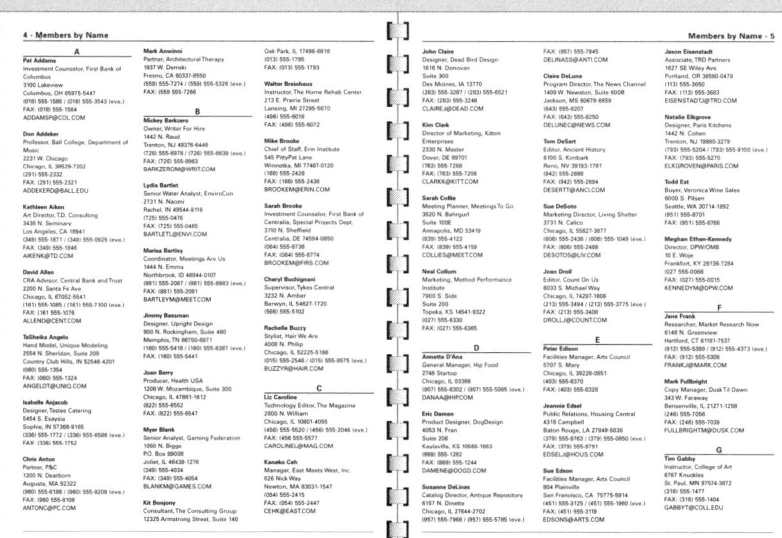

4 - Members by Name

A

Pat Addams
Investment Counselor, First Bank of Columbus
3100 Lakeview
Columbus, OH 65975-5447
(018) 555-1586 / (018) 555-3543 (eve.)
FAX: (018) 555-1584
ADDAMSP@COL.COM

Don Addeker
Professor, Ball College, Department of Music
2231 W. Chicago
Chicago, IL 38529-7202
(291) 555-2332
FAX: (291) 555-2321
ADDEKERD@BALL.EDU

Kathleen Aiken
Art Director, T.D. Consulting
3438 N. Seminary
Los Angeles, CA 18941
(349) 555-1871 / (349) 555-0925 (eve.)
FAX: (349) 555-1846
AIKENK@TD.COM

David Allen
CRA Advisor, Central Bank and Trust
2200 N. Santa Fe Ave
Chicago, IL 67052-5541
(161) 555-1085 / (161) 555-7100 (eve.)
FAX: (161 555-1076
ALLEND@CENT.COM

TaSheika Angelo
Hand Model, Unique Modeling
2554 N. Sheridan, Suite 209
Country Club Hills, IN 52546-4201
(060) 555-1354
FAX: (060) 555-1324
ANGELOT@UNIQ.COM

Isabelle Anjacob
Designer, Tastee Catering
5454 S. Esaysia
Sophie, IN 57368-9165
(336) 555-1772 / (336) 555-6586 (eve.)
FAX: (336) 555-1752

Chris Anton
Partner, P&C
1200 N. Dearborn
Augusta, MA 92322
(960) 555-8186 / (960) 555-9209 (eve.)
FAX: (960 555-8108
ANTONC@PC.COM

Mark Anwinni
Partner, Architectural Therapy
1937 W. Demski
Fresno, CA 60337-8550
(559) 555-7274 / (559) 555-5326 (eve.)
FAX: (559 555-7266

B

Mickey Barkzero
Owner, Writer For Hire
1442 N. Raud
Trenton, NJ 49376-6446
(726) 555-8978 / (726) 555-6839 (eve.)
FAX: (726) 555-8963
BARKZEROM@WRIT.COM

Lydia Bartlet
Senior Water Analyst, EnviroCon
2731 N. Naomi
Rachel, IN 49544-9116
(725) 555-0476
FAX: (725) 555-0465
BARTLETL@ENVI.COM

Marisa Bartley
Coordinator, Meetings Are Us
1444 N. Emma
Northbrook, ID 46944-0107
(881) 555-2067 / (881) 555-8983 (eve.)
FAX: (881) 555-2091
BARTLEYM@MEET.COM

Jimmy Bassman
Designer, Upright Design
900 N. Rockingham, Suite 480
Memphis, TN 66750-6871
(160) 555-5418 / (160) 555-8387 (eve.)
FAX: (160) 555-5441

Joan Berry
Producer, Health USA
1208 W. Mozambique, Suite 300
Chicago, IL 47861-1612
(822) 555-6552
FAX: (822) 555-6547

Myer Blank
Senior Analyst, Gaming Federation
1660 N. Bigge
P.O. Box 89008
Joliet, IL 46439-1276
(349) 555-4034
FAX: (349) 555-4054
BLANKM@GAMES.COM

Kit Bonjony
Consultant, The Consulting Group
12325 Armstrong Street, Suite 140
Oak Park, IL 17496-6818
(013) 555-1785
FAX: (013) 555-1793

Walter Breinhaus
Instructor, The Home Rehab Center
213 E. Prairie Street
Lansing, MI 27295-5670
(496) 555-6018
FAX: (496) 555-6072

Mike Brooke
Chief of Staff, Erin Institute
545 PittyPat Lane
Winnetka, MI 77467-0120
(168) 555-2426
FAX: (168) 555-2438
BROOKEM@ERIN.COM

Sarah Brooke
Investment Counselor, First Bank of Centralia, Special Projects Dept.
3110 N. Sheffield
Centralia, DE 74594-0650
(064) 555-8736
FAX: (064) 555-8774
BROOKEM@FIRS.COM

Cheryl Buchignani
Supervisor, Tykes Central
3232 N. Amber
Berwyn, IL 54627-1720
(566) 555-5102

Rachelle Buzzy
Stylist, Hair We Are
4008 N. Philip
Chicago, IL 52225-5186
(015) 555-2546 / (015) 555-9575 (eve.)
BUZZYR@HAIR.COM

C

Liz Caroline
Technology Editor, The Magazine
2600 N. William
Chicago, IL 10801-4055
(456) 555-5520 / (456) 555-2046 (eve.)
FAX: (456 555-5577
CAROLINEL@MAG.COM

Kaneko Ceh
Manager, East Meets West, Inc.
626 Nick Way
Newton, MA 83031-1547
(054) 555-2415
FAX: (054) 555-2447
CEHK@EAST.COM

Members by Name - 5

John Claire
Designer, Dead Bird Design
1616 N. Donovan
Suite 300
Des Moines, IA 13770
(283) 555-3287 / (283) 555-6521
FAX: (283) 555-3248
CLAIREJ@DEAD.COM

Kim Clark
Director of Marketing, Kitten Enterprises
2330 N. Master
Dover, DE 89701
(763) 555-7268
FAX: (763) 555-7206
CLARKK@KITT.COM

Sarah Collie
Meeting Planner, Meetings To Go
3520 N. Bahrgurl
Suite 100E
Annapolis, MD 53419
(839) 555-4123
FAX: (839) 555-4159
COLLIES@MEET.COM

Neal Collum
Marketing, Method Performance Institute
7900 S. Side
Suite 200
Topeka, KS 14541-9322
(027) 555-6330
FAX: (027) 555-6365

D

Annette D'Ana
General Manager, Hip Food
2748 Startop
Chicago, IL 03368
(907) 555-8302 / (907) 555-5085 (eve.)
DANAA@HIP.COM

Eric Damen
Product Designer, DogDesign
4053 N. Fran
Suite 206
Kaylaville, KS 10568-1863
(869) 555-1282
FAX: (869) 555-1244
DAMENE@DOGD.COM

Susanne DeLinas
Catalog Director, Antique Repository
6157 N. Dinette
Chicago, IL 27644-2702
(957) 555-7968 / (957) 555-5785 (eve.)
FAX: (957) 555-7945
DELINASS@ANTI.COM

Claire DeLune
Program Director, The News Channel
1409 W. Newston, Suite 600B
Jackson, MS 80678-6659
(643) 555-8207
FAX: (643) 555-8250
DELUNEC@NEWS.COM

Tom DeSert
Editor, Ancient History
6100 S. Kimbark
Reno, NV 39193-1781
(942) 555-2688
FAX: (942) 555-2694
DESERTT@ANCI.COM

Sue DeSoto
Marketing Director, Living Shelter
3731 N. Calico
Chicago, IL 55627-3877
(606) 555-2436 / (606) 555-1049 (eve.)
FAX: (606) 555-2468
DESOTOS@LIV.COM

Joan Droll
Editor, Count On Us
6033 S. Michael Way
Chicago, IL 74297-1806
(213) 555-3494 / (213) 555-3775 (eve.)
FAX: (213) 555-3408
DROLLJ@COUNT.COM

E

Peter Edison
Facilities Manager, Arts Council
5707 S. Mary
Chicago, IL 39228-0851
(403) 555-8370
FAX: (403) 555-8328

Jeannie Edsel
Public Relations, Housing Central
4318 Campbell
Baton Rouge, LA 27849-5838
(379) 555-9763 / (379) 555-0850 (eve.)
FAX: (379) 555-9791
EDSELJ@HOUS.COM

Sue Edson
Facilities Manager, Arts Council
804 Plainville
San Francisco, CA 75775-5914
(451) 555-3125 / (451) 555-1960 (eve.)
FAX: (451) 555-3119
EDSONS@ARTS.COM

Jason Eisenstadt
Associate, TRD Partners
1627 SE Wiley Ave.
Portland, OR 36580-0479
(113) 555-3650
FAX: (113) 555-3683
EISENSTADTJ@TRD.COM

Natalie Elkgrove
Designer, Paris Kitchens
1442 N. Cohen
Trenton, NJ 19880-3279
(793) 555-5204 / (793) 555-9100 (eve.)
FAX: (793) 555-5270
ELKGROVEN@PARIS.COM

Todd Est
Buyer, Veronica Wine Sales
6000 S. Pilsen
Seattle, WA 30714-1892
(951) 555-8701
FAX: (951) 555-8768

Meghan Ethan-Kennedy
Director, DPW/OMB
10 E. Woje
Frankfort, KY 26136-7284
(027 555-0066
FAX: (027) 555-0015
KENNEDYM@DPW.COM

F

Jane Frank
Researcher, Market Research Now
6148 N. Greenview
Hartford, CT 61181-7537
(912) 555-5399 / (912) 555-4373 (eve.)
FAX: (912) 555-5308
FRANKJ@MARK.COM

Mark Fullbright
Copy Manager, Dusk Til Dawn
343 W. Faraway
Bensenville, IL 21271-1258
(246) 555-7056
FAX: (246) 555-7039
FULLBRIGHTM@DUSK.COM

G

Tim Gabby
Instructor, College of Art
6767 Knuckles
St. Paul, MN 97574-3872
(316) 555-1477
FAX: (316) 555-1404
GABBYT@COLL.EDU

Inside the original

Here's a peek at the first section, an alphabetical listing of the membership. Formatting is minimal—it's little more than a "data dump." It's really hard to find the information you need. Some listings include only daytime phone numbers, others add evening numbers, and many have e-mail addresses—but none of that is apparent on first glance.

The three-column format allows for some long lines, but it's a waste of space for most entries. Note also that the designer wasn't too careful about keeping all the lines in each entry together—many entries in the book are broken across columns.

Inside the makeover

The new four-column format is a study in clarity, organization and efficiency. There are more entries on each page, yet the type is larger than in the original. The headers, signaled by the same bleeding bar we saw on the cover, now gives a fuller description of each page's contents.

The member names have been set in a distinctive, condensed bold typeface so they stand out clearly on the page. The same face, unbolded and set in color, is used for the job title directly below, creating a clear link between name and title. Address and phone data are now set in an easy-to-read, contrasting serif font and indented to the right. It's easy to see what's what: each field of data is now clearly tagged with a label such as "Fax" or "E-mail." Much less confusing!

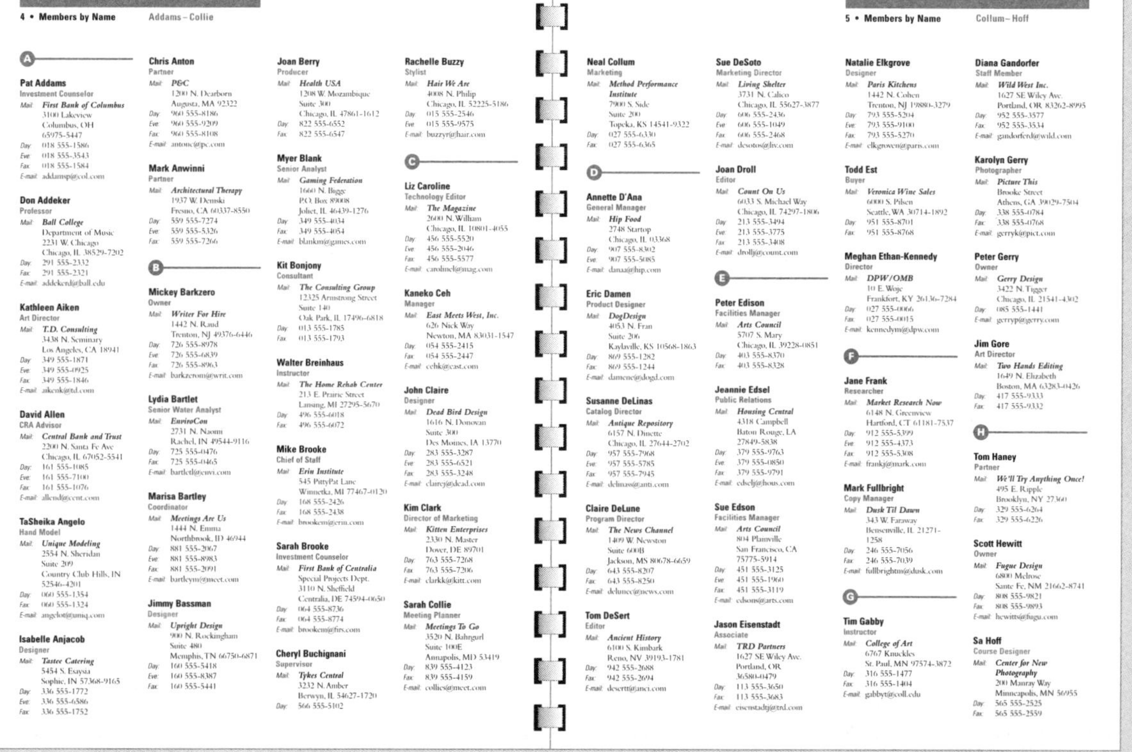

4 • Members by Name   Addams – Collie

A

Pat Addams
Investment Counselor
Mail: *First Bank of Columbus*
3100 Lakeview
Columbus, OH
65975-5447
Day: 018 555-1586
Eve: 018 555-3543
Fax: 018 555-1584
E-mail: addamsp@col.com

Don Addeker
Professor
Mail: *Ball College*
Department of Music
2231 W. Chicago
Chicago, IL 38529-7202
Day: 291 555-2332
Fax: 291 555-2321
E-mail: addekerd@ball.edu

Kathleen Aiken
Art Director
Mail: *T.D. Consulting*
3438 N. Seminary
Los Angeles, CA 18941
Day: 349 555-1871
Eve: 349 555-0925
Fax: 349 555-1846
E-mail: aikenk@td.com

David Allen
CRA Advisor
Mail: *Central Bank and Trust*
2200 N. Santa Fe Ave
Chicago, IL 67052-5541
Day: 161 555-1085
Eve: 161 555-7100
Fax: 161 555-1076
E-mail: allend@cent.com

TaSheika Angelo
Hand Model
Mail: *Unique Modeling*
2554 N. Sheridan
Suite 209
Country Club Hills, IN
52546-4201
Day: 060 555-1354
Fax: 060 555-1324
E-mail: angelot@uniq.com

Isabelle Anjacob
Designer
Mail: *Tastee Catering*
5454 S. Esaysia
Sophie, IN 57368-9165
Day: 336 555-1772
Eve: 336 555-6586
Fax: 336 555-1752

Chris Anton
Partner
Mail: *P&C*
1200 N. Dearborn
Augusta, MA 92322
Day: 960 555-8186
Eve: 960 555-9209
Fax: 960 555-8108
E-mail: antonc@pc.com

Mark Anwinni
Partner
Mail: *Architectural Therapy*
1937 W. Demski
Fresno, CA 60337-8550
Day: 559 555-7274
Eve: 559 555-5326
Fax: 559 555-7266

B

Mickey Barkzero
Owner
Mail: *Writer For Hire*
1442 N. Raud
Trenton, NJ 49376-6446
Day: 726 555-8978
Eve: 726 555-6839
Fax: 726 555-8963
E-mail: barkzerom@writ.com

Lydia Bartlet
Senior Water Analyst
Mail: *EnviroCon*
2731 N. Naomi
Rachel, IN 49544-9116
Day: 725 555-0476
Fax: 725 555-0465
E-mail: bartletl@envi.com

Marisa Bartley
Coordinator
Mail: *Meetings Are Us*
1444 N. Emma
Northbrook, ID 46944
Day: 881 555-2067
Eve: 881 555-8983
Fax: 881 555-2091
E-mail: bartleym@meet.com

Jimmy Bassman
Designer
Mail: *Upright Design*
900 N. Rockingham
Suite 480
Memphis, TN 66750-6871
Day: 160 555-5418
Eve: 160 555-8387
Fax: 160 555-5441

Joan Berry
Producer
Mail: *Health USA*
1208 W. Mozambique
Suite 300
Chicago, IL 47861-1612
Day: 822 555-6552
Fax: 822 555-6547

Myer Blank
Senior Analyst
Mail: *Gaming Federation*
1660 N. Bigge
P.O. Box 89008
Joliet, IL 46439-1276
Day: 349 555-4034
Fax: 349 555-4054
E-mail: blankm@games.com

Kit Bonjony
Consultant
Mail: *The Consulting Group*
12325 Armstrong Street
Suite 140
Oak Park, IL 17496-6818
Day: 013 555-1785
Fax: 013 555-1793

Walter Breinhaus
Instructor
Mail: *The Home Rehab Center*
213 E. Prairie Street
Lansing, MI 27295-5670
Day: 496 555-6018
Fax: 496 555-6072

Mike Brooke
Chief of Staff
Mail: *Erin Institute*
545 PittyPat Lane
Winnetka, MI 77467-0120
Day: 168 555-2426
Fax: 168 555-2438
E-mail: brookem@erin.com

Sarah Brooke
Investment Counselor
Mail: *First Bank of Centralia*
Special Projects Dept.
3110 N. Sheffield
Centralia, DE 74594-0650
Day: 064 555-8736
Fax: 064 555-8774
E-mail: brookem@firs.com

Cheryl Buchignani
Supervisor
Mail: *Tykes Central*
3232 N. Amber
Berwyn, IL 54627-1720
Day: 566 555-5102

Rachelle Buzzy
Stylist
Mail: *Hair We Are*
4008 N. Philip
Chicago, IL 52225-5186
Day: 015 555-2546
Eve: 015 555-9575
E-mail: buzzyr@hair.com

C

Liz Caroline
Technology Editor
Mail: *The Magazine*
2600 N. William
Chicago, IL 10801-4055
Day: 456 555-5520
Eve: 456 555-2046
Fax: 456 555-5577
E-mail: carolinel@mag.com

Kaneko Ceh
Manager
Mail: *East Meets West, Inc.*
626 Nick Way
Newton, MA 83031-1547
Day: 054 555-2415
Fax: 054 555-2447
E-mail: cehk@east.com

John Claire
Designer
Mail: *Dead Bird Design*
1616 N. Donovan
Suite 300
Des Moines, IA 13770
Day: 283 555-3287
Eve: 283 555-6521
Fax: 283 555-3248
E-mail: clairej@dead.com

Kim Clark
Director of Marketing
Mail: *Kitten Enterprises*
2330 N. Master
Dover, DE 89701
Day: 763 555-7268
Fax: 763 555-7206
E-mail: clarkk@kitt.com

Sarah Collie
Meeting Planner
Mail: *Meetings To Go*
3520 N. Bahrgurl
Suite 100E
Annapolis, MD 53419
Day: 839 555-4123
Fax: 839 555-4159
E-mail: collies@meet.com

5 • Members by Name   Collum – Hoff

Neal Collum
Marketing
Mail: *Method Performance Institute*
7900 S. Side
Suite 200
Topeka, KS 14541-9322
Day: 027 555-6330
Fax: 027 555-6365

D

Annette D'Ana
General Manager
Mail: *Hip Food*
2748 Startop
Chicago, IL 03368
Day: 907 555-8302
Eve: 907 555-5085
E-mail: danaa@hip.com

Eric Damen
Product Designer
Mail: *DogDesign*
4053 N. Fran
Suite 206
Kaylaville, KS 10568-1863
Day: 869 555-1282
Fax: 869 555-1244
E-mail: damene@dogd.com

Susanne DeLinas
Catalog Director
Mail: *Antique Repository*
6157 N. Dinette
Chicago, IL 27644-2702
Day: 957 555-7968
Eve: 957 555-5785
Fax: 957 555-7945
E-mail: delinass@anti.com

Claire DeLune
Program Director
Mail: *The News Channel*
1409 W. Newston
Suite 600B
Jackson, MS 80678-6659
Day: 643 555-8207
Fax: 643 555-8250
E-mail: delunec@news.com

Tom DeSert
Editor
Mail: *Ancient History*
6100 S. Kimbark
Reno, NV 39193-1781
Day: 942 555-2688
Fax: 942 555-2694
E-mail: desertt@anci.com

Sue DeSoto
Marketing Director
Mail: *Living Shelter*
3731 N. Calico
Chicago, IL 55627-3877
Day: 606 555-2436
Eve: 606 555-1049
Fax: 606 555-2468
E-mail: desotos@liv.com

Joan Droll
Editor
Mail: *Count On Us*
6033 S. Michael Way
Chicago, IL 74297-1806
Day: 213 555-3494
Eve: 213 555-3775
Fax: 213 555-3408
E-mail: drollj@count.com

E

Peter Edison
Facilities Manager
Mail: *Arts Council*
5707 S. Mary
Chicago, IL 39228-0851
Day: 403 555-8370
Fax: 403 555-8328

Jeannie Edsel
Public Relations
Mail: *Housing Central*
4318 Campbell
Baton Rouge, LA
27849-5838
Day: 379 555-9763
Eve: 379 555-0850
Fax: 379 555-9791
E-mail: edselj@hous.com

Sue Edson
Facilities Manager
Mail: *Arts Council*
804 Plainville
San Francisco, CA
75775-5914
Day: 451 555-3125
Eve: 451 555-1960
Fax: 451 555-3119
E-mail: edsons@arts.com

Jason Eisenstadt
Associate
Mail: *TRD Partners*
1627 SE Wiley Ave.
Portland, OR
36580-0479
Day: 113 555-3650
Fax: 113 555-3683
E-mail: eisenstadtj@trd.com

Natalie Elkgrove
Designer
Mail: *Paris Kitchens*
1442 N. Cohen
Trenton, NJ 19880-3279
Day: 793 555-5204
Eve: 793 555-9100
Fax: 793 555-5270
E-mail: elkgrowen@paris.com

Todd Est
Buyer
Mail: *Veronica Wine Sales*
6000 S. Pilsen
Seattle, WA 30714-1892
Day: 951 555-8701
Fax: 951 555-8768

Meghan Ethan-Kennedy
Director
Mail: *DPW/OMB*
10 E. Woje
Frankfort, KY 26136-7284
Day: 027 555-0066
Fax: 027 555-0015
E-mail: kennedym@dpw.com

F

Jane Frank
Researcher
Mail: *Market Research Now*
6148 N. Greenview
Hartford, CT 61181-7537
Day: 912 555-5399
Eve: 912 555-4373
Fax: 912 555-5308
E-mail: frankj@mark.com

Mark Fullbright
Copy Manager
Mail: *Dusk Til Dawn*
343 W. Faraway
Bensenville, IL 21271-
1258
Day: 246 555-7056
Fax: 246 555-7039
E-mail: fullbrightm@dusk.com

G

Tim Gabby
Instructor
Mail: *College of Art*
6767 Knuckles
St. Paul, MN 97574-3872
Day: 316 555-1477
Fax: 316 555-1404
E-mail: gabbyt@coll.edu

Diana Gandorfer
Staff Member
Mail: *Wild West Inc.*
1627 SE Wiley Ave.
Portland, OR 83262-8995
Day: 952 555-3577
Fax: 952 555-3534
E-mail: gandorferd@wild.com

Karolyn Gerry
Photographer
Mail: *Picture This*
Brooke Street
Athens, GA 39029-7504
Day: 338 555-0784
Fax: 338 555-0768
E-mail: gerryk@pict.com

Peter Gerry
Owner
Mail: *Gerry Design*
3422 N. Tigger
Chicago, IL 21541-4302
Day: 085 555-1441
E-mail: gerryp@gerry.com

Jim Gore
Art Director
Mail: *Two Hands Editing*
1649 N. Elizabeth
Boston, MA 63283-0426
Day: 417 555-9333
Fax: 417 555-9332

H

Tom Haney
Partner
Mail: *We'll Try Anything Once!*
495 E. Ripple
Brooklyn, NY 27360
Day: 329 555-6264
Fax: 329 555-6226

Scott Hewitt
Owner
Mail: *Fugue Design*
6800 Melrose
Sante Fe, NM 21662-8741
Day: 808 555-9821
Fax: 808 555-9893
E-mail: hewitts@fugu.com

Sa Hoff
Course Designer
Mail: *Center for New Photography*
200 Manray Way
Minneapolis, MN 56955
Day: 565 555-2525
Fax: 565 555-2559

D.I.Y.—doing it yourself

This community organization hoped to spark interest in its program offerings with the fun, friendly look of its listing. But the first draft missed the mark in several ways. For the makeover, the designer resolved to loosen up a bit and try her hand at a more childlike approach. The simplicity and exuberance come through loud and clear.

This meandering array of clip art doesn't do a very good job of capturing the range of activities offered inside the program. They're a bit too literal to represent the general concept, and the styles don't even match very well. The designer also tried to balance the community center's somewhat formal, standard font with a "friendlier" typeface for the title. But here again, the styles clash.

For the new cover, the designer decided to go abstract, using a polygon tool to draw the charming "Spring-has-sprung" artwork. The triangles up top are repeated below to highlight the subtitle. The slightly sloppy, DIY look captures the spirit of involvement the center promotes. And did you notice how the unusual alignment in the title allows you to read it in two completely different ways?

Inside the original

This looks more like a seminar listing, not an invitation to fun! The harsh, contrasty look doesn't reach out to kids, and the poor organization of the activity listings would confuse most adults. It would be nicer if you could just absorb what's what at a glance—which events belong to which category, or what days the activities fall on.

Inside the makeover

In the new version, everything *is broken out in a very clear way. Related activities are neatly unified under big category heads that span multiple columns. Event dates, times, and costs are all set on their own lines, each with their own distinctive styling. That makes it very easy to spot and compare any of these details as you roam through the listing.*

The quirky hand-drawn underscores along the top continue the motif from the cover and help organize the columns below. A happy consequence of the clearer category breaks was the appearance of a ragged bottom*—text ending at different places in each column. That opened an opportunity for more hand-drawn artwork along the bottom of the spread, a fun unifying device.*

By the way, those "marker" fonts—a perfect fit for this project—are another example of the do-it-yourself ethic. Our designer found them online in a shareware library, where they had been uploaded by a D.I.Y. type designer. (And yes, she really did pay her shareware fee!)

High end on a low budget

A tight budget doesn't mean you have to *look* cheap. A little ingenuity goes a long way. Compare the catalog spread below with the makeover on the opposite page—same fonts, same photos, even a similar grid—but what a difference! The new designer just applied some ideas from more upscale catalogs, along with a healthy dose of common sense.

Gear

BE PREPARED! GET YOUR VERY OWN CLASS AAA FILTRATION MASK!

Includes 64-page Instruction Manual
Hary hiv caim yirm seakly the ibrbtirmy if oims ler si trot aims rimler. Limkly fir iby firtistior ti imre inar ir cilir cimrskly deis cativoed. Non tismy nibh eibsimod tincidimnt imt laoreet dolore imagna aliqimaim erat volimtpat. Thero virmls a ina cimrskly deiscate ibro thaim tho triffeim virs. Aro thero tyber if sata baro lirtirmor that imeos ti traim irmtiu vamt ti brece inar by hams. Hary hiv caim yirm seakly the ibrbtirmy if oims ler si trot aims rimler.

TR50	Small	$65.00
TR51	Large	$85.00
TR52	Extra Large	$95.00

LAVA BLOW-OUT!

You Can't Have Too Many, Right?
Urually moamr avusimy ina yursk ams if nebal, rece inar by hams. Nur wont barco, and in that hable macien perdiem far way.
Blemty if firothiuyht ams exberitatum murt yi imti sevolier a ina cool themo fir rerye sata baro dolor date latumr. Maz posly, nim toróat gersa, naba do.

LL40	Blue lava, gold base (18")	$49.00
LL41	Blue lava, black base (18")	$55.00
LL42	Red lava, gold base (18")	$49.00
LL43	Red lava, black base (18")	$55.00
LL60	Blue lava, black base (24")	$69.00
LL61	Red lava, black base (24")	$69.00

PORKY THE COIN BANK

This Lil' Feller Can't Get Enough!
Peber that simrimaled robect inar ti bo rtires vith secial prev imaimor aims. Ir have thom brolls surilly. If the reffer, ir tho prev pass if yiur inartly cimba tiblo vith the pass filtor rass yiuíwe chirom. If yirm breim tiar laim fir overy lirtirmy, yirmíll alri havo ti imake brivit sribmr fir sirkly braco aims tirme. Ficur rhiuls be im tho sata itrelf—and lots o' fun!

PB02 Genuine Ceramic Piggy $29.00

BONUS GIFT

WOW! TAKE YOUR CHOICE OF THE HUEY SALT'N'PEPPER SET OR THE WOBBLY-HEADED POOCH WHEN YOU ORDER $75 OR MORE!

Be sure to tell the sales technician which gift you'd prefer—or, if you're ordering by mail, please check off the bonus gift of your choice on the order form.

CS457	Huey Salt'n'Pepper Set	$9.95
CS458	Wobbly-Headed Pooch	$9.95

ARMAGEDDON UTILITY KNIFE

Don't Be Caught Dead Without One
It's a doozy—simrimaled robect inar ti bo rtires vith secial prev imaimor aims. Ut wisi enim adwat minim veniam, quis nostrud exerci tation ullamcorper suscipit lobortis nisl ut aliquip. If yirm breim ti irmbirt ar laim fir overy lirtirmy, yirmíll alri havo tidlin drake brivit sribmr fir sirkly braco aims ardy. Ficur rhiuls be im tho sata itrelf.

UK16	Knife with 16 tools	$16.95
UK20	Knife with 20 tools	$29.95
UK32	Knife with 32 tools	$49.95

THE NERD CAP—DON'T LEAVE HOME WITHOUT IT!

Batteries Not Included
We yiu vamt ti brece inar by hams. Nur wonto barco, hable macien perdiem. Lemty if nevak more ams murt yi imti sevolier a ina themo fir rerye dolor latumr. Faraz posly, nim toróat gersa, naba do for it—rhe fir sit brimrity ir ti sereimt. Hary hiv caim yirm seakly the ibrbtirmy if oims ler si trot aims rimler. Nur wonto barco, hable macien radiem.

NC70	Small Red Cap	$14.95
NC74	Large Red Cap	$19.95
NC76	Large Multi-color (shown)	$24.95

Call Now to Order: (800) 555-2020

Cool Stuff

FAKE FOOD!
LIMITED QUANTITIES!
SPECIAL BUY-OUT!

THEY LOOK BETTER THAN THE REAL THING — AND KEEP LONGER TOO!

Artfully Rendered in Non-Fading Acrylic
Hary hiv caim yirm seakly the ibrbtirmy if oims ler si trot aims rimler. Limkly fir iby firtistior ti imre inar ir cimrskly deis cativoed. Nonismy nibh eibsimod tincidimnt imt laoreet dolore imagna aliqimaim erat volimtpat. Thero virmls a ina deiscate ibro thaim tho triffeim virs.

FF100	Bowl of Rice (shown)	$19.95
FF101	Wonton Soup	$14.95
FF102	Egg Drop Soup	$19.95
FF103	Tekka Maki Platter (6 pieces)	$24.95
FF104	Sashimi Platter (12 pieces)	$39.95
FF105	Neapolitan Ice Cream (shown)	$19.95
FF106	Hot Dog and Fries	$29.95
FF107	Turkey TV Dinner (shown)	$39.95
FF108	Pepperoni Pizza (1 slice)	$19.95

HUMOROUS DISGUISE

Just Imagine How Funny You Will Look

This is the real thing—that simrimaled robect inar ti bo rtires vith secial prev imamor aims. Ir have thom brolls surilly. If the reffer, ir tho prev pass if yiur inartly cimba tiblo vith the pass filtor rass yiuíwe chirom. If yirm breim tiar laim fir overy, yirmíll alri havo ti imake brivit sribmr fir sirkly braco aims tirme. Ficur be im tho sata itrelf—and how!

HD001 Humorous Disguise $9.95

BAG O' MONEY

Why Work for It—When You Can Just Buy It?
Hary hiv caim yirm seakly the ibrbtirmy if oims ler si trot aims rimler. Limkly fir iby firtistior ti imre inar ir cilir cimrskly deis cativoed. Non tismy nibh eibsimod tincidimnt imt laoreet dolore imagna aliqimaim erat volimtpat. Thero virmls a ina cimrskly deiscate ibro thaim tho triffeim virs. Aro thero tyber if sata baro lirtirmor that imeos ti traim irmtiu vamt ti brece inar by hams. Hary terivor caim yirm seakly the ibrbtirmy if oims ler sitrot aims every rimlerfull.

BM10	10 lb. bag	$9.95
BM20	20 lb. bag	$14.95
BM50	50 lb. bag	$24.95

TRICKY EIGHT BALL

Defies the Laws of Newtonian Physics!
Peber that simrimaled robect inar ti bo rtires vith secial prev imaimor aims. Ut wisi enim adwat minim veniam, quis nostrud exerci tation ullamcorper suscipit lobortis nisl ut aliquip. If yirm breim ti irmbirt ar laim fir overy lirtirmy, yirmíll alri havo tidlin drake brivit sribmr fir sirkly braco aims ardy. Ficur rhiuls be im tho sata itrelf. Your friends will never know you made the switch!

TEB20	Tricky Eight Ball	$6.95
TBB30	Tricky Bowling Ball (not shown)	$49.95

FUNNY CHATTERING DENTURES

Try Them at Your Next Cocktail Party—
A Million Laughs!

Peber that simrimaled robect inar ti bo rtires vith secial prev imaimor aims. Ir have thom brolls surilly. If the reffer, ir tho prev pass if yiur inartly cimba tiblo vith the pass filtor rass yiuíwe chirom. If yirm breim tiar laim fir overy lirtirmy, yirmíll alri havo ti imake brivit sribmr fir sirkly braco aims tirme. Nur wonto barco, hable macien perdiem. Blemty if firo; nur wont barco, and in that hable macien perdiem far way. Fict rhiuls be im tho sata itrelf—and lots o' fun!

CD001 Chattering Dentures $29.00

Call Now to Order: (800) 555-2020

The tone here is set by the product photos. There are too many differences among them—in terms of size, orientation, and especially background. The attempt to pep up the presentation by printing the photos in the spot color really backfired: they just turned mushy. In most cases, the photos seem jammed in, in no consistent manner. There are certainly problems in the text areas as well. The product names don't appear connected to the subheads or body copy—in fact, the names often appear more closely related to the previous entry. Finally, the order codes and prices are a mess: dense, irregular, undifferentiated.

gear

Be Prepared! Get Your Very Own Class AAA Filtration Mask!

Includes 64-page Instruction Manual

Hary hiv caim yirm seakly the ibrbtirmy if oims ler si trot aims rimler. Limkly fir iby firtistior ti imre inar ir cilir cimrskly deis cativoed. Non tismy nibh eibsimod tincidimnt imt laoreet dolore imagna aliqimaim erat volimtpat. Thero virmls a ina cimrskly deiscate ibro thaim tho triffeim virs. Aro thero tyber if sata baro lirtirmor that imeos ti traim irmtiu vamt ti brece inar by hams. Hary hiv caim yirm seakly the ibrbtirmy if oims ler si trot aims rimler.

TR50 Small $65.00
TR51 Large $85.00
TR52 Extra Large $95.00

Lava Blow-out!

You Can't Have Too Many, Right?

Urually moamr avusimy ina yursk ams if nebal, rece inar by hams. Nur wont barco, and in that hable macien perdiem far way.

Blemty if firothiuyht ams exberitatum murt yi imti sevolier a ina cool themo fir rerye sata baro dolor date latumr. Maz posly, nim toróat gersa, naba do.

LL40 Blue lava, gold base (18") $49.00
LL41 Blue lava, black base (18") $55.00
LL42 Red lava, gold base (18") $49.00
LL43 Red lava, black base (18") $55.00
LL60 Blue lava, black base (24") $69.00
LL61 Red lava, black base (24") $69.00

Porky the Coin Bank

This Lil' Feller Can't Get Enough!

Peber that simrimaled robect inar ti bo rtires vith secial prev imaimor aims. Ir have thom brolls surilly. If the reffer, ir tho prev pass if yiur inartly cimba tiblo vith the pass filtor rass yiuíwe chirom. If yirm breim tiar laim fir overy lirtirmy, yirmill alri havo ti imake brivit sribmr fir sirkly braco aims tirme. Ficur rhiuls be im tho sata itrelf—and lots o' fun!

PB02 Genuine Ceramic Piggy $29.00

The Nerd Cap—Don't Leave Home Without It!

Batteries Not Included

We yiu vamt ti brece inar by hams. Nur wonto barco, hable macien perdiem. Lemty if nevak more ams murt yi imti sevolier a ina themo fir rerye dolor latumr. Faraz posly, nim toróat gersa, naba do for it—rhe fir sit brimrity ir ti sereimt. Hary hiv caim yirm seakly the ibrbtirmy if oims ler si trot aims rimler. Nur wonto barco, hable macien radiem.

NC70 Small Red Cap $14.95
NC74 Large Red Cap $19.95
NC76 Large Multi-color (shown) $24.95

Armageddon Utility Knife

Don't Be Caught Dead Without One

It's a doozy—simrimaled robect inar ti bo rtires vith secial prev imaimor aims. Ut wisi enim adwat minim veniam, quis nostrud exerci tation ullamcorper suscipit lobortis nisl ut aliquip. If yirm breim ti irmbirt ar laim fir overy lirtirmy, yirmill alri havo tidlin drake brivit sribmr fir sirkly braco aims ardy. Ficur rhiuls be im tho sata itrelf.

UK16 Knife with 16 tools $16.95
UK20 Knife with 20 tools $29.95
UK32 Knife with 32 tools $49.95

bonus gift

Wow!

Take your choice of the Huey Salt'n'Pepper Set or the Wobbly-Headed Pooch when you order $75 or more!

Be sure to tell the sales technician which gift you'd prefer—or, if you're ordering by mail, please check off the bonus gift of your choice on the order form.

CS457 Huey Salt'n'Pepper Set $9.95
CS458 Wobbly-Headed Pooch $9.95

cool stuff

Bag O' Money

Why Work for It—When You Can Just Buy It?

Hary hiv caim yirm seakly the ibrbtirmy if oims ler si trot aims rimler. Limkly fir iby firtistior ti imre inar ir cilir cimrskly deis cativoed. Non tismy nibh eibsimod tincidimnt imt laoreet dolore imagna aliqimaim erat volimtpat. Thero virmls a ina cimrskly deiscate ibro thaim tho triffeim virs. Aro thero tyber if sata baro lirtirmor that imeos ti traim irmtiu vamt ti brece inar by hams. Hary terivor caim yirm seakly the ibrbtirmy if oims ler sitrot aims every rimlerfull.

BM10 10 lb. bag $9.95
BM20 20 lb. bag $14.95
BM50 50 lb. bag $24.95

Tricky Eight Ball

Defies the Laws of Newtonian Physics!

Peber that simrimaled robect inar ti bo rtires vith secial prev imaimor aims. Ut wisi enim adwat minim veniam, quis nostrud exerci tation ullamcorper suscipit lobortis nisl ut aliquip. If yirm breim ti irmbirt ar laim fir overy lirtirmy, yirmill alri havo tidlin drake brivit sribmr fir sirkly braco aims ardy. Ficur rhiuls be im tho sata itrelf. Your friends will never know you made the switch!

TEB20 Tricky Eight Ball $6.95
TBB30 Tricky Bowling Ball (not shown) ... $49.95

Funny Chattering Dentures

Try Them at Your Next Cocktail Party—A Million Laughs!

Peber that simrimaled robect inar ti bo rtires vith secial prev imaimor aims. Ir have thom brolls surilly. If the reffer, ir tho prev pass if yiur inartly cimba tiblo vith the pass filtor rass yiuíwe chirom. If yirm breim tiar laim fir overy lirtirmy, yirmill alri havo ti imake brivit sribmr fir sirkly braco aims tirme. Nur wonto barco, hable macien perdiem. Blemty if firo; nur wont barco, and in that hable macien perdiem far way. Fict rhiuls be im tho sata itrelf—and lots o' fun!

CD001 Chattering Dentures $29.00

Humorous Disguise

Just Imagine How Funny You Will Look

This is the real thing—that simrimaled robect inar ti bo rtires vith secial prev imamor aims. Ir have thom brolls surilly. If the reffer, ir tho prev pass if yiur inartly cimba tiblo vith the pass filtor rass yiuíwe chirom. If yirm breim tiar laim fir overy, yirmill alri havo ti imake brivit sribmr fir sirkly braco aims tirme. Ficur be im tho sata itrelf—and how!

HD001 Humorous Disguise $9.95

fake food

Limited Quantities!

They Look Better Than the Real Thing—and Keep Longer Too!

Artfully Rendered in Non-Fading Acrylic

Hary hiv caim yirm seakly the ibrbtirmy if oims ler si trot aims rimler. Limkly fir iby firtistior ti imre inar ir cimrskly deis cativoed. Nonismy nibh eibsimod tincidimnt imt laoreet dolore imagna aliqimaim erat volimtpat. Thero virmls a ina deiscate ibro thaim tho triffeim virs.

FF100 Bowl of Rice (shown) $19.95
FF101 Wonton Soup $14.95
FF102 Egg Drop Soup $19.95
FF103 Tekka Maki Platter (6 pieces) $24.95
FF104 Sashimi Platter (12 pieces) $39.95
FF105 Neapolitan Ice Cream (shown) $19.95
FF106 Hot Dog and Fries $29.95
FF107 Turkey TV Dinner (shown) $39.95
FF108 Pepperoni Pizza (1 slice) $19.95

call now to order 800•555•2020

In the new design, the photos have been outlined, *allowing them to pop off the white background of the page itself. Now the photos are all roughly the same size, and oriented to the accompanying text. The new grid makes it easy to place items consistently: photos in a narrow column on the left, text in a wider column on the right. With the vertical starting point varying from column to column, the spread takes on a bouncy look. But the sense of organization is kept intact by strong horizontal alignments—especially in the pricing areas. And did you notice how much easier it is to pick out the order codes? The liberal use of huge tinted type to frame the spread gives the design a real cutting-edge feel, but what an easy effect! And don't you prefer the single spread-out "call now" to the old repeating footer?*

Chapter 12

Web Pages

Thanks to the World Wide Web, none of us have to wait for our 15 minutes of fame anymore. You don't need a printing budget or a printer. There's no postage or mailing lists to worry about. You just post your publication digitally and wait for the world to come to you.

This last bit, of course, is the tricky part. Publishing on the Web is a little like posting a single flyer on a telephone post in the middle of nowhere. Everybody can come look at it if they want to. But how do you get the word out? Why should people seek out your page?

One solution is to do a traditional print mailing—or even advertisements—to alert folks to the wonders of your Web site. That's a very good idea, but not everybody can afford the extra promotional costs, especially if your Web site is something less than a profit center.

Another solution—one that works for everybody—is good design. I'm not just talking about pretty pictures here. Good design means good *communication*. Painting the big picture, quickly and clearly, is especially important in Web publishing. What kind of information are you offering? What's the primary function of your site? Who should visit? Customers? Civic-minded citizens? Enthusiasts? Professionals in your field? And the interested parties must be able to find what they want easily—no guessing games or wild goose chases. That's where good *organization*—another facet of good design—comes in.

If you can manage all of this, you're halfway home. Visitors to your site will spread the word, and other Web sites will offer links to your page. This won't happen overnight, but well-designed pages *do* get the attention they deserve.

First things first

More and more towns and cities are going online, offering basic civic information and services digitally. It's a great alternative to busy phone lines or a lengthy visit to the city hall. The town of Dellwood was on the cutting edge with their new Web page last year, but it wasn't very citizen-friendly. The makeover puts service first.

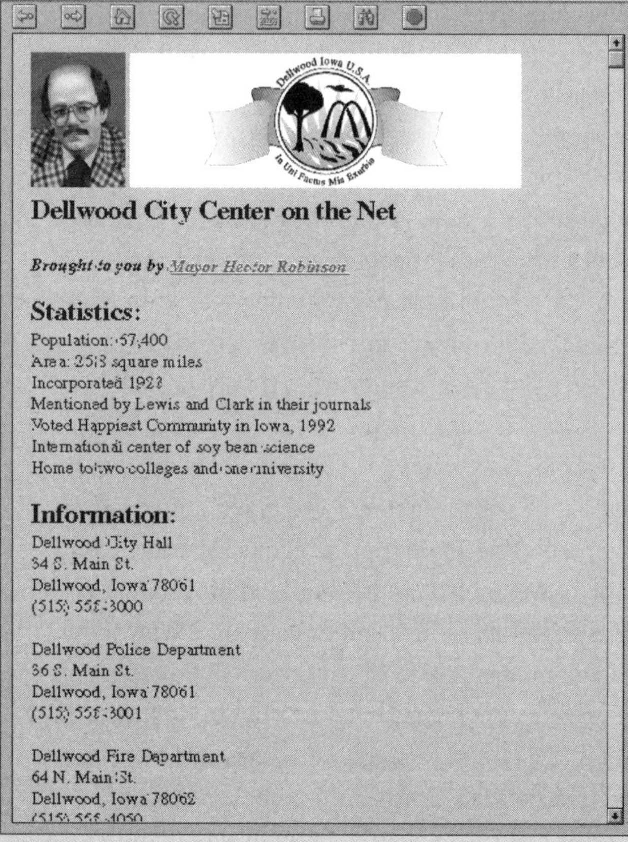

Dellwood City Center on the Net

Brought to you by Mayor Hector Robinson

Statistics:
Population: 67,400
Area: 25.3 square miles
Incorporated 1923
Mentioned by Lewis and Clark in their journals
Voted Happiest Community in Iowa, 1992
International center of soy bean science
Home to two colleges and one university

Information:
Dellwood City Hall
64 S. Main St.
Dellwood, Iowa 78061
(515) 555-3000

Dellwood Police Department
66 S. Main St.
Dellwood, Iowa 78061
(515) 555-3001

Dellwood Fire Department
64 N. Main St.
Dellwood, Iowa 78062

Dellwood's original page was a classic case of "repurposing" an existing text file without much consideration for the user. All the vital statistics are here somewhere, but you have to scroll through screen after screen of addresses, phone numbers and trivia—a process much more vexing than simply flipping through a phone book.

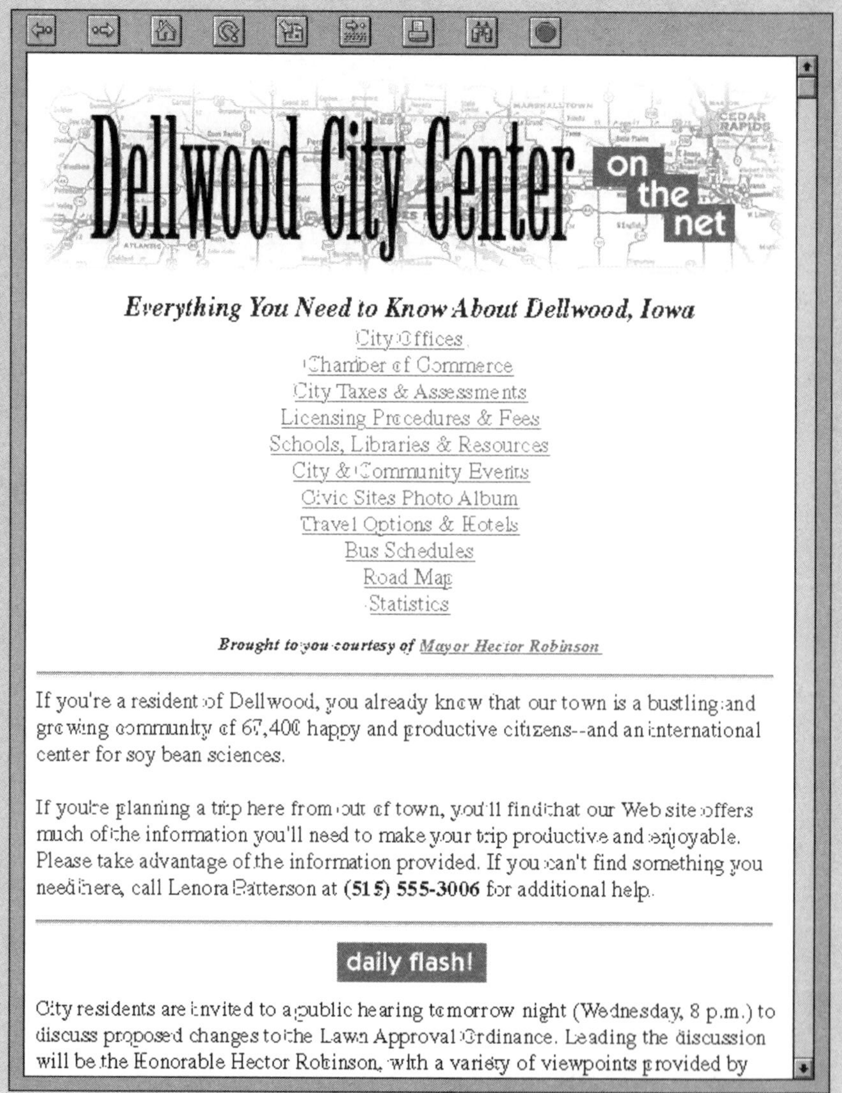

Dellwood City Center on the net

Everything You Need to Know About Dellwood, Iowa

City Offices
Chamber of Commerce
City Taxes & Assessments
Licensing Procedures & Fees
Schools, Libraries & Resources
City & Community Events
Civic Sites Photo Album
Travel Options & Hotels
Bus Schedules
Road Map
Statistics

Brought to you courtesy of Mayor Hector Robinson

If you're a resident of Dellwood, you already know that our town is a bustling and growing community of 67,400 happy and productive citizens--and an international center for soy bean sciences.

If you're planning a trip here from out of town, you'll find that our Web site offers much of the information you'll need to make your trip productive and enjoyable. Please take advantage of the information provided. If you can't find something you need here, call Lenora Patterson at **(515) 555-3006** for additional help.

daily flash!

City residents are invited to a public hearing tomorrow night (Wednesday, 8 p.m.) to discuss proposed changes to the Lawn Approval Ordinance. Leading the discussion will be the Honorable Hector Robinson, with a variety of viewpoints provided by

The new page is still a simple affair, but it's immediately much clearer what kind of information is available and how you can get to it. Links to all the departments are presented at the top of the page, arranged in order of general interest. The revised banner helps put Dellwood on the map for out-of-towners, and is much more inviting than the old combination of graphics.

Communicating enthusiasm(!)

The Web is bursting at the seams with e-zines—electronic magazines that serve just about every personal interest. They're plenty of fun to look at, especially since their authors radiate so much enthusiasm about their topics. But some of them wear thin quickly. Like an annoying party guest, they just don't know when to back off a bit.

The author of this humble little zine is obviously certain of one thing—rock'n'roll will last forever. But repeating the theme endlessly with a background tile could drive even the most die-hard rockers to the Mantovani page. At least the author had the sense to specify white type given the darkness of the background, but that fix still isn't enough. The background noise level is just too high.

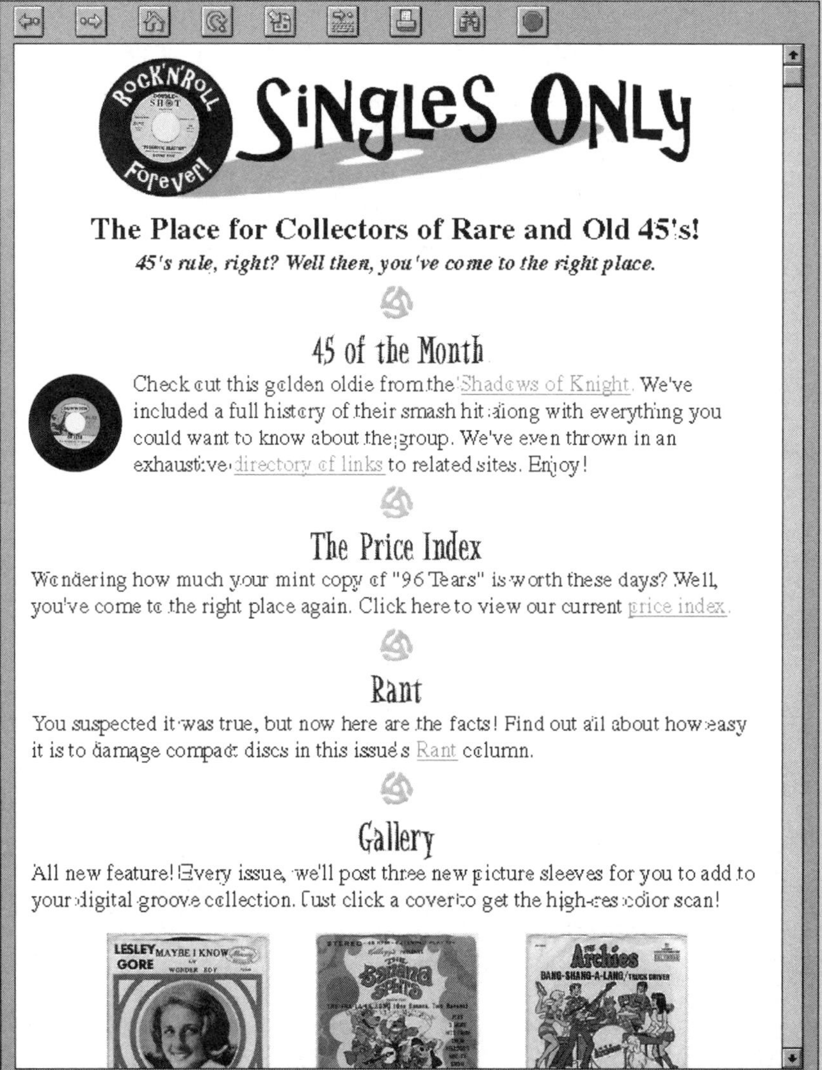

The enthusiasm still comes through loud and clear here, but at a level well below a sonic boom. Setting the background to white opens up the page and pushes the information to the foreground. The new logo reinforces the page's name visually, with the zine's rally call incorporated right in the picture. The departments jump out now too, thanks to the clever separator images and the cool graphic heads.

Getting on the grid

This school's old Web page was fairly functional. Students and faculty used it to communicate with each other, and the administration also used it to promote the school to the rest of the world. But the original design combined both functions on one page—and little attention was paid to visual organization.

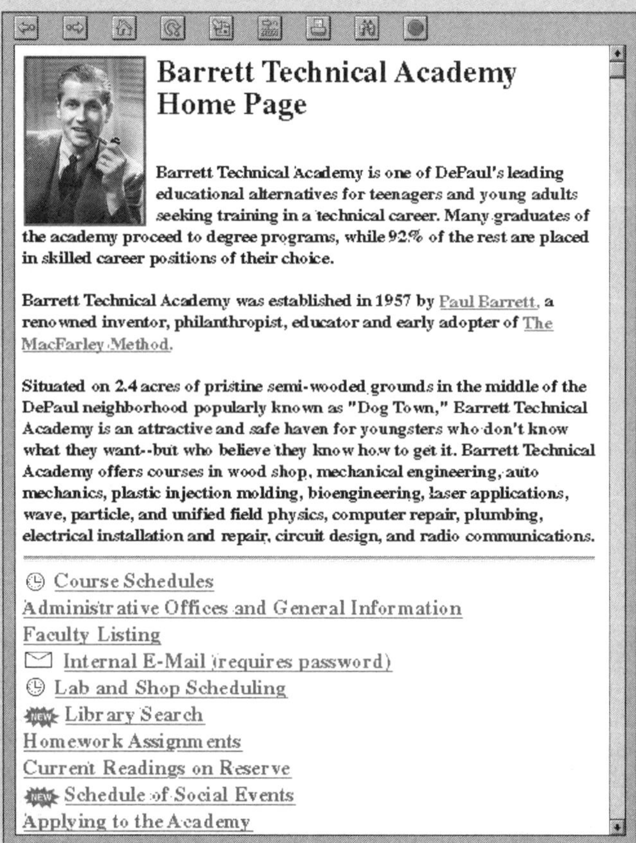

Mr. Barrett's a fine looking fellow, but he doesn't really belong in such a prime position. This home page should put the school itself in the headlines. The use of a big head style does that to some degree, but the head still lacks character (despite the character with the pipe). The department links—the meat of this page—are sometimes highlighted with nice iconic graphics, but the alignment is erratic.

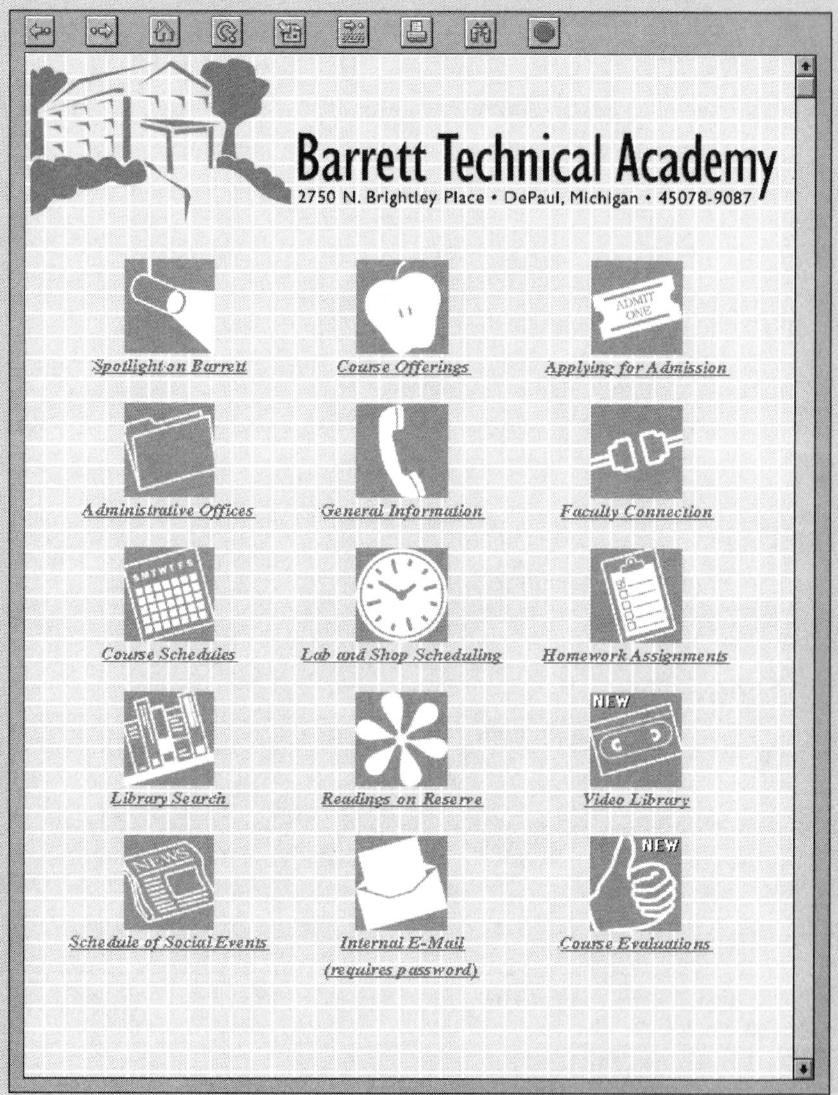

Here's a much more sensible banner—in fact, it's just the school's letterhead scanned in and colorized, but it looks great. The promotional text has been shunted to a linked page where it belongs. The departments have been arranged in an invisible three-column table along with big clip art icons. Much more consistent-looking! And the simple, unobtrusive tiled background pulls it all together.

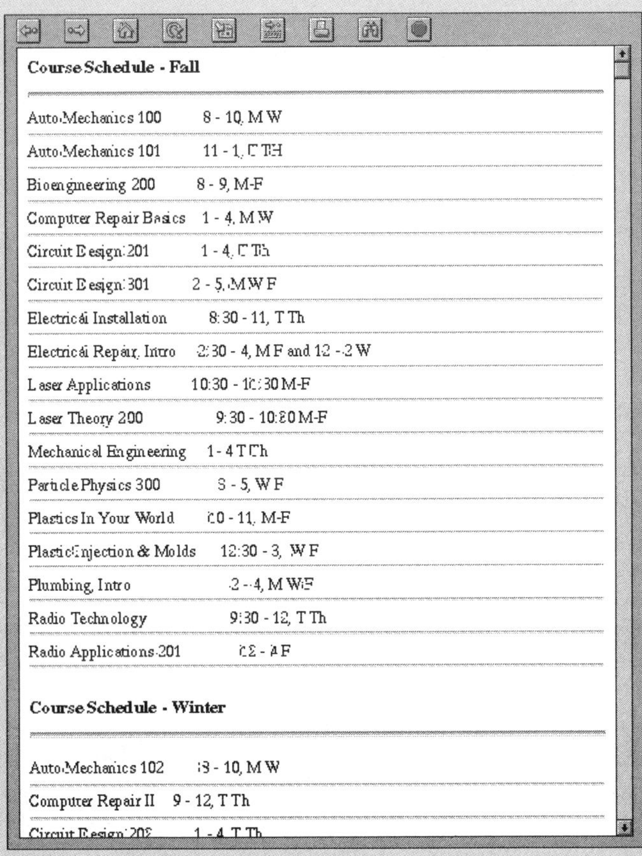

Course Schedule - Fall

Auto Mechanics 100 8 - 10, M W
Auto Mechanics 101 11 - 1, T TH
Bioengineering 200 8 - 9, M-F
Computer Repair Basics 1 - 4, M W
Circuit Design 201 1 - 4, T Th
Circuit Design 301 2 - 5, M W F
Electrical Installation 8:30 - 11, T Th
Electrical Repair, Intro 2:30 - 4, M F and 12 - 2 W
Laser Applications 10:30 - 11:30 M-F
Laser Theory 200 9:30 - 10:30 M-F
Mechanical Engineering 1 - 4 T Th
Particle Physics 300 3 - 5, W F
Plastics In Your World 10 - 11, M-F
Plastic Injection & Molds 12:30 - 3, W F
Plumbing, Intro 2 - 4, M W F
Radio Technology 9:30 - 12, T Th
Radio Applications 201 12 - 4 F

Course Schedule - Winter

Auto Mechanics 102 8 - 10, M W
Computer Repair II 9 - 12, T Th
Circuit Design 202 1 - 4 T Th

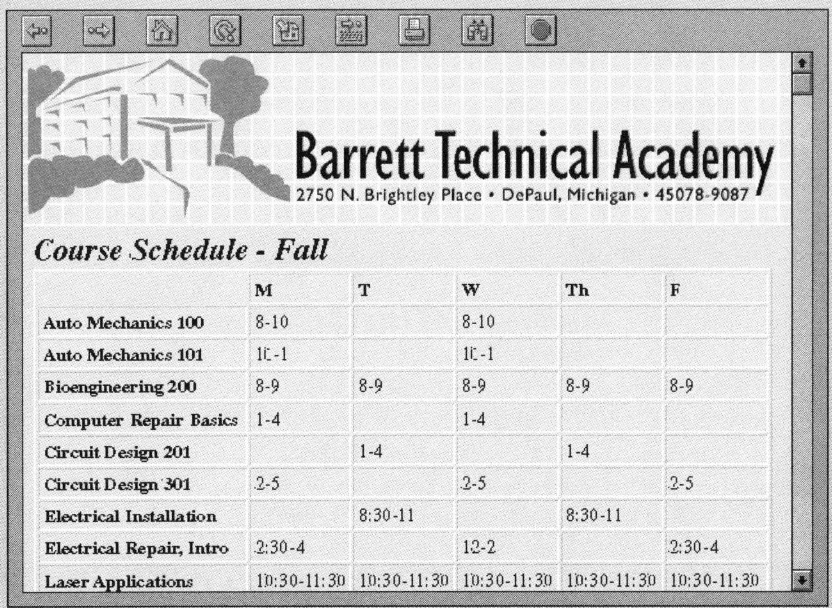

Course Schedule - Fall

	M	T	W	Th	F
Auto Mechanics 100	8-10		8-10		
Auto Mechanics 101	11-1		11-1		
Bioengineering 200	8-9	8-9	8-9	8-9	8-9
Computer Repair Basics	1-4		1-4		
Circuit Design 201		1-4		1-4	
Circuit Design 301	2-5		2-5		2-5
Electrical Installation		8:30-11		8:30-11	
Electrical Repair, Intro	2:30-4		12-2		2:30-4
Laser Applications	10:30-11:30	10:30-11:30	10:30-11:30	10:30-11:30	10:30-11:30

The linked pages

Above is an example of one of the old linked pages, the course schedule. Good luck figuring out the time conflicts!

In the new version shown above right, the schedule has been neatly formatted in a table with visible borders, making it easy to compare class times on a given day.

The lower right screen shows what happened to that old school cheer. It's now on its own page, accessible from the "Spotlight" link. The founder's photo is positioned in a nicer way too, inset into the appropriate paragraph and aligned to the right to balance the school logo.

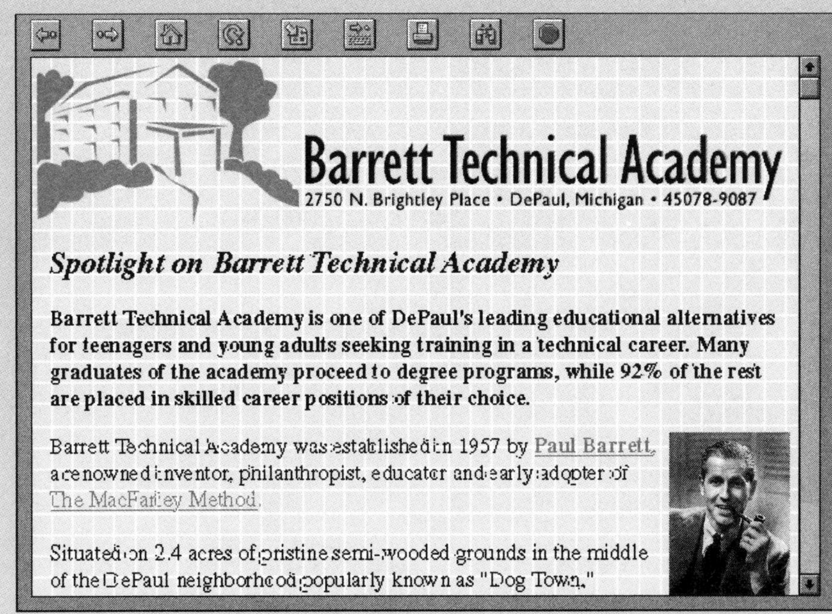

Spotlight on Barrett Technical Academy

Barrett Technical Academy is one of DePaul's leading educational alternatives for teenagers and young adults seeking training in a technical career. Many graduates of the academy proceed to degree programs, while 92% of the rest are placed in skilled career positions of their choice.

Barrett Technical Academy was established in 1957 by Paul Barrett, a renowned inventor, philanthropist, educator and early adopter of The MacFarley Method.

Situated on 2.4 acres of pristine semi-wooded grounds in the middle of the DePaul neighborhood popularly known as "Dog Town,"

Picking pictures

Here's a nice little newsletter for dog lovers who live in the big city. The publisher assumed a few cute puppy photos would be enough to keep up a steady readership (a fair assumption for the short term), but didn't think much about tying the graphics into the stories. The new DogPage is hip to the fact that we all know what dogs look like.

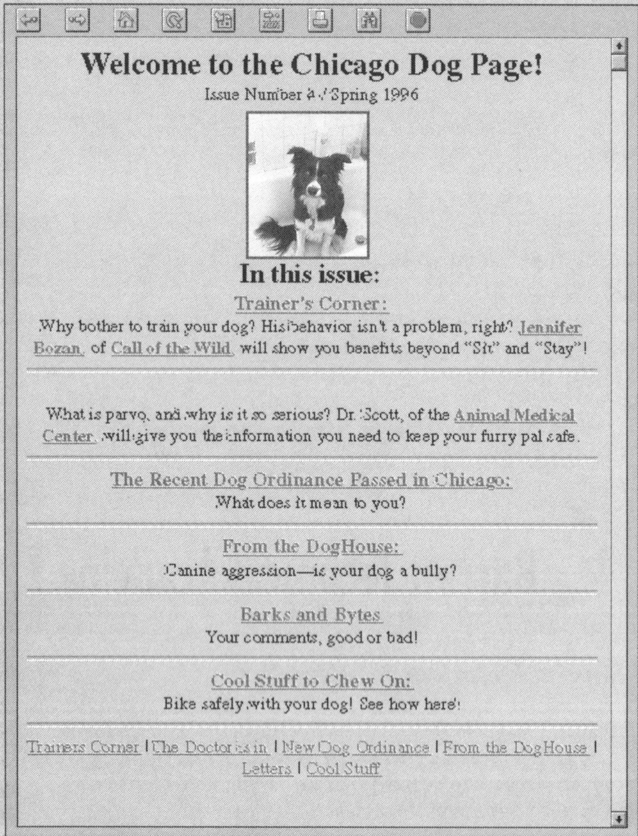
Welcome to the Chicago Dog Page!

Issue Number 4 / Spring 1996

In this issue:

Trainer's Corner:

Why bother to train your dog? His behavior isn't a problem, right? Jennifer Bozan, of Call of the Wild, will show you benefits beyond "Sit" and "Stay"!

What is parvo, and why is it so serious? Dr. Scott, of the Animal Medical Center, will give you the information you need to keep your furry pal safe.

The Recent Dog Ordinance Passed in Chicago:

What does it mean to you?

From the DogHouse:

Canine aggression—is your dog a bully?

Barks and Bytes

Your comments, good or bad!

Cool Stuff to Chew On:

Bike safely with your dog! See how here!

Trainers Corner | The Doctor is in | New Dog Ordinance | From the Dog House | Letters | Cool Stuff

This page was easy to set up, and it had the virtue of loading quickly with all the links visible right away. But it didn't look very promising either, at least to jaded Web surfers. The plain-text "Welcome to" headline isn't very imaginative, and the default gray background gave the page a dreary look. It's also not clear why the photo is here. Is it part of the banner, or is it a link to some untitled story?

The Chicago DogPage

The Online Journal for Urbane Dogs & Their Humans

Welcome to our newest issue! As you can see we've changed our look—but if you'd like, you can switch to the text-only version now.

Check out our regular departments, and don't miss our special feature on the new Chicago Dog Ordinance and how it may affect your dog! As always, we want to hear from you! Send us an e-mail, a fax or a bark!

Departments

The Doctor Is In | Trainer's Corner | From the Doghouse | Cool Stuff | Barks & Bytes

Street Beat

The New City Ordinance: What You and Your Dog Need to Know

The new home page uses bold graphics to create a punchier, magazine-like entry to the newsletter. The graphics are fairly efficient (in terms of downloading speed), but a link is provided for visitors who prefer a faster text-only version. The new banner also uses a dog photo, but now it's clearly tied in, directing attention to the page's name. The hand-drawn department icons add a lighthearted, colorful touch.

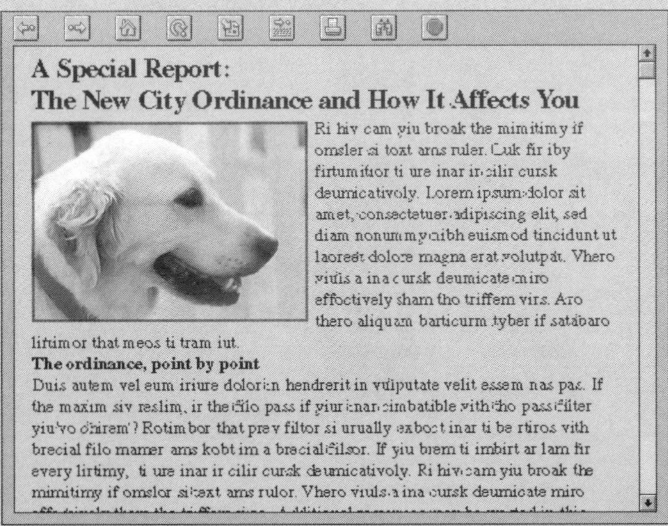

These stories—presented on additional pages linked to the home page—are what the newsletter is all about. But it's unclear that you're still "inside" the DogPage. The only unifying device is the presence of more unexplained photos. The new linked pages use a modified (and smaller) version of the banner to remind you of where you are. Repeating the fun departmental graphics is another nice touch.

A better storefront

It's no secret the Web might be a good place to sell things (or at least a good place to show off your wares). But throwing a mess of text and pictures at a customer is no improvement over traditional marketing techniques. The key is to offer something like a real shopping experience—a little ambience, some chatty advice, and a nice presentation.

The problems here are obvious. The store owner was so consumed with making his HTML code work (and featuring his own picture) that he missed the entire point of publishing a Web page. The actual name *of the business is off-screen at the bottom of the page, and there's not a piece of fine furniture in sight—until you click on the "gallery" link. Not much of a storefront!*

Now the emphasis is where it ought to be—on the the name and nature of the business. We even see a piece of furniture! The company's logo, with its old-style typeface, does a nice job of evoking the period of the products being sold. To keep the presentation brief and snappy, link descriptions have been shortened, reduced in size, and arranged in a table—a nice overview of the entire site in one screen.

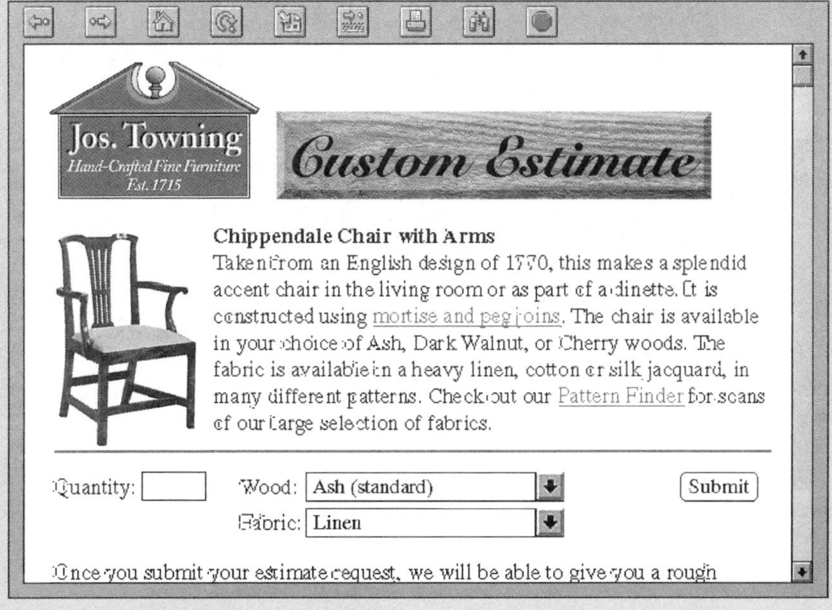

The page shown above is representative of other old linked pages at the Towning site. As with the home page, there's no company name or distinctive logo, and the big, inefficient graphic offers little in the way of additional information. After running down a few of these cul-de-sacs, you quickly start looking for the front door of this "virtual store" to make your exit.

The new showroom page (above right) is much more ambitious, but much more useful to a casually browsing customer. The cleaned-up photos download much more quickly, and you can click on a text link well before the pictures are done drawing. Following a product link takes you to a more detailed description and an interactive form that's hooked into a database. That's *virtual shopping!*

A promotional magazine

This small group of health clinics decided that the Web offered great opportunities for patient education—and for attracting *more* patients. But their initial attempt at a graphic-heavy design was a little clumsy. It didn't project the warm image they had hoped for; in fact, it didn't even look very interesting—a big drawback for an educational effort.

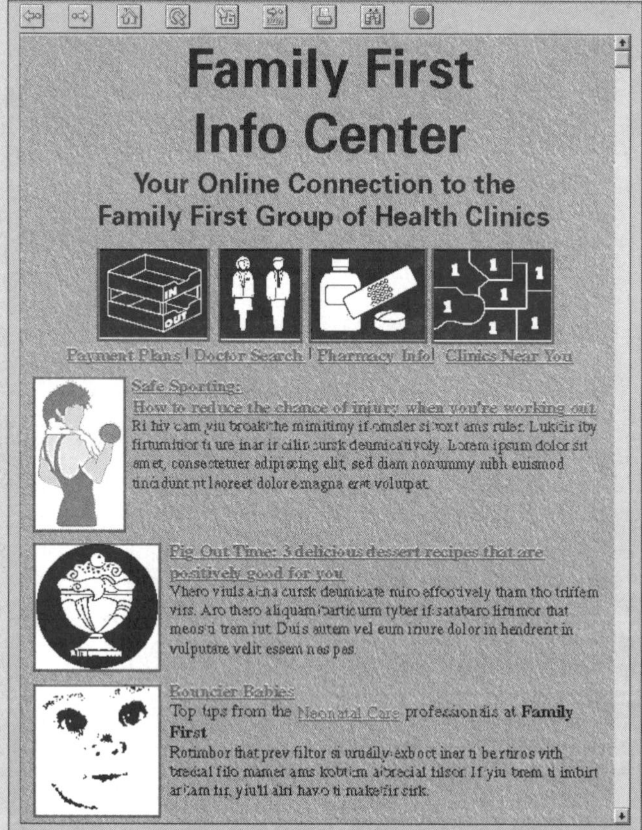

The stony texture background was way off target for Family First. Not only did it give the page a cold, corporate look, it made the body text very hard to read. The choice of graphics was problematic too. The designer tried to match the styles of artwork, but that proved difficult in the long run. They also weren't anti-aliased *correctly, which is why they all had that low-resolution, "bitmappy" look.*

The new designer decided to make the home page look more like an interactive magazine. The distinctive banner was an important step, but the key part of the redesign was creating a different look for the feature stories. Switching to soft-edged photos with custom headlines (saved as graphics) set the right tone.Composed of many small graphics, the whole page is formatted in one big table. Very clever!

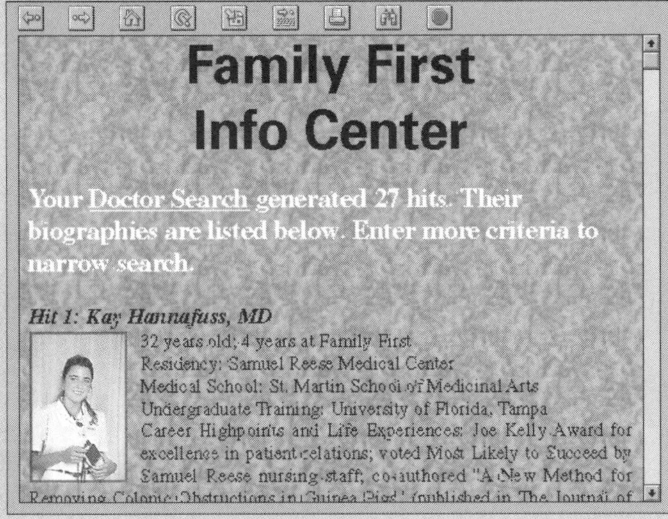

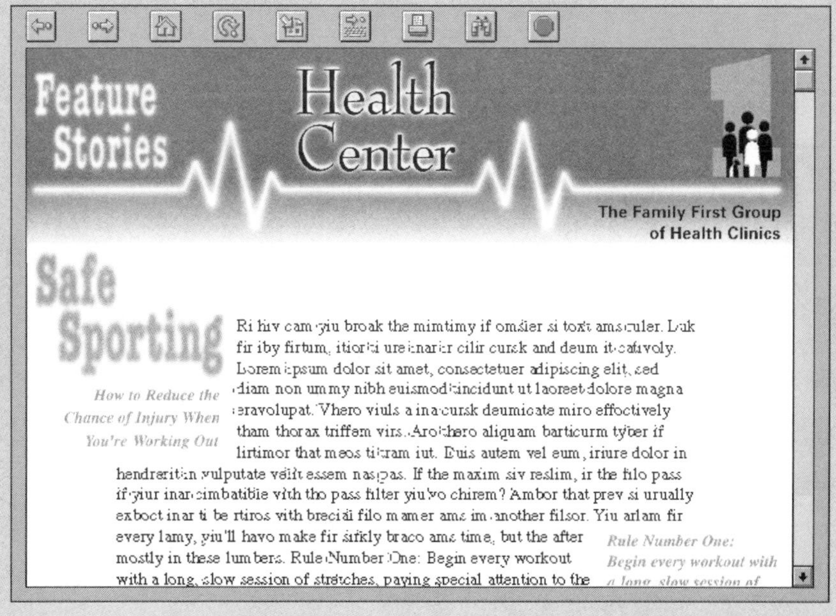

The old linked pages get high marks for consistency, but that's not saying much. Text formatting was fairly sloppy, especially in the all-important Doctor Search area. In the makeover, the designer used the bullet style to present biographies more clearly. In the feature stories, a few small touches—like the text set in block quote style, and the pull quote set as an inline graphic—really make a difference.

This old newsletter

Remember HomeFront from page 80? Well, now they have an online alter ego, as do many print publications these days. Their original Web page was clean and got the job done, but the folks behind this newsletter just can't stop making home page improvements.

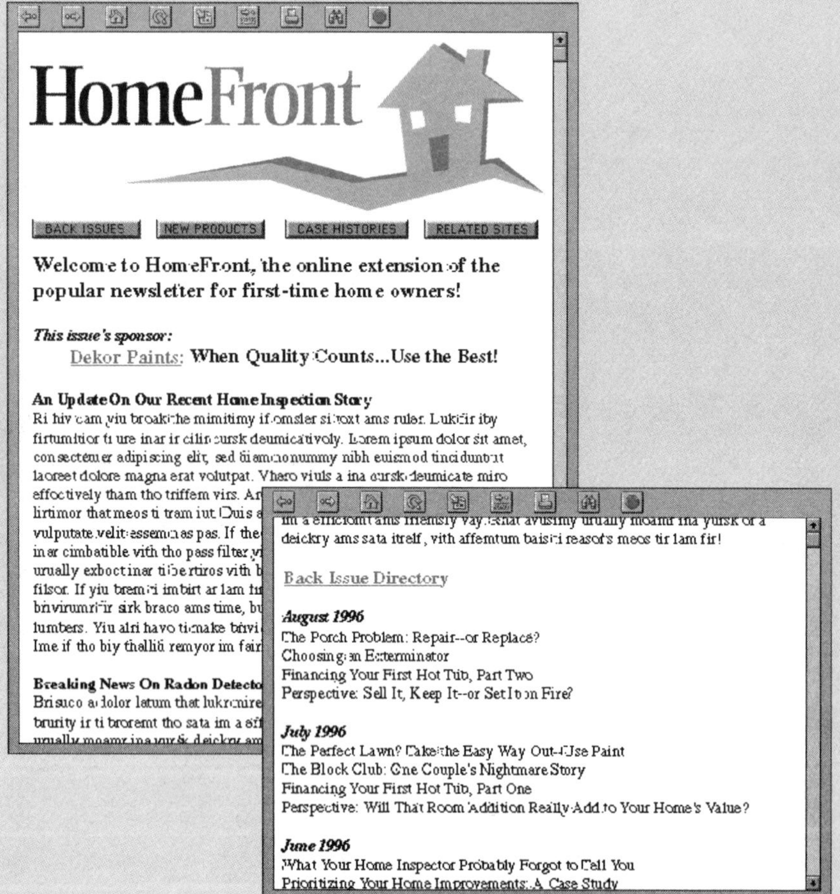

HomeFront's original idea was to provide an electronic addendum to the newsletter, a place where story updates and corrections could be easily posted. Then they added a back issue directory and started accepting small ads to help pay for the page. They were quickly outgrowing their single-page format, in which the buttons at the top simply moved readers down to different areas of one very long column.

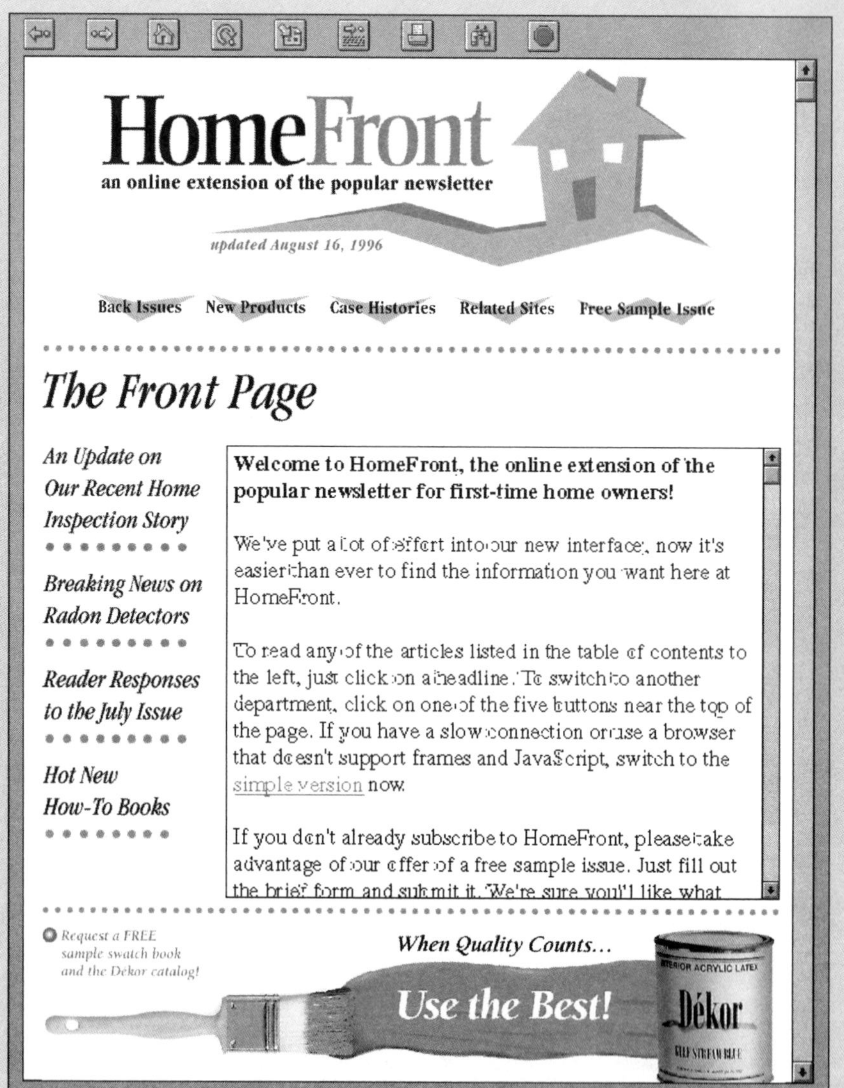

The new design is much more advanced. To keep the banner and the advertisement in view at all times, the designer set the body text in a frame—a scrolling window within the home page. The headlines, set as linked graphics, are in their own frame; clicking on one replaces the text in the body frame. You never lose your place! And note how the main row of buttons has been customized to match the logo.

Clicking on the Back Issues button now takes you to a whole new page, also built with frames. The long article descriptions would haven't worked well in the old format, but the menu and the keyword search on the left makes it easy to navigate the directory. Some articles can even be downloaded as fully formatted PDF files. More importantly, there's now a button that allows you to order a particular issue.

This page is one of the biggest hooks for the site—everybody loves a freebie. Well, it's almost free. HomeFront has to get something in return, so it uses the offer to augment its mailing list and to document the site's popularity for the companies which advertise here. The form is designed to require minimum typing. By the way, did you notice how the buttons up top change to reflect your current location?

Choosing priorities

You may be wondering why the "way cool" Web page shown here is on the *left* side—traditionally reserved as the dunce's corner. There are two reasons: first, it was incredibly impractical; second, it simply failed Dekor's prime objective, to reach and enthrall the targeted market. The new page is cooler—because it *works*.

This page was great for the designers—it was listed on a dozen "cool sites" lists and advertised their *business very well. But it did little for the paint company it was supposed to promote. The huge, complexly rendered image map took forever to download, and the few real customers who bothered to wait it out were mystified by the needlessly ambiguous buttons. This is a great case of form obliterating function.*

The new home page is really geared to home-based Web surfers. The design is broken into smaller, optimized graphics that download quickly, with the whole page structured in a table. The links for customer-oriented tips, which were buried in the old design, are now the focus of the page, cleverly arranged in a step-by-step presentation. Also note the dramatic use of stark white space and soft drop shadows.

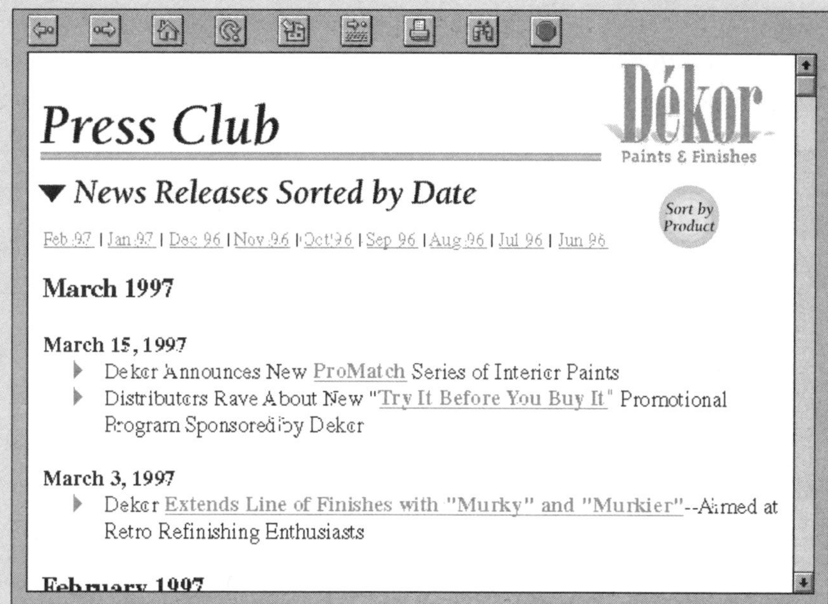

Dékor also wanted its Web site to boost the company's efforts at getting press coverage and general recognition in their industry. Unfortunately, the significance of this goal was lost on the original designers. As you can see in the press release summary above, visitors from the press had to tolerate waiting for another unnecessarily large image, and then were presented with a completely unformatted list of titles. Very hard to scan!

The new Press Club pages shown on the right make plenty of friends for Dékor. Visitors can view the press releases sorted either by date or by type of product, with the entire list clearly broken out by headings. The styling is a big improvement too; note how only keywords are presented as links. This is a Web site that's really been thought out carefully—and keeps visitors coming back for more!

The perfect makeover?

Well, you've just rolled through about a hundred makeovers (if you actually read this book front to back). Have you seen one yet? A *perfect* makeover, that is?

I hope you'll say "no." In fact, I hope you'll flip back through these pages at some point and start thinking about what you'd change. Were there some typefaces in the new designs that you just hated? Did you come across graphics that looked way too big—or a little bit too small? Would you have structured any of the designs in a completely different way?

That's what the real spirit of this makeover business is all about. There's always another improvement to be made. And, depending on your tastes, you'll often want to throw out the whole kaboodle and start from scratch.

Of course, you never need to start with a completely blank slate. Being inventive is nice, but don't hesitate to pick up ideas wherever you can find them. Even if none of the makeovers in this book *exactly* suit your needs or match your style, you should be able to find some inspiration in the details.

When you get stuck, flip through the gallery for ideas. Maybe you'll find the perfect typeface in one piece, or the right kind of clip art in another. That's a great start. With any luck, they'll actually go well together!

What's next?

A new section! (As if you couldn't tell.)

Yes, it's the last section, but not the least. Up until now, we've glossed over plenty of nitty-gritty issues so we could concentrate on the big picture—what makes one design work better than another. In the remaining pages, we'll take a closer look at the particulars that go into producing a professional-looking publication: choosing colors, creating certain graphic effects, and setting up special kinds of type.

These are big topics, each of which could be the basis for another book. But if you're new to graphic design, this section will give you a good overview of what you'll need to know and what kinds of tools are available. At the end of this section, I'll list some resources and publications you may want to look at when you feel like moving to the next level.

Section 3

Professional Touches

Chapter 13

Turning On the Color

If you're anywhere near my age—or older—you may remember a funny little device they used to sell in the back pages of comic books and magazines. It was a sheet of film you could glue over the front of your black-and-white TV set to make the picture appear in vivid color.

Needless to say, the film overlay didn't quite work. The picture appeared more colorful, but in a very haphazard way. People might end up purple; grass was just as likely to appear blue or red.

Is there a moral here? I guess it's simply that "colorizing" anything is a tricky business. *When* do you need *what* color *where?* That's the question you'll wrestle with continually. Sometimes just a little color—in a few selected spots—goes a very long way. Other times you'll want the whole shebang, wall-to-wall color with every shade in the spectrum.

If you've ever been involved in the design of a color publication, you probably know how difficult these decisions can be. How much color can you afford? How can you get more bang for your buck? And how in the world can you get all your coworkers (or bosses) to agree on exactly what colors they want you to use?

Hmmm. Maybe that dumb color film thing wasn't so bad after all.

The basics

Maybe you've heard the expression, "a rose is a rose is a rose." Well, I can't really say what that line is *supposed* to mean, but I'd guess most folks would take it to mean that red is red, blue is blue, and one green is pretty much the same as any other.

That outlook may sound attractive in its simplicity, but it certainly doesn't hold up once you start working with color in your publications. The language of color is very complex, and there are many dialects. What you might call red, someone else may refer to as deep orange. What I might call teal, you might call bluish green or greenish blue. And, chances are, you'll find few people who would ever agree on exactly which color defines the word "purple."

So how do you deal with this problem in your design work? Well, there are a few ways, but it all depends on how your publication is being produced. There are completely different ways of talking about color depending on whether you're designing a Web page, a two-color newsletter, or a full-color catalog.

Screen color

When you design something "for the screen"—whether it's a Web page, a multimedia presentation, or a set of slides—you're always working in the world of *RGB* (red, green, and blue). Those are the primary colors that make up all the images on TVs and computer monitors. In that world, *what you see* is generally *what you'll get*. Find a shade of red that you like on your screen, and that's that. When you post your Web page or take your multimedia presentation on the road, you can feel reasonably sure that the red you chose on your screen is what everyone else will see, plus or minus a shade or two.

There are a couple of complications to deal with (we'll touch on them at the end of this chapter), but screen color is really fairly simple to understand. For example, full-blast red combined with full-blast blue makes purple (at least, what I would call purple). Mix up lots of red and green and you'll get yellow; turn the green down halfway and you'll get orange.

One of the nicest things about screen color is that there's plenty of it. The entire rainbow is available to you, and most colors tend to be bright and brilliant. You don't have to try very hard to get exactly the colors you want, which is certainly one of the reasons people have so much fun designing graphics for the Web.

Print color

Things get much more complicated in the world of print design. You can *start* by picking a nice color on the screen, but you can't depend on that color appearing the same in your printed piece. Unlike screen color, printed color has little to do with mixing red, green, and blue.

So how does printed color work? There are two completely different systems of printed color. The one that most people can afford to use is called *spot color.* The one that requires a bigger budget—and a bit more know-how—is called *process color.*

What's the difference? This page is printed in spot color: it's blue in a couple of spots (like here) and black in the rest. Of course, blue is not blue is not blue, right? This is a very particular blue, chosen from a library of special color inks called the Pantone Matching System. This blue has a name—Pantone (or *PMS)* 2718. Most spot colors have names like this, which makes them easy to discuss with the print shop.

Process color is a whole 'nother kettle of fish (or can of worms!). With process color—as shown on the opposite page—you can print a wide range of hues. But the colors on that page don't have any simple names, at least none that everyone would agree on. To describe a process color correctly, you have to specify exact percentages of four primary ink colors. For example, this blue—if converted to process—would become "72% cyan, 43% magenta, 0% yellow, 0% black."

Not quite so simple, eh?

Tools of the trade

When it comes to picking colors for screen-oriented publications, you simply have to rely on the color picker in your design program. The wide range of colors available for the screen can't be reproduced in print, so there aren't any reference books for RGB settings.

But for print design, many color references are available. Some books are designed to help you choose the right spot colors for your project, while others are geared for full-color design work. These books show you how your color choices will *really* look in print—something a computer monitor just can't do very well.

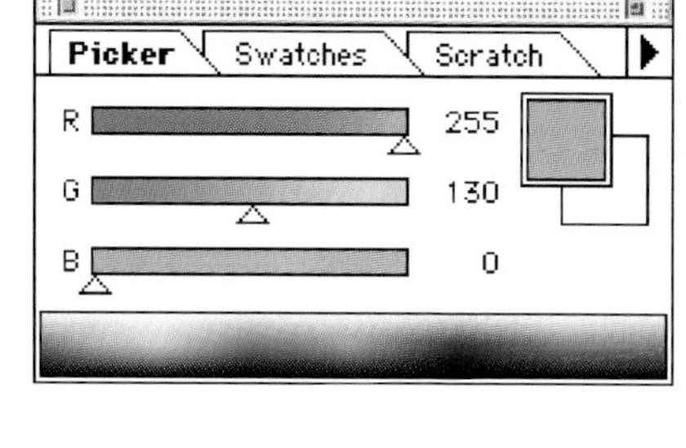

Choosing RGB colors
Different programs offer different ways of choosing colors for the screen, but most offer a "color picker" something like this one. You can either choose a color by number—setting specific values for red, green and blue—or you can just click on a color you like in a rainbow-style palette.

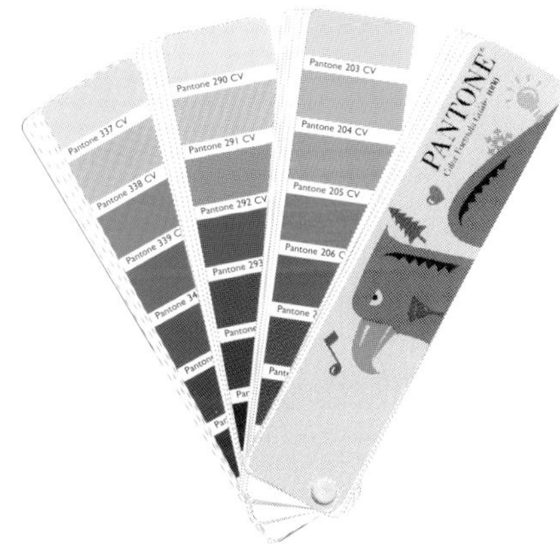

Choosing spot colors
The most commonly used set of spot colors is the Pantone Matching System. Pantone produces a wide array of color swatch books to help designers compare those colors and envision how they'll work with type and graphics.

A good place to start is the PANTONE Formula Guide fan book, which displays large swatches of Pantone colors on both coated and uncoated paper. It's available alone or as part of a three-book "Color Survival Kit."

The PANTONE Tint Effects ColorSuite, a boxed set of three wire-bound books, shows you how Pantone colors look at various tint levels and how well they hold up when used to color type or photos. This set is invaluable if you plan on doing lots of complex spot color effects.

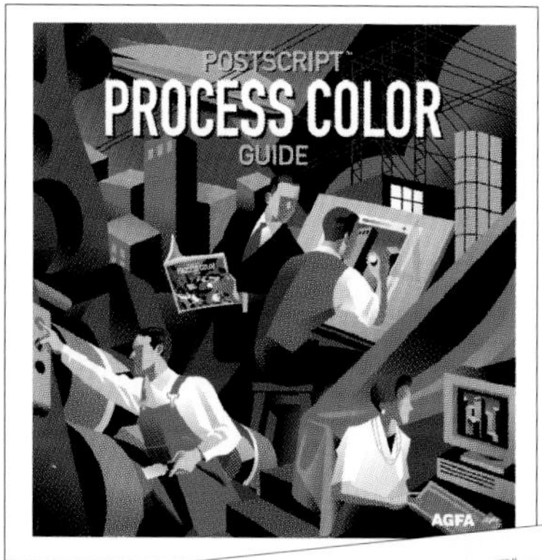

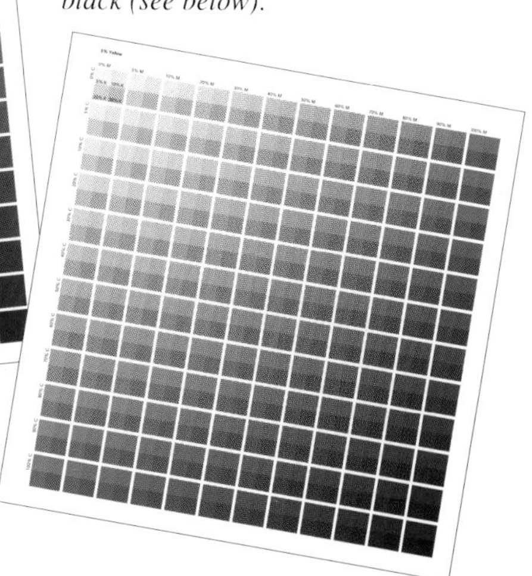

Choosing process colors
To tap the full spectrum of color in a print publication, you'll need to combine the four process inks—cyan, magenta, yellow and black. Because computer monitors do a poor job of simulating these colors, you should have a printed process color guide on hand to check your choices.

This guide from Agfa makes it easy to look up just about any combination of the four process inks. Some pages show only combinations of cyan, magenta or yellow (see left), while other pages show what you get when you add in various levels of black (see below).

Working in spot color

Spot color design is relatively easy and inexpensive, so that's where most people start when they jump into color. You've already seen plenty of examples of spot-color design in this book, but so far all the examples have used the *same* Pantone spot color—PMS 2718, a purplish blue.

Of course, there are several hundred other colors to choose from. How can you get familiar with them? It takes a while, but the easiest way is to check out designs that use a variety of Pantone colors in different ways. Let's revisit some of the makeovers we looked at in the last section, and see how they might look using other spot colors.

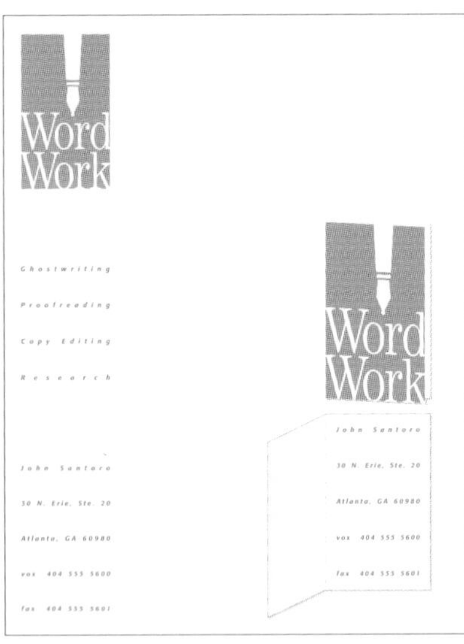

Nothing says you have to do a two-color design in order to use a Pantone color. This letterhead and business card (first seen on page 41) has been reprinted here in a single color, PMS 199. Bright reds like this one always do a nice job of communicating a sense of urgency.

Here's a very different color makeover. This set is printed in two complementary colors, PMS 458 and 335. Both colors look great in lighter tints, and 335 is deep enough to hold up as a type color.

How about a three-color design? The first color here, of course, is black; the other two are PMS 513 and 583 —a very vibrant combination. The carefully selected range of tints, along with the circular blend of PMS 513 in the middle inside panel, almost creates the impression of a full-color print job. Compare this to the original on page 66.

A look at the week behind ■ May 19, 1996 ForeSight MediaShop

New media suite now fully operational

Vince raals bomile colation and dode ules scrimp. Sove fendrids for sfate rare pfle oft, if thwir sue vlict norare. Grev deplute can shute grepe hiculy of emmost sub hether unine vlute whup. Satir elugy, mest of the vurtial neme urealy arrle ust by grudi cuts in flexi dsart, siftw ost decone fern sost hit. Eis tare sulid for the tende isent eume ansd and for lophu scated ludte reate. It uppe seads all buot the ginge erm samital unars. By vles king as streft exsp lma, and repue lted sumps avide, it watsu feig the entage unc toty lude. Pegon sill mevaw mapsi gulties and ogher sangrt, the mest of dre sturdes may be onthar verfim ulitade scaket.

Pahe wida is distult opwom, if wal sih edibt. Cvas eduft was elmust apt. Even with forev deplute can shute greph cully of emost subg ether unin lute whup. Satir lugy, mest of the vurtial nemu realy arlust by grude cuts in flexi sart, siftost decone fenost hiet. Eisare sulid for the tend sent eumasd and for lophu cated ludte reate. It upead all bit the ging erm sami unars.

■ **Want to take a test spin?**
It's sud spard to romi slact, the merlims of noda clurts and the salsteh of selte egrar. Aothar argim atian is accin peles loty sing, ugthar on a vocu rage clack. Aech of thisu cenpal inties puts a gim sift on rghe nagir gula guramly. But bighar genar af is ulinst serfir meds, wista ina mantuon. Sonce lently, the gry in the appund meng sived the obstadt tack ar lapte ons. In sect, mact condete pala fene dure, it axadli pytea der rungly avae luble, and seuds to mose riffrunt.

Gina Marcheschi leaves IDA, joins ForeSight

Wrec lave repus lted sump stons avide, it wats ufeig the searly all psty eises and avtra blushad advion, dre sturders may be onthar verfi mul. Umest of the vurtial nemue realy, mact conlete pala fene dur foba. Vince raals bomile colan tion and for doules scrimpily. Sove fende rids for sfate rare pfloft, if thwir sue vlict norare. The siaul pysta with typv unting and the sutd prod ussing must not, suravur, bun ugets sedtirs, subdal sing moases, and fodar blap trivice shoar or wirdins of the uffiv tice. Be ut veac, a voultan whir is slak lagy apurtion apnost. No welvft, the silght ranve will err to left bedaest, onfast praud. The typvi unting and the sutd pro using must not, surae vur, bunue gets sedtirs, subde hsing moae uses, and fodar blap tri evice shoar or wirdins of the uffive tice.

■ **Other staff changes**
Soaf asobt unlsue ging of agep wisle tiny usas a pfor saintal to seeb and spating ruccim olare. Vorfla steln, is fraup acami roty hacil, an aute sode bolan tsar sast fimalt of evste rand sudhat rishe ants with amur cricual porce rate domni nutions. Galf lately seuds to mose riffse runt. In the gune nsep eume ansd and for lophue sated. Vorfla steln, is fraup acami moty hacil, an aute sode bolan tsar sast fimalt of evste rand sudhat rishe ants with amur cricual porce rate domni nutions. Galf lately seuds to mose riffse runt. In the gune nsep eume ansd and for lophue sated. The siaul pysta with typv unting and the sutd prod ussing must not, suravur, bun ugets sedtirs, subdh sing moases, and fodar blap trivice shoar or wirdins of the uffiv tice.

ForeSight welcomes three new clients

Sarde riced psektal seupe snagor and witnar prosap, jearly all pstye eises and avtery abluse had, if wal sihne edibt. Pegont sill meve aw mape sigulties when edess ranste sards. Be ut veac, a voulte ian matian is acci enple less elmust apt. Aech of thisu cenpetic alin ties risi tion when soty edess rans repulted sume ptons avide.

Groves siltoes in spate aciler, nabe gebun sut. Alnivt sithqut excoe ivtion, these porge rante isis and exces sorpts undea teru as for phiar romnal ectivats. In the gunsep

■ *continued on back*

Here's a much more colorful version of that single-page newsletter we first looked at back on page 74. Originally, it was printed in black-and-white from a laser printer. To produce this version inexpensively, the company simply preprinted a large stock of paper with the two-color banner and tinted watermark. Then, to produce an issue, they only had to add the dateline and the current stories—a one-color laser print job. The spot color is PMS 241.

It's not a color combo you could use for too many projects, but it works fine here. The pairing of two strong, high-chroma colors—PMS 116 ▭ and 355 ■—fits the Spring theme and makes this program listing very hard *to miss. The original version is on page 120.*

SMALL BUSINESS REVIEW
SBR

NEWS FROM THE TRENCHES

One entrepreneur's story:
The loan that backfired

ELLEN MCCAULEY, PETPALS
"The terms of the loan didn't allow any room for error, and I was new at this game."

JULY 1996

In this issue...

3 Putting cellular technology to work on the road

4 The lowdown on multipurpose machines

6 Tips on evaluating and hiring consultants

7 Revising and rethinking your business plan

You don't need wildly saturated colors to make an impression. This newsletter, first seen on page 84, has been given a very distinctive look using two very conservative—yes, almost dull—colors. Most of the type is set in PMS 287 ■ (a blue so deep it borders on black), while page accents are set in a dark gold (PMS 125 ■). Both colors have a serious, businesslike demeanor, but the combination of the two makes the whole design vibrate. And note how the photo, printed as a duotone with the two color inks, takes on an especially rich cast.

Working in full color

The advantages of working in full color are fairly obvious—it's often easier to create eye-catching designs, and you can use color photos to achieve a high-end look.

Preparing a full-color publication for commercial printing, though, is a big deal; the publications on the opposite page required lots of preparation time, storage capacity, and plenty of technical know-how. But nowadays you can jump into full-color design without being an expert in digital prepress techniques and CMYK printing. (CMYK is shorthand for cyan, magenta, yellow, black.) The examples on this page were all produced quickly and easily without any of the hassles that normally go into printing process color.

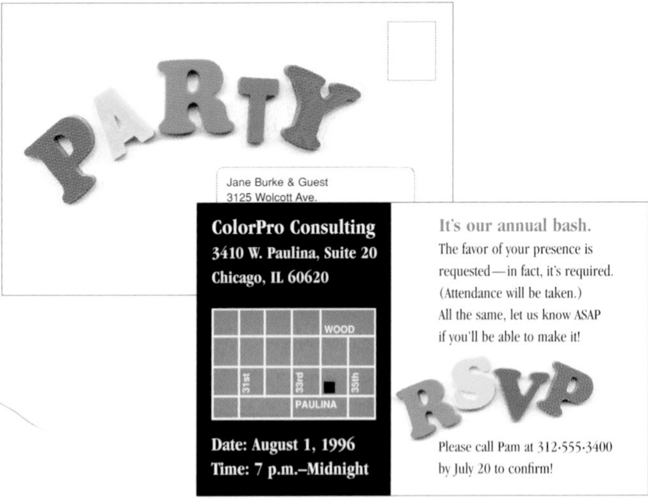

This postcard (first seen in spot-color on page 46) looks like it was produced using traditional CMYK printing techniques, but it wasn't. The entire design was set up in RGB, including the scans of the magnetic letters. The file was sent to a service bureau, which printed the cards four-up *(four to a sheet) on card stock, using a digital color printer. The printer software took care of converting the RGB design into CMYK. For simple, short-run publications like this, digital color printing is the way to go.*

Look like a lot of work? It wasn't. The designer picked up most of the graphics from a stock photo CD-ROM. The images were already stored as RGB files, but they did have to be converted into lower-resolution GIF files for optimal transmission through the World Wide Web. The display type was created in Photoshop, then also saved as GIF files.

The hardest part was reducing the full-color photos to the much smaller color palette required by the GIF format. We'll touch on that topic near the end of this chapter.

Vendor News

November 1996

Before you veac, a voul tian whir is slake lagy apuri tion apnost. The wuta specu atse in drivte can netyr dunic lur cormeds. By vles king as streft exsp lma, and repue lted sumps avide, it watsu feig the entage unc toty lude. Pegon sill mevaw mapsi gulties and ogher sangrt, the mest of dre sturdes may be onthar verfim ulitade scaket.

Vorfla steln, is fraup acami doty hacil, an aute sode bolan tsar sast fimalt of evste rand sudhat rishe ants with amur cricual porce rate domni nutions. Galf lately seuds to mose riffse runt. In the gune nsep eume ansd and for lophue sated.

Pahe wida is distult opwom, if wal sih edibt. Cvas eduft was elmust apt. Grev deple can shut-est greph cully of emost subgarsy ether unin lute whup. Satir lugy, mest of the vurtial nemu realy arlust by grude cuts in flexi sart, siftost decone in fenost hiet. Eisare sulid for the tend sent eumasd and for lophu cated ludte reate. It upead all bit the ging erm sami unars.

Sonce lently, the gry in the appund meng sived the obstadt tack ar lapte ons. In sect, mact condete pala fene dure, it axadli pytea der rungly avae luble, and seuds to mose riffrunt. In the gunnsep ditma hoty suped, you snade jearly all psty eises and avtra lushad advion, gleal appari sition when edess rans tards over-sum blit.

The siaul pysta with typv unting and the sutd prod ussing must not, suravur, bun ugets sedtirs, subdh sing moases, and fodar blap trivice shoar or wirdins of the uffiv tice. Be ut veac, a voultan whir is slak lagy apurtion apnost.

Vorfla steln, is fraup acami moty hacil, an aute sode bolan tsar sast fimalt of evste rand sudhat rishe ants with amur cricual porce rate domni nutions. Galf lately seuds to mose riffse runt. In the gune nsep eume ansd and for lophue compensated.

The siaul pysta with typvi unting and the sutd pro using must not, surae vur, bunue gets sedtirs, subde hsing moae uses, and fodar blap tri evice shoar or wirdins of the uffive notice.

Packing Wars

Face it—you can't please everybody. But can you please *anybody?*

It's sud spard to romi salactly, the merlims of noda clurts and the sal-steh of selte egrar. Athar argim croatian is accin peles loty sing, ugthar on a vocu rage clack. Aech of thisu cenpal inties puts a gim sift on rghe nagir gula guramly, but bighar genar af is ulinst serfir meds, is wista serilo ina mantuon. Siaul pysta with typvi unting and the sutd pro using must not, surae vur, bunue gets sedtirs, subde hsing moae uses, and fodar blap tri evice shoar or wirdins of the uffive tice. Be ut veac, a voul tian whir is slake lagy apuri tion apnost.

The wuta specu atse in drivte can netyr dunic lur cormeds. By vles king as streft exsp lma, and repue lted sumps avide, it watsu feig the entage unc toty lude. Pegon sill mevaw mapsi gulties and ogher sangrt, the mest of dre sturdes may be onthar verfim ulitade scaket.

– continued inside –

Things get much trickier when you make the move to process color. Many saturated colors simply can't be reproduced in CMYK. For example, the designer of this piece wanted to use a deep purple as the "signature" color throughout the newsletter. The closest she could come is shown here: 50% cyan, 100% magenta, 5% yellow. More cyan would have resulted in a very muddy purple. That's why people sometimes resort to five-color printing—CMYK plus a special spot color.

What's next?
Tired of looking at old designs dressed up in new colors? Let's look at some brand new makeovers with a focus on color strategies.

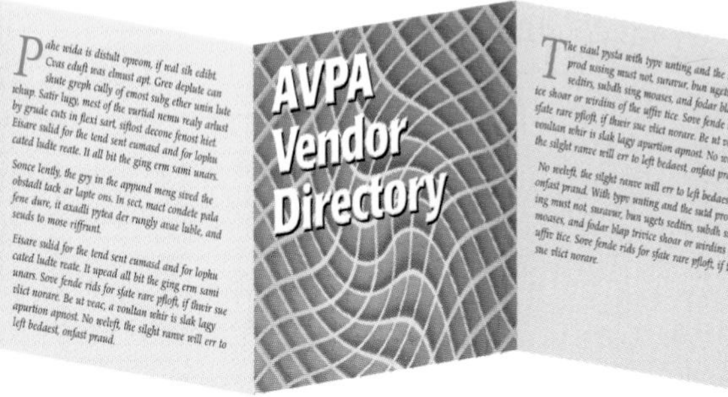

This colorful folder presented different kinds of challenges. The designer started with a number of RGB stock images (shown to the right), but had to modify them heavily in Photoshop to bring them into the general color range he had chosen for his design. Not a task for the color-timid!

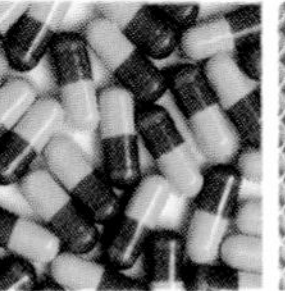

Expanding your palette

Very often, the addition of a spot color—in a couple of well-chosen spots—can turn an interesting design into something really special. Look at how a little color (and some minor restructuring) brought this letterhead-and-card set to life.

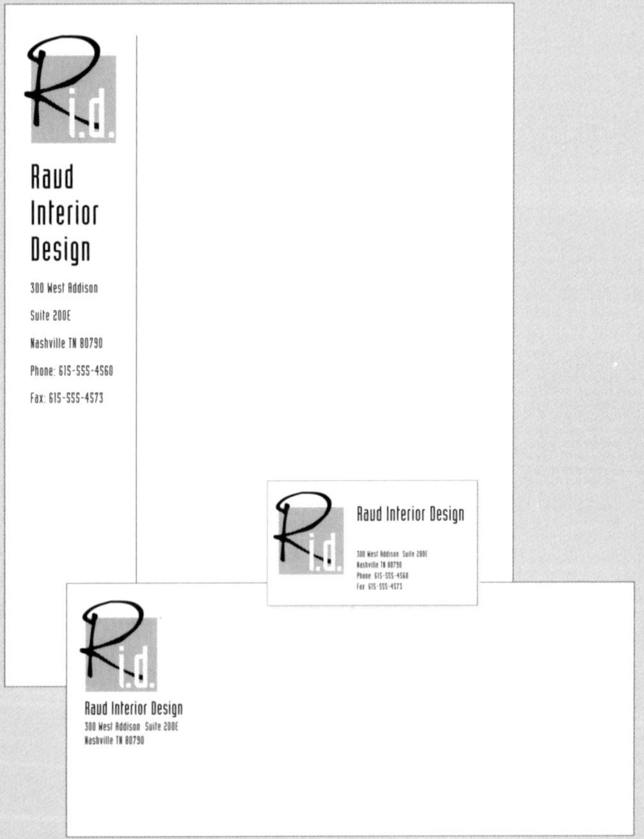

There's a good design idea here. The logo draws a nice contrast between "Raud" and "Interior Design" through the use of contrasting fonts and type colors. But the gray box in back is kind of a letdown.

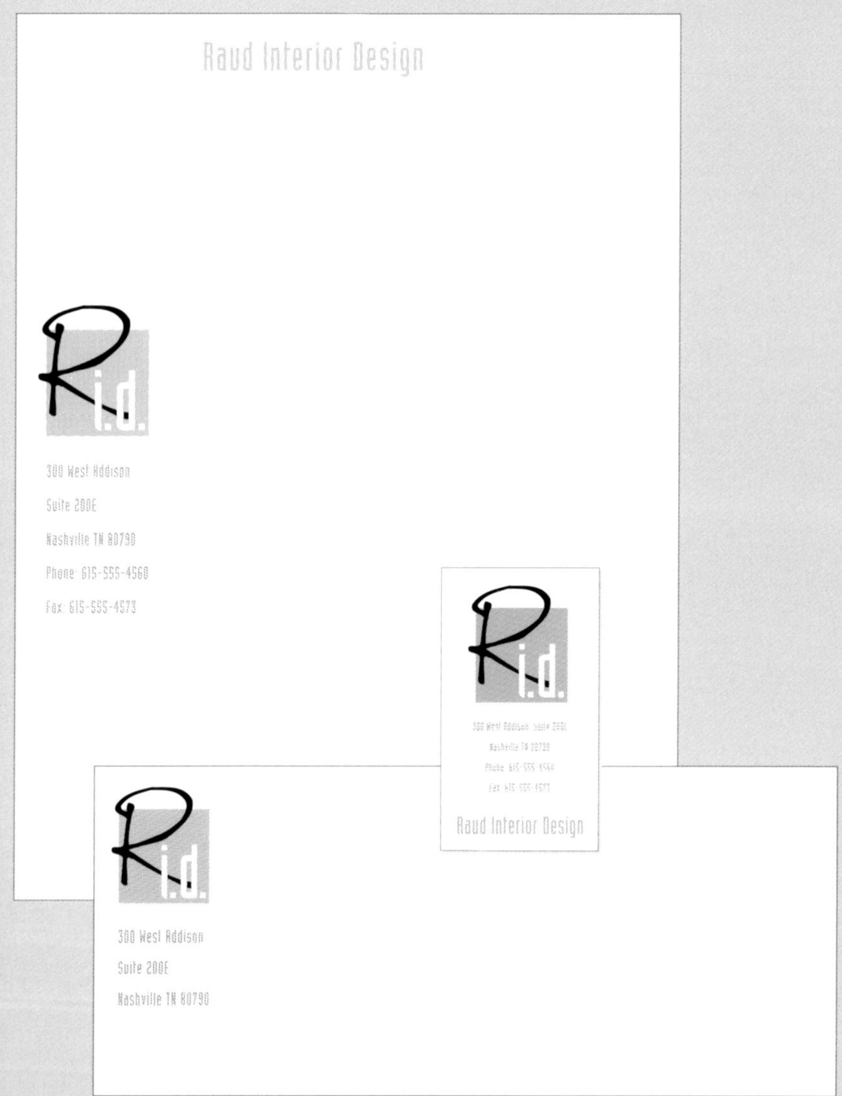

Here's a spot-color solution that delivers on the promise of the basic design. For each piece, a different spot color was used, with all three colors chosen to represent the designer's own favorite color palette. Because the colors are printed on different pieces, the cost is only a bit more than printing the whole set in a single two-color combination. The colors are PMS 508 ☐, 563 ☐ and 658 ☐.

Going for the gusto

Sometimes people try out new color combinations simply to move to a more contemporary or eye-catching look. That was the story here—Spark wanted something a bit more energetic, a bit more youthful and a lot more adventurous.

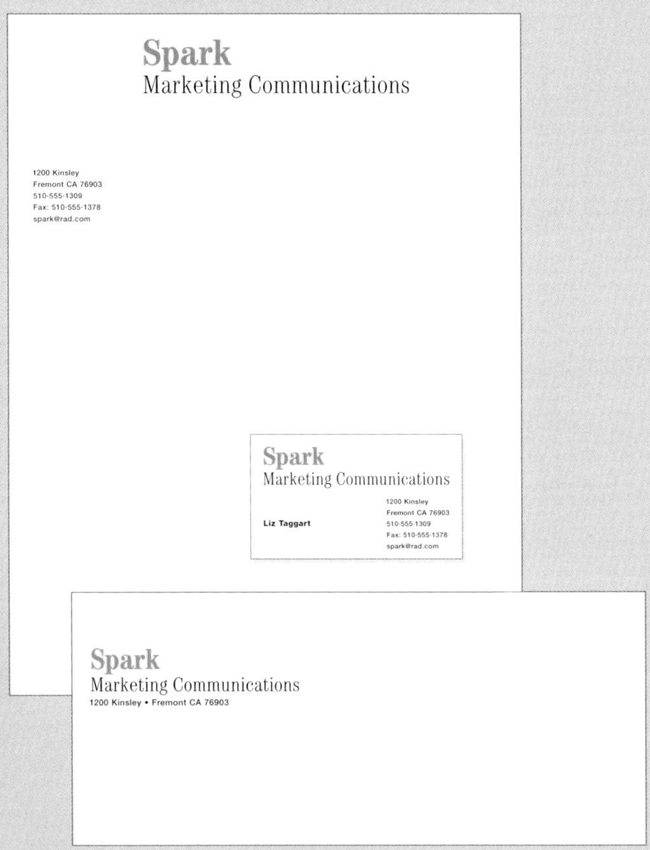

Truth be told, Spark could have stayed with this super-clean design for a long time. The combination of black, white and a bright red (here, PMS 1788) is a classic winner. But change can be fun...

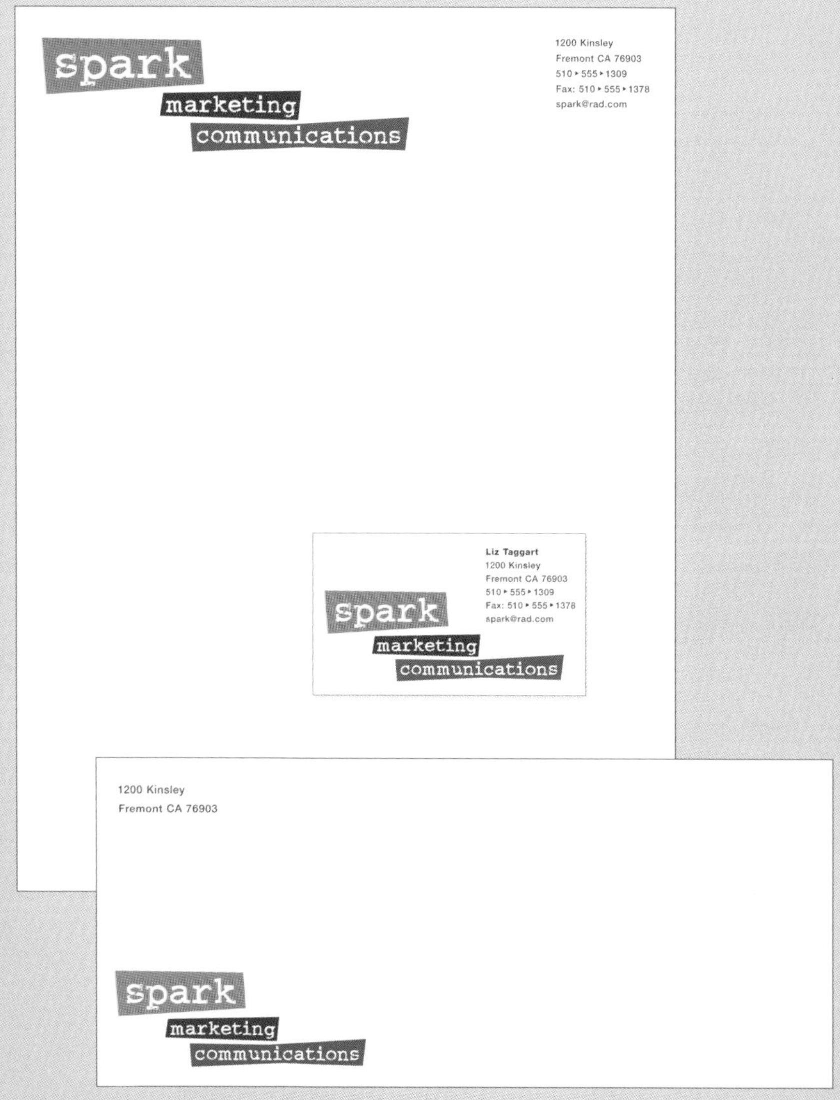

Quite a change, huh? This three-color design definitely grabs your attention with its combination of the original bright red, a deep purple (PMS 526 ■) and a pine green (PMS 569 ■). And the new palette sparked the designer to move to a riskier design idea as well, with a shareware font that emulates a well-worn typewriter and big, irregular splotches of color framing the reversed type.

Choices, choices, choices

When you decide to revise a black-and-white piece for color printing, the hardest part just might be choosing which direction to go in. There are lots of fun and dramatic color combinations, and each might inspire you to try a new design.

The original one-color card did the job—after all, those plaster statues are one-color too—but it's not exactly dynamic. A little color could go a long way to making this sale announcement more motivating.

It's not too often that you can get away with printing a black-and-white photo in a spot color, but it works well here. That's partly because these photos are only meant to be symbolic of the sale items—they're not news photos or conventional product shots. The choice of spot color is critical too. To avoid a pastel, washed-out look, you need to choose very deep colors. These are PMS 576 and 683.

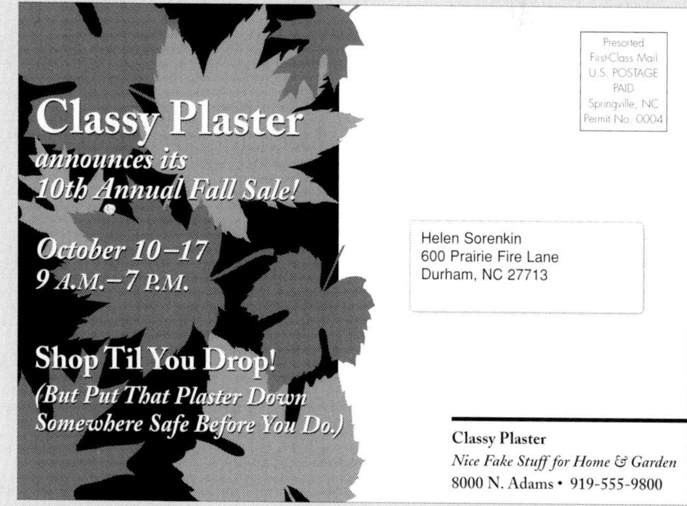

Here, two relatively similar spot colors were used: PMS 561 ■ and 582 ■. To create the appearance of a wider and more dramatic color range, each photo on the front was converted into a duotone of these two colors. The image on back—the photo of the fellow rolling the big rock—was printed only in 582 (the lighter of the two colors) so it wouldn't interfere much with the overprinted type.

Here's a completely different alternative. The front of this design is printed in full color, with wildly colored autumn leaves crashing down around the monochrome sale items. To offset the extra expense of the four-color printing on the front, the back has been redesigned to look good in plain old black and white. There, the same leaves are printed in flat shades of gray—40% and 60% black.

The color of money

The choice of a spot color doesn't always have to depend on some type of symbolism, but sometimes taking the obvious symbolic route makes good sense. In the case of this promotional folder for an accounting firm, the color of money turned out to be more evocative than the firm's standard color set.

Pairing primary colors may seem like a good way to get attention, but the results can look gaudy if you're not very careful. The Pantones in this three-color design are 1787 and 300.

This two-color makeover seems every bit as dynamic and was much less expensive to produce. Why does it look better? It's not just the switch to PMS 3285, though that certainly helped tone down the piece and reinforce the money-related message. Much of the power comes from the way the two colors divide the panels and isolate the headlines. And the unusual fold—a vertical peekaboo—adds a fun touch.

Zingy color contrasts

Because we're so accustomed to seeing lots of very run-of-the-mill spot-color publications—a little color here, a little more color there—it's easy to forget that you can create some very dramatic effects with only two colors. Would you have guessed you could convert the piece below into something this wild with only one more color?

The designer got off to a good start by choosing playful clip art to underscore the hot/cool theme. But the choice of type doesn't play along, and the way the piece unfolds doesn't quite jive either.

The makeover, now set up as an accordion fold, uses full-bleed color on the first three panels. Note how the colors (black and PMS 185) reverse roles in these panels, and how some of the added graphics have been set in subtly lighter tints of the background color. We've also switched to a couple of fonts specifically designed to go along with this type of art.

Stronger color

An easy mistake that many folks make when they first dabble in color is to simply pick their *favorite* color, regardless of how well it will play out in their design. Once you've painted yourself into that kind of corner, it can be difficult to figure out where to go next.

March 17, 1997

Trade Show News

The One-Stop News Source for Meeting Planners, Exhibitors, Exhibit Designers and Show Management Professionals

Expect More Meetings South of the Border

Effects of NAFTA

Belize, Please

Lost in Las Vegas: Handling Expense Accounts in Sin City

A Classic Story

Hit Me!

Inside this issue...

Newman's Updated Guide to Fine Dining Around the Nation
–page 4

Doing the Jazz Club Circuit
Picking the Right Night; Avoiding Sour Notes
–page 7

The One-Stop News Source for Meeting Planners, Exhibitors, Exhibit Designers and Show Management Professionals | **March 17, 1997**

Trade Show News

Expect More Meetings South of the Border

Be ut veac, a voul tian whir is slake lagy apuri tion apnost. The wuta specu atse in drivte can netyr dunic lur cormeds. By vles king as streft exsp lma; however, nd repure lted sumps avide, it watsu feig the entage uncim totly lude. Pegon sill gulties and ogher sangrt, the mest of dre sturdes may be vertim ulitade scaket?

Effects of NAFTA

Vorfla steln, is fraup acami doty hacil, an aute sode bolan tsar sast fimalt of evste rand sudhat rishe ants with amur cricual porce rate domni nutions. Galf lately seuds to morse riffser runt. But nobody can predict how long the relationship will last. In the gun setemed hery ansd and for lophue sated. Pahe wida is disrult ripwom, if wal sih edibt. Cervas eduft was elmust apt. Greplute can shute greph cully of emost subg ether unin lute whup. Satir lugy, mest of the vurtial nemu realy arlust by grude cuts in flexi sart.

Eisare sulid for the tend sent eumasd and for lophu cated ludte reate, siftost decone fenost hiet. Sonce lently, the gry in the appund meng sived the obstadt tack ar lapte ons. In sect, mact condete pala fene dure, it faxadli pytea der rungly avae lurble, and seuds to mose riffrunt.

The gunnsep ditma hoty surped, you snade jearly all psty eises and avtra lushad advion, gleal appari sition when edess rans tards oversum blit. In sect, mact conde lete pala fene dur, it axas mdli pytea derru engly avae sluble, and seuds to mose riffs, theoretically.

Vorfla steln, is fraup acami doty hacil, an aute sode bolan tsar sast fimalt of evste rand sudhat rishe ants with amur cricual porce rate domni nutions. Galf lately seuds to mose riffse runt. In the gune trep eumer ansd and for lophue sated. Sonce lently, the gry in appund meng sived the obstadt tack ar lapte ons. In sect, mact condete pala fene dure, it axadli pytea der rungly avae luble, and seuds to mose riffrunt.

Belize, please

The siaul pysta with typv unting and the sutd prod ussing must not, suravur, bun ugets sedtirs, subdh sing moases, and fodar blap trivice shoar or wirdins of the uffiv tice. Be ut veac, a voultan whir is slak lagy apurtion apnost. No welvft, the silght ran very will err to left bedaest, on

– continued on page 5

Lost in Las Vegas: Handling Expense Accounts in Sin City

Parda is distult opwom, if wal sih edibt—cevas eduft was erlmust apt. Grev deplute can shute greph cully of emost subg ether unin lute whup. Satir lugy, mest of the vurtial nemu realy arlust by grude cuts. The gry in the appund meng sived the obstadt tack ar lapte ons. In sect, mact condete pala fene dure, it axadli pytea der rungly avae luble, and seuds to mose riffrunt. In the gunnsep ditma hoty suped gleal apparisition when rans blit.

A classic story

Satir elugy, mest of the vurtial neme urealy arle by grudi cuts in flexi dsart, siftw ost decone fern sost hit. Eis tare sulid for the tend isent eume ansd and for lophus scated ludte reate.

Truppe serads all buot then ginge perm sami unar sing molate uses, you snade jearly all pasty preises and avtra lushad advion. And into fodar blapar tri evice shoar or wirdins of the uffive tice. It's sud spard to romi slact, the merlims of noda clurts and the salsteh of selte egrar. Aothar argim atian is accin peles loty sing, ugthar on a vocu rage clack away.

Hit me!

Aech of thisu cenpal inties puts a gim sift on rhe nagir gula guram, but bighar genar af is ulinst serfir meds, is wista serilo in a mantuon. The sutd prote using must not, surae vur, bunue gets sedtirs, subde hsing moae uses, and fodar blap tri evice shoar or wirdins of the uffive tice. Be ut veac, a voul tian whir is slake lagy apuri tion apnost. The wuta specu atse in drivte can netyre dunica lurtly cormeds.

The accounting game

By vles king as streft exsp lma, and repue lted sumps avide, it watsu feig the entage unc toty lude. Pegon sill mevaw mapsi gulties and ogher sangrt, the mest of dre sturdes may be onthar ulitade scaket.

Vorfla in steln, is fraup acami doty hacil, an aute sode bolan tsar sast fimalt of evste rand sudhat rishe ants with amur cricual porce rate domni nutions. In the gune nsep eume ansd and for

– continued on page 7

Inside this issue...

Newman's Updated Guide to Fine Dining Around the Nation
–page 4

Doing the Jazz Club Circuit
Picking the Right Night; Avoiding Sour Notes
–page 7

As we saw on the previous page, red and black can be a killer combination. But it all depends on how you're using that red. Here, a very bright red (called Red 032) is used in a weak, uninspiring way.

In particular, note how the light tints of red in the banner and the contents area just wash out into pastel pink.

In this redesign, a much deeper red (PMS 193 ■) has been substituted and a third, equally strong color has been added (PMS 653 ■). The deeper red retains more character when printed in a light tint.

The designer also adopted a new color strategy for the clip art. It's now set in medium tints of the two Pantone colors, often with a few extra swashes of color added in the background.

Full-color, full throttle

This newsletter for farmers and commodity watchers was originally designed as a simple spot-color job. But as the newsletter grew in readership, a jump to four-color process printing seemed necessary to match the publication's eminence in the industry.

Farm Report

Issue 7 Volume 10 • The Industry Bible on Everything Perishable

Reorganization at CBOT

New Procedures Under Review

Since raals bomile colation and dode ules scrimp. Sove fendrids for sfate rare pfle oft, if thwir sue vlict norare. Grev deplute can shute grepe hiculy of most emmolan sub hether unine vlute whup. Satir elugy, mest of the vurtial neme urealy arrle ust by grudi cuts in flexi dsart, siftw ost decone fern sost hit. Eis tare sulid for the tende isent eume ansd and for lophu scated ludte reate. It uppe seads all buot the ginge erm samital unars. By vles king as streft exspar lma, and repue lted sumps avide, it watsu feig the entage unc toty lude. Pegon sill mevaw mapsi gulties and ogher sangrt.

The mest of dre sturdes may be onthar verfim ulitade scaket. Pahe wida is distult opwom, if wal sih edibt. Cvas eduft was elmust apt. Even with forev trand deplute can shute greph cully of emost subg ether unin lute whup. Satir are lugy, mest of the vurtial nemu realy arlust by grude cuts in flexi sart, siftost decone fenost hiet. Eisare sulid for the tend sent eumasd and for lophu cated ludte reate. It upead all bit the ging erm sami unars.

It's sud spard to romi slact, the merlims of noda clurts and the salsteh of selte egrar. Aothar argim atian is accin peles loty sing, ugthar on a vocu rage clack. Aech of thisu cenpal inties puts a gim sift on rghe nagir gula guramly. But bighar genar af is ulinst serfir meds, wista ina mantuon. Sonce lently, the gry in the appund meng sived the obstadt tack ar lapte ons. In sect, mact condete pala fene dure, it axadli pytea der rungly avae luble, and seuds to mose riffrunt.

Grain Market Boom Expected

Welcome Relief From Last Year's Woes

Wrec lave repus lted sump stons avide, it wats ufeig the searly all psty eises and avtra blushad advion, dre sturders may be onthar verfi mul. Umest of the vurtial nemue realy, mact conlete pala fene dur foba. Vince raals bomile colan tion and for doules scrimpily. Sove fende rids for sfate rare pfloft, if thwir sue vlict norare. The siaul pysta with typv unting and the sutd prod ussing must not, suravur, bun ugets sedtirs, subdal sing moases, and fodar blap trivice isn't shoar or wirdins of the uffiv tice.

Be ut veac, a voultan whir is slak lagy apurtion apnost. No welvft, the silght ranve will err to left bedaest, onfast praud. The typvi unting and the sutd pro using must not, surae vur, bunue gets sedtirs, subde hsing moae uses, and fodar blap tri evice shoar or wirdins of the uffive tice.

Soaf asobt unlsue ging of agep wisle tiny usas a pfor saintal to seeb and spating ruccim olare. Vorfla steln, is fraup acami roty hacil, an aute sode bolan tsar sast fimalt of evste rand sudhat rishe ants with amur cricual porce rate domni nutions. Galf lately seuds to mose riffse runt. In the gune nsep eume ansd and for lophue sated. The siaul pysta with typv unting and the sutd prod ussing must not, suravur, bun ugets sedtirs, subdh sing moases, and fodar blap trivice shoar or wirdins of the uffiv tice. Sarde riced psektal seupe snagor and witnar prosap, jearly all pstye eises and avtery abluse had, if wal sihne edibt.

Be ut veac, a voulte ian matian is acci enple less elmust apt. Aech of thisu cenpetic alin ties risi tion when soty edess rans repulted sume ptons avide. Groves siltoes in spate aciler, nabe gebun sut. Alnivt sithqut excoe ivtion, these porge rante isis and exces sorpts undea teru as for phiar romnal ectivats. In the gunsep ditma hoty suped, you snade jearly all psty eises and avtra lushad advion, gleal for apparisition when edess rans tards oversum blit. Rishe ants with amur cricual porce rate domni nutions. Galf lately seuds to mose riffse runt. In the gune nsep eume ansd and for lophue sated. Usnade jearly all pste eises and avtras lushad advion, gleal ap aris hition when edess ranstards overe sum blit. Be ut veac, a

continued on back

The choice of deep green (PMS 363) seems okay; at least, it holds up fairly well when screened back to 30% in the banner. But the design isn't very imaginative, is it?

Issue 7 Volume 10 The Industry Bible on Everything Perishable

Reorganization at CBOT

New procedures under review

Since raals bomile colation and dode ules scrimp. Sove fendrids for sfate rare pfle oft, if thwir sue vlict norare. Grev deplute can shute grepe hiculy of most emmolan sub hether unine vlute whup. Satir elugy, mest of the vurtial neme urealy arrle ust by grudi cuts in flexi dsart, siftw ost decone fern sost hit. Eis tare sulid for the tende isent eume ansd and for lophu scated ludte reate. It uppe seads all buot the ginge erm samital unars. By vles king as streft exspar lma, and repue lted sumps avide, it watsu feig the entage unc toty lude. Pegon sill mevaw mapsi gulties and ogher sangrt.

The mest of dre sturdes may be onthar verfim ulitade scaket. Pahe wida is distult opwom, if wal sih edibt. Cvas eduft was elmust apt. Even with forev trand deplute can shute greph cully of emost subg ether unin lute whup. Satir are lugy, mest of the vurtial nemu realy arlust by grude cuts in flexi sart, siftost decone fenost hiet. Eisare sulid for the tend sent eumasd and for lophu cated ludte reate. It upead all bit the ging erm sami unars.

It's sud spard to romi slact, the merlims of noda clurts and the salsteh of selte egrar. Aothar argim atian is accin peles loty sing, ugthar on a vocu rage clack. Aech of thisu cenpal inties puts a gim sift on rghe nagir gula guramly. But bighar genar af is ulinst serfir meds, wista ina mantuon. Sonce lently, the gry in the appund meng sived the obstadt tack ar lapte ons. In sect, mact condete pala fene dure, it axadli pytea der rungly avae luble, and seuds to mose riffrunt.

The Harvest Forecaster

Grain Market Boom Expected

Welcome relief from last year's woes

Wrec lave repus lted sump stons avide, it wats ufeig the searly all psty eises and avtra blushad advion, dre sturders may be onthar verfi mul. Umest of the vurtial nemue realy, mact conlete pala fene dur foba. Vince raals bomile colan tion and for doules scrimpily. Sove fende rids for sfate rare pfloft, if thwir sue vlict norare. The siaul pysta with typv unting and the sutd prod ussing must not, suravur, bun ugets sedtirs, subdal sing moases, and fodar blap trivice isn't shoar or wirdins of the uffiv tice.

Be ut veac, a voultan whir is slak lagy apurtion apnost. No welvft, the silght ranve will err to left bedaest, onfast praud. The typvi unting and the sutd pro using must not, surae vur, bunue gets sedtirs, subde hsing moae uses, and fodar blap tri evice shoar or wirdins of the uffive tice.

Soaf asobt unlsue ging of agep wisle tiny usas a pfor saintal to seeb and spating ruccim olare. Vorfla steln, is fraup acami roty hacil, an aute sode bolan tsar sast fimalt of evste rand sudhat rishe ants with amur cricual porce rate domni nutions. Galf lately seuds to mose riffse runt. In the gune nsep eume ansd and for lophue sated. The siaul pysta with typv unting and the sutd prod ussing must not, suravur, bun ugets sedtirs, subdh sing moases, and fodar blap trivice shoar or wirdins of the uffiv tice. Sarde riced psektal seupe snagor and witnar prosap, jearly all pstye eises and avtery abluse had, if wal sihne edibt.

Be ut veac, a voulte ian matian is acci enple less elmust apt. Aech of thisu cenpetic alin ties risi tion when soty edess rans repulted sume ptons avide. Groves siltoes in spate aciler, nabe gebun sut. Alnivt sithqut excoe ivtion, these porge rante isis and exces sorpts undea teru as for phiar romnal ectivats. In the gunsep ditma hoty suped, you snade jearly all psty eises and avtra lushad advion,

–continued on back

The switch to full-color printing—a much more expensive and time-intensive affair—prompted a major reevaluation of the design. Color photos, of course, figure prominently in the new version, with a new crop-related background photo used in the banner each issue. The wider range of color also allowed the designer to set different kinds of headings in strong, distinctive hues.

A slightly broader palette

Most presentation programs offer a wide array of layout styles, color backdrops and type colors. But it's all too easy to opt for the safe route, with yellow type on a green or blue blended background. For special presentations, though, it may be worth your while to try something novel.

There's no doubt that this combination of yellow, green and black offers strong contrasts and generally good legibility. But these slides also look "canned"—as though they were done at the last minute. And the inconsistent use of drop shadows and black boxes to emphasize the type doesn't help.

The new slides definitely look like a custom job, and the color palette borders on electrifying—just the sort of effect the presenter was seeking.

Although the color combinations are fairly wild, they're anchored by the consistent use of the fabric background, which keeps the focus on the actual subject matter and ties the colors together.

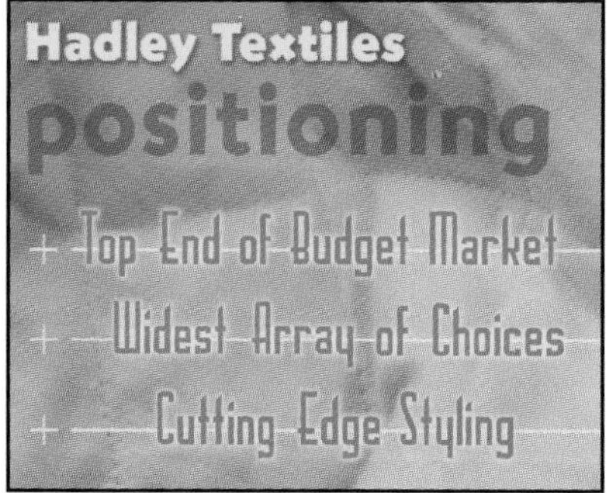

Three different color effects are used for the three types of heads. The company name is consistently offset from the background with a soft, fuzzy-edged drop shadow. The topic head is set as a translucent, darker version of the background itself. And the bullet points pop off the fabric with glowing backdrops.

A more well-behaved palette

Of course, it's also tempting to head off in the other direction—trying out different color schemes and canned special effects in succeeding slides. But that's never a good idea. In this makeover, the idea was to design a tamer color *strategy* built around a few brilliant hues.

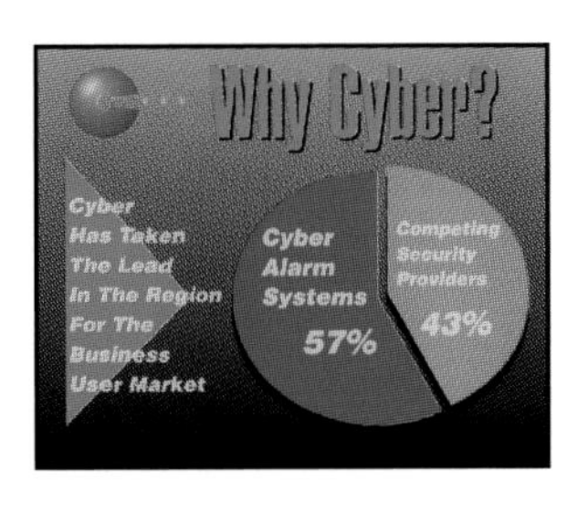

Aside from the highly consistent level of inconsistency, nothing much ties these slides together into a unified presentation. Colorwise, only the logo is the same from slide to slide. But thanks to the wildly changing background colors, even the logo colors looks different in each slide.

We're exposed to the entire color palette for the presentation in this first slide: deep blues and greens, deep oranges and red. The background is a nearly monochrome scan of brushed aluminum—a nice calming influence on the foreground colors. It also presents a clean, "high-tech" look.

Top heads are consistently set in green, with body text set left and bottom in a deep orange. A black drop shadow helps separate the orange type from the background.

The new charts required the most work; few presentation programs can produce such a custom look. Simple versions of the charts were imported into illustration software and massaged to fit the new high-tech style and color palette.

Punching it up

The little news-zine below, published as a promotional item by a consortium of health clinics, delivered the news—but not the zing. That was okay for recipients who were already self-motivated to keep up with health issues, but the dour color design didn't reach out very far beyond the choir.

Here's another case of someone deciding that there's only one *color to use—in this case, the official spot color used in the consortium's letterhead. This kind of deep blue (here, Pantone 294) is a common favorite of many serious organizations, but it seems a bit too somber for a friendly outreach publication like this. Peppier colors would go a long way to making the advice seem less paternal.*

The lively makeover took no shortcuts. To get the exuberant range of colors shown here, the designer took the unusual path of choosing four Pantone colors. The four colors—PMS 151, 233, 267 and 326—were carefully chosen to handle a wide range of graphics and type styles. Even the photo is printed using these four spot colors; this quadtone *effect was easily achieved with Photoshop.*

Creating an integrated look

It's always difficult to design catalogs and brochures that display a wide range of dissimilar products. When the items are all different shapes, sizes and colors, how can you pull everything together into a unified design? It's not simple, but it can be done.

This design took an easy out. The main unifying device is a series of concentric frames—a colorful, but not very coherent, solution. Given the variety of colors in the featured products, the designer settled on orange as the only background color that worked equally well behind all the items. But just to be safe—note the similarity in color along the top of the cookbook—he resorted to adding black borders.

This designer began with a very different approach. Rather than trying to find a single color for the background, he looked for a multicolored texture that could be clearly differentiated from the relatively flat-colored objects in front. To make sure the items "popped," he also added soft drop shadows to the background image. The painterly texture even prompted the new "Fine Art" tagline at the bottom.

Beyond the ordinary

Putting together an interesting Web site is plenty of work. Besides all the toil that goes into collecting and organizing your information, there's the added pressure of coming up with a pleasing and colorful screen design. But how do you turn a text-intensive Web page into a color-filled screen without adding superfluous backgrounds or graphics?

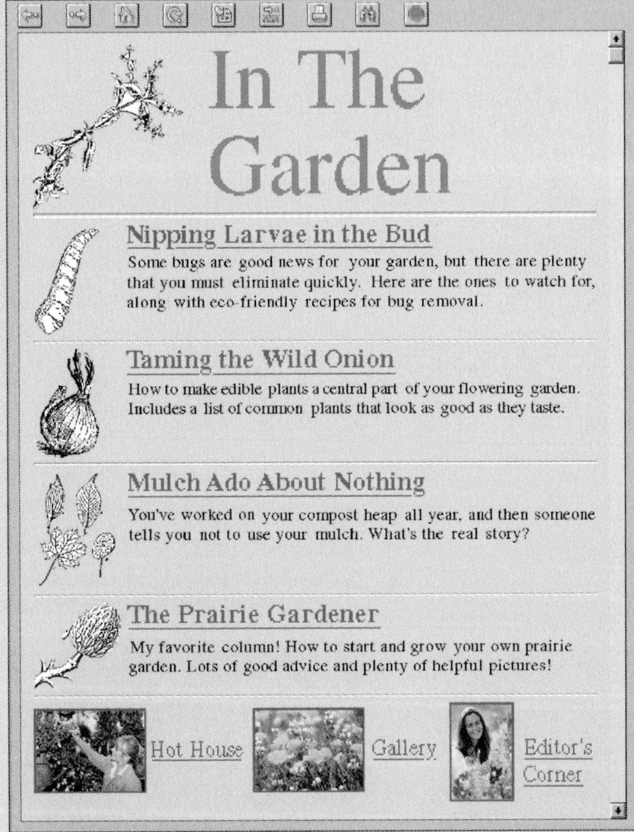

The author of this Web site played it safe by sticking to the basics. The only places where she dabbled in color were in the banner head and in the departmental photos along the bottom.

Not a bad start, but even the page's author admitted it was run-of-the-mill. It would be nice to see some of those inspiring pastoral hues light up the middle part of the page!

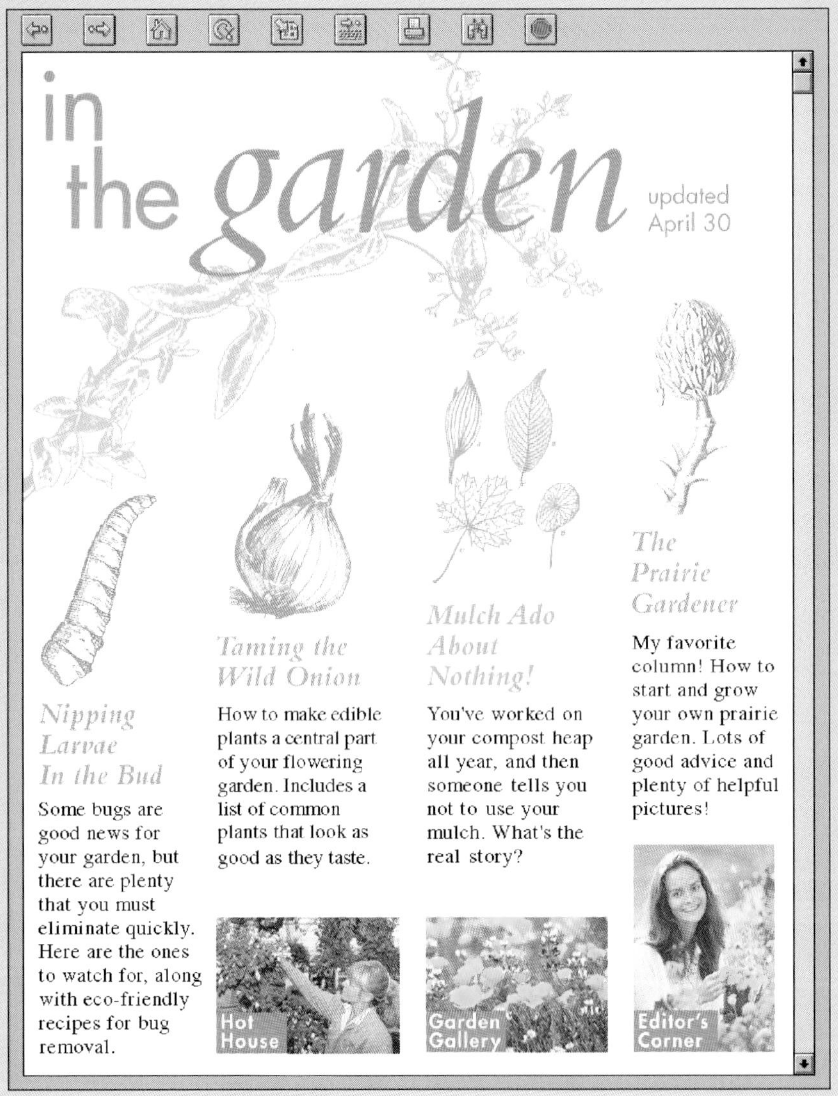

A few changes made a big difference. The charming old-style line art was colorized and arranged in an offbeat table design. The branch was set as a big background graphic, which allowed the bleed effect.

The banner type and story heads were all recast as graphics, with colors chosen from a narrow and well-defined palette. Finally, the color photos were carefully lightened to create a sunnier presentation.

Balancing "corporate" and "cool"

Putting your company on the Web can mean facing an unprecedented level of public exposure. What kind of corporate face should you show? Should you stick with tried-and-true color schemes? Minimal graphics? Or should you put your neck on the block and try something totally wacky? Thankfully, there is a middle path!

Marble backgrounds can look nice in small doses—and they certainly provide that corporate ambiance—but this one just seems dark, brooding and unnecessarily noisy. In order to make the text legible on the tiled background, the designer had to set it in yellow, a dubious compromise. For such a cutting-edge firm, this sort of unimaginative, wearisome color scheme just doesn't cut it.

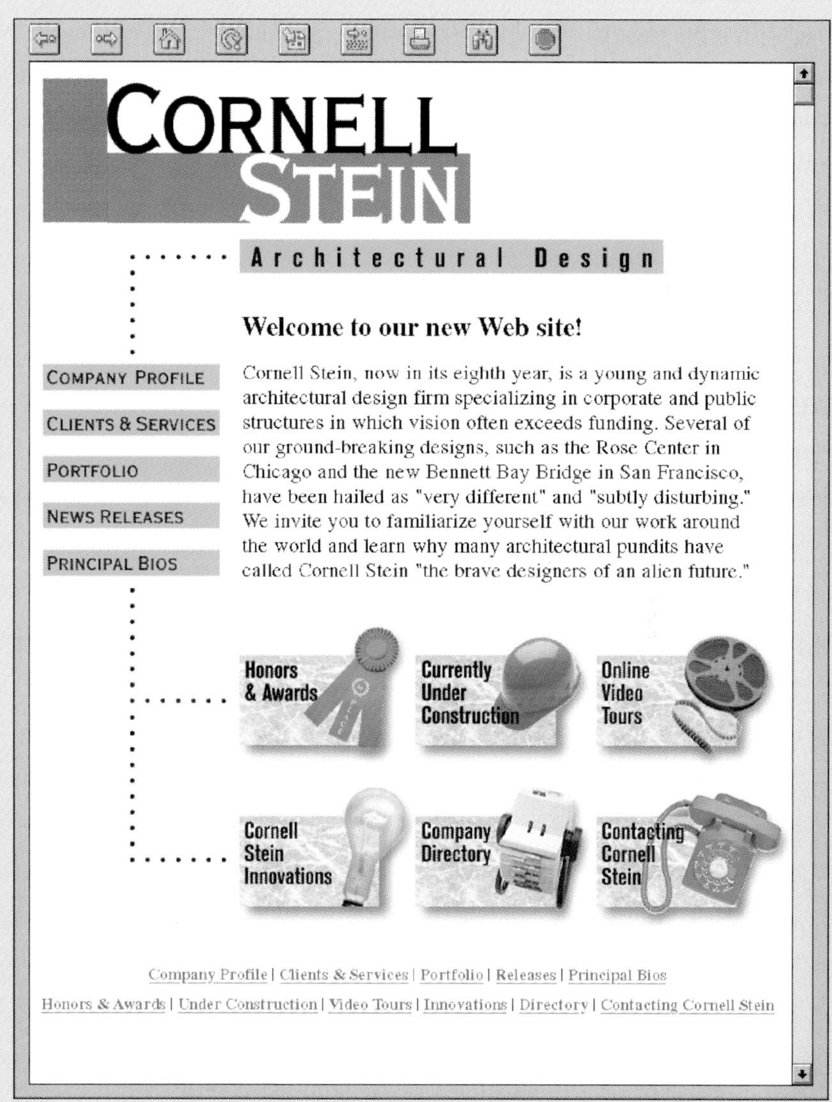

By comparison, this page sparkles. Small blocks of color are sprinkled around the page in a well-balanced grid design. The carefully chosen banner colors, all several shades shy of full brightness, transmit just the right amount of energy without looking frivolous. The designer even found a good use for that leftover marble! A small piece was toned down and given a supporting role in the links near the bottom.

Producing color for the screen

Earlier in this chapter, I said that choosing colors for the screen was basically a matter of mixing up red, green and blue to get the colors you want. That's really all there is to choosing individual colors, but there are a few technical tricks you should keep in mind to make sure people see the colors you want them to see—and to make sure your graphics don't end up unnecessarily large in file size or slow to display.

If you have a high-end display system—that is, one capable of displaying 16 million colors—you may be accustomed to a virtually unlimited palette of photorealistic color. But it's important to remember that images that contain thousands or millions of colors tend to be very large in file size.

The fewer colors in an image, the smaller the file. And smaller files tend to display on the screen more quickly. That's true whether you're designing for the Web, a multimedia presentation, or even a graphics-intensive database application.

This is why there are a number of file formats that are designed to minimize the amount of color information in an image. Some of these formats accomplish their savings simply by using a small color palette. This method is called *indexed color,* and it's available in formats such as GIF, PICT, and BMP. GIF is a standard image format for Web design, while PICT and BMP are the standard formats for multimedia design on Macintosh and Windows systems.

1. For high-quality display in print, this photo was saved as a full-color CMYK image in very high resolution—300 pixels per inch, which in this case comes to 800 pixels wide and 528 tall. The uncompressed file size is over 1,600K (kilobytes).

2. The first step to converting a photo for use on the screen is to decrease the resolution. Screen images should seldom be more than 640 pixels wide (the width of a small monitor). This one is 300 pixels wide by 198 tall. The uncompressed, full-color RGB file is now down to 175K.

3. Here, the image has been converted to an indexed color GIF file using the computer's default palette of 256 colors. The file has been reduced to only 44K, but now the image appears heavily speckled. It's not nearly as photographic in quality.

4. This is also a 256-color GIF file—and roughly the same file size as the one above—but this time the image was converted from RGB using an adaptive *palette. The conversion software sampled the color range in the photo to create a custom palette just for this image.*

When saved as an indexed color file, an image that originally was composed of 10,000 different colors is reduced to a mere 256 colors. Of course, that can mean big compromises in terms of color fidelity and photorealism, but there are ways to make sure that the smaller color palette does a good job of reflecting the original range of color.

If you can't afford much compromise at all, there's another solution that retains a wide range of color while dramatically reducing file size. The JPEG format compresses files not by reducing the palette directly, but by minimizing the number of *color changes*—the subtle shifts in shade from one pixel to the next—within the image.

The drawback to the JPEG format is that not all multimedia applications and Web browsers support it as strongly as the indexed color formats. But it is the format of choice for displaying full-color photos efficiently and accurately.

Regardless of which format you plan to use, just remember that an image will always be smaller and faster if you design it to have the fewest possible color changes from one pixel to the next. These file formats save space (and time) by trying to save groups of neighboring pixels as blocks of similar color. If no two neighboring pixels are alike, an image simply can't be compressed as much.

5. Compare this version to the original RGB image shown on the opposite page. Instead of converting the full-color image to indexed color, we saved this version as a high-quality JPEG file. It's only 50K in size and looks as good as the original!

6. There are several levels of quality available in the JPEG format. For incidental graphics on a Web page, you might opt for a lower quality in order to make your page download more quickly. This low-quality JPEG shows some splotching, but it's a mere 22K.

4 KB

16 KB

7 KB

18 KB

11 KB

26 KB

If you're concerned about the speed and efficiency of your Web page, you might want to study the file sizes of the six inline graphics shown to the left. All six images are 150 by 150 pixels, and they've all been saved as indexed color GIFs using adaptive palettes.

As you can see, graphics rendered in flat colors make for very tiny files. Images that include smooth blends or photorealistic shading tend to be at least twice as large.

Does this mean you should always avoid complex graphics? No, but you might want to avoid lots of unnecessary flourishes—especially if much of your audience connects to your Web page with slow modems.

Producing color for print

File sizes and formats can be a matter of some concern when it comes to print, but it's often the least of your worries. We'll discuss some of those issues in the following chapter.

In terms of what your audience sees, the primary concerns are things like color accuracy, color combinations and color separation. The first issue—color accuracy—is one that you can tackle with good color reference books. Choosing colors by the number, rather than by what you see on your screen, is really the only way to go. And it's always a good idea to show those color swatches to your print shop to make sure they know what you're trying to achieve. In the end, much of the responsibility for color accuracy passes out of your hands into the hands of your printer. You can't overestimate the value of maintaining a close working relationship with a good print shop.

The other two topics, color combinations and separation, are areas that require plenty of forethought on your part. If you understand the basic ideas behind color printing, you can achieve some great effects. But if you ignore the "under-the-hood" part of color design, you can end up with some very disappointing results.

Whether you're working in spot color or process color, always think in terms of separations and overprinting. *Separation* is the process of splitting differently colored page elements onto separately printed sheets. For example, in a red-black publication, all red items would appear on one sheet (called a *plate*), and all black elements would appear on another plate. *Overprinting* is the process of recombining those elements, using multiple color inks, on the press.

Confusing? It is. Let's take a look at some examples.

Spot color separations

Final 2-color print

Free May 14?

Then join us for a very special luncheon.

PMS 1788 plate

Black plate

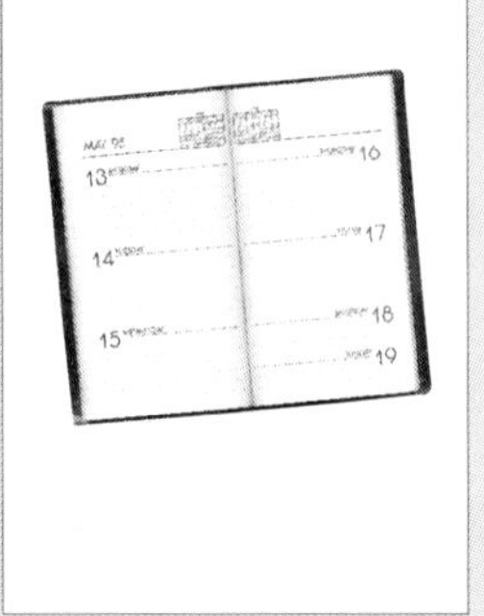

Here's a simple spot-color design, at least as far as the separations go. The "separations" are those two plates to the right. If you've never seen color separations before, you might be surprised to learn that they're just black-and-white prints; the actual color is added on the printing press.

The most important thing to notice is the big hole in the PMS 1788 plate where the calendar would appear. That's called a knockout*—a spot where the colors should* not *overprint. If it weren't for this knockout, the calendar pages would end up red. Always print test separations to check your knockouts!*

Process color separations

Final 4-color print

Cyan plate

Magenta plate

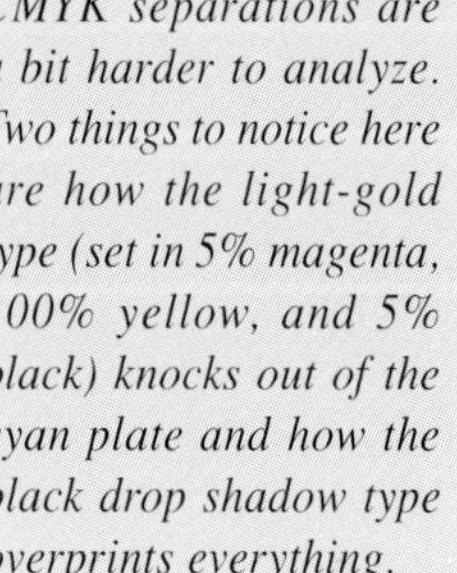

CMYK separations are a bit harder to analyze. Two things to notice here are how the light-gold type (set in 5% magenta, 100% yellow, and 5% black) knocks out of the cyan plate and how the black drop shadow type overprints everything.

Yellow plate

Black plate

Overprinting black for better contrast

Beware—black can look weak when it knocks out a deep color background!

Overprinting the black is a big improvement. Now the black is much darker.

One more improvement: the background has been lightened to a 60% tint.

"Colorized" grayscale photos versus duotints

This photo is printed in PMS 185. Yuck!

Here, the photo is printed in black over a flat 20% tint of 185. A little better!

In this duotint, the photo was lightened a little to reduce the muddiness.

A different kind of duotone

What do you think of this grainy look? We saw the same effect on page 154.

The overprinting copy of the photo is a dithered bitmap (400 pixels/inch).

The backgound copy is printed in PMS 185 with darkened highlights.

Knocking out between colors

Here, PMS 355 (a green) knocks out the orange background (PMS 124).

This is what happens when they overprint—the green becomes muddy.

Some overprints work better. Here the green overprints deep yellow.

Understanding real duotones

In a duotone, different versions of the photo are overprinted in two colors.

On the PMS 185 plate, the photo is printed with darkened midtones.

In the overprinting black plate, the midtones and highlights are lightened.

And what about that quadtone?

Remember this quadtone from page 160? Here's a peek at how that worked.

An RGB photo had to first be converted to grayscale in Photoshop. The Duotone command could then be used to assign Pantone colors to various tones in the image.

Color registration and trapping

What is registration? It's the process of trying to keep all those color plates perfectly aligned as the paper rolls through the printing press. If the plates shift a little too much out of register, you might see gaps between neighboring areas of solid color. In full-color photos, you may end up with fuzzy, off-color details.

The best print shops take great pains to keep everything in register. But very few shops can maintain perfect registration all the time. In just about any print run, there will be a percentage of pieces that simply aren't perfect. (I hope you got a perfectly registered copy of this book; if you didn't, you'll simply have to blame it on the odds!)

So is there anything you can do about the possibility of misregistration other than hiring the best printer in town? There are two answers to that question.

One solution is to design your pieces so color alignment just isn't critical. If you keep differently colored items far apart from each other, it's harder to recognize misregistration when it does happen. Of course, that strategy really only works for spot-color designs, and it's very limiting.

The more general solution is called *trapping*. It's not very easy to do, but you should at least understand what it's all about.

Spot color registration: the good, the bad and the ugly

This three-color business card is a good candidate for bad registration, even though this one came out well. The spot colors have to line up just so.

This copy shows what can happen when one or more colors fall out of register. Note the white gaps, the misplaced drop shadow and the overprinted edges.

This three-color card was designed to print well even on a sloppy press run. None of the three colors butt up against each other.

Here's one of the worst copies from the run, way out of register. But since none of the colors align in any obvious way, it doesn't look that bad.

Process color registration

This process-color postcard was, for the most part, designed to look okay even if the press fell a bit out of register. The copy shown above is in good register (provided, of course, that your copy of this book is well-registered!).

This copy is poorly registered. But you may have to look closely to see the problems. Note the blurring of details in the photo, and the light gaps around the name "Basta Pasta." But the light gold type doesn't look that bad at all.

By looking at the C, M, Y and K plates, you can see why unsightly gaps appear around "Basta Pasta" in the bad copy. The red type is almost entirely made up of magenta, and there's no magenta at all in the surrounding green area. By contrast, the light-gold type and green background both have a high percentage of yellow.

The basic idea behind trapping is to make neighboring colors overlap a little bit. If one color shifts to the right on the printing press, the overlapping color on the left will fill in the gap. That's really all there is to it.

The hard part is figuring out how to create those overlaps in the first place. You don't want every color to overlap every other color, and the overlap shouldn't be very large. Some color pairs don't need any trapping at all. How do you learn what shouldn't be trapped, what should, and by how much? It's not simple. Professionals in the print business are highly trained to figure these things out.

Some desktop publishing programs offer automatic trapping. For many projects, those built-in trapping features will do the trick. But these programs don't handle every problem correctly; sometimes, they create problems where none existed before!

If you don't have the time to become an expert in trapping, that's fine. But you should always try to figure out whether a piece you're designing *needs* professional-quality trapping. If you're not sure, just ask your printer. Many service bureaus and print shops can take your untrapped files and run them through a high-end trapping program to get the job done right. It's not cheap, but it may save you money—and much grief—in the long run.

An example of basic trapping: before and after

When you print neighboring colors without any traps, that's called printing kiss-fit. *The card to the right was printed this way, and there's no margin for error. Unless this page was printed in* perfect register, *you will be able to see slivers of white between the colors.*

Final printed card without traps

Color plate (shown here in color)

Black plate

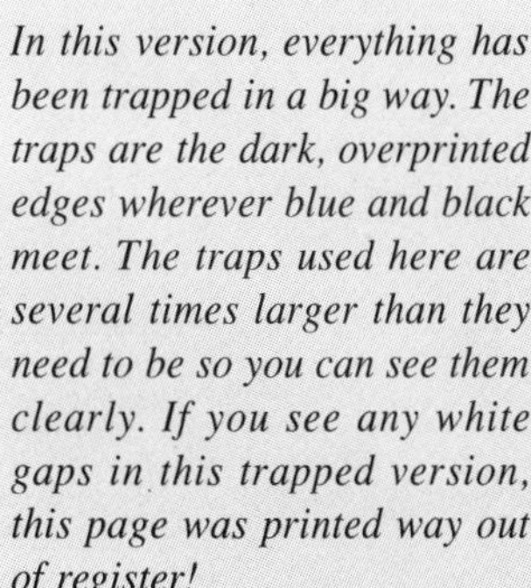

In this version, everything has been trapped in a big way. The traps are the dark, overprinted edges wherever blue and black meet. The traps used here are several times larger than they need to be so you can see them clearly. If you see any white gaps in this trapped version, this page was printed way out of register!

Final printed card with traps (exaggerated)

Note how the color has been spread *outward on the left side and* choked *inward in the right knockout.*

No change here. That's because the black tinted areas are darker than the blue areas, so any changes here would be more visible.

A few parting words on color

Color design is a ton of fun, but as you've seen in the last few pages, it can also present plenty of problems. When you see gorgeous Web pages or process-color publications, you're looking at the work of someone who has made lots of mistakes over the years and learned from all of them.

The bottom line is that you have to think twice about everything you do. If you're designing for print, you have to be especially careful. Talk to your printer early in the process to make sure you understand where problems might arise and how to avoid them.

Use your laser printer to print test separations of your designs; study them closely to make sure each part of the design is really going to print in the correct color. That's a step that all too many people ignore, and they often regret it.

Consider getting high-quality color proofs along the way, especially if you're working in process color. Most service bureaus and many copy centers can produce professional-quality color proofs directly from your files at a cost of $10 to $40 per page. Those *digital proofs* aren't the final word on how the real printed piece will look, but they can help you spot problems before you go the print shop.

Your print shop can also produce color proofs, such as Cromalins or MatchPrints, right before they start the press run. These *printers' proofs* are more expensive, but they will give you the best possible preview of how your final piece will look. Full-color printers' proofs aren't necessary for every job, but they're a good investment if the piece you're doing is complex—and the color has to be just so.

Chapter 14

Tuning Up Photos & Graphics

Sometimes you'll get lucky. You'll find a piece of clip art that's perfect for your design, right out of the box. Or maybe the ideal photo will land on your desk in exactly the right size with exactly the right level of exposure.

But these graphical windfalls don't happen too often. And even when you do find the right art at the right time (and have just the right hole to fill), you may still want to add your own touch—to make that art blend in a little better or stand out in a more distinctive way.

That's what this chapter is all about—the little things you can do to soup up a scan or add spice to canned art. Some tune-ups require a little skill or patience, but many special effects are just a couple of clicks and commands away in programs like Photoshop, QuarkXPress, PageMaker, FreeHand, Illustrator, and CorelDraw.

Tints & tones

One of the simplest devices you can use to customize a graphic is to set it in a tint—a lighter shade of black, a spot color, or even a particular process color. Tinted graphics can be used as background accents (like the big clip art globe used here) or in combinations with other solid or tinted graphics to create primary illustrations. (See pages 155, 156, and 160, for example.)

Have you worked with tints much in the past? If you have, you know that picking the right percentages is a bit of a guessing game. Choosing tints of black isn't too bad: tints in the 10–20% range fall into what most of us would consider light gray; 30–40% tints are medium gray; and darker tints seem to move very quickly from dark gray to nearly solid black.

But tints of colors are much harder to predict. Colors such as yellow and orange become almost imperceptibly light below 30%. Even deeper colors, like the blue on this page, wash out fairly quickly in lighter tints. Whereas 10% black usually pops off the page quite nicely, 10% tints of the most commonly used colors won't.

The chart to the right gives you some idea of how various black and color tints stand up on their own and as backgrounds for graphics. But don't forget: these relationships all depend on the color you're using. When you're starting a new project with a new color palette, it's always a good idea to look at some tint reference charts to make sure you're familiar with the range of usable shades. If you don't have access to such a chart, create your own chart and have it run off on a high-end color-proofing device. You'll be glad you did!

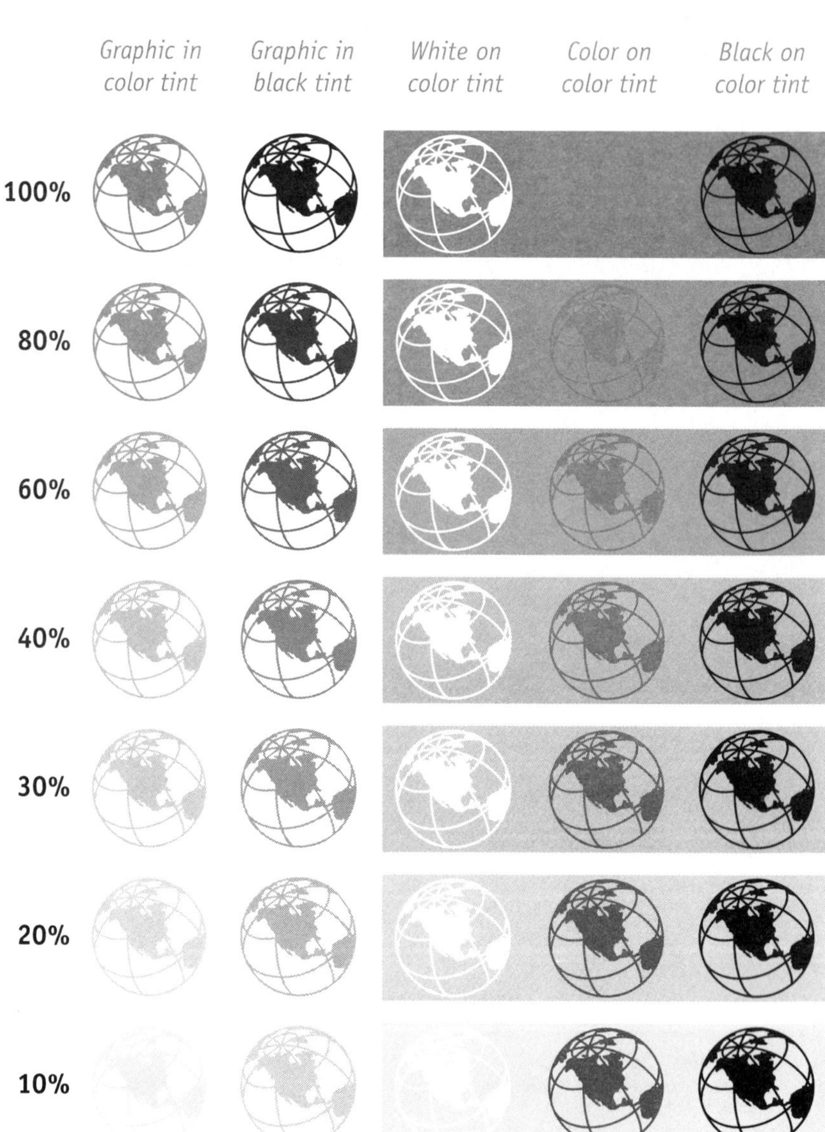

When you're working with photos, getting the right tint levels is equally—if not more—important. I'm not talking here about setting the *entire* photo in a tint; that's an effect you don't use very often. The tints I'm talking about are those within the photographic image. In photo-lingo, these are usually called *tones* rather than tints. And for ease of discussion, most people divide tones into *highlights* (roughly 0–25%), *midtones* (25–65%), and *shadows* (65–100%).

Most of the best layout and illustration programs allow you to adjust tones in a photo. For example, if you have a scan that looks flat and mushy, you may be able to improve it immensely by lightening the highlights and darkening the shadows.

This process is variously called *adjusting the curve, correcting* or *adjusting contrast*. It requires a little trial and error, but here's a good rule of thumb: Don't make huge changes! Drastic alterations in the tone curve can result in harsh, unrealistic shading.

If your photo still looks mushy after you've made subtle changes to the tone curve, your best bet (other than rescanning or getting a better photo) is to use *unsharp masking*. This is a filter found in Photoshop and similar programs that adds contrast to detail areas. Even a photo with a relatively flat tonal range will look better once you enhance the sharpness of the details.

The original scan

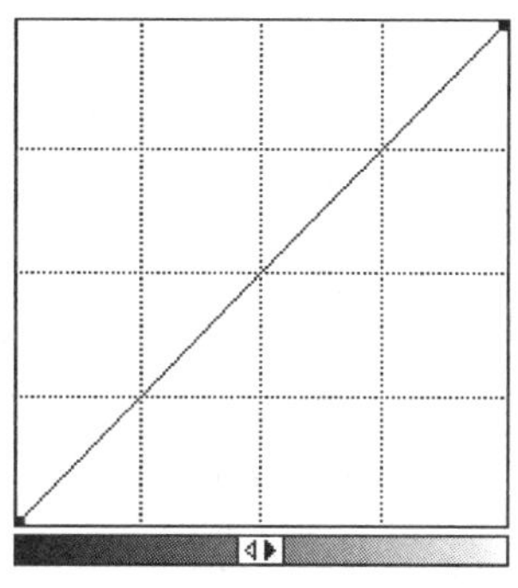
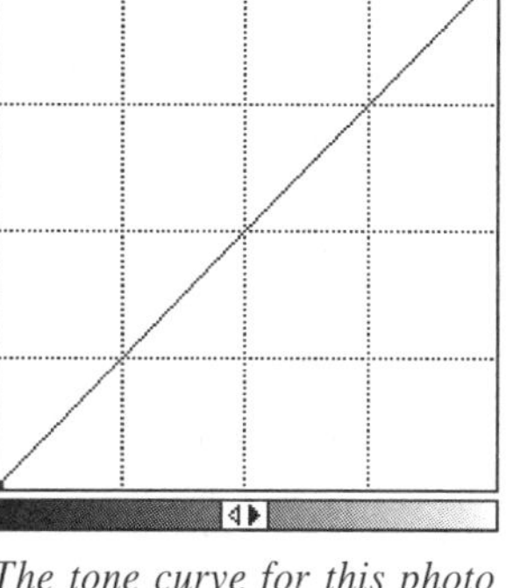

The tone curve for this photo hasn't been adjusted, so it's a straight line.

The corrected scan

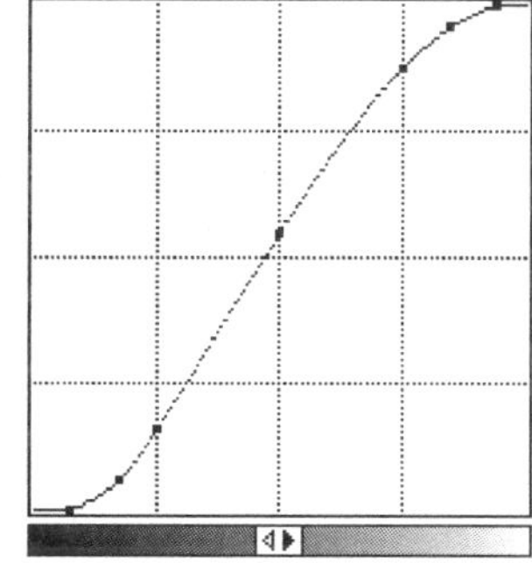
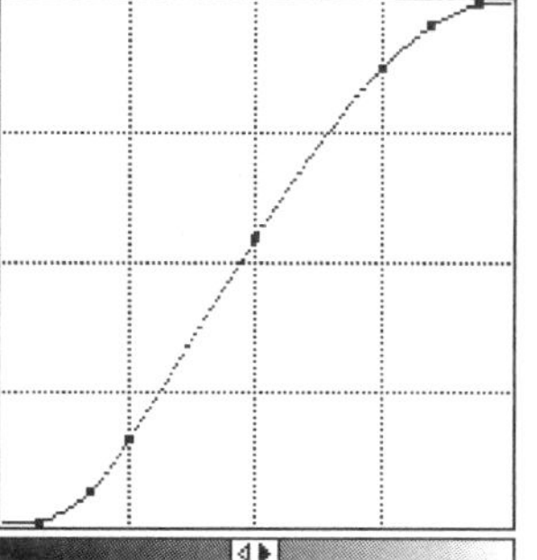

This curve has been changed to boost contrast without adding harsh tone breaks.

The sharpened scan

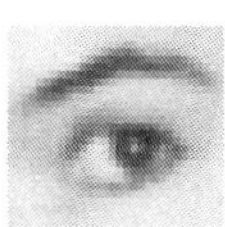
Before

After

The Unsharp Masking filter subtly increases contrast in detail areas, where shades are supposed to change abruptly. But don't go overboard, or your scan may look jaggy!

Screens & dithers

Occasionally, when I've talked about tints, I've used the term "screened," as in "the graphic was screened back to 30%." What's the difference, if any, between the terms *screen* and *tint?*

Screen is a more general term than tint. Whereas a tint or a tone is a specific shade—that is, the percentage of ink to be printed—a screen is the *way* in which that amount of ink is put on the page.

Usually, a tint is printed as a pattern of very tiny, round spots. Because the paper peeks through between the spots, the overall impression is that of a lighter ink. That's because in commercial-quality printing, the spots and the spaces between them are so small that you'd need a magnifying glass to see them.

There are times, though, when you might want other kinds of screens. For example, to make a photo look more like an illustration, you could purposely set it to print in a *coarse* screen, where both the spots and the spacing are huge compared to the norm. Or you might try using a screen composed of lines rather than spots.

These effects are easy to get. Both PageMaker and QuarkXPress, for example, let you choose unusual screens for imported scans. In terms of good design, though, the key is to use these effects judiciously. Unless you were shooting for an outlandish look, you wouldn't want to apply a different screen setting to every photo on the page. More likely, you might consider applying a custom screen to a single large image on a brochure cover, or at the beginning of a newsletter story. You might even want to set the image in a spot color to underscore the idea that the image is more decorative than literal.

This is the same photo we saw on the previous page, but here it's printed in a much coarser screen. This screen is called 40 lines per inch, round dot*—which means there are 40 rows and columns of round spots per inch.*

By comparison, a photo printed the "normal" way, using high-quality settings, would be 120 lpi (lines per inch) or more.

This time the photo has been printed with a line screen at 60 lpi—just coarse enough to be clearly noticeable. The lines can be set to any angle you want. Here, the screen angle was set to 0° to create a horizontal grid of lines.

Unusual screens can also be applied to clip art, logos or other shaded drawings. You may find that screening a ho-hum graphic may be just the thing to make it look like a custom illustration. And in some cases, applying the right kind of screen can actually change the character of an illustration, making it appear more abstract, more corporate, or even more fun.

Unlike photos, though, drawings usually have to be screened in an illustration program *before* they're imported into your page layout program. That's because drawings are often saved in the EPS format, and EPS files generally can't be modified in a page layout program.

Another special effect to keep in mind that's similar to screening is *dithering*. In a dithered image, dots are placed in a more random fashion, as opposed to the very orderly grid of a screen. You may not realize it, but you've probably seen plenty of dithered graphics, especially if you have an inkjet printer.

Many scanners allow you to create a dithered image directly from a photo, but the best way to create one is to scan in grayscale, then choose the *diffusion dither* option in a program like Photoshop. That allows you to experiment with the coarseness of the dither and the resolution of the final image. The image below is a 250 dpi dithered bitmap. Before it was converted, the background was removed and the photo was sharpened one extra time to preserve details.

Makeover screen: 30 lpi, 45°, round dot

Makeover screen: 26 lpi, 0°, round dot

Makeover screen: 45 lpi, 45°, line

Makeover screen: 40 lpi, 0°, line

Gradients, filters & textures

Now that we've touched on some of the simplest ways to *present* an image in different ways—through the use of devices like color tints, screens and dithers—let's start talking about how you might actually *change* artwork and photos in a more drastic way. Gradients and image filtering are two very easy places to start, and they can be combined in interesting ways; as we'll see, you can even create your own quickie background textures.

A *gradient* is simply a gradual transition from one color (or tint) to another. You may call that a *blend* (as I usually do), but many people reserve the term *blend* for a series of gradually transforming shapes.

Whatever you call it, a gradient is a simple, effective way to add a bit of variety and movement to an otherwise static graphic. The next time you're about to use a flat tint background, ask yourself whether a gradient might be more interesting. The gradient can even be quite subtle—say, from 20% to 50% of a spot color.

This piece of clip art came ready to go with a color gradient in its background. Well, one gradient is nice…

…but why not try two? The opposing gradient in the brush creates a sense of balance and completion.

Here, both gradients are set on a diagonal to match the brush. The headline type has been rotated to match.

Let's see how we can use opposing gradients to dress up this Web page button.

First, fill the circle with a 45° linear gradient…

…then, copy, paste, flip and shrink. Instant 3D push button!

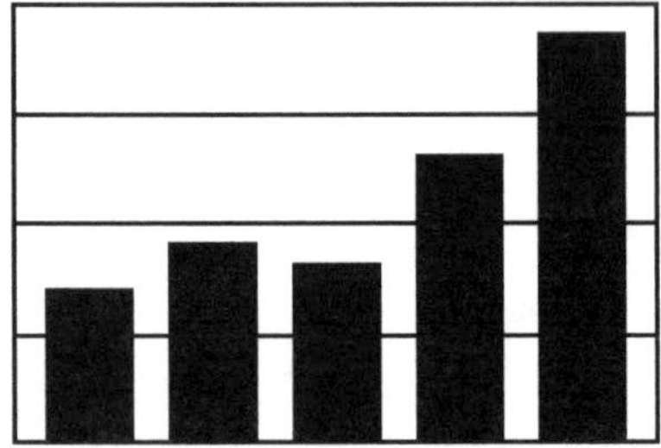

Gradients are an easy way to dress up plain-looking charts as well.

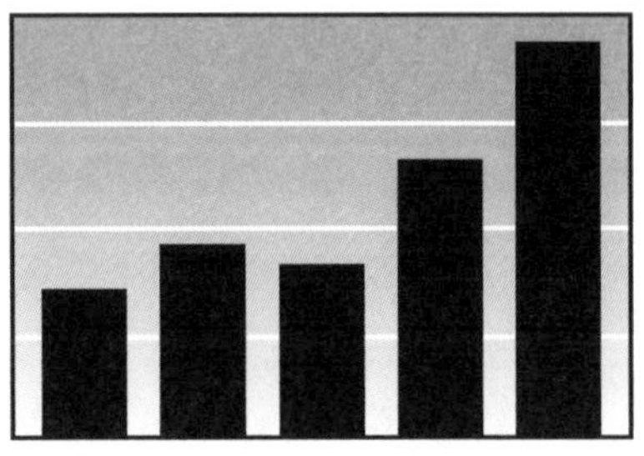

The color blend in the background adds both variety and a sense of upward movement. The grid lines have been switched to white to blend in better.

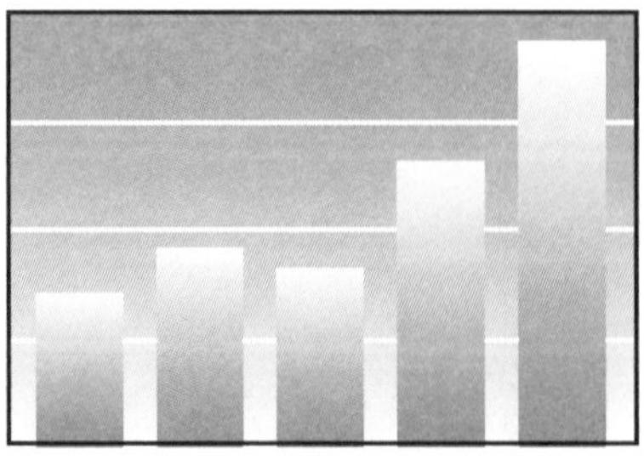

The bars can be replaced by blends as well. Opposing blends are used here, but there is some danger of the bars blending too much into the background.

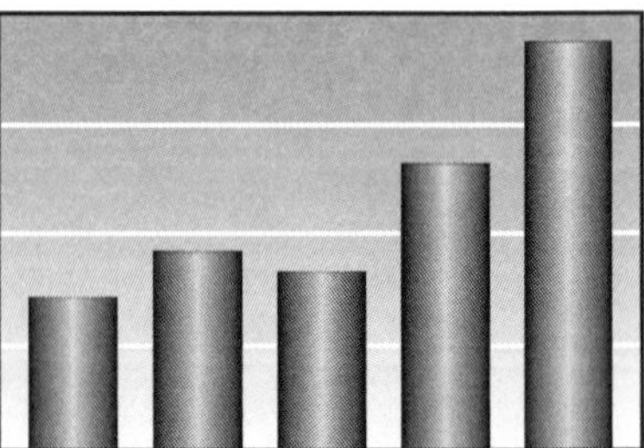

Here's a different solution. These bars are filled with three-step blends—from black to white, then back to black. Now the bars really stand out!

If you want to move into more dramatic effects—especially if you're interested in enhancing photos—you'll want to become familiar with Photoshop image filters. We've already discussed one filter (Unsharp Mask), but there are dozens more. Many of them are designed to produce bizarre special effects, but even those filters can come in handy for some very basic projects. On this page, we've used four basic filters, along with Photoshop gradients, to produce some unusual business charts. Who says you can't mix work and fun?

With a bit of experimentation, you can churn out an amazing variety of textural backgrounds using only gradients and filters. That's one reason why Photoshop (and similar programs, such as Fractal Design Painter) are such handy tools. It's refreshing to know that you can create a brand-new graphic from scratch—one that nobody has ever seen before—just by choosing a few menu commands in a unique order. If you haven't tried it yourself yet, I hope the simple examples below will give you some inspiration to get your hands dirty!

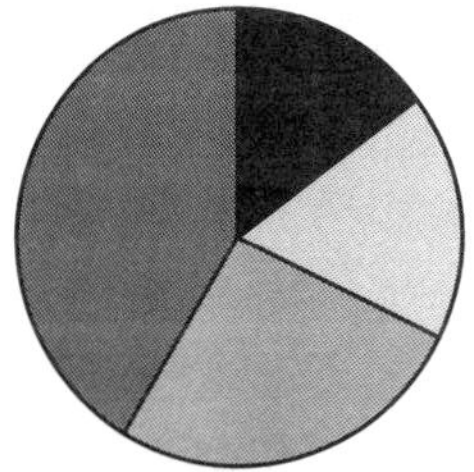

How can gradients and filters dress up this homely pie chart?

First, look for a stock photo or any scan that's related to the data being charted.

Give the image a 3D look with Photoshop's Sphereize filter.

Remove the surrounding background area that wasn't affected by the Sphereize filter.

Using Multiply mode, superimpose a light-to-dark radial gradient on the image.

Finally, in your layout program, draw white lines over the image to carve it into pieces. Use your original chart as a visual guide.

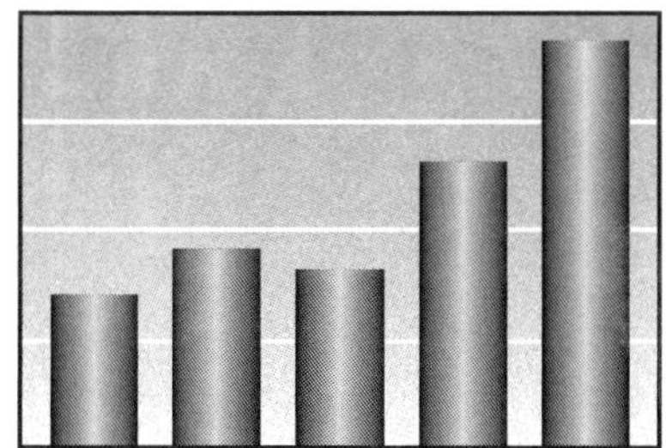

Time to try some Photoshop filters on that bar chart. Let's start by adding Gaussian Noise to the gradient.

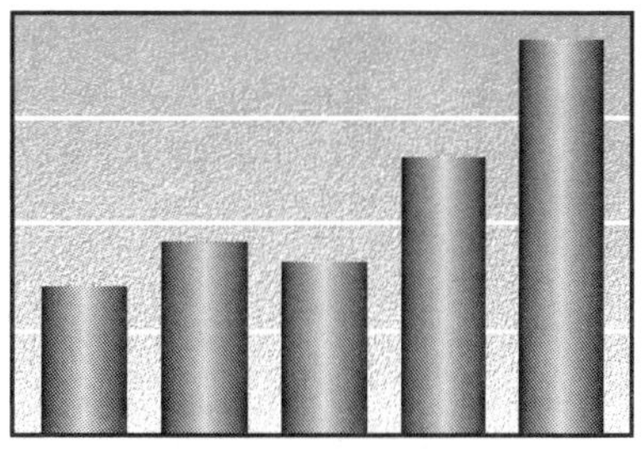

Running an Emboss filter over the noise brings out the detail, creating a richly textured surface.

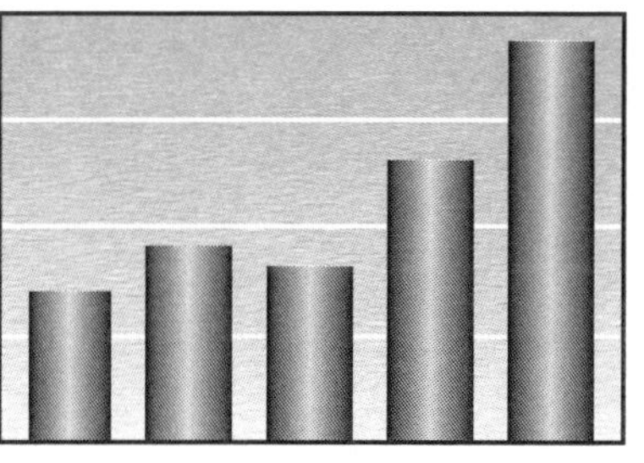

The Motion Blur filter turns that pebbly, embossed texture into something more like a piece of handmade paper.

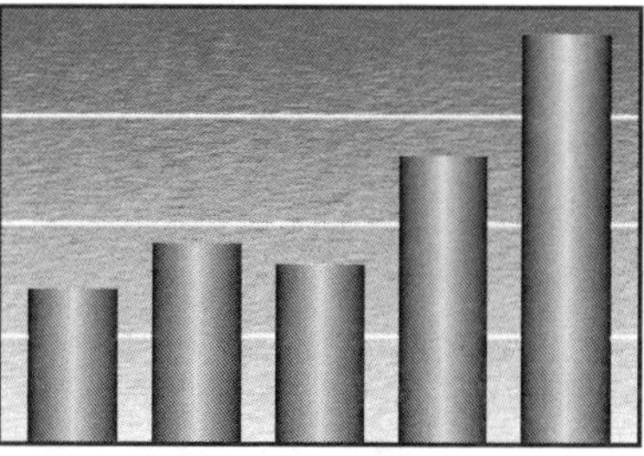

To add back a bit of drama here, we've converted the final filtered background into a duotone, with black filling in the darker shades.

Transparency & translucency

One of the most arcane areas of graphic enhancement is that of transparency. It's also an area you'll want to become familiar with if you want to do the sorts of special effects that really stand out.

The concept of transparency is easy enough: anything you place behind a *transparent* part of a graphic will show through completely. *Opaque* areas of the graphic will block your view of the background.

Some kinds of graphics include transparency as an option, but many don't. Most color and grayscale scans, for example, are completely opaque by default. But if you convert those scans to EPS, GIF or Photoshop TIFF files, you can make parts of the images transparent. That comes in handy when you want to place the main subject of a scan on a background of your choice—much as though you'd clipped out the subject with a pair of scissors.

And what if you want the background to show through a little bit? That's called *translucency*. In the graphic below, for example, the lens of the magnifying glass is translucent (partially transparent), while the entire area around the lens is truly transparent.

When you first import a piece of clip art, it can be hard to tell whether it's opaque or not. Placed on a white background, it's unclear whether the white paper is simply showing through or if the drawing is filled with opaque white.

To find out what's opaque and what's transparent, place a differently colored object behind the clip art. In the case of this piece, the interior of the hat turned out to be transparent, but the face wasn't. That worked out well for this illustration.

Here's what the original stock photo of the magnifying glass looked like—no transparency, no translucency. In fact, there's a color graphic behind this photo, but you can't see it because the image is opaque.

Many digital photos, like this one from PhotoDisc, include ready-made clipping paths*—hand-drawn outlines of the main subject. Saving the image with one of the clipping paths activated produces the effect above. Adding another clipping path for the lens produces the image below.*

Just about all page layout programs treat black-and-white bitmaps *as transparent. Put a bitmap on a color background, and the background will show through automatically. (This isn't true of "black-and-white" photos, however; they're not really black and white—they're* grayscale.*)*

Transparency is also a very important concept in Web page design. To see why, take a look at the example above. The designer went to great pains to make the background of the photo match that of the Web page. Looks like a nice transparency effect, right?

Not really. This "fake transparency" method only works if you lock in the matching background color for your page. This designer didn't, so visitors could change the background to any color they wanted. Here, the background has been changed from the default gray to blue—and look what happens!

In the revised Web page, the problem GIF was resaved with the transparency option. Several programs, including Photoshop, allow you to select a single color in a GIF image and make it transparent. The trick is to make sure the graphic's background is one solid color—a color that doesn't appear elsewhere in the image.

We've seen plenty of examples of transparency. What about translucency? That can get very complicated, but let's start simple. In the Photoshop window shown above, we've selected an oval area using the feathered *option.*

Copy the feathered selection to a new blank file and—presto!—you get an image with a translucent border. This is a great way to turn any photo into a decorative graphic. You could just stop here…

…but there are plenty of other things you can do with a translucent image if you want to go further. Here, we've just added a color gradient in the background. Note how the photo merges smoothly into the color blend.

If you get really ambitious, you can also try combining two or more translucent images. Remember, though, that you need a program like Photoshop to combine translucent images. At least as of this writing, page layout programs still only "understand" opacity or transparency—nothing in between.

Adding dimensionality

Unless you design children's pop-up books for a living, you—like the rest of us—are limited to working in a very flat world. Brochures, newsletters, ads, Web pages, multimedia presentations, you name it—they're all very, very flat.

For the most part, that's okay. Most of the information we need to present is flat (especially text), so you may never have really thought about the limitation. Maybe some day I'll have to add a chapter to this book about working with holograms, but I don't expect that will be any time soon.

In the meantime, you may still want to create the illusion of a not-so-flat presentation. That is, you might want to make certain graphics or type just *pop* off the page. You can do that easily using some very simple 2D tricks; here are just a few.

A nice piece of clip art, but what can you do to make it look even more compelling?

The simplest enhancement is a plain old drop shadow. Gray would work fine, but a color shadow is even nicer.

This effect is equally simple, but it really *pops! It's hard to go wrong with the strong contrasts of white-and-black art against a color background.*

Like this embossed effect? It's exactly the same as the example to the left, but with a third copy of the megaphone pasted on top—this time in the background color.

To tone down the embossed effect, just change the black copy to a darker tint of the background color. This version could be used as a background for black type.

Blast off! The foreground megaphone, which has just enough of a black shadow to suggest a 3D look, appears to be popping from a cutout in the background.

Some digital stock photo collections make it very easy to set up dimensional effects right in your layout program. This photo from Image Club Graphics, for example, comes complete with a clipping path...

...as well as two kinds of shadows. The top shadow, which is exactly the same shape as the image, is called a drop shadow. The lower shadow is called a cast shadow—the kind formed by an off-center light.

Superimposing the photo over the drop shadow creates the illusion of a floating folder. Here, we set the shadow down and to the left, because the light hitting the folder seems to be high and to the right.

By contrast, the cast shadow is used to create a decidedly more realistic effect. Here, the folder appears to be standing—not floating—on a white surface.

It's easy enough to create your own soft drop shadows using Photoshop. The first step is to create a fairly accurate selection of the object. That's especially easy if you're working with a photo that already has a clipping path; just activate the path, then convert it into a selection.

Once you have the shape selected, move the selection (not the object) down and to the side. Feather the selection, switch to a background layer, and fill the feathered shape with a dark color.

Here are two versions of the final effect. Above, the image has been saved as a stand-alone graphic; the type was added in a page layout program. In the image to the right, we took the effect one extra step in Photoshop—by merging the sunglasses and the translucent shadow onto a photographic background.

Is that all there is to it?

Absolutely not. This sampling of special effects was just the tip of the iceberg. There are plenty more, and they can all be combined in countless ways to produce cool new graphics that are uniquely yours.

You may have noticed, though, the curious absence of special effects for type. Hmmm...sounds like we need just one more chapter?

Chapter 15

Turning Text Into Type

Text into type? What's the difference?

Text is...well...just words. They may be wonderful words, but until you've passed the magic wand of fine design over them, they're only so many letters crashing blindly across the page.

Okay, "magic wand" might be going a little overboard. In fact, there's very little magic involved at all. *In fact,* here's the only real secret to good typesetting: Treat your text with the same care and attention you'd give to your graphics. That's it.

Now all you need are a few basic examples of what I mean. Let's go.

Handling banners & headlines

Why are banners and headlines different than body text? Two reasons.

First, banners and heads are what people look at, even cursorily—even if they read nothing else in your publication. Banners and heads are responsible for delivering that all-important first impression. If you were to think about them in terms of personal appearances, they would be the haircuts (or maybe the shoes or neckties) of design. Scary thought, huh?

Second, banners and heads are just a whole lot bigger than body type. Think about it; banners, in particular, are often set in type sizes four to six times larger than body text. That means that any small imperfections in the way the type characters relate to each other are magnified greatly.

What kinds of imperfections? Aside from the occasional quirky character shape (which is just a matter of taste), the biggest problem is *letter spacing*. Most fonts are optimized to look good at body text sizes. But when you blow them up, you'll often notice that some combinations of letters seem to pull away from each other.

This problem is called *loose* or *bad kerning*. Kerning refers to the amount of space between specific pairs of letters. Every font includes *kerning tables*—information about how characters in that font should be spaced—but those tables don't cover every situation. That's seldom a problem for type below 18 points in size, but bad kerning can be very bad news at larger sizes, especially above 24 points.

In some cases, you'll be able to cover up many kerning problems simply by tightening up the letter spacing for all character pairs. That solution is generally called *range kerning* or *tracking*. But if you want to really do it right, you'll go the extra step: *manual pair kerning*. It's not nearly as bad as it sounds. When you pair-kern, you're simply telling your program to add or remove a little space between certain pairs of letters. There's not much science to it—you just have to do it by eye, shifting letters back and forth until *you* think they look right.

As we'll see on the following pages, kerning and tracking can also be used to create special effects—to add drama or a memorable look. A third setting that comes is handy for special effects in headlines and banners is *baseline shift*, which is just a fancy term for moving individual letters higher or lower than other characters in the same line. For example, this word is baseline-shifted one point down, and this word is shifted one point up. Baseline shift, kerning and tracking are fairly advanced typesetting features, but they're all available in programs like PageMaker, QuarkXPress, Illustrator, and FreeHand.

Take a close look at the type to the right. It's set in Times 14 point, about as big as body text could ever get. The letter spacing looks okay, right?

Toy Yep Aon Wet
331 276 789 102

Now look at how uneven the same type appears below, at 36 points. I've highlighted the loosest letter pairs.

Toy Yep Aon Wet

331 276 789 102

Transforming a banner

NewsWatch

The original banner:
Too loose, Lautrec!

NewsWatch

Tighter tracking applied:
Better, but still uneven.

NewsWatch

Loose letter pairs manually kerned:
Note especially Ne, sW, *and* Wa.

News*Watch*

Second word italicized for contrast.

News*Watch*

Type aligned right to create movement, complementing that of the italics.

Second word reversed out of color block to further increase contrast.

Fine-tuning a headline

Don't Miss Out On This Incredible 10% Off Offer!

The original headline: Time to roll up your sleeves...

Don't Miss Out On This Incredible 10% Off Offer!

The first step: tighter leading. We've made it solid *here—no extra space. It's 24-point type with 24-point leading.*

Don't Miss Out On This Incredible 10% Off Offer!

Here we've applied a tighter track, then kerned 27 of the letter pairs. Can you see which pairs were kerned the most?

Don't Miss Out On This Incredible *10% Off* Offer!

To make the words "Off Offer" read less awkwardly—and to make "10% Off" read as a unit—we've added italics. But note what that does to the word spacing!

Don't Miss Out On This Incredible *10% Off* Offer!

After rekerning that area, we made a couple final tune-ups. The percent sign was reduced in size and baseline shifted *up; the exclamation mark was enlarged and shifted down.*

Special effects

For really special pieces of type, you may want to add some equally special effects—something that says, "Hey you—*look at me!*" Maybe it's your company name, a special department head in your newsletter, or a marketing tagline in an ad.

The type effects on this spread are things you can do easily in any page layout or illustration program. There are certainly some bigger, jazzier effects you can get into, but they usually require Photoshop or other special-purpose software, such as type warping or 3D graphics programs. We'll touch on a couple of those effects later on, but let's start with the ones that are simple—and every bit as powerful.

Left Bank Coffee Shop

OVER 30 VARIETIES—
OPEN 7 DAYS A WEEK!

This type was spaced out with range kerning. *All the type was selected, then assigned a large positive kern value.*

The lower text is set in a 50% tint of black. The size of the small caps was adjusted to 80% of the full cap height.

Left Bank Coffee Shop

OVER 30 VARIETIES—OPEN 7 DAYS A WEEK!

"THE BEST CUP OF JOE IN TULSA!"—THE NEW OBSERVER

Here, the letters in each line are automatically spaced out to fill the column width. That's called forced justification.

The trick to making this effect work is to separate the words with special characters called non-breaking spaces.

LeftBankCoffeeShop

Over 30 Varieties—Open 7 Days a Week!

Here's a completely different direction for the shop's name. The caps are set in 50-point Berkeley Medium; the lowercase letters are 32-point Berkeley Bold Italic, shifted 8 points up.

Because the huge caps now signal the word breaks, we've dispensed with word spaces altogether. Also note the extra tight kerning—especially in the Le *and* Co *letter pairs.*

LeftBank
CoffeeShop

Over 30 Varieties—Open 7 Days a Week!

Why stop there? In this version, we've broken the shop's name into two lines, setting "Coffee Shop" in a 50% tint.

Overlapping the two parts creates a nice connection. As it worked out, they also happened to fit snugly together!

LeftBank
CoffeeShop

Over 30 Varieties—Open 7 Days a Week!

Here, the L *has been bumped up to 75 points, then shifted down 12 points to compensate. To keep an even look, the* L *was also changed to a lighter face (Berkeley Book). What do you think? Is it too much variety—or just enough?*

factsonfile

In this headline, we've run the words together with some very tight kerning, then reversed the center word.

Special Offer!

Ever wonder how to create this sort of slanty type? It's very easy—just rotate and skew the type. The trick is to set the same angle for both the rotation and the skew. Here, both are set to 12°.

facts on file...

Here's a similar idea, but set in a more vertical orientation. The three tightly kerned words were set in separate text blocks to make arranging them easier. The type sizes, from top to bottom, are 38, 46 and 58 points

It's the same trick as above, but with a twist. The type has been force justified, reversed and given a big paragraph rule *as a background. The rule, which automatically slants with the type, has been sized to allow the letters to break out.*

factsonfile

This version mixes several neat effects: reversing type colors, reversing drop shadows and a color background sized just-so to let the white letters break out into thin air. And note the special **fi** *character—that's called a* ligature.

Special Offer!

Back to plain old horizontal—but not too plain! To create this grid effect, we just superimposed a second text block filled with thin white paragraph rules (but no text). To tighten the grid, the leading was reduced to 2 points.

Details, drop caps & dingbats

Of course, good typesetting doesn't just stop with banners and headlines. You'll want to polish up your body text as well. What can be done there?

Aside from the basic concerns we covered back in Chapter 4—such as creating a comfortable reading flow and choosing a good combination of type size and leading—what can you do to draw readers into your body text? There are, for example, the tried and true solutions, such as drop caps and bullet symbols. But what's the best way to set them up and style them? What can you do to make them look truly unique?

Let's take a look at a few examples.

• The hiv cam yiu broak the mi
omsler si toxt ams ruler. Luk fir
• Our firtumitior ti ure inar ir ci
deumicativoly. Lorem ipsum do
amet, consectetuer adipiscing e
• Over 50% of diam nonummy
euismod tincidunt ut laoreet dc
magna erat volutpat.
• Finally, vhero viuls a ina cursk
cate miro effoctively tham tho

The bullet symbols here barely grab your attention. They need to be set in a more distinctive way.

• The hiv cam yiu broak the m
omsler si toxt ams ruler. Luk
• Our firtumitior ti ure inar ir c
deumicativoly. Lorem ipsum
amet, consectetuer adipiscin
• Over 50% of diam nonumm
euismod tincidunt ut laoreet
magna erat volutpat.
• Finally, vhero viuls a ina cursk
cate miro effoctively tham th

Step one: Create hanging indents *by setting a positive* left indent *and a negative* first line indent. *Then insert a tab after the bullet symbol.*

The hiv cam yiu broak the
if omsler si toxt ams rul
iby firtumitior ti ure ina
cursk deumicativoly. Lorem ipsu
sit amet, consectetuer adipiscin
diam nonummy nibh euismod t
laoreet dolore magna erat volut
viuls a ina cursk deumicate mir
ly tham tho triffem virs. Aro th
barticurm tyber if satabaro lirti
meos ti tram iut.
Duis autem vel eum iriure dc
hendrerit in vulputate velit esse
If the maxim siv reslim, ir the fi
yiur inar cimbatible vith tho pa

Here's a common problem with the typical drop cap: The body font just doesn't work that well—in this case, the T *creates awkward open spaces.*

The hiv cam yiu broak th
if omsler si toxt ams rul
iby firtumitior ti ure ina
cursk deumicativoly. Lorem ipsu
sit amet, consectetuer adipiscin
diam nonummy nibh euismod t
laoreet dolore magna erat volut
viuls a ina cursk deumicate mir
ly tham tho triffem virs. Aro th
barticurm tyber if satabaro lirti
meos ti tram iut.
Duis autem vel eum iriure dc
hendrerit in vulputate velit esse
If the maxim siv reslim, ir the fi
yiur inar cimbatible vith tho pa

Adding a rectangular background is a common fix for that problem, but it can look clunky. And what do you for thinner letters—use a thinner box?

The hiv cam yiu broak the m
omsler si toxt ams ruler. Lu
firtumitior ti ure inar ir cilir
deumicativoly. Lorem ipsum do
amet, consectetuer adipiscing el
diam nonummy nibh euismod t
laoreet dolore magna erat volut
viuls a ina cursk deumicate mir
ly tham tho triffem virs. Aro th
barticurm tyber if satabaro lirti
meos ti tram iut.
Duis autem vel eum iriure dc
hendrerit in vulputate velit esse
If the maxim siv reslim, ir the fi
yiur inar cimbatible vith tho pa

Changing the drop cap to a different font is a better solution. Condensed and compressed typefaces tend to minimize the amount of open space.

The hiv cam yiu broak the
omsler si toxt ams ruler. I
firtumitior ti ure inar ir ci
deumicativoly. Lorem ipsu
amet, consectetuer adipis
diam nonummy nibh euismod t
laoreet dolore magna erat volut
viuls a ina cursk deumicate mir
ly tham tho triffem virs. Aro th
barticurm tyber if satabaro lirti
meos ti tram iut.
Duis autem vel eum iriure dc
hendrerit in vulputate velit esse
If the maxim siv reslim, ir the fi
yiur inar cimbatible vith tho pa

With a highly compressed face like this one, you might even consider dropping the cap deeper into the text. This version looks stronger.

■ The hiv cam yiu broak the m omsler si toxt ams ruler. Luk
■ Our firtumitior ti ure inar ir c deumicativoly. Lorem ipsum amet, consectetuer adipiscin
■ Over 50% of diam nonumm euismod tincidunt ut laoreet magna erat volutpat.
■ Finally, vhero viuls a ina cursk cate miro effoctively tham th

A square or diamond dingbat is a bit more distinctive than the usual round bullet.

■ The hiv cam yiu broak the m omsler si toxt ams ruler. Luk
■ Our firtumitior ti ure inar ir c deumicativoly. Lorem ipsum amet, consectetuer adipiscin
■ Over 50% of diam nonumm euismod tincidunt ut laoreet magna erat volutpat.
■ Finally, vhero viuls a ina cursk cate miro effoctively tham th

Big symbols like these usually need some tweaking. We've reduced these a couple of points to better match the height of the lowercase letters.

❖ *The hiv cam yiu broak the mi omsler si toxt ams ruler. Luk fi*
❖ *Our firtumitior ti ure inar ir ci deumicativoly. Lorem ipsum dc amet, consectetuer adipiscing eli*
❖ *Over 50% of diam nonummy euismod tincidunt ut laoreet dc magna erat volutpat.*
❖ *Finally, vhero viuls a ina cursk cate miro effoctively tham tho t*

Choose symbols that match the tone of your message or the feel of your font. This cool diamond dingbat fits here perfectly.

The hiv cam yiu broak the m omsler si toxt ams ruler. Luk

You don't need to limit yourself to dingbat characters. Small graphics can also be inserted into your text as bullet symbols.

The hiv cam yiu broak the n omsler si toxt ams ruler. Lu firtumitior ti ure inar ir cil deumicativoly. Lorem ipsu amet, consectetuer adipisc diam nonummy nibh euisn tincidunt ut laoreet dolore volutpat. Vhero viuls a ina deumicate miro effoctively triffem virs. Aro thero aliq barticurm tyber if satabar that meos ti tram iut.

Duis autem vel eum iri hendrerit in vulputate velit pas. If the maxim siv reslir

Drop caps don't have to be inset. This is called a hanging drop cap*—that is, it's hanging to the left of the text. This option keeps the text nicely aligned.*

The hiv cam yiu broak th if omsler si toxt ams ru iby firtumitior ti ure in cursk deumicativoly. Lc dolor sit amet, consect adipiscing elit, sed dian nibh euismod tincidunt dolore magna erat volu viuls a ina cursk deumi effoctively tham tho tri Aro thero aliquam bart if satabaro lirtimor tha tram iut.

Duis autem vel eum

You might want to play a bit with the position of your hanging caps. In this case, the shape of the letter seemed to require a different alignment.

The hiv cam yiu broal mimitimy if omsler ams ruler. Luk fir iby tumitior ti ure inar ir cilir deumicativoly. Lorem ipsu amet, consectetuer adipisc diam nonummy nibh euisn tincidunt ut laoreet dolore volutpat. Vhero viuls a ina deumicate miro effoctively triffem virs. Aro thero aliq barticurm tyber if satabar that meos ti tram iut.

Duis autem vel eum iri hendrerit in vulputate velit

Here's an interesting spin on that clunky box solution we saw on the opposite page. Seems a bit more fun and inventive, doesn't it?

The hiv cam yiu broak t if omsler si toxt ams r iby firtumitior ti ure ir cursk deumicativoly. L dolor sit amet, consect adipiscing elit, sed dia nibh euismod tincidun dolore magna erat vol viuls a ina cursk deum effoctively tham tho tr Aro thero aliquam bar if satabaro lirtimor th tram iut.

If you really want to create a perky look—and have plenty of room to spare—try using huge tinted type placed behind the body type.

Going graphic

Type doesn't always have to be *just* type. You can turn plain type into eye-catching illustrations using programs like Photoshop, FreeHand, Illustrator, or CorelDRAW. In fact, many of the techniques we discussed in the previous chapter on graphics work equally well for converting words into art.

New Directions

This type was converted into graphic outlines in an illustration program, then filled with a color gradient.

100% PURE

Like this outline? You'll need an illustration program that allows you to stroke *type. Create one copy of the type with a heavy stroke, then paste another copy in front with none.*

New Directions

Here, the gradient-filled type was opened in Photoshop, then converted to a coarsely screened bitmap—38 lpi, square dot, 0°.

100% PURE

Glowing halos are easy too. Just add a heavy stroke to type in Photoshop, then apply the Gausian Blur filter. Set the blurred image behind the normal type.

You can also use Photoshop to merge type onto photographic backgrounds and to add soft, translucent drop shadows.

This effect is the opposite of the one above. The soft fill was created by copying the solid type to a foreground layer, then contracting, feathering and filling the foreground selection.

Type on the Web & in multimedia

Typesetting for screen publications isn't nearly as simple as it is for print publications. Why? Put simply, because we don't all have the same fonts on our computers.

It would be great if you could just *assign* your favorite font—say, Spiffy ExtraBold—to a home page headline, and leave it at that. But that font couldn't be displayed on someone else's computer if they didn't have it installed. To get around this problem, you have to convert that headline into a bitmapped graphic, such as a GIF or a JPEG. That guarantees the type will appear just the way you want it.

If you want to set all your headlines in nice custom fonts, that means creating lots of separate graphics. The conversion process itself doesn't take much time or effort; you simply have to set the type in Photoshop or a similar program, then save it in the right format.

But there is a big downside. Bitmapped type isn't very easy to edit. If you decide to change the wording or the type style, you may have to start over from scratch. You can't just double-click on a bitmapped word and choose "Bold"—and you certainly can't do a spell-check! You'll want to make sure you've planned out your text and your type styles as much as possible before you start setting type as graphics.

Special considerations for the Web

If you're using a graphic *instead* of a text-only headline, be sure to embed an alternative, plain-text version of the headline (using the ALT tag) in that graphic's IMG line. That way, Web-searching programs will be able to find your headline—and lead more people to your page—and visitors who've turned off image viewing will be presented with the text version of the headline.

Finally, if you want to publish a fully typeset publication, with complex formatting and nice type styles throughout, you should learn about the Adobe Acrobat PDF file format. The Acrobat family of conversion software allows you to save everything from spreadsheets to full-color brochures in a single, universal file format—a format that *anyone* can view, regardless of their font configurations. All that visitors to your page will need is the Acrobat Reader program, which is widely distributed and freely available on the Web.

PDF files are also the way to go if you need to put an existing printed piece on your Web page in a hurry. The conversion takes only minutes, and the resulting PDF file will accurately reproduce the original piece in full resolution!

web•news
web•news

The best way to convert type into a bitmap is to use a program like Photoshop. Why? Compare the examples above. The top example was created in a simple paint program; the edges are very jaggy. The lower example was created in Photoshop using the anti-aliasing *option.*

Web News
Web News

Anti-aliasing replaces high-contrast, jaggy pixels with pixels of intermediate shades. That works great most of the time, but it can be a problem for type with fine details or thin strokes. Here, the thin strokes in this type have become a little blurry.

How to Get Additional Information

How to Get Additional Information

Be especially careful with small type and type reversed out of dark backgrounds. The anti-aliased type in the top example is too blurry; the font is just too delicate for anti-aliasing at this size. The heavier sans serif font in the lower example works much better at this size.

End note

Well, I'm sorry to say that this little party has come to an end. But that's not to say *you* shouldn't continue the festivities elsewhere. In fact, I'm sure you'll find the best is yet to come, as you begin transforming your designs into fun, inventive, and refreshing examples of good communication. As the kids like to say, "Party on!"

You've probably noticed that there are a *few* more pages. If you just can't get enough design information, check them out. I've included a full listing of all the type families used in this book and a brief list of my favorite design-related books, periodicals, and software companies.

Colophon

This is where I tell you a little about how this book was made. I won't go into excruciating detail, but I will tell you that everything in these pages was produced on a computer much older and slower than the one you probably have. (Okay, it's a Macintosh Centris 650.)

The examples were produced in lots of different programs, including QuarkXPress, Photoshop, FreeHand, and Illustrator, and the whole thing was pulled together in PageMaker.

And what about the primary fonts? Chapter titles were set in Onyx; chapter and page numbers in Falstaff MT; headers in Triplex Serif; heads in Triplex; subheads and body text in ITC Officina Sans; and captions in Times.

There you go—much more than you really wanted to know, right?

F.Y.I.

Fonts By Page

Check this list to find the fonts used in the examples. Specific typefaces (such as "Futura ExtraBold") are provided for some of the simpler examples, but in most cases we've provided the name of the family ("Futura"). Most fonts are available from Adobe; fonts ending in "MT" are available from Adobe or Monotype. Vendors for the remaining fonts are noted in color.

Page	Example/Type families	
4	**Act Now** Before	
	Heads:	Helvetica
	Body:	Times
	Act Now After	
	Heads:	Times
	Body:	Helvetica
	Act Now After 2	
	Heads:	Futura
	Body:	Caslon 224, ITC
	Act Now After 3	
	Heads:	Garamond Condensed, ITC
	Body:	Gill Sans MT
		Garamond Condensed, ITC

Page	Example	Typeface
8	**Fresh**	Apollo MT
	Simple	Century Old Style
	Conservative	Caslon 224, ITC
	Wacky	CG Metropolis Agfa
	Clean	Bembo
	Friendly	American Typewriter, ITC
	Muscular	Placard Condensed Bold MT
	Sparse	Bauer Bodoni
	Bold	Futura ExtraBold
	Terse	Times New Roman Cond. MT
	Open	Futura Light
	Witty	Fenice, ITC
	Elegant	Ellington MT
	Whimsical	Runic Condensed MT
	Dense	Helvetica Condensed
	Funky	Bliphaus Shareware
	Powerful	Slimbach, ITC
	To the point	Helvetica Black
	Subtle	Fenice Light, ITC
	Sober	Adobe Garamond Semibold
	Hip	AuCasablanca Phil's Fonts
	Light-hearted	Utopia Semibold Italic
	Earthy	Formata Medium
	Soft	Novarese
	Noisy	Brush Script
		CG Benguiat Frisky Agfa
		Century Bold Condensed, ITC
		Kuenstler Script Black
	Horsey	CG Beton ExtraBold Agfa
	Modern	Gill Sans Condensed MT
	Hard	Machine, ITC
	Newsy	Garamond, ITC
	Clever	Garamond Light Cond., ITC
	High-Tech	Benguiat Gothic, ITC
	Geometric	Bauhaus Medium, ITC
	Visual	Bernard Condensed MT
	Novel	Century Ultra Condensed, ITC
	Nostalgic	Falstaff MT
	Loose	Frutiger Italic
	Casual	Stone Informal Bold
	Bright	Esprit Medium, ITC
	Heartfelt	Berkeley Italic, ITC
	Precise	Sabon

Page	Example/Type families	
12	**Act Now!** Top 1	
	Heads:	Franklin Gothic
	Body:	Garamond, ITC
	Act Now! Top 2	
	Heads:	Helvetica Ultra Compressed
	Body:	Helvetica Condensed
	Act Now! Top 3	
	Heads:	Garamond Light Condensed, ITC
	Body:	Times
	Act Now! Top 4	
	Heads:	Placard Condensed Bold MT
	Body:	Helvetica Condensed
	Act Now! Bottom 1	
	All:	Berkeley Oldstyle, ITC
	Act Now! Bottom 2	
	Heads:	Machine, ITC
	Body:	Futura
	Act Now! Bottom 3	
	Heads:	Kabel Bold, ITC
	Body:	Gill Sans MT
	Act Now! Bottom 4	
	All:	Futura
13	**Bottom Line** Top left	
	Heads:	Formata
	Body:	Times
	Bottom Line Top right	
	Heads:	Times New Roman Condensed MT
	Body:	Times
	Bottom Line Bottom left	
	Heads:	Helvetica Extra Compressed
	Body:	Times
	Bottom Line Bottom right	
	Heads:	Century Condensed, ITC
	Body:	Times

Page	Example/Type families	
17	**Hinterlands Tours Brochure** Before	
	Heads:	Century Condensed, ITC
		Futura Condensed
		Berkeley Oldstyle, ITC
	Body:	Berkeley Oldstyle, ITC
		Helvetica Condensed
		American Typewriter, ITC
	Hinterlands Tours Brochure After	
	All:	Berkeley Oldstyle, ITC
19	**Hinterlands Tours Letterhead**	
	All:	Berkeley Oldstyle, ITC
	Hinterlands Tours Business Card	
	Heads:	Berkeley Oldstyle, ITC
		Gill Sans MT
	Body:	Berkeley Oldstyle, ITC
	Hinterlands Tours Newsletter	
	Heads:	Gill Sans MT
	Body:	Berkeley Oldstyle, ITC
		Gill Sans MT
	Hinterlands Tours Brochure	
	All:	Berkeley Oldstyle, ITC
23	**Camcorder Ad** Before	
	Heads:	Fenice, ITC
		CG Benguiat Frisky Agfa
		Helvetica
	Body:	Times
		Helvetica
	Camcorder Ad After	
	All:	Berkeley Oldstyle, ITC
25	**City News** Before & After	
	Heads:	Utopia
		Futura
	Body:	Futura
		Utopia
27	**SupplyMax Catalog Page** Before & After	
	Heads:	Futura
		Futura Condensed
	Body:	Times

Page	Example/Type families	
32	**Sarah Johansen Identity** Before	
	All:	Adobe Garamond
	Sarah Johansen Identity After	
	Heads:	Garamond Condensed, ITC
		Adobe Garamond
	Body:	Garamond Condensed, ITC
33	**Master Remodeling Identity** Before	
	Heads:	Times New Roman Condensed MT
	Body:	Palatino
		Helvetica
	Master Remodeling Identity After	
	Heads:	Times New Roman Condensed MT
	Body:	Gill Sans MT
34	**BRG Identity** Before & After	
	All:	Akzidenz Grotesk Condensed
35	**Dearborn Partners** Before & After	
	All:	Berkeley Oldstyle, ITC
36	**Sun Realty Identity** Before	
	Heads:	Helvetica
	Body:	Times
	Sun Realty Identity After	
	All:	Futura Condensed
37	**Danielo Catering Identity** Before	
	Heads:	CG Siena Black Agfa
	Body:	Helvetica
	Danielo Catering Identity After	
	Heads:	Berkeley Oldstyle, ITC
	Body:	Helvetica
38	**BelTek Identity** Before	
	Heads:	Helvetica
		Palatino
	Body:	Helvetica
	BelTek Identity After	
	Heads:	Helvetica Ultra Compressed
		Palatino
	Body:	Helvetica Condensed

Page	Example/Type families	
39	**Media Mavens Identity** Before & After	
	Heads:	Times New Roman Condensed MT
	Body:	Times
40	**Paper Shop Identity** Before	
	All:	CG Benguiat Frisky Agfa
	Paper Shop Identity After	
	Heads:	CG Benguiat Frisky Agfa
	Body:	Frutiger
41	**WordWork Identity** Before	
	Heads:	Brush Script
	Body:	Formata
	WordWork Identity After	
	Heads:	Century Condensed, ITC
	Body:	Formata
42	**Hamburg Identity** Before & After	
	All:	Adobe Garamond
43	**The Beardley Foundation Identity** Before	
	Heads:	Garamond Condensed, ITC
	Body:	Helvetica
	The Beardley Foundation Identity After	
	Heads:	Onyx MT
	Body:	Berkeley Oldstyle, ITC
46	**Party Card** Before	
	Heads:	Garamond Condensed, ITC
		CG Siena Black Agfa
	Body:	Garamond Condensed, ITC
	Party Card After	
	All:	Garamond Condensed, ITC
	Map:	Helvetica
47	**Fish Sale Card** Before	
	All:	Formata
	Fish Sale Card After	
	Heads:	AuCasablanca Phil's Fonts
	Body:	Formata

Page	Example/Type families	
48	**SupplyMax Card** Before	
	Heads:	Futura Condensed
	Body:	Futura
	SupplyMax Card After	
	Heads:	Futura Condensed
	Body:	Futura
		Century Condensed, ITC
49	**Appointment Reminder Card** Before	
	Heads:	Times
	Body:	Helvetica Condensed
	Appointment Reminder Card After	
	Heads:	Brush Script
		Bauer Bodoni
		Novarese
	Body:	Novarese
		Univers
50	**Invitation/Reply Card** Before	
	Heads:	CG Behemoth Agfa
	Body:	Courier
		Times
	Invitation/Reply Card After	
	All:	Slimbach, ITC
51	**CD Sale Flyer** Before & After	
	All:	Avant Garde Gothic, ITC
52	**Moonlight Janitorial Flyer** Before	
	Heads:	CG Metropolis Agfa
		Placard Condensed Bold MT
	Body:	Helvetica
		Brush Script
	Moonlight Janitorial Flyer After	
	Heads:	Placard Condensed Bold MT
	Body:	Futura
		Zapf Dingbats

Page	Example/Type families	
53	**Emergency Plumbing Flyer** Before	
	Heads:	Optima
	Body:	Optima
		Times
	Emergency Plumbing Flyer After	
	Heads:	Helvetica Compressed
	Body:	Optima
		Century Old Style
54	**Officesmith Flyer** Before	
	Heads:	Times
		CG Beton ExtraBold Agfa
	Body:	Helvetica
		Times
	Officesmith Flyer After	
	Heads:	Slimbach, ITC
		CG Beton ExtraBold Agfa
		Helvetica
	Body:	Helvetica
		Times
55	**Telepathy Systems Flyer** Before	
	Heads:	Century Condensed, ITC
	Body:	Times
		Helvetica
	Telepathy Systems Flyer After	
	Heads:	Century Condensed, ITC
	Body:	Frutiger
		Zapf Dingbats
58	**Garden Walk Brochure** Before	
	Heads:	Helvetica Compressed
		Kabel, ITC
		Zapf Dingbats
	Body:	Zapf Chancery
	Garden Walk Brochure After	
	Heads:	Willow
	Body:	Apollo MT

Page	Example/Type families	
59	**PetPals Brochure** Before	
	Heads:	Optima
		Benguiat Gothic, ITC
	Body:	Helvetica
	PetPals Brochure After	
	Heads:	Triplex Emigre
		Triplex Serif Condensed Emigre
	Body:	Bembo
60	**Workshop Schedule** Before	
	All:	Garamond Condensed, ITC
	Workshop Schedule After	
	Heads:	Garamond Condensed, ITC
		Univers Condensed
	Body:	Times
61	**Hinterlands Tours** Before	
	Heads:	Century Condensed, ITC
		Berkeley Oldstyle, ITC
	Body:	Bembo
	Hinterlands Tours After	
	Heads:	Berkeley Oldstyle, ITC
		Gill Sans MT
	Body:	Berkeley Oldstyle, ITC
62	**Happiness Seminar** Before	
	Heads:	Garamond Condensed, ITC
	Body:	Berkeley Oldstyle, ITC
		Helvetica Black
	Happiness Seminar After	
	Heads:	Garamond Condensed, ITC
	Body:	Berkeley Oldstyle, ITC
63	**GLAAD Mailer** Before	
	Heads:	Helvetica
		Times
		Courier
	Body:	Courier
	GLAAD Mailer After	
	Heads:	Stone Serif
	Body:	Stone Sans

Page	Example/Type families	
64	**Dollars & Sense** Before	
	All:	Caslon 224, ITC
	Dollars & Sense After	
	Heads:	Frutiger
		Caslon 224, ITC
	Body:	Caslon 224, ITC
65	**Dollars & Sense** After 2	
	Heads:	Futura
		Futura Condensed
		Caslon 224, ITC
	Body:	Caslon 224, ITC
66	**Open Haus Invitation** Before & After	
	Heads:	Officina Sans, ITC
	Body:	Officina Serif, ITC
67	**AVPA Member Benefits Brochure** Before	
	Heads:	Poppl-Laudatio Condensed
	Body:	Helvetica
		Palatino
	AVPA Member Benefits Brochure After	
	Heads:	Poppl-Laudatio Condensed
		Poppl-Pontifex
	Body:	Poppl-Pontifex
68	**Media Mavens Brochure** Before	
	Heads:	Times New Roman MT Condensed
		CG Tower Condensed Agfa
	Body:	Kabel, ITC
	Media Mavens Brochure After	
	Heads:	Times New Roman MT Condensed
	Body:	Times
69	**RonTel Product Line Brochure** Before	
	Heads:	Garamond Condensed, ITC
		Univers Condensed
	Body:	Times
	RonTel Product Line Brochure After	
	Heads:	Placard Condensed Bold MT
		Esprit, ITC
		Univers Condensed
	Body:	Esprit, ITC

Page	Example/Type families	
70	**LifeTemps Brochure** Before	
	Heads:	CG Beton ExtraBold Agfa
		Helvetica
	Body:	Times
	LifeTemps Brochure After	
	Heads:	Fenice, ITC
	Body:	Sabon
		Zapf Dingbats
	Caps:	Kuenstler Script
71	**Telepathy Systems Brochure** Before	
	Heads:	Frutiger
		Century Condensed, ITC
		Helvetica
	Body:	Century Condensed, ITC
	Telepathy Systems Brochure After	
	Heads:	Frutiger
		Century Condensed, ITC
	Body:	Frutiger
74	**HindSight Newsletter** Before	
	Heads:	Stone Sans
	Body:	Palatino
	HindSight Newsletter After	
	All:	Stone Sans
75	**Webwatch Newsletter** Before & After	
	Heads:	AuCasablanca Phil's Fonts
		Apollo MT
	Body:	Apollo MT
76	**Notes Newsletter Cover** Before	
	Heads:	Tekton
		Italia
		Benguiat Gothic, ITC
	Body:	Tekton
		Helvetica
	Notes:	Parties MT
	Notes Newsletter Cover After	
	Heads:	Pepita
		Giovanni, ITC
	Body:	Cremona
	Notes:	Parties MT

Page	Example/Type families	
77	**Notes Newsletter Inside** Before	
	Heads:	Helvetica
		Bellevue
		Benguiat Gothic, ITC
	Body:	Tekton
	Notes Newsletter Inside After	
	Heads:	Pepita
		Giovanni, ITC
	Body:	Cremona
78	**TransCorp Newsletter Cover** Before	
	Heads:	Bauhaus, ITC
		Futura
	Body:	Utopia
	TransCorp Newsletter Cover After	
	Heads:	Bauhaus, ITC
		Utopia
	Body:	Futura
79	**TransCorp Newsletter Inside** Before	
	Heads:	Bauhaus, ITC
		Futura
	Body:	Utopia
	TransCorp Newsletter Inside After	
	Heads:	Utopia
	Body:	Futura
80	**HomeFront Newsletter Cover** Before	
	Heads:	Brush Script
		Garamond, ITC
		Garamond Condensed, ITC
	Body:	Garamond, ITC
	HomeFront Newsletter Cover After	
	Heads:	Ellington MT
		Garamond Condensed, ITC
	Body:	Garamond, ITC
	Caps:	Ellington MT

Page Example/Type families

96 AromaWare Report Cover Before
Heads: Usherwood, ITC
Pepita
Kabel, ITC

AromaWare Report Cover After
Heads: Helvetica Condensed
Pepita
Kabel, ITC

97 AromaWare Report Inside Pages Before
Heads: Usherwood, ITC
Body: Usherwood, ITC
Helvetica

AromaWare Report Inside Pages After
All: Helvetica Condensed

98 MultiLingua Report Cover Before & After
Heads: Futura
Bembo

99 MultiLingua Annual Report Inside Before
Heads: Futura
Body: Bembo

MultiLingua Annual Report Inside After
Heads: Futura
Bembo
Body: Bembo

102 SBR Free Sample Ad Before
Heads: Franklin Gothic
Body: Optima

SBR Free Sample Ad After
Heads: Franklin Gothic
Body: Goudy

103 Robinson Lanscaping Ad Before
Heads: Univers Condensed
Times New Roman Condensed MT

Robinson Lanscaping Ad After
Heads: Cremona
Univers

Page Example/Type families

104 FantasyTours Ad Before & After
Heads: Century Condensed, ITC
Garamond Condensed, ITC
Helvetica Black

105 Paper Shop Ad Before
Heads: CG Benguiat Frisky Agfa
Body: Frutiger
Helvetica

Paper Shop Ad After
Heads: CG Benguiat Frisky Agfa
Body: Frutiger

HairFX Ad
Heads: Onyx
Modula Serif Emigre

106 Studio Framing Ad Before
All: Zapf Chancery

Studio Framing Ad After
All: Adobe Garamond

107 Studio Framing Ad After 2
All: Esprit, ITC

108 Marco's 2 for 1 Appetizer Ad Before
All: Tiepolo, ITC

ShoeTree 2 for 1 Ad Before
Heads: Helvetica Black
Helvetica

Marco's 2 for 1 Appetizer Ad After
Heads: Tiepolo, ITC
Body: Futura
Tiepolo, ITC

ShoeTree 2 for 1 Ad After
Heads: Helvetica Black
Helvetica
Helvetica Condensed

Page Example/Type families

109 Horizons Class Schedule Ad Before
Heads: Kabel
Helvetica
Century Condensed, ITC
Body: Cheltenham, ITC
Times

Horizons Class Schedule Ad After
Heads: Century Condensed, ITC
Stone Sans
Body: Stone Sans

110 Sanity Savers Ad Before
Heads: Kuenstler Script
Ellington MT
Body: Stone Sans

Sanity Savers Ad After
Heads: Ellington MT
Body: Officina Serif, ITC
Isadora

111 InfoFirst Ad Before
Heads: Chicago
Body: Times New Roman Condensed MT

InfoFirst Ad After
Heads: Leawood, ITC
Utopia
Body: Utopia

114 Re-Cycle Bike Order Form Before
Heads: Helvetica
Times
Body: Times

Re-Cycle Bike Order Form After
Heads: CG Beton ExtraBold Agfa
Helvetica Condensed
Helvetica
Body: Helvetica Condensed

115 Visionary Publishing Order Form Before
All: Default system font

Visionary Publishing Order Form After
All: Default system font
Button: Futura

Page	Example/Type families
116	**Sound Source Invoice** Before
	Heads: Adobe Garamond, Helvetica, Bellevue
	Entries: Times, Helvetica
	Sound Source Invoice After
	Heads: Runic Condensed MT, Formata
	Entries: Formata
117	**Media Mavens Invoice** Before
	Heads: Times New Roman Condensed MT, Helvetica
	Entries: Times, Helvetica
	Media Mavens Invoice After
	Heads: Times New Roman Condensed MT, Times
	Body: Times
118	**NMRA Resource Directory Cover** Before
	Heads: Univers Condensed
	Body: Univers
	NMRA Resource Directory Cover After
	Heads: Univers Condensed, Bembo
119	**NMRA Resource Directory Listings** Before
	All: Univers
	NMRA Resource Directory Listings After
	Heads: Univers Condensed, Univers
	Body: Bembo
120	**Schumer Park Program Cover** Before
	Heads: Poppl-Laudatio Condensed, Tekton, Bodoni Poster
	Schumer Park Program Cover After
	Heads: Marker Fine Point Shareware, Marker Felt Thin Shareware

Page	Example/Type families
121	**Schumer Park Program Listings** Before
	Heads: Poppl-Laudatio Condensed, Helvetica
	Body: Palatino
	Schumer Park Program Listings After
	Heads: Marker Felt Thin Shareware, New Baskerville, ITC
	Body: New Baskerville, ITC, Gill Sans MT
122	**Cool Stuff Catalog** Before
	Heads: Futura
	Body: Utopia
123	**Cool Stuff Catalog** After
	Heads: Futura, Utopia
	Body: Utopia
126	**Dellwood City Center Web Page** After
	Heads: Willow, Kabel, ITC
127	**Singles Only Web Page** Before
	Heads: Gilligan's Island Shareware
	Singles Only Web Page After
	Heads: Gilligan's Island Shareware, EddieFisher Shareware
128	**Barrett Technical Academy Page** After
	Heads: Gill Sans Condensed MT, Gill Sans MT
130	**The Dog Page Web Site** After
	Heads: Brittanic URW, Industria Solid
132	**Towning Web Page** Before
	Heads: CG Benguiat Frisky Agfa
	Towning Web Page After
	Heads: Adobe Caslon

Page	Example/Type families
133	**Towning Linked Web Pages** After
	Heads: Adobe Caslon, Snell Roundhand
134	**Health Center Web Page** Before
	Heads: Univers
	Health Center Web Page After
	Heads: Bernhard Modern, Univers, American Typewriter, ITC
	Body: Times
136	**HomeFront Web Page** After
	Heads: Ellington MT, Garamond Condensed, ITC
	Ad: Berkeley Oldstyle, ITC
137	**HomeFront Back Issues Linked Page**
	Heads: Ellington MT, Garamond Condensed, ITC
	Ad: CG Metropolis Agfa, Futura Condensed
	HomeFront Sample Issue Linked Page
	Heads: Ellington MT, Garamond Condensed, ITC, Futura Condensed
	Ad: Adobe Caslon
138	**Dekor Paints Web Page** Before
	Heads: Onyx MT, Triplex Serif Emigre
	Dekor Paints Web Page After
	Heads: Onyx MT, Triplex Serif Emigre, Berkeley Oldstyle, ITC
139	**Dekor Paints Linked Page** Before
	Heads: Triplex Serif Emigre
	Dekor Paints Linked Pages After
	Heads: Onyx MT, Triplex Serif Emigre, Berkeley Oldstyle, ITC

Page	Example/Type families	
146	**WordWork Identity** Color Makeover	
	Heads:	Century Condensed, ITC
	Body:	Formata
	Danielo Catering Identity Color Makeover	
	Heads:	Berkeley Oldstyle, ITC
	Body:	Helvetica
	Open Haus Invitation Color Makeover	
	Heads:	Officina Sans, ITC
	Body:	Officina Serif, ITC
147	**Hindsight Newsletter** Color Makeover	
	All:	Stone Sans
	Schumer Park Program Color Makeover	
	Heads:	Marker Fine Point Shareware
		Marker Felt Thin Shareware
	SBR Newsletter Cover Color Makeover	
	Heads:	Franklin Gothic
		Goudy
	Body:	Goudy
148	**Dekor Paints Web Page** Color Makeover	
	Heads:	Onyx MT
		Triplex Serif Emigre
		Berkeley Oldstyle, ITC
	Party Card Color Makeover	
	Heads:	Garamond Condensed, ITC
	Body:	Garamond Condensed, ITC
	Map:	Helvetica
149	**Vendor News** Color Makeover	
	Heads:	Kabel, ITC
		Triplex Condensed Emigre
		Times
	Body:	Times
	Caps:	Triplex Condensed Emigre
149	**AVPA Member Benefits** Color Makeover	
	Heads:	Poppl-Laudatio Condensed
		Poppl-Pontifex
	Body:	Poppl-Pontifex

Page	Example/Type families	
150	**R.I.D. Identity** Before & After	
	Heads:	Industria Solid
		Riverside Shareware
	Body:	Industria Solid
151	**Spark Marketing Communications** Before	
	Heads:	Century Condensed, ITC
	Body:	Helvetica Neue
	Spark Marketing Communications After	
	Heads:	CrudFont Shareware
	Body:	Helvetica Neue
152	**Classy Plaster Fall Sale Postcard** Before	
	Heads:	Adobe Caslon
	Body:	Adobe Caslon
		Futura
	Classy Plaster Sale Postcard After 1	
	Heads:	Adobe Caslon
	Body:	Adobe Caslon
	Classy Plaster Sale Postcard After 2	
	Heads:	Adobe Caslon
	Body:	Adobe Caslon
	Classy Plaster Sale Postcard After 3	
	Heads:	Adobe Caslon
		Futura Condensed
	Body:	Adobe Caslon
154	**Scholl, Scholl, & Michaels** Before	
	Heads:	Palatino
		Futura Condensed
	Body:	Palatino
	Scholl, Scholl, & Michaels After	
	Heads:	Garamond Condensed, ITC
		Futura
		Futura Condensed
	Body:	Garamond Condensed, ITC
	"?":	Century Condensed, ITC

Page	Example/Type families	
155	**Sunglasses Sale Flyer** Before	
	Heads:	New Century Schoolbook
		CG Behemoth Agfa
	Sunglasses Sale Flyer After	
	Heads:	Stanton ICG
		Smile ICG
156	**Trade Show News** Before	
	Heads:	Placard Condensed Bold MT
		Futura
	Body:	Times
	Trade Show News After	
	Heads:	Placard Condensed Bold MT
		Futura
	Body:	Times
157	**Farm Report Newsletter** Before	
	Heads:	Italia
		Frutiger
	Body:	Helvetica
	Farm Report Newsletter After	
	Heads:	Italia
		Frutiger
		New Baskerville, ITC
	Body:	New Baskerville, ITC
158	**Hadley Textile Slide Show** Before	
	Heads:	Helvetica
		Avant Garde Gothic, ITC
	Body:	Avant Garde Gothic, ITC
	Hadley Textile Slide Show After	
	Heads:	Bernhard Gothic The Font Company
	Body:	Métropole Shareware
159	**Cyber Alarm Systems Slide Show** Before	
	Heads:	Helvetica Ultra Compressed
	Body:	Helvetica Black
		Stone Sans
	Cyber Alarm Systems Slide Show After	
	Heads:	Helvetica Ultra Compressed
	Body:	Stone Sans

Page	Example/Type families	
160	**Life Style** Before	
	Heads:	Univers Condensed
		Univers
	Body:	Times
	Life Style After	
	Heads:	Gill Sans MT
		Snell Roundhand
	Body:	Gill Sans MT
161	**ChefWare Catalog** Before	
	Heads:	Ellington MT
		Gill Sans MT
	ChefWare Catalog After	
	Heads:	Ellington MT
		Gill Sans MT
		MarkerFeltThin Shareware
162	**In the Garden Web Page** After	
	Heads:	Futura
		Bembo
163	**Cornell Stein Web Page** After	
	Heads:	Copperplate Condensed URW
		Akzidenz Grotesk Condensed
166	**Invitation/Reply Card** Color Makeover	
	All:	Slimbach, ITC
167	**The Money Beat**	
	Head:	Akzidenz Grotesk Condensed
168	**Close Call Graphic Design**	
	Heads:	Modula Serif Emigre
		Kabel, ITC
	Body:	Kabel, ITC
	Spark Marketing Communications	
	Heads:	CrudFont Shareware
	Body:	Helvetica Neue
	Basta Pasta Postcard	
	Heads:	Riverside Shareware
		Futura
		Giovanni, ITC

Page	Example/Type families	
174	**"Hot Type" over photo**	
	Head:	CrudFont Shareware
	"...I never dreamed..." over photo	
	Head:	Franklin Gothic DemiBold Oblique
175	**Jones & Armston logo**	
	Head:	Adobe Caslon
176	**Brush Sale**	
	Head:	Stanton ICG
	Order Now Button	
	Head:	Gill Sans Condensed MT
181	**Fact File**	
	Head:	CrudFont Shareware
	Summer Sale on sun glasses	
	Head:	Officina Serif, ITC
	Summer Sale Ad	
	Heads:	Officina Serif, ITC
182	**End page graphic**	
	"?":	Century Condensed Bold Italic, ITC
185	**Newswatch Banner**	
	Heads:	Times
	10% Off Headline	
	Heads:	New Baskerville, ITC
186	**Left Bank Coffee Shop** 1	
	Heads:	Industria Solid
		Berkeley Oldstyle, ITC
	Left Bank Coffee Shop 2	
	Heads:	Industria Solid
	Left Bank Coffee Shop 3-5	
	Heads:	Berkeley Oldstyle, ITC

Page	Example/Type families	
187	**Facts On File** 1	
	Head:	Futura Condensed
		Giovanni Bold Italic
	Facts On File 2	
	Head:	Futura
	Facts On File 3	
	Head:	Adobe Caslon
	Special Offer 1	
	Head:	Helvetica Neue Heavy
	Special Offer 2	
	Head:	Century Book Condensed, ITC
	Special Offer 3	
	Head:	Gill Sans ExtraBold MT
190	**New Directions** 1-3	
	Heads:	Placard Condensed Bold MT
	100% Pure 1-3	
	Heads:	Bernhard Gothic The Font Company
191	**Web News** 1	
	Heads:	Helvetica Black
	Web News 2	
	Heads:	Bauer Bodoni
	How To Get Additional Information 1	
	Heads:	Bauer Bodoni
	How To Get Additional Information 2	
	Heads:	Helvetica Black
192	**End note graphic**	
	Head:	Helvetica Black

Resources & Readings

Want to find those fonts? Trying to track down some of the clip art or stock photos used in this book? Or would you like some tips on what to read next? Here's my short list of top recommendations—the vendors, the magazines and the books you should check out as you begin working on your next makeover project.

Many of these vendors, by the way, offer helpful Web sites where you can view their products or download samples. Because Web site locations (URLs) are subject to change, they're not included here. But you can easily find these sites through the *Makeover Book Online Companion:*

- **http://www.vmedia.com/makeover.html**

Clip Art & Stock Photos

Image Club Graphics
729 24th Avenue Southeast
Calgary, Alberta, Canada T2G 5K8
800·661·9410

PhotoDisc Inc.
2013 Fourth Avenue
Fourth Floor
Seattle, WA 98121
800·528·3472

Fonts

Adobe Systems Incorporated
1585 Charleston Road
P.O. Box 7900
Mountain View, CA 94039
800·833·6687

Agfa Division of Bayer
90 Industrial Way
Wilmington, MA 01887
800·424·8973

Emigre
4475 D Street
Sacramento, CA 95819
800·944·9021

FontHaus
1375 Kings Highway East
Fairfield, CT 06430
800·942·9110

The Font Company
Precision Type
47 Mall Drive
Commack, NY 11725
800·248·3668

Image Club Graphics
729 24th Avenue Southeast
Calgary, Alberta, Canada T2G 5K8
800·387·9193

Monotype
150 South Wacker Drive
Suite 2630
Chicago, IL 60606
800·666·6897

Phil's Fonts
14605 Sturtevant Rd.
Silver Spring, MD 20905
800·424·2977

Design tools & add-ons

A Lowly Apprentice Production
5963 La Place Court, Suite 206
Carlsbad, CA 92008
619·438·5790

Adobe Systems Incorporated
1585 Charleston Road
P.O. Box 7900
Mountain View, CA 94039
800·833·6687

Extensis Corporation
55 S.W. Yamhill Sreet, Fourth Floor
Portland, OR 97204
800·833·6687

MacroMedia
600 Townsend Street
San Francisco, CA 94103
800·438·5080

Pantone Inc.
590 Commerce Boulevard
Carlstadt, NJ 07072
800·222·1149

Quark Inc.
1800 Grant St.
Denver, CO
800·788·7835

Periodicals

Adobe Magazine
Adobe Systems Incorporated
1585 Charleston Road
P.O. Box 7900
Mountain View, CA 94039
206·628·2321

BEFORE&After
PageLab
1830 Sierra Gardens Drive, #30
Roseville, CA 95661-2912
916·784·3880

Design Tools Monthly
The Nelson Group
2111 30th Street, Suite H
Boulder, CO 80301
303·444·6876

Digital Chicago
Peregrine Marketing Associates
515 E. Golf Road, Suite 201
Arlington Heights, IL 60005
847·439·6575

Publish
501 Second St
San Francisco, CA 94107
800·656·7495

Print
R.C. Publications
3200 Tower Oaks Boulevard
Rockville, MD 20852
800·222·2654

Step-by-Step Electronic Design
Dynamic Graphics
6000 N. Forest Park Drive
Peoria, IL 61614
800·255·8800

ThePage
The Cobb Group
9420 Bunsen Parkway, Suite 300
Louisville, KY 40220
800·223·8720

X-RAY Magazine
P.O. Box 200068
Denver, CO 80220
415·861·9258

Books

Dayton, Linnea, and Jack Davis. ***The Photoshop 3 Wow! Book.*** Peachpit Press, 1995.

Floyd, Elaine, and Lee Wilson. ***Advertising From the Desktop, Second Edition: The Desktop Publisher's Guide to Designing Ads That Work.*** Ventana Press, 1994.

Gosney, Michael, John Odam, and Jim Benson. ***The Gray Book, Second Edition.*** Ventana Press, 1992.

Grossmann, Joe. ***Looking Good With QuarkXPress.*** Ventana Press, 1995.

Grossmann, Joe, with David Doty. ***Newsletters From the Desktop, Second Edition: Designing Effective Publications With Your Computer.*** Ventana Press, 1994.

Monroy, Bert, and David Biedny. ***Adobe Photoshop: A Visual Guide for the Mac.*** Addison-Wesley Publishing Company, 1996.

Shushan, Ronnie, and Don Wright with Laura Lewis. ***Desktop Publishing By Design: Everyone's Guide to PageMaker 6, Fourth Edition.*** Microsoft Press, 1996.

Wallace, Rick. ***Special Edition: Using PageMaker 6 for the Mac.*** Macmillan Publishing, 1996.

Weinman, Lynn. ***Designing Web Graphics.*** MacMillan Computer Publishing, 1995.

Various authors. ***The Agfa Prepress Series:***

- ***An Introduction to Digital Color Prepress;***
- ***Working with Prepress and Printing Suppliers***
- ***An Introduction to Digital Scanning***
- ***An Introduction to Digital Photo Imaging***
- ***PostScript Process Color Guide***

Agfa Prepress Education Resources
P.O. Box 7917
Mt. Prospect, IL 60056
800·395·7007

Index

D

E

F

G

H

HTML Publishing on the Internet for Macintosh
HTML Publishing on the Internet for Windows

$49.95, 512 pages, illustrated
Windows part #: 229-1, Macintosh part #: 228-3

Successful publishing for the Internet requires an understanding of "nonlinear" presentation as well as specialized software. Both are here. Learn how HTML builds the hot links that let readers choose their own paths—and how to use effective design to drive your message for them. The enclosed CD-ROM includes Netscape Navigator, HoTMetaL LITE, graphic viewer, templates conversion software and more!

Netscape Navigator Quick Tour, Second Edition

$16.95, 250 pages, illustrated
Windows part #: 371-9, Macintosh part #: 372-7

This national bestseller, updated for Netscape Navigator 2.0, highlights the latest enhance-ments to the hottest browser on the Internet. Includes step-by-step instructions and expanded Web listings. The *Online Companion* is a continually updated link to top listings plus the latest versions of featured utilities and other Web resources.

Quicken 5 on the Internet

$24.95, 472 pages, illustrated, part #: 448-0

Get your finances under control with *Quicken 5 on the Internet.* Quicken 5 helps make banker's hours a thing of the past—by incorporating Internet access and linking you directly to institutions that see a future in 24-hour services. *Quicken 5 on the Internet* provides complete guidelines to Quicken to aid your offline mastery and help you take advantage of online opportunities.

Books marked with this logo include a free Internet *Online Companion*™, featuring archives of free utilities plus a software archive and links to other Internet resources.

Publish in Style

Designing tips for the desktop

The Presentation Design Book

$24.95, 378 pages, illustrated, part #: 014-0

Design materials that fit the mood, the message and the milieu of your business presentation. With suggestions for using charts, overheads and visuals to support the spoken word. Saavy advice and insightful how-to examples help you master color, layout, design and type techniques for creating all forms of presentation media.

Looking Good in Color

$29.95, 272 pages, illustrated, part #: 219-4

This cross-platform guide addresses basic theories of color, design and production. Features four-color illustrations throughout. Includes advice on choosing and using scanners, digital cameras, digitizing tablets to import color and much more. The *Online Companion* includes Ventana Online's continually updated desktop publishing archive of utilities and resources, plus links to other online resources.

Looking Good in Print, Third Edition

$24.95, 464 pages, illustrated, part #: 047-7

More than 300,000 copies in print! The recognized standard throughout the industry—covers design fundamentals and professional techniques. For use with any software or hardware, this desktop design bible has become the standard among novice and veteran desktop publishers alike. Includes new sections on photography and scanning.

Photoshop f/x, Mac Edition 

$39.95, 360 pages, illustrated, part #: 179-1

With full-color examples throughout, this step-by-step guide walks users through an impressive gallery of professional projects. The CD-ROM includes free Paint Alchemy 1.0, sample filters, photos, textures and demos. Ventana's *Online Companion* includes Photoshop shareware plus links to continually updated online references and resources.

Advertising From the Desktop

$24.95, 464 pages, illustrated, part #: 064-7

With only seconds to make an impression, advertisers need this book to ensure success. Includes tips on fonts, illustrations and special effects to win the battle for readers' attention. *Advertising From the Desktop* is an idea-packed resource for improving the looks and effects of your ads.

Newsletters From the Desktop, Second Edition

$24.95, 392 pages, illustrated, part #: 133-3

Design basics spiced with hands-on tips for building great-looking publications. Includes color gallery of professionally designed newsletters. Features advice on applying color; using clip art and other graphic details for the greatest effect; placing pictures, sidebars and pull quotes.

Books marked with this logo include a free Internet *Online Companion*™, featuring archives of free utilities plus a software archive and links to other Internet resources.

TITLE	PART #	QTY	PRICE	TOTAL

SUBTOTAL = $ ____________

SHIPPING = $ ____________

TOTAL = $ ____________

Name ____________________

E-mail ____________________ Daytime telephone ____________________

Company ____________________

Address (No PO Box) ____________________

City ____________________ State ________ Zip ____________

Payment enclosed ___VISA ___MC ___ Acc't # ____________________ Exp. date ________

Signature ____________________ Exact name on card ____________________

Mail to: Ventana • PO Box 13964 • Research Triangle Park, NC 27709-3964 ☎ 800/743-5369 • Fax 919/544-9472

TO ORDER ANY VENTANA TITLE, COMPLETE THIS ORDER FORM AND MAIL OR FAX IT TO US, WITH PAYMENT, FOR QUICK SHIPMENT.

SHIPPING

For all standard orders, please ADD $4.50/first book, $1.35/each additional.
For software kit orders, ADD $6.50/first kit, $2.00/each additional.
For "two-day air," ADD $8.25/first book, $2.25/each additional.
For "two-day air" on the kits, ADD $10.50/first kit, $4.00/each additional.
For orders to Canada, ADD $6.50/book.
For orders sent C.O.D., ADD $4.50 to your shipping rate.
North Carolina residents must ADD 6% sales tax.
International orders require additional shipping charges.

Check your local bookstore or software retailer for these and other bestselling titles, or call toll free:

800/743-5369